D1520569

RACE, ETHNICITY, AND EDUCATION

Racism and Antiracism in Education

RACE, ETHNICITY, AND EDUCATION

E. WAYNE ROSS AND VALERIE OOKA PANG, General Editors

VOLUME 4

Racism and Antiracism
in Education

Edited by

E. WAYNE ROSS

PRAEGER PERSPECTIVES

Westport, Connecticut
London

Library of Congress Cataloging-in-Publication Data

Race, ethnicity, and education / E. Wayne Ross and Valerie Ooka Pang, general editors.
   p. cm.
   Includes bibliographical references and index.
   ISBN 0-275-98596-2 (set : alk. paper)—ISBN 0-275-98691-8 (vol. 1 : alk. paper)—ISBN 0-275-98728-0 (vol. 2 : alk. paper)—ISBN 0-275-98722-1 (vol. 3 : alk. paper)—ISBN 0-275-98600-4 (vol. 4 : alk. paper)   1. Multicultural education—United States.   2. Educational equalization—United States.   3. United States—Race relations.   4. United States—Ethnic relations.   I. Ross, E. Wayne, 1956–   II. Pang, Valerie Ooka, 1950–   III. Title.
   LC1099.3.R33 2006
   370.1170973—dc22   2006010359

British Library Cataloguing in Publication Data is available.

Library of Congress Catalog Card Number: 2006010359
ISBN: 0-275-98596-2 (set)
      0-275-98691-8 (vol. 1)
      0-275-98728-0 (vol. 2)
      0-275-98722-1 (vol. 3)
      0-275-98600-4 (vol. 4)

First published in 2006

Praeger Publishers, 88 Post Road West, Westport, CT 06881
An imprint of Greenwood Publishing Group, Inc.
www.praeger.com

Printed in the United States of America

The paper used in this book complies with the
Permanent Paper Standard issued by the National
Information Standards Organization (Z39.48-1984).

10 9 8 7 6 5 4 3 2 1

For

My Dad

Rev. Bobby G. Ross

who has always done his best to desegregate 11:00 AM Sunday

Contents

General Editors' Introduction to *Race, Ethnicity, and Education*

Valerie Ooka Pang and E. Wayne Ross

WE BELIEVE IN students, all students. We also believe that we as educators can make a difference in the lives of students.

This set is based on the belief that education must be a life-giving process of joy and growth founded on the ethic of care and action for social justice. Caring in partnership with social justice form a powerful foundation for schooling because this orientation perceives each student as a precious human being and member within a country that values social justice, democracy, and moral courage.[1] This orientation affirms the belief in human dignity and our commitment to care for each other.[2] The ethic of care must be understood to be intimately connected to our national commitments to freedom and equality within (and outside of) schools. When we care, we act. Our laws, policies, politics, and methods for achieving social justice flow directly from what we care about and our commitment to a socially just society. bell hooks, the Black feminist, reminds us, "The civil rights movement was such a wonderful movement for social justice because the heart of it was love—loving everyone."[3] Within this orientation each student is seen as a whole person who finds happiness in learning and reaching her or his potential. The student is not passive but rather an active learner and participant and citizen who thinks, questions, collaborates, and acts to make our democracy more just and compassionate.[4]

Every day there are numerous editorials and articles appearing in newspapers and magazines across the country about solutions to problems in our schools. These pieces are often written by individuals who have not studied schools or had extensive experiences working in schools. Some of these individuals believe that they know about schools because they were once students. Having been a student does not mean a person is an expert about schools. However, many individuals believe that their successes in corporations, for example, can also be transferred to schools because they see schools as businesses or profit centers rather than communities of learners.

Therefore, many recommended reform measures strive to make schools more like businesses, where the bottom line is a narrow conception of productivity. This orientation reflects the current social direction toward efficiency and output in schools, usually in the form of test scores. We ask: When did children become products? How has school curriculum become the arena for lawyers and politicians, an arena where they decide the future of millions of students with little input from educators? We do not believe schools should be thought of as an assembly line for children or as for-profit business investments for distant shareholders. Pauline Lipman calls for schools that do not bombard students with testing but rather are communities where creative and engaging learning occurs.[5] Just as Lipman does, the authors in these four volumes clarify the complex issues that face our increasingly culturally and linguistically diverse schools. The authors share the aim that all citizens become more fully informed, so that they better understand how issues of race, ethnicity or culture, and language influence schooling and education.

We are concerned for public schools because there are many forces outside the control of local school communities that shape schools. Recently many districts have hired noneducators to run school districts. For example, the superintendent of San Diego City Schools for seven difficult years was Alan Bersin, former U.S. Attorney for the Southwest region who many people knew as the "Border Czar." His role was to coordinate relationships of the federal government with numerous agencies in the area dealing with trade and patrolling the border. He became superintendent of the seventh largest urban district in the country, where approximately 70 percent of students are from culturally and linguistically diverse families. Bersin's major goal seemed to be to raise the test scores of students at almost any cost. His tenure with the teachers in the district was rocky, at best, because of his dictatorial leadership style. However, many business executives supported Bersin's reform program called *Blueprint for School Success*. Between 2000 and 2002, the *San Diego Union-Tribune* reported that the scores of Hispanic elementary children on reading measures showed a narrowing of the gap between their achievement with White children by 15 percent; however in middle-school scores the gap was decreased by a mere 2 percent.[6]

Many parents may not know that the change in reading achievement may be due not only to the infusion of literacy programs but also to the massive increase of time spent on reading due to a three-hour literacy time block every morning required for most students and the increase in after-school programs focusing on literacy. Therefore the success of his programs may be due, in part, to the increase in time dedicated to the instruction of reading and the incessant focus on teaching test-taking skills. Fortunately, many teachers were concerned with the removal of class time spent on subject areas such as art, music, social studies, math, and science during the first years of the Blueprint program. Though Bersin's reform efforts have been called a success, many teachers have questioned the cost of the literacy reform on student and teacher morale and the teaching of core subject area knowledge. Through the efforts of the teachers in the district, Bersin was pushed out. However Governor Arnold Schwarzenegger quickly named Bersin as Secretary of Education for the state of California. Again we ask, "Who is best qualified to direct the schooling of millions of children?" and "What are the goals of schools?"

We do believe one of the most important goals of schools is academic achievement of our students. However, we perceive the role of schools to be much more extensive than high scores on tests. We are committed to schools where all students are respected and provided an equitable education so they reach their potential. They must be guided in an educational environment that empowers them to think, analyze, build communities of learners, and develop citizenship skills. Can our students work together? Can they analyze social problems? Do they speak up and take leadership in the creation of action plans to address issues such as oppression?

These volumes rose out of the belief that in our society, race and ethnicity matter. We believe it is critical for the general public to understand issues of equity from the view of educators. We see many inequalities in schools. For example, academic tracking, where a disproportionate number of students of color can be found in remedial classes, continues to be an issue. In addition, resegregation continues to be the norm in many urban schools. Schools are more segregated today than when the Civil Rights Act of 1964 was passed.[7]

Through this four-volume set, we believe it is important for the reader to do the following: become familiar with philosophy and instructional practices of multicultural education, more fully understand issues of language and literacy, examine issues of ethnic identity, and examine the complexities of racism still present in schools and society today. Therefore, the first volume, edited by Valerie Ooka Pang, is dedicated to providing background information, identifying principles, and discussing successful practices of the interdisciplinary field of multicultural education.

The second volume, edited by Robert T. Jiménez and Valerie Ooka Pang, is devoted to issues dealing with language and literacy. Millions of students arrive at school speaking a home language other than English. Teachers can provide rich and successful learning environments for them by respecting diverse languages, building on the cultural knowledge of their students, and employing strategies designed for English learners. Developing partnerships with parents of English learners can also be an effective strategy because parents can then become involved in activities that extend learning into the home.[8]

In volume 3, editors H. Richard Milner and E. Wayne Ross present a comprehensive discussion of ethnic identity. Our nation is made up of individuals from many diverse cultural communities. Ethnic identity is a core component of how students see themselves. This volume examines foundational concepts of racial identity development as well as racial identity development in diverse contexts, with chapters focusing on Latina and African American females, Asian Americans, mixed-heritage people, and the intersections of race, ethnicity, and sexual identities. A substantial part of this volume is devoted to examining implications of our knowledge about racial identity development for teaching and learning.

The final volume, edited by E. Wayne Ross, addresses the challenging issue of racism in society and more specifically in our schools. Many people do not appreciate how pervasive racism is within schools and society. Racism is often hidden because elements are subtly inserted within classrooms. For example, an elementary schoolteacher may read with expression and humor the stereotypical picture book *The Five Chinese Brothers* by Claire Bishop, where Chinese protagonists are portrayed with buckteeth, without eyes, and as less than human people. High school teachers may unconsciously teach prejudicial ideas about people of color in the content of the materials they develop for use in their classroom. The following is an example of materials used in a vocabulary lesson in an English lesson.

> Students were asked to memorize the definitions and companion sentences . . .
> 2. Ambush—to lie in wait or hiding for an attack.
> *The Indians tried to ambush the settlers as they went by.* The teacher has positional power in a school. When she presents information as if it is true, students may believe what she teaches.[9]

Although this was an English class, the social science content was presented as a statement of truth. The sentence reinforces the stereotypical image of savage Native Americans without a context. Having students memorize this sentence is also problematic because the statement reinforces a stereotypical image. However even the most dedicated teacher whose goal is to develop a classroom where students become aware of social inequities finds obstacles that are difficult to overcome in our schools.[10] To provide equitable schools, we must examine all aspects of schooling, such as policies, practices, and curriculum, in light of a society where inequalities have been legalized and legitimated. The plight of folks in New Orleans after Hurricane Katrina clearly demonstrated that our nation is stratified by race and social class.[11]

The issues of race and ethnicity are powerful forces in education, and it is imperative that each citizen is well informed and understands how these issues can be addressed in schools to ensure equal education for all students. We hope that this set engages you in an in-depth analysis and understanding of issues of equity.

NOTES

1. David W. Hursh and E. Wayne Ross, *Democratic Social Education: Social Studies for Social Change* (New York: RoutledgeFalmer, 2000); Valerie Ooka Pang, *Multicultural Education: A Caring-Centered, Reflective Approach* (Boston: McGraw-Hill, 2005).

2. Pauline Lipman, *High Stakes Education: Inequality, Globalization, and Urban School Reform* (New York: RoutledgeFalmer, 2004); Daniel Liston and Jim Garrison, *Teaching, Learning, and Loving* (New York: RoutledgeFalmer, 2004); Nel Noddings, *The Challenge to Care in Schools* (New York: Teachers College Press, 1992).

3. bell hooks, "How Do We Build a Community of Love?," *Shambhala Sun* 8, no. 3 (2000): 32–40.

4. John Goodlad, Corrine Mantle-Bromley, and Stephen Goodlad, *Education for Everyone: Agenda for Education in a Democracy* (San Francisco: Jossey-Bass, 2004).

5. Lipman, *High Stakes Education*.

6. Julian Betts, "Evidence Suggests Bersin Reforms Working," *San Diego Union-Tribune* (October 15, 2005). Available online at www.signonsandiego.com/union-trib/20051014/news_lz1e14betts.html.

7. Jonathan Kozol, *The Shame of Our Nation: The Restoration of Apartheid Schooling in America* (New York: Crown, 2005).

8. Patrick H. Smith, Robert T. Jiménez, and Natalia Martínez-León, "Other Countries' Literacies: What U.S. Educators Can Learn from Mexican Schools," *Reading Teacher* 56, no. 8 (2003): 2–11.

9. Pang, *Multicultural Education*, 185–186.

10. H. Richard Milner, "Developing a Multicultural Curriculum while Teaching in a Predominantly White Teaching Context: Lessons from an African American Teacher in a Suburban English Classroom," *Curriculum Inquiry* 35, no. 4 (2005): 393–427.

11. E. Wayne Ross, "Introduction: Race, Ethnicity, and Education: Racism and Antiracism in Schools," in E. Wayne Ross (ed.), *Race, Ethnicity, and Education: Racism and Antiracism in Schools* (Westport, CT: Praeger, 2006).

Introduction: Racism and Antiracism in Education

E. Wayne Ross

"IT WAS TO HELL WITH US NEGROES"

Hurricane Katrina made landfall on the Gulf Coast of the United States on August 29, 2005, devastating coastal communities in Louisiana, Mississippi, and Alabama. In Katrina's aftermath the levees protecting New Orleans failed and tens of thousands of poor and overwhelmingly Black residents, who were without the means to evacuate before the hurricane hit, became refugees in their own hometown. The initial response from the federal government to one of the deadliest and most powerful hurricanes to ever hit the nation was woefully inadequate.[1] New Orleans was declared "America's Third World Hell Hole."[2]

Katrina made America's urban poor suddenly visible to the media (who somehow manage not to pay much attention to the 37 million Americans below the poverty line)[3] and they (and others) seemed stunned that most of those left behind to face the toxic stew in New Orleans were poor and Black. How could this happen in the United States they asked? The preconceptions of at least some in the media were confirmed and captured in the descriptions of White survivors "'finding' bread and soda from a local grocery store" and Black survivors "'looting' a grocery store."[4]

The federal government was not paying attention either. Michael D. Brown, director of the Federal Emergency Management Agency, told CNN that he was unaware local officials had housed thousands of evacuees, who had quickly run out of food and water, in the Convention Center—even though city officials had been telling people for days to gather there and major news outlets had been reporting the plight of evacuees in the center.[5] Brown also criticized the people who were stuck in New Orleans as those "who chose not to evacuate, who chose not to leave the city," disobeying the city's mandatory evacuation order, despite the fact that those remaining were there because they lacked a place to go and the means to get there.[6] The conditions in the makeshift shelters at the Superdome and the New Orleans convention center quickly disintegrated, becoming horrendously appalling.[7]

Newspaper columnist Christine Blatchford described the situation at the convention center:

> The people crowded into the convention centre are overwhelmingly black, yet the Big Easy is—was?—a relatively diverse city, with about 62 per cent of the population black and 28 per cent white. Yet rare are the white faces to be seen among these folks who have suffered so dreadfully, and rare are the white faces who even dare enter the fetid, revolting building.[8]

After giving Blatchford a tour of the convention center, New Orleans resident Autherine Algere summed up the racial divide in the city: "Miss, with great respect for your race, I don't see no White people here. Where they at? I live here, I know there's plenty of White folk in New Orleans."[9] Blatchford then reports that, "Ms. Algere, who clutched her Bible in her right hand, looked upward to beg the Lord's forgiveness for what she was about to say. 'It was to hell with us Negroes.'"

Days later, in a theatrically staged speech from New Orleans, President George W. Bush admitted the role race and poverty played in the response to the aftermath of Katrina, promising an urban renaissance that would address poverty, race, and the country's massive disparities. In the speech, Bush admitted that "poverty has roots in a history of racial discrimination, which cut off generations from the opportunity of America."[10]

And it still does.

THE RACIAL DIVIDE

The devastation wrought by Hurricane Katrina and the failure of the government to adequately respond to the needs of its largely poor and Black victims in New Orleans has spotlighted the racial divide in the United States and provided a formidable challenge to beliefs of some people—those in the privileged position to ignore certain realities—that the nation has overcome its apartheid past.

For folks who have been paying attention or don't have the privilege to ignore such things, the racial divide brought to light in the aftermath of Katrina fits quite comfortably within the lived experience of many Americans regarding, for example, the economy, health care, the judicial system and, the subject of this book, education. Below are a few selected examples of the racial divide in the United States that have deleterious effects for millions of people every day, although these issues have not captured people's attention in any sustained way as have the cataclysmic events of Hurricane Katrina.

The Economic Divide

It's news when the President admits that poverty is directly connected to racial discrimination. But history shows that poverty is systematic. African Americans and Latinos are more susceptible to poverty than Whites as the result of inherited inequalities, discrimination, unemployment, and holes in the social safety net. According to the Center for Popular Economics:

> Between 1959 and 1978, government antipoverty programs and relatively low unemployment rates decreased the overall poverty rate and reduced the differences in poverty rates among ethnic groups. Things got worse in the 1980s and 1990s. Unemployment went up, and cuts in federal social spending had a particularly ugly impact on people of color. Public support for families with dependent children declined, leaving many kids vulnerable to squalor and violence. Poverty rates fell with the economic expansion of the late 1990s. But even in 2001, after ten years of uninterrupted economic growth, close to a quarter of all African Americans and Latinos lived below the poverty line [compared to ten percent of whites].[11]

Although progress has been made in reducing the racial divides that mark per-capita income, poverty, homeownership, education, and median wealth, these gaps remain so large that at the current rate of progress it would take centuries to eliminate racial inequities in these areas.[12] For example:

- At the slow rate that the Black-White poverty gap has been narrowing since 1968, it would take 150 years, until 2152, to close.

- For every dollar of White per-capita income, African Americans had 55 cents in 1968—and only 57 cents in 2001. At this pace, it would take Blacks 581 years to get the remaining 43 cents.
- Almost a third of Black children live in poverty—32.1 percent in 2002. The child poverty gap would take 210 years to disappear, not reaching parity until 2212.
- Although White homeownership has jumped from 65 to 75 percent since 1970, Black homeownership has only risen from 42 to 48 percent. At this rate, it would take 1,664 years to close the homeownership gap—about fifty-five generations.[13]

When it comes to the wealth gap there is not even an excruciatingly slow improvement as the Black-White gap in average household wealth is *increasing*. United for a Fair Economy reports that "White households had an average net worth of $468,200 in 2001, more than six times the $75,700 of Black households. This includes home equity. In 1989, average white wealth was five-and-a-half times Black wealth." And the same dynamic is at work in the Latino-White wealth gap. In 2004, the Pew Hispanic Center reported that the jobless recovery of the economy has been "much harder on the net worth of minority households."

> The wealth gap between Hispanic and non-Hispanic White households has increased in the recent past. And the gap in wealth is far greater than the gap in income. According to [this] study, the median net worth of Hispanic households in 2002 was $7,932. This was only nine percent of $88,651, the median wealth of non-Hispanic White households at the same time. The net worth of Non-Hispanic Blacks was only $5,988. Thus, the wealth of Latino and Black households is less than one-tenth the wealth of White households even though Census data show their income is two-thirds again as high.[14]

The Pew study also reports that 26 percent of Hispanic, 32 percent of non-Hispanic Black, and 13 percent of non-Hispanic White households had zero or negative new worth in 2002, and those proportions are unchanged since 1996. Fewer than 40 percent of Black and Hispanic households have "middle-class levels of wealth," although nearly 75 percent of White households have middle-class or higher levels of wealth.

There is an additional wealth gap within the Black and Hispanic populations, as the wealthiest 25 percent of Hispanic and non-Hispanic Black households own 93 percent of the total wealth of each group (among non-Hispanic White households the top 25 percent own 79 percent of the total wealth).

The Health Divide

In terms of health care, the racial divide is stark and deadly. In 1970, Blacks had a life expectancy 90 percent that of Whites (64.2 years compared to 71.6 years). By 2000, life expectancy for Blacks was only 93 percent that of Whites (71.7 years to 77.4 years). African Americans have higher HIV/AIDS infection rates than other racial and ethnic groups. In December 1999, African Americans accounted for an estimated 37 percent of HIV/AIDS cases nationwide. Almost half of the HIV/AIDS cases reported in 1999 were among African Americans, and 63 percent of HIV/AIDS infected women were Black. HIV/AIDS was the ninth-leading cause of death among African Americans in 1998. Black men ages twenty-five to forty-four have significantly higher death rates than White men due to HIV/AIDS and homicide.[15]

A major contributing factor to the Black-White life expectancy gap is the high infant mortality rates among Blacks. In 2000, the infant mortality rate for African American infants was 14.1 per 1,000 live births (more than twice the national average) and less than half the rate for Whites (6.0 per 1,000 live births).[16] African American infants are at greater risk of death than infants in much poorer countries (e.g., Bulgaria, Cuba, Jamaica, Uruguay, etc.).[17] Infant mortality rates are, of course, connected to the polarization of income in the U.S. economy and the resulting lack of access to health care. In 1998, 85 percent of all White mothers received prenatal care during the first trimester compared to 73 percent of African American mothers.

Latinos have lower mortality rates than non-Hispanic Whites. However, of all major racial and ethnic groups Latinos have the lowest rates of health insurance coverage. Food insufficiency is an important health risk factor, particularly in Mexican American families. Latinos also have significantly higher rates of some chronic and infectious diseases including diabetes, tuberculosis, and AIDS.[18]

The Justice Divide

According the U.S. Justice Department, there are more than two million men and women behind bars in the United States.[19] Presently, more people—literally and proportionally—are incarcerated in the United States than at any time in history and the United States has a higher percentage of its population in prisons than any other country in the world. In 2002, the U.S. rate of incarceration was 700 prisoners per 100,000 population (that is seven times the rate of incarceration in China, for example).[20] These astonishing rates of incarceration come at a time when violent crime rates have been relatively constant or declining for two decades.[21] Perhaps even more astonishing is the extraordinary magnitude of minority incarceration and the stark disparity in their rates of incarceration compared to those of Whites. "Out of a total population of 1,976,019 incarcerated in adult facilities, 1,239,946 or 63 percent are Black or Latino, though these two groups constitute only 25 percent of the national population. The figures also demonstrate significant differences among the states in the extent of racial disparities."[22]

The Education Divide

Despite public support for desegregated schools, federal court decisions and education reform legislation have led to the resegregation of students and erection of barriers that limit racial diversity in the teaching profession. Though public schools were continuously desegregated from the 1950s to the 1980s, the past fifteen years have seen a rapid retreat from these efforts as federal courts terminated major and successful desegregation orders.

In the 1990s, U.S. Supreme Court rulings made it easier for school districts to be declared unified or desegregated. In the past seven years, in the wake of these decisions, the court-ordered desegregation plans of fifty districts across the country have been abolished. Key findings in a study released in 2003 by the Harvard Civil Rights Project illustrate how these rulings have contributed to the resegregation of public schools across the nation.[23]

Whites are now the most segregated group in public schools, attending institutions that on average are 80 percent White. White students are attending majority White schools at a time when minority students make up nearly half the public school enrollment. During the 1990s, the proportion of Black students in majority White schools decreased by 13 percent, a level lower than any year since 1968.

Only two states have not shown an increase in Black segregation in recent years. Michigan and New Jersey are highly segregated and showed virtually no change. States with large increases in segregation—such as Florida, Missouri, and North Carolina—are home to school districts whose long-running desegregation orders were ended in the 1990s.

In the past two decades in Kentucky, there has been a nearly 10 percent decrease in the percentage of White students in schools attended by Blacks. Despite the decrease, the Harvard report notes that Kentucky has had the highest level of Black-White exposure in schools since 1980. This is largely the result of consolidation of city and county school systems in metro Louisville, which remains under a desegregation plan.

The Harvard study also identifies the emergence of a substantial number of public schools that are virtually all non-White. These apartheid schools, as they are labeled in the report, educate a quarter of the students in the Midwest and Northeast and are often plagued by poverty and social and health problems. In addition to racial segregation of students, there is a serious racial and cultural gap between teachers (86 percent are White) and the nearly fifty percent of students who are minorities.

State and federal legislation has actually become a serious barrier to achieving quality education for all children and increasing diversity among teachers in public schools, compounding the deleterious effects of rese-gregated schools.

The No Child Left Behind Act (NCLB) relies on standardized tests to improve education and teacher quality.[24] But there is overwhelming evi-dence that standardized tests are primarily measures of race and class rather than educational achievement. In her article "The Accumulation of Disad-vantage: The Role of Educational Testing in the School Career of Minority Children," Sandra Mathison demonstrates that test-driven education (à la NCLB) is not the great equalizer it is portrayed to be in the mythical meri-tocracy of U.S. public schools. Rather, "standardized testing puts children of color and children living in poverty at a disadvantage. This disadvantage begins early in the school career of a child and repeats itself again and again."[25] Students of color are at a disadvantage before they even start school. Analysis of data from the U.S. Department of Education Early Childhood Longitudinal Study shows that,

> there are substantial differences by race and ethnicity in children's test scores as they begin kindergarten . . . the average cognitive scores of children in the highest SES group are 60% above the scores of the lowest SES group. Moreover, average math achievement is 21% lower for blacks than whites, and 19% lower for Hispanics.[26]

Mathison says that "setting aside the unjustified confidence in the mean-ingfulness of standardized test scores for young children, this report illus-trates just the beginning of a lifetime of characterizations and decisions that will be made and, indeed institutionalized for children of color and those living in poverty" as test results are used "to sort, track, and monitor the abilities, achievements, and potentials of students."[27]

Black and Latino students are also subject to more high-stakes testing—tests that have serious consequences attached to the results—than their White counterparts. The National Educational Longitudinal Survey shows that 35 percent of African American and 27 percent of Latino eighth-graders will take a high-stakes test compared with 16 percent of Whites.[28] Along class lines, 25 percent of lower socioeconomic status eighth-graders compared to 14 percent of high SES eighth-graders will take a high-stakes test.

High-stakes tests diminish the quality of education for all students by contributing to the deprofessionalization of teachers—narrowing the curriculum; eliminating challenging, project-based work in favor of test preparation; and creating unproductive stress. But high-stakes tests also have a disproportionate and negative impact on grade retention and dropout rates for minorities. (Being retained in grade at least triples a student's likelihood of dropping out.)[29]

Perhaps most important, Mathison points out that the focus on testing in schools and concern for the so-called achievement gap does not improve education; indeed, it diminishes quality.

> The rhetoric of the achievement gap looks for solutions that alter children and families of color and those living in poverty but not for solutions that alter teacher competencies, curriculum, pedagogy, school organization, and school finance . . . The "achievement gap" is more accurately a *test score gap*. It's also an *opportunity gap*.[30]

And these gaps are closely related to the resource and income gaps that are routinely found between affluent White suburban schools and schools the Harvard Civil Rights Project has labeled "apartheid schools." "Focusing on the test scores gap without attention to these other gaps," says Mathison, "will do little to alleviate the inherent racism in educational opportunity and achievement."[31]

The research findings on high-stakes testing for kindergarten through twelfth-grade students are consistent with what we know about the effects of college admissions and teacher licensure tests, which contribute to educational inequality by denying education, scholarships, and access to the teaching profession to minority students, thereby sustaining the race gap between teachers and students.[32] ACT college admissions test scores, for example, are directly related to family income (the richer the students' parents, the higher the average scores across income groups) and race (Whites outscore all groups when factors such as course work, grades and family income are equal). ACT or SAT test scores above a specified level are required for admission to most teacher education programs. As a result of biases in both tests, large numbers of potential minority teachers are being excluded from opportunities to become classroom teachers.[33]

A detailed study of the impact of standardized tests on the teacher candidate pool in Florida indicated that test score requirements eliminated 80 percent of Black and 61 percent of Latino applicants to teacher education programs, but only 37 percent of Whites. There is also a long history of cultural bias on teacher licensure tests.[34] A recent National Research Council report on teacher tests concludes that raising cut-off scores on these tests will reduce racial diversity in the teaching profession without improving quality. Most important, the council found that these tests do not predict who will become effective teachers.[35]

RACIAL JUSTICE AND EDUCATION

"Justice is about who should get what and why," said philosopher Charles W. Mills to a group of educators gathered in Kansas City in 2004 for a conference highlighting the fiftieth anniversary of the *Brown v. Board of Education* decision.[36] Williams noted that racial justice is only part of justice, but in our world racial injustice has obviously been central to the modern history of the West in general and the United States in particular, yet the discussion of racial justice has not been correspondingly central to philosophy or education.

Williams pointed out the "pattern of differential and inferior treatment of nonwhites" that is the history of education in the United States. In the antebellum period, teaching Black slaves to read was a crime. Following the Civil War, during Reconstruction, freedmen were not given adequate resources to start lives on a level playing field. In the 1896 U.S. Supreme Court decision *Plessy v. Ferguson* "separate but equal" became the law of the land, but the reality was "separate and *unequal.*" *Brown v. Board of Education*, along with the Civil Rights Act (1964), Voting Rights Act (1965), and Fair Housing Act (1968) ended *de jure* segregation.[37] But segregation didn't vanish, as a result as the Harvard Civil Rights Project report, mentioned previously, makes clear.

Williams notes that for the struggle for racial justice to be taken seriously "requires a battle on the conceptual front." This struggle is made more difficult by the widely held but erroneous belief that racism stands as an anomaly in the otherwise egalitarian liberal democracy of the United States. But this belief is disconnected from the historical record. For example, Rogers M. Smith in his path-breaking book *Civic Ideals* has documented how most adults were legally denied access to full citizenship, including political rights, solely because of their race, ethnicity, or gender, not in anomalous circumstances but as the order of the day from the colonial period through the Progressive era in the United States.[38]

The strategy Williams suggests for this conceptual battle—a strategy adopted by many of the contributors to this book—is the "retrieval and elaboration of [the] concept of *white supremacy*, to characterize a system of pervasive illicit structural white advantage and corresponding nonwhite disadvantage." This approach shifts the debate on racial justice from the more familiar conservative and left-liberal positions—that is, acting and designing public policy in a color-blind way versus acting and designing public policy in a color-sensitive way.[39]

As you read the chapters that follow it's important to note that all of the authors are concerned about understanding and advancing racial justice in our society, particularly in educational contexts. However, even though they all share a vision of racial justice, they offer a wide variety of perspectives; many of them are engaged in the conceptual battle to recast the issues along the lines that Williams suggests and others focus on what is possible to achieve within the lines as currently drawn. Our aim is to provide readers with thorough analyses of what is the case as well as what ought to be regarding both racism and antiracist responses in schools, universities, and other educational settings.

THE PLAN OF THE BOOK

Race, Ethnicity, and Education: Racism and Antiracism in Education is divided into three parts. Authors in part I, "Conceptualizing Racism and Antiracism," take their lead from Williams and interrogate meanings of racism (and, as a result, define a foundation for antiracist education). The two opening chapters offer sociological perspectives on color-blind racism. In chapter 1, Eduardo Bonilla-Silva and David G. Embrick document the frames, styles, and stories that constitute the "new dominant racial ideology in town." George J. Sefa Dei then confronts the either-or arguments of the dominant conservative and liberal color-blind discourses and describes why and how the dominant frameworks for thinking about race should be subverted.

The next two chapters offer Marxian and anarchist analyses of capital, the state, and racism and discuss the limitations and possibilities of educational responses. In chapter 3, Rich Gibson explicates the relationship between capitalism and racism and how the latter serves to further the goals of the former. This is a wide-ranging chapter that covers issues of history and sociological theory as well as racism as a practical and pedagogical problem.

Then, in chapter 4, John F. Welsh critiques multiculturalism as process and ideology in higher education and explores theoretical alternatives to multiculturalism that critique racism but provide individualist visions of social relations.

Part II, "Racism and Antiracism in Schools," focuses on how racism operates in schools and classrooms and offers examples of how educators can strategize, organize, and teach against it. Jay P. Heubert begins this section with the chapter "High-Stakes Testing, Nationally and in the South." With particular attention to schools in the Southern United States and the role of courts in judging what constitutes racial discrimination, Heubert examines how high-stakes testing—the engine of current approaches to educational reform (e.g., NCLB)—affects the education and life chances of students of color. In "Whole Schooling As a Framework for Antiracist Education," Michael Peterson describes a systemic approach to school reform that aims to move beyond repression, punishment, rejection, boredom, and isolation to create schools that lead to communities that are empowering, democratic, inclusive, engaging, and based on a sense of partnership, support, and care.

"Antiracist Education in Majority White Schools," by Christine Sleeter and Linda Turner Bynoe, describes what antiracist education is and why it is important to pursue in majority White schools. Sleeter and Bynoe explore race, racism, and White identity development and describe how to successfully engage in antiracist education in majority White schools. In chapter 8, Marvin Lynn describes the theoretical foundations of critical race pedagogy and presents findings from a study of social justice–oriented African American teachers. Lynn's findings provide important insights into what critical race pedagogy looks like in the classroom and contributes theoretically to an emerging paradigm of critical race pedagogy in education.

Part III tackles the key problem of "Preparing Antiracist Educators." In chapter 9, Joyce E. King focuses analytical attention on ideological representations of the Middle Passage and how slavery began, as depicted in classroom textbooks adopted by the state of California in the early 1990s. The clash that ensued in California over the adoption of these controversial textbooks foreshadowed ongoing struggles concerning what and how students are learning about the Black experience. In "Demystifying Our Reality: Deconstructing Our Politics of Nonengagement," Rudolfo Chávez Chávez and Jeanette Haynes Writer adopt a Freirean perspective in exploring how a praxis of engagement can inform preparation of insightful and intuitive practitioners willing to struggle and to be challenged to understand their unique realities.

Chapters 11 and 12 peel back the layers of teacher education to reveal how White privilege and White supremacy operate in the classroom and at a programmatic level. In "'If Only We Could Find Some!' The White Privilege of Teacher Education," Rasheeda Ayanru, Eugenio Basualdo, and Stephen C. Fleury describe a unique urban education collaborative that aims to increase the number of teachers of color working in public schools. Their narrative of successes and failures is a story of how White privilege operates in teacher education (and public schools) and offers valuable insights into the politics of education and institutional racism. "Avoidance, Anger, and Convenient Amnesia" chronicles teaching and learning in a social studies teacher education course. Luis Urrieta Jr. and Michelle Reidel present an ethnographic case study of a professor of color engaging primarily White students in a critical, multicultural, social justice–oriented curriculum. Urrieta and Reidel raise important questions regarding the emotional terrain of race, ethinicity, and critical teaching and learning.

The volume closes with "Overcoming Disparity: Repositioning Leadership to Challenge the Conceptual Underpinnings of Antiracist Education" by Carolyn M. Shields and Russell Bishop. Drawing on examples from various countries, most prominently New Zealand, Shields and Bishop illustrate how as we "reposition ourselves discursively" the educational experiences of students who have traditionally been marginalized and unsuccessful can be transformed. The approach they offer aims to empower all learners, while members of a community develop new knowledge, new understanding, new norms, beliefs, and assumptions, which is also the aim we collectively have for this volume.

NOTES

1. See "Katrina Timeline." Available online at www.thinkprogress.org/katrina-timeline. Accessed August 30, 2005.

2. Margaret Wente, "The Real Storm Has Just Begun; How Did A Piece Of America Become a Third World Hellhole?," *Globe and Mail* (September 3, 2005): A23.

3. Howard Kurtz, media critic for the *Washington Post*, reported that a database search of that paper's stories for the past decade found one story prominently mentioning the poor of New Orleans. More typical were stories of Mardi Gras on how "the city's Black neighborhoods come alive" with Sunday parades in the fall. Kurtz also reports that "*New York Times* ombudsman Byron Calame found a similar record at his newspaper, unearthing only two articles about New Orleans in ten years that 'contained a few paragraphs on poverty and race.'" (Howard Kurtz, "Wiped Off the Map, and Belatedly Put Back on It," *Washington Post* [September 19, 2005]: C01. Available online at www.washingtonpost.com/wp-dyn/content/article/2005/09/18/AR2005091801265.html.)

4. Document available online at weblogs.elearning.ubc.ca/ross/archives/016535.html.

5. "Military Due to Move in to New Orleans," CNN (September 2, 2005). Available online at www.cnn.com/2005/WEATHER/09/02/katrina.impact.

6. "FEMA Chief: Victims Bear Some Responsibility," CNN (September 1, 2005). Available online at www.cnn.com/2005/WEATHER/09/01/katrina.fema.brown.

7. "A 2-year-old girl slept in a pool of urine. Crack vials littered a restroom. Blood stained the walls next to vending machines smashed by teenagers. 'We pee on the floor. We are like animals,' said Taffany Smith, 25, as she cradled her 3-week-old son, Terry. . . . By Wednesday, it had degenerated into horror. . . . At least two people, including a child, have been raped. At least three people have died, including one man who jumped 50 feet to his death, saying he had nothing left to live for. There is no sanitation. The stench is overwhelming." ("Katrina's Rising Toll; Trapped in an Arena and Suffering," *Los Angeles Times* [September 1, 2005]: A1.)

8. Christine Blatchford, "Katrina's Unequal Toll," *Globe and Mail* (September 3, 2005): A1.

9. Ibid.

10. "'This Great City Will Rise Again' Bush Promises," *New York Times Online* (September 16, 2005). Available online at www.nytimes.com/2005/09/16/politics/16btext.html.

11. The Center for Popular Economics, "4.10 The Color of Poverty (updated 8/19/04)," *Ultimate Field Guide to the U.S. Economy* (Amherst, MA: Center for Popular Economics, 2004). Available online at www.fguide.org/Update/4_10u.htm; U.S. Department of Commerce, Census Bureau, *Historical Poverty Tables*, Table 2. Available online at www.census.gov/hhes/poverty/histpov/hstpov2.html.

12. Dedrick Muhammad, Attieno Davis, Meizhu Lui, and Betsy Leondar-Wright, *The State of the Dream 2004: Enduring Disparities in Black and White* (Boston: United for a Fair Economy, 2004).

13. Ibid.

14. Pew Hispanic Center, "Wealth Gap Widens between Whites and Hispanics," (October 19, 2004). Available online at pewhispanic.org/newsroom/releases/release.php?ReleaseID=15.

15. Joshua Bonilla and Linda Rosen, *Black Americans: A Demographic Perspective* (Washington, DC: Population Resource Center, 2002).

16. U.S. Centers for Disease Control, "Infant Mortality Fact Sheet." Available online at www.cdc.gov/omh/AMH/factsheets/infant.htm.

17. Infant mortality comparison table on Yahoo! Education. Available online at education.yahoo.com/reference/factbook/countrycompare/imort/4a.html.

18. Pew Hispanic Center, "Hispanic Health: Divergent and Changing," (January 2002). Available online at pewhispanic.org/files/factsheets/1.pdf.

19. Department of Justice, Bureau of Justice Statistics, "Prison and Jail Inmates at Midyear 2002," (April 6, 2003). Available online at www.ojp.usdoj.gov/bjs /abstract/pjim02.htm.

20. Now with Bill Moyers, "Society and Community: Prisons in America." Available online at www.pbs.org/now/society/prisons2.html.

21. According to Human Rights Watch, "Nearly three quarters of new admissions to state prison were convicted of nonviolent crimes. Only 49 percent of sentenced state inmates are held for violent offenses. Perhaps the single greatest force behind the growth of the prison population has been the national war on drugs."

"The number of incarcerated drug offenders has increased twelvefold since 1980. In 2000, 22 percent of those in federal and state prisons were convicted on drug charges." (Human Rights Watch, "Incarcerated America" [April 2003]. Available online at www.hrw.org/backgrounder/usa/incarceration.)

22. Human Rights Watch, "Race and Incarceration in the United States," (February 27, 2002). Available online at www.hrw.org/backgrounder/usa/race/#P13_2990.

23. Erica Frankenberg, Chungmei Lee, and Gary Orfield, "A Multiracial Society with Segregated Schools: Are We Losing the Dream?" (Cambridge, MA: Harvard University Civil Rights Project, 2003). Available online at www.civilrightsproject.harvard.edu/research/reseg03/resegregation03.php.

24. For more on NCLB and its impact on public schools see E. Wayne Ross (ed.), *Defending Public Schools*, vols. 1–4, (Westport, CT: Praeger, 2004).

25. Sandra Mathison, "The Accumulation of Disadvantage: The Role of Educational Testing in the School Career of Minority Children," in Sandra Mathison and E. Wayne Ross (eds.), *Defending Public Schools: The Nature and Limits of Standards-Based Reform and Assessment* (Westport, CT: Praeger, 2004), 121–135. (An earlier version of this chapter is freely accessible online in *Workplace: A Journal for Academic Labor* at www.cust.educ.ubc.ca/workplace/issue5p2/mathison.html.)

26. V. E. Lee and D. T. Burkham, *Inequality at the Starting Gate* (Washington, DC: Economic Policy Institute, 2002).

27. Mathison, "The Accumulation of Disadvantage," 121–122.

28. Ibid.

29. Ibid.

30. Ibid., 129.

31. Ibid., 130.

32. Ibid.

33. National Center for Fair and Open Testing, "University Testing: Problems." Available online at www.fairtest.org/univ/univproblems.htm.

34. G. Pritchy-Smith, *The Effects of Competency Testing on the Supply of Minority Teachers: A Report Prepared for the National Education Association and the Council of Chief State School Officers* (Washington, DC: National Education Association, 1987).

35. Committee on Assessment and Teacher Quality, National Research Council, *Tests and Teaching Quality: Interim Report* (Washington, DC: National Academy Press, 2000). Efforts to improve learning and teacher quality rest on a misguided use of standardized tests. But the latest research indicates that an emphasis on testing results actually lowers student academic performance, increases dropout rates, and is a barrier to diversifying the teaching profession while improving teacher quality (for more technical, social, and political aspects of test-driven education reform see Ross, *Defending Public Schools*).

36. Charles W. Williams, "Education and Racial Justice." Speech to the American Educational Studies Association, Kansas City, MO, November 2004.

37. It is important to note that the *Brown v. Board of Education* decision did not apply to Latino students until 1970.

38. Rogers M. Smith, *Civic Ideals* (New Haven: Yale University Press, 1999).

39. Williams, "Education and Racial Justice,"2.

I

CONCEPTUALIZING RACISM AND ANTIRACISM

The (White) Color of Color Blindness in Twenty-First-Century Amerika

Eduardo Bonilla-Silva and David G. Embrick

INTRODUCTION

In the post–civil rights era, nothing seems racist in the traditional sense of the word. Even David Duke, Tom Metzger, and most members of the Ku Klux Klan and other old-fashioned White supremacist organizations claim they are not racist, just pro-White. Moreover, the "White street" asserts that Whites "don't see any color, just people."[1] They assume that although the ugly face of discrimination is still around, it is no longer the central factor determining minorities' life chances. Finally, they claim to aspire, much like Dr.Martin Luther King Jr., to live in a society where "people are judged by the content of their character, not by the color of their skin."

However, regardless of Whites' "sincere fictions,"[2] racial considerations shade almost everything in America. Blacks and dark-skinned minorities lag well behind Whites in virtually every area of social life; they are about three times more likely to be poor than Whites, earn about 40 percent less than Whites, and have about a tenth of the net worth of Whites. They also receive an inferior education compared to Whites even when they attend so-called integrated (at best, desegregated) schools.[3]

How is it possible to have this tremendous degree of racial inequality in a country where most Whites claim that racism is a thing of the past? More important, how do Whites explain the apparent contradiction between their professed color blindness and the U.S. color-coded inequality? Bonilla-Silva refers to this as the strange enigma of racism without racists. In his 2003 book *Racism without Racists*, he attempts to solve this enigma by arguing that Whites as a social collectivity have developed a new, powerful, and effective racial ideology to account for contemporary racial matters that he labels *color-blind racism*.[4] Whereas Jim Crow racism explained minorities' standing mainly as the result of their imputed biological and moral inferiority, color-blind racism avoids such simple arguments. Instead, Whites rationalize minorities' status as the product of market dynamics, naturally occurring phenomena, and their presumed cultural deficiencies. Despite its apparent "racism-lite" character, this ideology is as deadly as the one it replaces.

Before we attempt to deconstruct color-blind racism, let us explain why a new racial ideology is at play in the first place. Color-blind racism acquired cohesiveness and dominance in the late 1960s as the mechanisms and practices for keeping Blacks and other racial minorities at the bottom of the well changed. We argue that contemporary racial inequality is reproduced through new racism practices that are predominantly subtle, institutional, and apparently nonracial.[5] In contrast to the Jim Crow era, where racial inequality was enforced through overt means (e.g., signs saying "No Negroes Welcomed Here" or shotgun diplomacy at the voting booth), systemic White privilege is maintained nowadays in a "now you see it, now you don't" fashion. For example, residential segregation, which is almost as high today as it was in the past, is no longer accomplished through overtly discriminatory practices (e.g., bombs, housing covenants, etc.).[6] Instead, covert behaviors such as not showing all the available units, steering minorities and Whites into certain neighborhoods, quoting higher rents or prices to minority applicants, the racialization of credit scores, or not advertising units at all are the weapons of choice to maintain separate communities. New racism practices have been documented in a variety of venues: schools, jobs, banks, restaurants, and stores. Hence, as we will illustrate, the contours of color-blind racism fit quite well the way racial inequality is reproduced these days.

METHODOLOGY

The data for this chapter come from two sources: the 1997 Survey of Social Attitudes of College Students and the 1998 Detroit Area Study (DAS) on White Racial Ideology. The Survey of Social Attitudes of College Students is based on a convenient sample of 627 (including 451 White) students from large universities in the South and Midwest and a midsize university on the

West Coast. Of the White students who provided contact information (about 90 percent), 10 percent of them were randomly selected for interviews (forty-one students altogether, of which seventeen were men and twenty-four women, and of which thirty-one were from middle- and upper-middle-class backgrounds and ten were from working-class backgrounds).

The 1998 DAS is a probabilistic survey based on a representative sample of 400 Black and White Detroit metropolitan-area residents (323 White and 67 Black). The response rate to the survey was 67.5 percent. In addition, eighty-four respondents (sixty-seven White and seventeen Black) were randomly selected for in-depth interviews. The hour-long interviews were race-matched, followed a structured protocol, and were conducted in the subjects' home.

THE FRAMES OF COLOR-BLIND RACISM

The frames of any dominant racial ideology are *set paths for interpreting information* and *operate as cul-de-sacs* because, after people invoke them, they explain racial phenomena in a predictable manner—as if they were getting on a one-way street without exits. [7] Frames provide the intellectual and moral road map Whites use to navigate the always rocky road of domination and derail non-Whites from their track to freedom and equality.[8] The four central frames of color-blind racism are *abstract liberalism, naturalization, cultural racism,* and *minimization of racism,* and we illustrate each one separately in subsequent sections.

Abstract Liberalism: Unmasking Reasonable Racism

This frame incorporates tenets associated with political and economic liberalism in an abstract and decontextualized manner. By framing race-related issues in the language of liberalism, Whites can appear reasonable and even moral while opposing all practical approaches to deal with de facto racial inequality. For instance, by using the tenets of the free market ideology in the abstract, they can oppose affirmative action as a violation of the norm of equal opportunity. The following example illustrates how Whites use this frame. Jim, a thirty-year-old computer software salesperson from a privileged background, explained his opposition to affirmative action as follows:

> I think it's unfair top to bottom on everybody and the whole process. It often, you know, discrimination itself is a bad word, right? But you discriminate every

day. You wanna buy a beer at the store and there are six kinda beers you can get from Natural Light to Sam Adams, right? And you look at the price and you look at the kind of beer, and you . . . *it's a choice.* And a lot of that you have laid out in front of you, which one you get? Now, should the government sponsor Sam Adams and make it cheaper than Natural Light because it's brewed by someone in Boston? That doesn't make much sense, right? Why would we want that, or make Sam Adams eight times as expensive because we want people to buy Natural Light? And it's the same thing about getting into school or getting into some place. And universities it's easy, and universities is a hot topic now, and I could bug you, you know, Midwestern University I don't think has a lot of racism in the admissions process. And I think Midwestern University would, would agree with that pretty strongly. So why not just pick people that are going to do well at Midwestern University, pick people by their merit? I think we should stop the whole idea of choosing people based on their color.

Because Jim assumes hiring decisions are like market choices (e.g., choosing between competing brands of beer), he embraces a laissez-faire position on hiring. The problem with Jim's view is that labor market discrimination is alive and well (e.g., it affects 30 to 50 percent of Black and Latino job applicants) and most jobs (as much as 80 percent) are obtained through informal networks.[9] Jim's abstract position is further cushioned by his belief that although Blacks perceive or feel like there is a lot of discrimination he does not see much discrimination out there.

Hence, by upholding a strict laissez-faire view on hiring and, at the same time, ignoring the significant impact of discrimination in the labor market, Jim can safely voice his opposition to affirmative action in an apparently race-neutral way. This abstract liberal frame allows Whites to be unconcerned about school and residential segregation, oppose almost any kind of government intervention to ameliorate the effects of past and contemporary discrimination, and even support their preferences for Whites as partners or friends as a matter of choice.

Naturalization: Decoding the Meaning of "That's the Way It Is"

A frame that has not yet been brought to the fore by social analysts is the naturalization of race-related matters. The word *natural* or the phrase *that's the way it is* are often interjected to normalize events or actions that could otherwise be interpreted as racially motivated (residential segregation) or racist (preference for Whites as friends and partners). But as social scientists know quite well, these are not natural but socially produced outcomes. An example of how Whites use this frame is Bill, a manager in a manufacturing firm in his fifties, who explained the limited level of school integration as follows:

> I don't think it's anybody's fault. Because people tend to group with their own people. Whether it's White or Black or upper-middle-class or lower-class or, you know, Asians. People tend to group with their own. Doesn't mean if a Black person moves into your neighborhood, they shouldn't go to your school. They should and you should mix and welcome them and everything else, but you can't force people together. If people want to be together, they should intermix more. [Interviewer: OK. So the lack of mixing is really just kind of an individual lack of desire?] Well, individuals, it's just the way it is. You know, people group together for lots of different reasons: social, religious. Just as animals in the wild, you know. Elephants group together, cheetahs group together. You bus a cheetah into an elephant herd because they should mix? You can't force that. [laughs]

Although most respondents were not as crude as Bill, they still used this frame to justify the racial status quo.

Cultural Racism: "They Don't Have It Altogether"

Pierre Andre Taguieff has argued that modern racial ideology does not portray minorities as inferior biological beings.[10] Instead, it biologizes their presumed cultural practices (i.e., presents them as fixed features) and uses that as the rationale for justifying racial inequality (he labels this *differentialist racism*). This cultural racism is very well established in the United States.[11] The newness of this frame resides in the centrality it has acquired in Whites' contemporary justifications of minorities' standing. The essence of the frame, as William Ryan pointed out a long time ago, is blaming the victim by arguing that minorities' status is the product of their lack of effort, loose family organization, or inappropriate values.[12] An example of how Whites use this frame is Kim, a student at Midwestern University. When asked, "Many Whites explain the status of Blacks in this country as a result of Blacks lacking motivation, not having the proper work ethic, or being lazy ... what do you think?," Kim said,

> Yeah, I totally agree with that. I don't think, you know, they're all like that, but, I mean, it's just that if it wasn't that way, why would there be so many Blacks living in the projects? You know, why would there be so many poor Blacks? If they worked hard, they could make it just as high as anyone else could. You know, I just think that's just, you know, they're raised that way and

they see that parents are so they assume that's the way it should be. And they just follow the roles their parents had for them and don't go anywhere.

Although not all Whites were as crude as this student, most subscribed to this belief whether in its nastiest, most direct versions or in a so-called compassionate conservative manner.

Minimization of Racism: Whites' Declining Significance of Race Thesis

Most Whites do not believe that the predicament of minorities today is the product of discrimination. Instead, they believe that it's because of their culture, class, legacies from slavery, Mexican/Puerto Rican backward culture, culture of segregation, lack of social capital, poverty, and so on. It's anything but racism! An example of how Whites use this frame is Sandra, a retail salesperson in her early forties, who explained her view on discrimination as follows:

> I think if you are looking for discrimination, I think it's there to be *found*. But if you make the best of any situation, and if *you don't use it as an excuse*. I think sometimes it's an excuse because people felt they deserved a job, whatever! I think if things didn't go their way I know a lot of people have a tendency to use prejudice or racism as whatever as an *excuse*. I think in some ways, *yes* there is [*sic*] people who are prejudiced. It's not only Blacks, it's about Spanish, or women. In a lot of ways there [is] a lot of *reverse* discrimination. It's just what you wanna make of it.

This needs very little comment. Because most Whites, like Sandra, believe discrimination has all but disappeared, they regard minorities' claims of discrimination as excuses or as minorities playing the infamous race card.

THE STYLES OF COLOR BLINDNESS: HOW TO TALK NASTY ABOUT BLACKS WITHOUT SOUNDING RACIST

Ideologies are not just about ideas. For the frames of an ideology to work effectively, those who invoke them need rhetorical devices to weave arguments in all kinds of situations. In the case of color-blind racism, given the post–civil rights normative context, Whites need these devices to save face and still be able to articulate their racial views. Hence, we define the style of a racial ideology as its peculiar *linguistic manners and rhetorical strategies* (or *race talk*), that is, the technical tools that allow users to articulate its frames and racial stories. Because a full comprehensive analysis of the five stylistic components of color blindness is beyond the scope of this chapter, we only illustrate three: semantic moves, projection, and rhetorical incoherence.

Semantic Moves

Semantic moves—phrases that protect a user's moral standpoint (e.g., "I am not a racist, but ... ")—allow Whites to express their racial views in a coded and safe way—safe because they can always go back to the safety of the disclaimers ("I didn't mean that because I am not a racist" and "Some of my best friends are Black"). However, because statements such as "I am not a racist" or "Some of my best friends are Black" have become clichéd and, therefore, less effective, Whites have developed new ways to accomplish the same goals.[13]

One such rhetorical way to state racial views without opening yourself to the charge of racism is taking apparently all sides on an issue. We label this as the "Yes and no, but ... " move. Sandra, the retail person cited previously, answered the question "Are you for or against affirmative action?" in the following apparently cryptic manner:

> Yes and no. I feel someone should be able to have *something,* education, job, whatever, because they've earned it, they deserve it, they have the ability to do it. You don't want to put a six-year-old as a *rocket scientist.* They don't have the ability. It doesn't matter if the kid's Black or White. As far as letting one have the job over another, one just because of their race or their gender, I don't believe in that.

Sandra's "yes and no" stand on affirmative action is truly a *strong* no because she does not find any reason whatsoever for affirmative action programs to be in place.

"It Wasn't Me!": The Role of Projection in Color-Blind Racism

Psychologists know that projection is part of our normal equipment to defend ourselves. It is also an essential tool in the creation of a corporate identity (us versus them). More significantly, projection helps us escape from guilt and responsibility and affix blame elsewhere. Thus it was not surprising to find that Whites projected racism or racial motivations onto Blacks as a way of avoiding responsibility and feeling good about themselves.

The following example illustrates how Whites project racial motivations onto Blacks. In her answer to the interracial marriage question, Janet, a student at Southern University, projected onto people who marry across the color line:

> I would feel that in most situations they're not really thinking of the, the child. I mean, they might not really think anything of it, *but* in reality I think most of the time when the child is growing up, he's going to be picked on because he has parents from different races and it's gonna ultimately affect the child and, and the end result is they're only thinking of them. Both their own happiness, not the happiness of, of the kid.

By projecting selfishness onto those who intermarry, Janet was able to safely voice her otherwise problematic opposition to these marriages.

Rhetorical Incoherence

Finally, we want to provide one example of rhetorical incoherence. Although incoherence (e.g., grammatical mistakes, lengthy pauses, or repetition) is part of all natural speech, the level of incoherence increases noticeably when people discuss sensitive subjects. And because the new racial climate in America forbids the open expression of racially based feelings, views, and positions, when Whites discuss issues that make them feel uncomfortable, they become almost incomprehensible.

For example, Ray, a Midwestern University student and a respondent who was very articulate throughout the interview, became almost incomprehensible when answering the question about whether he had been involved with minorities while in college.

> Um so to answer that question, no. But I would not, I mean, I would not ever preclude a Black woman from being my girlfriend on the basis that she was Black. Ya' know, I mean, ya' know what I mean? If you're looking about it from, ya' know, the standpoint of just attraction, I mean, I think that, ya' know, I think, ya' know, I think, ya' know, all women are, I mean, all women have a sort of different type of beauty, if you will. And I think that, ya' know, for Black women, it's somewhat different than White women. But I don't think it's, ya know, I mean, it's, it's, it's nothing that would ever stop me from like, I mean, I don't know, I mean, I don't if that's, I mean, that's just sort of been my impression. I mean, it's not like I would ever say, "No, I'll never have a Black girlfriend," but it just seems to me like I'm not as attracted to Black women as I am to White women, for whatever reason. It's not about prejudice, it's just sort

of like, ya' know, whatever. Just sort of the way, way like I see White women as compared to Black women, ya' know?

The interviewer followed up Ray's answer with the question, "Do you have any idea why that would be?" Ray replied: "I, I, I [sighs] don't really know. It's just sort of hard to describe. It's just like, ya' know, who you're more drawn to, ya' know, for whatever reason, ya' know?" Ray's answer suggests that he is not attracted to Black women and has serious problems explaining why.

RACIAL STORIES

The last component of color-blind racism is racial stories. In this chapter we examine two kinds of racial stories, namely, *story lines* and *testimonies*.[14] We define story lines as the socially shared tales that incorporate a common scheme and wording. These racial story lines are often legend- or fable-like because, unlike testimonies (discussed later), they are most often based on impersonal, generic arguments with little narrative content—they are readily available ideological "of course" narratives that actors draw on in explaining personal or collective social realities. In story lines, characters are likely to be underdeveloped and are usually social types (e.g., the Black man in statements such as "My best friend lost a job to a Black man" or the welfare queen in "Poor Black women are welfare queens"). The ideological nature of such story lines is revealed by the similar intention and wording interlocutors employ in their execution (e.g., "the past is the past") and by the way they are deployed in a range of locations by a wide range of actors for similar ends.

Testimonies, on the other hand, are accounts where the narrator is a central participant in the story or is close to the characters in the story.[15] Testimonies provide the aura of authenticity that only firsthand narratives can furnish ("I know this for a fact because I have worked all my life with Blacks"). Therefore, these stories help narrators gain sympathy from listeners or persuade them about points they wish to convey. Although testimonies involve more detail, personal investment, and randomness than story lines, they are not just plain stories.[16] They serve rhetorical functions with regard to racial issues, such as saving face, signifying nonracialism, or bolstering their arguments on controversial racial matters. Moreover, they are often tightly linked to the story lines as these personal experiences are understood and framed through the lens of more general racial narratives and understandings about the world.

Story Lines

If racial stories were unchangeable, they would not be useful tools to defend the racial order.[17] Thus racial stories are intricately connected to specific historical moments and change accordingly.[18] For example, during the Jim Crow era, the myth of the Black rapist became a powerful story line that could be invoked to keep Blacks, particularly Black men, in their place.[19] Today new story lines have emerged to keep Blacks in their new (but still subordinate) place.[20] The most common story lines we identified were "the past is the past"; "I did not own slaves"; "If (other ethnic groups such as Italians or Jews) made it, how come Blacks have not?"; and "I did not get a (job or promotion) because of a Black man." Because most people are somewhat familiar with these stories, we will just provide a few examples.

The Past Is the Past.   The core of this story line is the idea that we must put our racial past behind and affirmative action–type programs do exactly the opposite by keeping the racial flame alive. Moreover, as the story line goes, these policies are particularly problematic because they attempt to address a long-past harm by doing a similar harm today (i.e., affirmative action regarded as reverse racism). This story line was used by more than 50 percent of college students (twenty-one out of forty-one) and by most DAS respondents usually in discussions on race-targeted programs for Blacks. A perfect example of how respondents used this story line is Emily, a student at Southern University, who told the story line in an exchange with the interviewer over the meaning of affirmative action.

> I have, I just have a problem with the discrimination, you're gonna discriminate against a group and what happened in the past is horrible and it should never happen again, but I also think that to move forward you have to let go of the past and let go of what happened um, you know? And it should really start equaling out 'cause I feel that some of, some of it will go too far and it's swing the other way. One group is going to be discriminated against, I don't, I don't believe in that. I don't think one group should have an advantage over another regardless of what happened in the past.

Clear in Emily's logic is the idea that "two wrongs don't make a right." Thus to compensate Blacks for a history of White advantage or Black oppression would involve unjustified, unfair advantage today. Note this view does not involve a denial of past injustice. Instead, it regards the past as unrelated or irrelevant to current realities. Hence, programs designed to redress the horrible past are constructed as discriminating in reverse.

Almost all DAS respondents resorted to a version of this story line to express their displeasure with programs they believe benefit Blacks solely because of their race. However, these older respondents were more likely to use the story line while venting lots of anger. John II, for instance, a retired architect and homebuilder in his late sixties, used a version of the story line in his response to the question on reparations.

> Not a nickel, not a nickel! I think that's ridiculous. I think that's a great way to go for the Black vote. But I think that's a ridiculous assumption because those that say we should pay them because they were slaves back in the past and yet, how often do you hear about the people who were Whites that were slaves and the White that were ah? Boy, we should get reparations, the Irish should get reparations from the English.

John's statement suggests not only that it is ridiculous to give Blacks even a nickel in compensation for a history of slavery but that Blacks have no special claim with regard to poor treatment ("the Irish should get reparations from the English").

But what is ideological about this story? Is it not true that "the past is the past?" First, whether Whites inserted this story line or not, most interpreted the past as slavery even when in some questions we left it open (e.g., questions regarding the history of oppression) or specified we were referring to slavery and Jim Crow. Because Jim Crow died slowly in the country (and lasted well into the 1960s to 1970s), the reference to a remote past ignores the relatively recent overt forms of racial oppression that have impeded Black progress. Second, such stories ignore or effectively erase the effects of historic discrimination on limiting minorities' and Blacks' capacity to accumulate wealth at the same rate as Whites. According to Oliver and Shapiro, the "accumulation of disadvantages" has "sedimented" Blacks economically so that even if all forms of economic discrimination Blacks face ended today, they would not catch up with Whites for several hundred years.[21] Third, this story of discrimination exclusively as a factor in a long-distant past is important to Whites' explanations for their staunch opposition to all race-based compensatory programs. This story line then is not merely used to deny the enduring effects of historic discrimination or the significance of contemporary discrimination but to explain why certain social programs are unnecessary and problematic.

If Jews, Italians, and Irish Have Made It, How Come Blacks Have Not?   Another popular story line of the post–civil rights era is "If Jews,

Italians, and Irish (or other ethnic groups) have made it, how come Blacks have not?" This story is used to suggest that because other groups who experienced discrimination are doing well today, Blacks' predicament must be their own doing. Although fewer respondents explicitly deployed this story in the interviews, a significant percentage (60 percent of DAS respondents and 35 percent of college students) agreed with a survey question on this matter. An example of how Whites used this story is Kim, a student at Southern University, who inserted it to explain why she does not favor government intervention on minorities' behalf.

> No. I think that a lot of bad things happened to a lot of people, but you can't sit there and dwell on that. I mean, like the Jewish people, look what happened to them. Do you hear them sitting around complaining about it and attributing anything bad that happens to them? I've never heard anyone say, "Oh, it's because I'm Jewish." And I know it's a little different because a Black, I mean, you can't really, a lot of—you can't really tell on the outside a lot of times, but they don't wallow in what happened to them a long time ago. It was a horrible thing I admit, but I think that you need to move on and try to put that behind you.

Here, this story line is told as evidence to question Black claims to harm. This story also presents a moral racial tale: the way to deal with hard times is to work hard and not dwell on or wallow in what happened a long time ago, which, according to the story, is presumably what other racial and ethnic groups did.

An example of how DAS respondents used this story line is Henrietta, a transvestite schoolteacher in his fifties, who inserted the story to answer a question on compensatory government spending on Blacks' behalf.

> As a person who was once reversed discriminated against, I would have to say no. Because the government does not need programs if they, if people would be motivated to bring themselves out of the poverty level. Ah . . . when we talk about certain programs, when the Irish came over, when the Italians, the Polish, and the East European Jews, they all were immigrants who lived in terrible conditions, who worked in terrible conditions too. But they had one thing in common; they all knew that education was the way out of that poverty. And they did it. I'm not saying the Blacks were brought over here maybe not willingly, but if they realize education's the key, that's it. And that's based on individuality.

What is ideological about this story? Have not Jews, Irish, Chinese, and other groups moved up and even assimilated in America? The problem is that this story line equates the experiences of immigrants groups with those of involuntary "immigrants" (enslaved Africans, etc.). But as Stephen Steinberg pointed out some time ago, most immigrant groups were able to get a foothold on certain economic niches or used resources such as an education or small amounts of capital to achieve social mobility.[22]

> In contrast, racial minorities were for the most part assigned to the pre
> industrial sectors of the national economy and, until the flow of immigration
> was cut off by the First World War, were denied access to the industrial jobs
> that lured tens of millions of immigrants. All groups started at the bottom, but
> as Blauner points out, "the bottom" has by no means been the same for all
> groups.[23]

Thus comparing these groups is comparing groups with quite different historical experiences and opportunities. It is a story line that is an updated form of what Ryan called blaming the victim, suggesting that the problem lies within those who have not made it, and thus the solution is for them to work harder.[24] These are not stories that a typically told about a relative, or even a group of which the speaker is a descendant. Instead, these are abstract stories of White ethnic triumph in the face of adversity deployed specifically to demonstrate that those who are motivated can succeed.

Racial Testimonies

During the course of the interviews, respondents also told more personal stories that although connected to the story lines, were different enough in style, content, and function to warrant analytic distinction. For example, testimonies tapped into aspects of color-blind ideology, such as the claim that traditional racism has all but disappeared. They also were extremely valuable for image restoration (in case of mistakes, such as saying something that sounds racist) or for self-presentation (presentation of self as color-blind). In what follows we examine the two most recurring testimonies.

Testimonies of Disclosure of Knowledge of Someone Close Who Is Racist.   Twelve students disclosed information about someone close (usually a parent or grandparent) being racist. The narrative form used to reveal this information resembles confession in church because by disclosing this sensitive information to the audience, respondents seem to be attempting to strategically absolve themselves from the possibility of being regarded as racist. By identifying a bad White individual, respondents could situate themselves among the nonracist. One example is Mike, a Midwestern University student who, in response to the question, "Do you ever talk about racial issues at home?" said,

> Yeah we do. I mean, my dad came from a pretty racist background, I mean, not, you know, like—well, actually, his grandfather, I think, was in the Ku Klux Klan until he got married. And my great-grandmother, who I knew—she died, but I knew her—was completely the opposite. And basically when they got married, she said "no way." So *that* ended, but I mean, there was still a certain, you know, racism that pervaded. In his family they were pretty racist, so you'll still hear, you know, racial slurs slip out every once in a while, but I think he makes a conscious effort not to, I mean, he certainly didn't ever try to teach me things like that, you know. For one thing, my dad was in the navy for a long time, so I grew up with my mom for the first five years or so, and then he worked and my mom stayed at home with me. So my dad's influence was not nearly as much as my mom's to begin with, and even when it was, I wouldn't say that influenced me a lot, but there were definitely, I mean, racist ideas in his family. And I see that with my grandparents, you know, his parents.

In all twelve cases, these testimonies had a similar narrative structure. First, the respondent confesses or reveals relatives who express explicit racist beliefs and gives examples to illustrate racial behavior among these family members. The respondent then ends the story by explaining why she or he is not racist. In this case, Mike confesses that his dad comes from a pretty racist background. Then he mentions that his father's grandfather was in the KKK. Finally, he concludes the story by showing that he was not substantially influenced by these ideas because his father "didn't try to teach me things like that" and because his mother raised him.

DAS respondents used this testimony, too. For example, Jenny, a public school administrator in her fifties, in response to the question on how she felt about the neighborhood where she grew up, stated that many of her neighbors were closed-minded and labeled them as Archie Bunkers. After narrating an incident in which a girl in her school refused one Black kid as a dance partner, Jenny said:

> My grandmother, who was—she was Scandinavian, used to make fun of Blacks. And when we would drive through a Black neighborhood she would say things like, "Look at all the little chocolate drops." And I can remember being a young child—maybe five, six, or seven years old—and being offended by her remarks. My parents never, ever said anything like that. My parents were very open-minded and broad-minded.

Similar to Mike, Jenny also used a similar narrative structure in her telling of this testimony. First, she discloses in an almost confessional tone that her grandmother harbored racist views. Then, she supplies the example of her grandmother's mocking remarks about Blacks. Finally, she distances herself from this relative by pointing out that even at a young age she was offended by her grandmother's remarks and that her parents were very open-minded and never said such things.

Why do we regard these stories as racial? Are they not just stories? We suggest these testimonies are not random because they all have a similar structure, often emerge at the same point in the interview and in response to similar questions, and have rhetorical and ideological functions. Furthermore, as we will discuss next, when White racial progressives or Blacks narrated stories about racist family members, they were significantly less likely to use the formula uncovered here. Our point about these testimonies then is that they serve strategic purposes: they are deployed to carry a message about self (as color-blind) through discussing others (the bad racist Whites).

Testimonies of Interactions with Blacks.   Other testimonies involved stories of interactions (negative or positive) with Blacks. In the first type, respondents narrate a negative incident with Blacks as an example to justify a position taken on some issue. In the other type, respondents narrate a positive incident or relationship with Blacks as a way to signify the narrator's good relationship or views about Blacks (positive self-presentation through a personal story). About a third of the students and DAS respondents inserted one of these stories.

Stories of positive interactions with Blacks have a function similar to the stories about a racist relative—all are used for the goal of representing oneself as color-blind. For instance, John II inserted a positive story of interaction with Blacks in World War II in response to the question on whether Blacks are hard to approach or are not made to feel welcome by Whites. After stating he had no experiences on which to issue an opinion on this matter, John II narrated the following story:

> [So] the Filipino scouts stood farther away from me and they got the cover and I got behind the curb. It wasn't quite enough curb to hide me and the fellow was shooting a full automatic [weapon?]. A jeep came in out of one of the roads and slid to a stop and, about the time he said, "Get in!," they said "Let's go!," because I was in laying across the back seat and he took off. When we got down the road, I climbed out of the back seat into the front seat and it was a colored captain. He wouldn't give me his name or anything. He said, "That's all

right," but I've always remembered that. He put himself at risk and under fire to pick up a man and take him out of a line of fire.

John II's story served as a vehicle to state his view that Blacks and Whites can act civil toward each other. His story resembles those many veterans tell of interracial solidarity during war. However, for John II, as for so many White veterans, these experiences do not seem to have penetrated very deeply as he did not have an interracial lifestyle after he returned to the United States. The telling of this story in some way serves a strategic function to demonstrate abstract acceptance or tolerance rather than as evidence of real racial openness. For example, John II, who used the term *colored* to refer to the Black man who saved his life, opposed interracial marriage and acknowledged that he is "more comfortable around Whites because I've grown up with them" and, thus, had no qualms about neighborhoods or schools being almost completely White. In some ways, John II's stance on these issues amounts to almost a modern version of the separate but equal policy: Blacks and Whites can be civil toward each other, but they should not live near each other or marry each other.

Stories of negative interactions with Blacks serve to reinforce the notion that Blacks and Whites are different. For example, Mickey, a student at Midwestern University, acknowledged that his family talks about racial matters often because of the area they live in (Benton Harbor, a formerly mostly White area that has become a predominantly Black area). After pointing out that Benton Harbor has "one of the highest crime rates in, like, the country" and that "now it's, it's a really dirtiest [*sic*] place," the interviewer asked him if people in his community ever worried about violence and crime spreading into their community. After Mickey acknowledged he thought about that a lot, he added,

> But I mean, nothing really happened horribly. Actually, a neighbor of mine [laughs], kind of a grim story. I have a younger brother who's friends with one of my neighbors just down the street who hangs out with him sometimes. And he was drivin' downtown in Benton Harbor, about a couple of months ago, and I think he was trying to get some, marijuana or somethin' stupid like that, and he, got beat over the head with a baseball bat, got some Black eyes, and he had brain damage. He's okay now, but he was in a coma for a little bit. And he's like, I think he's got minor brain damage, irreversible. But nothing that's affecting him, like, too bad, but that was just one incident that happened a couple of months that made me think about stuff like this.

Mickey deployed this story in expressing ambivalence about whether the problems of Benton Harbor were rooted in economics or morality. It was an example used to illustrate or explain his belief that Blacks are more aggressive than Whites.

DAS respondents also told negative stories of interaction with Blacks. Bill, a retired schoolteacher in his eighties, offered testimony to explain why he thinks Blacks and Whites are different. After pointing out that Blacks had bought a church in his neighborhood, he claimed they forced a restaurant in the area out of business. He narrated the following testimony to explain this situation:

> They like to eat. They pile their dishes just loaded with that stuff and, I actually didn't see it, but I saw one lady come in with a full plate of chicken. I didn't pay much attention, but the next thing I know, they are leaving. Now I know she didn't eat all that chicken. She probably put it in her purse and walked out with it. I didn't see that. Lot of them are doing that, how can they make any money? And seeing that they are all heavy people, it seems like they do a lot of eating and so I don't know what to say about something like that.

Here there is no question that Bill's facts are fuzzy (and racist in the traditional sense of the term). That a restaurant would go out of business because of too many customers who ate too much is unlikely. Nevertheless, the ideological importance of this testimony, as well as all the racial stories we have discussed, is not based on whether the facts are wrong but rather to the way they are deployed as evidence to validate Whites' beliefs about minorities (in this case, Bill's belief that they are different and qualitatively lesser than Whites) or about themselves.

DISCUSSION

In this chapter we suggest that there is a new dominant racial ideology in town: color-blind racism. This ideology is suave but deadly—hence the "k" in the spelling of the word Amerika in the title we used for this chapter.[25] Whites, as we show, need not use the tropes of the past to keep minorities in their new but still subordinate place.

What is fundamentally ideological about this new ideology is the myth that keeps all its components together: the idea that race has all but disappeared as a factor shaping the life chances of people in the United States. This myth is the central column supporting the house of color blindness. Remove this column from the house's foundation and the house collapses. Removing this column, however, will not be an easy task because Whites' racial views are not mere erroneous ideas to be battled in the field of rational discourse. They constitute, as we argued in this chapter, a racial ideology, that is, a loosely organized set of frames, phrases, and stories that help Whites justify contemporary racial inequality. These views, then, are symbolic expressions of Whites' dominance and cannot just be eradicated with facts because racial facts are highly contested. In the eyes of Whites, evidence of racial disparity in income, wealth, and education is evidence that there is something wrong with minorities; evidence of Blacks' overrepresentation in the criminal justice system or on death row is proof of Blacks' criminal tendencies.

Given that this chapter is in a collection pertaining to educational matters in the United States, we want to sketch a few of the ways in which color-blind racism will affect education in the twenty-first century.

1. Classroom discussions on race as well as the curricula on race have become as bland as color blindness and, hence, are not helping youths develop the skills they need to understand and be able to fight the evils of racism in the United States. Rather than discussing the continuing significance of discrimination, teachers prefer a view of the country in which all colors share an equal space in the rainbow.

2. The impact of Whites' segregation is never analyzed or discussed as a factor, limiting how teachers perceive and treat minority students. Teachers who constantly navigate what Bonilla-Silva has labeled as the "White habitus"[26] have serious difficulties educating minority youths because they have absorbed all sorts of stereotypes about them and have not developed the necessary emotional and cultural skills to interact effectively with minorities.

3. Color-blind racism limits the discussions on Whiteness in schools as Whites play their race card (I am not White! I am just a human being). Unless we recognize that the race of the teacher is likely to have an impact on school outcomes, we will not be able to begin a serious educational reform.

4. Race has become Black (and slowly Latino) in the United States. Hence, Whites can proclaim color blindness and still blame minorities for all the ills in the educational system. This is reflected in schools across the nation where White teachers who preach color blindness have no qualms about blaming all sorts of school problems on minority students ("They are not respectful," "They are not too smart," etc.) and teachers ("They are so aggressive," "They are this and they are that").

5. In so-called integrated schools, within-school segregation is rampant. However, White teachers and students only see so-called minority self-segregation and hardly acknowledge how tracking keeps White students out of reach for meaningful social interaction with minority students. Again, this is another case of the pot calling the kettle black.

CONCLUSIONS

Ending a chapter such as this one without offering potential solutions to the road blocks that color blindness poses could be a disempowering exercise. Hence, to prevent this from happening, we conclude this chapter with several concrete things we can all do to fight color-blind racism. First, we need to nurture a large cohort of antiracist Whites to begin challenging color-blind nonsense from within.[27] Whites' collective denial about the true nature of race relations may help them feel good, but it is also one of the greatest obstacles to doing the right thing. In racial matters, as in therapy, the admission of denial is the preamble for the beginning of recovery.

To make things clear, we are not suggesting that all Whites are racist. This would violate our theoretical frame and lead us into an essentialist position.[28] As a matter of fact, we classified 10 to 15 percent of the White respondents as racial progressives. [29] However, the identity of these respondents may be surprising: young working-class women. Why would this segment of the White population be more likely to be racially progressive? We suggest that because they experience the double whammy (being women and workers), they are therefore in a better position to empathize with minorities' plight. Equally important is that they are more likely to share intimate social spaces (neighborhoods, jobs, schools, etc.) with minorities, which combined with their low status produces the kind of race contact that Gordon Allport believed would result in better race relations.[30]

Second, researchers and educators need to provide counterideological arguments to each of the frames of color-blind racism. We need to counter Whites' abstract liberalism with concrete liberal positions based on a realistic understanding of racial matters and a concern with achieving real racial equality. Are Blacks color-blind, too? The answer is that color-blind racism has a small direct and a larger indirect effect on them that blunts the potential all-out character of their oppositional ideology. This means that color-blind racism is a dominant ideology because it makes those at the top of the racial order happy and confuses those at the bottom; that is, it has become a hegemonic ideology (similar to capitalism, patriarchy, etc.).

Third, we need to undress Whites' claims of color blindness. We must show in creative ways the myriad facets of contemporary Whiteness: Whites living in White neighborhoods, sending their kids to White schools, associating primarily with Whites, and having their primary relationships with Whites. And because of the subtle character of modern White supremacy, new research strategies, such as audits (Housing and Urban Development), mixed research designs (surveys and interviews), and racial treason will be required to unveil the mask of Whiteness.[31] Given the new demography of the United States, why the focus on the Black-White dyad? On this, our answer is twofold. First, a new research project by Bonilla-Silva and Emerson is being conducted to assess the parameters of the new racial stratification order (the Latin Americanization of race relations) and can offer arguments and preliminary data on how other groups might fit in the ideological constellation. In this project, they are positing that a new racial order is emerging in the United States, characterized by a triracial rather than biracial division, and the increasing salience of skin tone as a stratification element.[32] Second, despite the new racial demography, we believe, like Joe Feagin and others, that the Black-White paradigm still ordains the macroracial issues in the country; it is still through this prism that newcomers are assessed (close to Whiteness or Blackness).[33]

Fourth, modern White supremacy must be challenged wherever it exists—churches, neighborhoods, schools, places of work, and even academic organizations such as the American Educational Research Association and the American Sociological Association. Those committed to racial equality must develop a personal practice to challenge White supremacy. Is this a racial ideology or a general, post–civil rights ideology? In this chapter, we described the racial ideological aspects of the larger ideological ensemble, which always includes a plurality of subjects of domination (gender, race, class, etc.). At least one analyst makes the case that post–civil rights ideology is characterized by "muted hostility." [34]

Finally, the most important strategy for fighting new racism practices and the ideology of color blindness is to re-create a civil rights movement. Changes in systems of domination and their accompanying ideologies are never accomplished by racial dialogues ("Can we all just get along?"), workshops on racism, education, or through moral reform alone. Moral, counterideological, and educational appeals always need a social movement—in our case, a new civil rights movement that demands equality of results now! Only by demanding what seems impossible now will we be able to make genuine racial equality possible in the future.

NOTES

1. We are using the notion of "White street" to refer to how average Whites think and talk about race. The idea is similar to the way that American commentators talk and write about the "Arab street."
2. Joe R. Feagin, *Racist America: Roots, Realities, and Future Reparations* (New York: Routledge, 2000); Joe R. Feagin and Eileen O'Brian, *White Men on Race: Power, Privilege, and the Shaping of Cultural Consciousness* (Boston: Beacon Press, 2003).

3. For details on all these statistics, see chapter 4 in Eduardo Bonilla-Silva, *White Supremacy and Racism in the Post-Civil Rights Era* (Boulder, CO: Lynne Rienner, 2001).

4. We define racial ideology as the broad racial frameworks or grids that racial groups use to make sense of the world and to decide what is right or wrong, true or false, and important or unimportant. And given that all societies are structured in dominance, the frameworks of the rulers (whether men, the bourgeoisie, or Whites) are more likely to crystallize as common sense. See Teun Van Dijk, *Ideology: A Multidisciplinary Approach* (London: Sage, 1999).

5. See Bonilla-Silva, *White Supremacy*, chapter 4.

6. Douglas S. Massey and Nancy A. Denton, *American Apartheid: Segregation and the Making of the Underclass* (Cambridge, MA: Harvard University Press, 1993).

7. In this chapter we only examine the dominant racial ideology. However, we would be remiss if we did not point out that not all Whites spout this ideology. In fact we document the views of White racial progressives, who comprise about 10 percent of the White respondents in these samples, in chapter 6 of Bonilla-Silva, *White Supremacy*.

8. Here we are using the notion of ideology in the Althusserian sense, that is, ideology as a practice that allows users to accomplish tasks.

9. Jomills Braddock and James McPartland, "How Minorities Continue to Be Excluded from Equal Employment Opportunities: Research on Labor Market and Institutional Barriers," *Journal of Social Issues* 43, no.1 (1987): 5–39; Deirdre A. Royster, *Race and the Invisible Hand: How White Networks Exclude Black Men from Blue-Collar Jobs* (Berkeley: University of California Press, 2003).

10. Pierre-Andre Taguieff, *The Force of Prejudice: Racism and Its Doubles* (Minneapolis: University of Minnesota Press, 2001).

11. Although some analysts believe that the idea of the culture of poverty, as elaborated by Oscar Lewis in the 1960s, was the foundation of a racialized view on poverty, historians have documented the long history of this belief in America (Oscar Lewis, "The Culture of Poverty," *Scientific American* 215, no. 4 [1966]: 19–25.) See, for example, Michael A. Katz, *In the Shadow of the Poorhouse: A Social History of Welfare in America* (New York: Basic Books, 1986).

12. William Ryan, *Blaming the Victim* (New York: Vintage Books, 1976).

13. These moves have not disappeared completely as many respondents still used them. However, because ideologies are always in processand under construction, new and more refined moves have emerged.

14. Eduardo Bonilla-Silva, *Racism without Racists: Color-Blind Racism and the Persistence of Racial Inequality in the USA* (Boulder, CO: Rowman and Littlefield, 2003).

15. Norman K. Denzin, *The Research Act* (Englewood Cliffs, NJ: Prentice Hall, 1989).

16. In truth, there are no plain stories as all stories are imbued in ideology. See Jeremy Tambling, *Narrative and Ideology* (Bristol: Open University Press, 1991).

17. Mary R. Jackman, *Velvet Glove: Paternalism and Conflict in Gender, Class, and Race Relations* (Berkeley: University of California Press, 1994).

18. Michael Omi and Winant Howard, *Racial Formation in the United States: From the 1960s to the 1980s* (New York: Routledge, 1994); Stuart Hall, "The Whites

of Their Eyes: Racist Ideologies and the Media," in Manuel Alvarado and John Thompson (eds.), *The Media Reader* (London: British Film Institute, 1990), 18–22.

19. Patricia Hill-Collins, *Black Feminist Thought* (Boston, MA: Unwin Hyman, 1994).

20. Kimberlé W. Crenshaw, "Color-Blind Dreams and Racial Nightmares: Reconfiguring Racism in the Post–Civil Rights Era," in T. Morrison and C. B. Lacour (eds.), *Birth of a Nation'hood* (New York: Pantheon Books, 1997), 97–168.

21. Melvin Oliver and Thomas M. Shapiro, *Black Wealth/White Wealth: A New Perspective on Racial Inequality* (New York: Routledge, 1995).

22. Stephen Steinburg, *The Ethnic Myth* (Boston, MA: Beacon Press, 1989).

23. Ibid., 101.

24. Ryan, *Blaming the Victim.*

25. To those offended by our spelling of the word Amerika we say that we will remove the *k* from Amerika when Amerika removes racism from the country.

26. Bonilla-Silva, *Racism without Racists.*

27. Feagin and O'Brien, *White Men on Race.*

28. Eduardo Bonilla-Silva, "Rethinking Racism: Toward a Structural Interpretation," *American Sociological Review* 62, no. 3 (1997): 465–480; Eduardo Bonilla-Silva, "The Essential Social Fact of Race," *American Sociological Review* 64, no. 6 (1999): 899–906.

29. We classify as racial progressives respondents who support affirmative action and interracial marriage and who recognize the significance of discrimination in the United States.

30. Gordon Allport, *The Nature of Prejudice* (New York: Doubleday/Anchor Books, 1958).

31. Joel Ignatiev and John Garvey, *Race Traitor* (New York: Routledge, 1996).

32. Eduardo Bonilla-Silva, "From Bi-Racial to Tri-Racial: Towards New System of Racial Stratification in the USA," *Racial and Ethnic Studies* 27, no. 6 (2004): 1–20.

33. Feagin, *Racist America.*

34. In *The Velvet Glove*, Jackman (1994) argues that in the post-civil rights era, gender, class, and race ideology has shifted from overt to covert or muted hostility. Thus in Jackman's estimation, men, capitalists, and Whites are less likely to employ the nasty tropes of the past and hit women, workers, and minorities with a velvet glove.

2

"We Cannot Be Color-Blind": Race, Antiracism, and the Subversion of Dominant Thinking

George J. Sefa Dei

INTRODUCTION

Let me begin by making clear that I see myself as fully complicit in the discussion that I undertake in this chapter. The "we" that I write about therefore includes all who read this and share in the ideas espoused. The emerging challenges of educating for power and difference requires that we all leave the confines of the gated-community mentality of education—the thinking that difficult issues and challenges facing education can be hidden from view in our classrooms, whether in academia or the local elementary or secondary school—to engage these issues. Silence on such critical issues as dealing with difference and diversity do not augur well for educating a community. Christine Sleeter, in her work with U.S. educators, observed how some, in trying to appear not to be racist, would often claim not to see color in their classrooms.[1] The view is that by seeing color one necessarily acts in ways that would privilege some and disadvantage others. Yet the issue of differential negative treatment by race must be distinguished from the salient recognition of racial differences as important sites of strengths, with contributions to societies as communities of differences. To deny color and profess color blindness is very problematic, especially when this approach is pursued to deny one's racial privilege or the attempt to assert one's dominance. As many others have argued, the categories of "Black," "White," "Brown," and so on—no matter how imperfect—are not the problem in themselves. Working with these categories does not mean one is reproducing race or racism. It basically means becoming realistic that these categories organize our society. Omi and Winant astutely comment that race being a fundamental principle of social organization and identity formation in society cannot be dismissed.[2] Therefore, rather than deny them, we must challenge the interpretations put on them.

In this chapter I take the intellectual and political position that those who speak about race do not create a problem that is nonexistent in the first place. Antiracists speak, write, and discuss race as a problem that already exists. What is important is to subvert the interpretation we put on these categories. Refusing to speak race does not enable any resistance to the negative interpretation of racial differences. To argue that we should be color-blind misses the point. In fact, it is an insult to human intelligence to enthuse that "we should not see color." Color is not the problem; it is the interpretation and judgments that we put on color that makes the problem. Those who feel threatened when their race privilege is questioned would quite often rationalize their stance by charging that so-called antiracists have an obsession with race. But as Jewel Smith long ago noted, it is "exceedingly misguided for anyone to simply overlook, or de-emphasize, the destructive and ubiquitous presence of race. . . . Rather than an emphasis on race, what is truly excessive, it seems, is the amount of time spent avoiding a direct hit on the issue."[3]

In not speaking of race, what are we truly afraid of? Can we meaningfully have a discussion of antiracism without engaging race? Who are we kidding when we deny race with its political, material, and emotional currencies? This chapter is about bringing race to the foreground of any critical antiracist academic and political engagement. My focus is looking at the significance of race and difference for schooling and education. In articulating antiracist education, we cannot skirt around the key questions of race and difference. We must be bold to speak about the cultural injury done to racialized bodies in our classrooms, the social exclusions of their knowledges and experiences from official school curriculum and texts, the commodification of their cultures (as seen particularly in case of the presentation of Black male masculinities and Black sexuality for consumption), and the complicities of White privilege in enacting violence of Othered bodies. My point is that the racist moments—racist muggings and the egregious display of race privilege (e.g., White dominance) that certain bodies experience in our school systems (and in fact in the wider society)—are all enacted and played on race signifiers using racial tropes and imageries.

The power of race talk resides in the making and experiencing of the "Other" and the creation of othered subjects. Anticolonial thinker Albert

Memmi long ago informed us about the process of othering as initiated in the dominant's construction of imaginary differences.[4] These differences are seen as real and are assigned important social values. Through time these differences provided a justification for conferring rewards and benefits to some while subjecting the racialized "Other" to differential and unequal treatment. In the same vein the Martinique anticolonial theorist Aime Cesaire spoke of the equation of colonization with "thingification."[5] We continue to see this even today when some racialized bodies (e.g., Blacks, Aboriginals, and other racial minority groups) are objectified through the continual denial of their basic humanity. We are constantly blamed and pathologized for our perceived lack of certain basic qualities, neither understanding our own problems nor having the ability to think through solutions to these problems. Increasingly such discursive stances have become convenient grounds and excuses for failing to critically look at how systems marginalize and inferiorize groups and individuals. It is important to note that not everyone in society necessarily has to agree to these mischaracterizations to make them stick on groups and communities. The propensity to blame the victim is generally unquestioned. A blaming-the-victim mentality is cultivated and rewarded to avoid implicating larger systemic and structural forces of society. So we fail to look at structures and how institutions function to create marginality for racialized subjects. Of course it could be argued that racialized bodies resist and challenge these perceptions. But it is beside the point. We must ask: Resistance at what costs? What do we do with the emotional and spiritual consequences and the damage of everyday resistance?

Today the concept of racialization is frequently referred to in discussions on race and racism. Robert Miles and others have alluded to this as the process(es) through which groups come to be designated as different and, on that basis, subjected to differential and unequal treatment.[6] Earlier reference to racialization was to political and economic processes that ensured labor supply for the social formation and, specifically, how immigrant workers were scripted and racialized for work. Today we can speak of this process in relation to the evocation of ethnicity, language, economics, religion, culture, and politics. It is important to acknowledge that racialization entails the notion of biological determinism, that is to say, the concept of particular human traits as biologically determined and thus consistent both for individuals and for the group they belong to. For example, the idea that the working class are dirty, lazy, violent, of inferior intelligence, have low standards of morality, and so forth is one that has been deployed as biologically determined. Of course these same discursive practices have fixed people of color in exactly the same settled, "natural" position.

The most important point here is that racialization is a historical construction, one that allows for White supremacist systems of power to suppress
racial minority resistance. By way of understanding the project of racialization,
we look to those historical processes and trajectories that allowed dominant
groups to call on culture, gender, ethnicity, language, religion, sexuality, and
race (as skin color) as a way of distinguishing groups for differential and unequal treatment. As a historical construction, the process of racialization allows
for White supremacist systems of power to suppress racial minorities as unequal
and different to justify their suppression and domination.

Closely aligned with the processes of racialization is the making of racialized subjects. As Lawson notes, we must take racialized as a verb, that is,
the act of doing something to the body based on its phenotypical features.[7]
In the broader sense, the making of racialized subjects points to how bodies
are read negatively according to skin color and other phenotypical features as
an epidemically correct casting. Black skin is associated with deviance and
dishonesty, brown is associated with terrorism, and so on, and the subject
becomes racialized through such casting. In framing the issue as racialized
subjects, the gaze is placed more appropriately on the one racializing the
subject as such. In other words, we uphold and counter the view that
the subject remains embodied and therefore is not intrinsically bad because
of her or his race and, for that matter, gender, class, ethnicity, language, or
religion. Therefore it is the process of racializing the subject that is at fault and
must be dealt with. So the process of racializing is external, strategic, and not
the responsibility of the person who is targeted. Again, this distinction is
crucial because of the tendency for some to argue that those who do antiracist
work by working with race actually create the problem. As already noted, antiracist workers speak of race not to create it but to gesture to what already exists.

In looking at racialization processes and the making of racialized subjects, we see how these same biologically determined and thus racist ideas of
behavior, values, beliefs, cultural practices, and so on are grafted onto particular social relations and issues, such as immigration, education, and crime
in our communities. Dominant systems of racialized power construct ideas
of criminality through particular bodies. We begin to see how crime and
gang violence are viewed largely through (and in terms of) black and brown
bodies and communities because it is they who have been invested with a biological propensity to commit violence and crime. Discussions about terrorism and today's terrorists and gun violence are a case in point. We know
particular bodies are now invested with terrorism, they are viewed as a group
to be possessed of certain biological traits that lead to the nurturing of suicide
bombers, fanatical hatred of the West, sexist oppression, and so forth.

Consequently, it can be argued that the whole process of racialization and the making of racialized subjects is indicative of larger cultural, institutional, and social forces. Certain bodies are not encoded with such negative images and messages. In fact, some bodies are racialized for privilege. Hence, we need to ask, for example, why it is that Canadian families of European ancestry largely constitute themselves as White? What does this practice tell us about race and racism in Canadian history and contemporary politics and culture?

Antiracism challenges White power and its rationality for dominance. It is about resisting colonial and neocolonial privileges. As argued elsewhere, I see "colonial" as anything imposed and dominating, and not simply foreign or alien.[8] As argued elsewhere, the academic and political project of antiracism is to uncover how Western civilization scripts communities through the fabrication of Whiteness and the racial boundary policing that comes with it.[9] In fact, White racial supremacy is itself anchored in a fabrication of Whiteness. Historically, this fabrication has required an immense psychological, physical, and intellectual energies to keep up the alleged purity of Europe and the West. One can only point to the so-called enlightened European scholars' attempts to deny Egyptian and Nubian influence on European history or Western (Greek) civilization. Today, this fabrication continues exacting a heavy material, physical, psychological, and emotional toll on racialized subjects (e.g., spirit injury, the emotional harm of racism).

Antiracism also challenges the problem of fixed social categories and designations because, paraphrasing Edward Said, none of us has even been just one thing. We cannot discuss our identities in fragments, stripped of their complexities and specificities. Although antiracist practice requires the recognition of the saliency of race, it is also imperative for us to work with the intersections of difference (race, gender, class, disability, sexuality) if we are to address the myriad forms of oppressions we encounter in daily lived experiences. Given that the collective quest for solidarity in antioppression work can mask some underlying tensions and ambivalences, a critical antiracist practice must broach questions of power and privilege. Often the separation of the politics of difference from the politics of race allows dominant bodies to deny and refuse to interrogate White privilege and power.

Intersectional analysis always maintains blind spots. Primarily because of the reluctance to speak race, the complexities of difference must neither obscure nor deny the saliency of race in antiracist work. Antiracism highlights Whiteness because it guarantees racial privilege irrespective of gender, sexuality, or class. Whiteness must be viewed foremost as a system of dominance. However, it is how we use our individual and collective identities (e.g., White identities) that matter most in the way we pursue antiracist practice. For example, for dominant groups there must be a critical understanding of the connections between Whiteness and White racial identity. Howard argues that Whites cannot escape their implication and complicity in Whiteness in a White supremacist society.[10] To claim otherwise negates or compromises the ability of Whites to do serious antiracist work because "it exposes a gross misunderstanding of the structural and embedded nature of racism." Antiracist Whites must clearly acknowledge and demonstrate the tensions and difficulties of their grappling with racism to gain credibility and solidify the grounds for antiracist coalition politics. By the same token, for racial minorities we must recognize when we are working with dominant tropes and lenses.

Kincheloe and Steinberg's observation that Whiteness has become the tacit norm everyone references resonates powerfully with me.[11] Eurocentric knowledge masquerades as universal knowledge. In schools and other social settings, White power and privilege masquerade as excellence, and we often know and claim excellence if it looks like us. But it does not mean it is only those with White identities that usually work with and through such dominant tropes. Racial minorities at times encounter the easy and seductive slippage into the form, logic, and implicit assumptions of the very things we are contesting, in part, because of the ways we have been schooled and our comfort level working with and through the dominant's gaze. Sometimes we internalize our own racism and revisit it others. It is important, however, for a critical antiracist reading to understand how these things play out, the source of these oppressions, and the history and contexts from which the myriad forms of oppression in society emerge.

RACE AND ANTIRACISM

There is no doubt that in today's society, education is a force to be reckoned with. It may not be a panacea for all problems, but it is definitely something to be taken seriously. Either education does something *for* you or *to* you. This is why there is the ongoing contestation about what exactly constitutes education and how the different knowledges, experiences, and histories are situated in the struggle. Schools cannot write their students out of history. In education the question of difference is central if we are to respond to the diversity of the school population. To this end, I offer that perhaps difference is more appropriate than sheer sameness. It is always important for us as educators to bring openness and humility to the work we do and, particularly, to the pursuit of education and knowledge. I would like to think that nothing discussed and written about today has never been said before. If we do not know this, it is more because of our ignorance and a refusal to know. This is the gist of bringing humility to the process of seeking knowledge.

Some form of education is still mired in a missionary and neocolonialist view of the world. Students are taught to believe that if one learns about other people's cultural ways, then the learner will know how to help the other. Our schools are still mired in the missionary view of the world because we work more with diversity and not the pointed notions of difference and power. Difference gets us to acknowledge and deal with power issues and the question of social identities. The way educators impart knowledge to the students has some effect on schooling outcomes. Schools do not always consider the level of damage done when dominant knowledges and practices are reproduced. To take just one example, it should be of little wonder when a social worker is hired by a children's aid society, he or she encounters families where the children have been placed in foster care. No consideration is given to the social, economic, and racist pressures on that family, so it becomes pathologized and detrimental decisions are made on behalf of that family.

All this calls for rethinking schooling in our communities today. There have been some successes in the school system that we should be proud of. As already noted, there are also good intentions on the part of many hard-working educators and school administrators. But the fact remains that we all need to do more. Complacency is a recipe for disaster. In fact, despite successes, we have students at school having serious concerns. What I am getting at here is that I would like to see a situation where educators are able to take credit for their students' success and be prepared to accept responsibility for educational failures as well. We know from existing educational research that some students have difficulties in negotiating power and authority structures of schools.[12] The saliency and visibility of race in the schooling experiences of African Canadian youth is a case in point.[13] Power can, at times, be employed in racist ways to alienate or disengage minority students. The fact of differential (negative) treatment by race coupled with the lack of curricular and pedagogic sophistication in schools mean some students are bound to feel out of place in the educational system. When students complain about the lack of diverse staff representation they are also making a reference to the importance of being able to situate identity and schooling to knowledge production. Of course, the home is implicated in the search for educational excellence. All students see parents and local communities as sites and sources for political and social action for educational change. There is the need for communities and parents to act as sounding boards. The complex dynamics of the culture, environment, and organizational lives of mainstream schools and their intersections with societal and family forces make schooling a socially, politically, and culturally mediated experience for most students.[14]

SCHOOLING IN THE CONTEXT OF SOCIAL DIFFERENCE: THE CHALLENGE FOR THE RACIALIZED SUBJECTS

Using the Ontario context, I want to highlight some issues in the public domain of everyday conversations that have implications for how we engage difference and diversity within our communities and specifically within school settings. To set the tone, some figures from one school board are revealing if nothing else. In the Toronto District School Board (TDSB), Canada's largest school board, we learn that approximately 41 percent of students have a first language other than English; over 70 different languages are spoken at home by students. TDSB elementary schools (grades one through eight) receive 8,000 newcomers each year, representing more than 170 countries, and 12 percent of secondary students have been in Canada for three years or less. Overall, TDSB secondary schools receive approximately 4,000 newcomers every year. In effect, our schools are not simply multilingual and multiracial, they are *truly* diverse.[15]

Diversity should be operationalized in terms of the bodies, curriculum and text, knowledge and instruction, and the representation of identities in schools. The different bodies we have in our schools only confirm that we are dealing with heterogeneous communities. So how do schools, and particularly educators and administrators, ensure that the needs and concerns of a diverse body politic are addressed? Some of these concerns stem from the feeling, making, and othering of bodies as different. Embedded in such interpretations are encounters with racial, class, gender, [dis]ability, and sexual hostilities for many students and learners in the educational system. For particular groups the issues are further compounded by the broader questions of history and politics. For example, there are integration challenges for newcomers in our schools. Some of these students feel alienated, trying to fit in with a socially devalued identity. Many youths face problems of racialized and gendered poverty. The problem is acute among Somali and Afghani students. The chronic social problems of homelessness, nonstatus refugees, posttraumatic stress (among those coming from war zones), and discrimination in housing and social service sectors all implicate their schooling and educational success. And as schools are having to confront these challenges, we see the devastation of education through reductions in English as a second language (ESL) programs, elimination of entire equity departments, and the reduction of curriculum specialists in school boards in the province. As the state continues to shirk its responsibilities to a larger citizenry, we are beginning to see the creation of a two-tiered school system, one for the poor and the other for the wealthy and privileged citizens.

Among the six issues of public conversations, I want first mention the problematic misrepresentation of immigrant and racial minority cultures as something that fundamentally impinge on students' self-esteem. For example, on the question of violence, the pejorative term *Black-on-Black violence* stereotypes a whole community as violent. Of course we must be concerned with youth violence, but not at the expense of stereotyping a whole community. Tamil and other South Asian youth are continually stigmatized with youth gangs and crime. The messages conveyed in official school texts and curricular and instructional practices, when coupled with the negative media portrayals of racialized groups and the failure to look at history and contexts, all help cultivate and nurture a low sense of self-worth and self-esteem in some students. Similarly the overemphasis on the failures of racialized communities have tended to create a situation where communities are stigmatized. Through official school discourse (as conveyed in texts, curriculum, and everyday conversations) the critical eye can gauge how the vibrancy of the culture and histories of racialized groups are subsumed in discussions about crime and youth violence.

Second, we witness how in everyday discourse and practice racialized immigrant identities can be paired with punishment and repulsion. Current discussions regarding racial profiling and testimonies presented to the Ontario Human Rights Commission,[16] the rise in Islamophobia, and the hysteria around terrorism and what it means to be a brown body, Asian, or Muslim are clear cases of racial hostility and punishment.[17] Within the school system we see the constant struggles over identity and identifications as learners try to rid themselves of negative portrayals of their identities. Such portrayals carry huge personal, social, spiritual, and psychological costs to students.

Third, there is the economics of everyday living or material economics. The rising unemployment among racialized groups, many with highly qualified credentials (e.g., professionals driving taxis in Toronto due to the lack of accreditation of their foreign expertise and qualifications) implicate our schools. The issue is how do and can our schools prepare bodies for social participation and citizenship responsibility? There is a connection between the deterioration of racialized neighborhoods and these spaces becoming sites for violence and crime. In effect, crime is not inherent in these bodies. The connection of these bodies with crime speaks more about how structures and institutional forces function to foster social, spiritual, material, and psychological violence. These social problems are not innate in racialized subjects. Race and poverty intersect in powerful ways primarily because as a society we fail to address the challenges of difference and diversity. For our schools what this means is that we cannot divorce the difficulties such racialized subjects encounter in the school system from the wider social environments in which they live.

Fourth, on the issue of power sharing, whereby there is the absence of diverse physical representation to deal with institutional access for all peoples, there is a grave concern for racialized communities. We must seriously link identity, schooling, and knowledge production. Collins writes of how, for racial minorities, our absence in the academy itself becomes the norm. The knowledge that circulates in our institutions is often said to be "neutral."[18] Schools, colleges, and universities may claim to hire bodies on merit and excellence and that somehow these bodies, when hired, come into these institutions as disembodied persons with no race, ethnicity, class, gender, or sexuality. Nothing is further from the truth. Decisions and determinations about who gets in can be framed in dominant discourses of excellence and merit whereby Whiteness becomes the tacit norm that is continually referenced.[19] The harm that is perpetuated is that learners are not presented with difference in ways that can enrich the learning process. Students do not get the learning opportunities to benefit from the diversity that can be reflected in the teaching staff.

Fifth, on the broader question of the intersections of race, difference, power, and education we require a critical interrogation of our institutions and structures for educational delivery. As already alluded to, we are having to deal with the sidelining of race and equity work as "special interest."[20] In Ontario, the repeated cutbacks in education to frontline services—such as school community advisors; equity departments; and programs like ESL, African heritage, and adult education—all serve to disadvantage learners. In fact, in most cases what these cuts have meant is that community organizations have had to step in and fill the gap to make sure that the needs of children from racialized communities are met. This has not always been easy on these communities. Meanwhile, the wealthy and powerful have found ways to address these concerns more so than others.

Racism in schools has been a contested terrain afflicted with denials and defensive postures.[21] But there exists a tremendous amount of educational research attesting to how racism manifests itself in everyday student–student relations, student–teacher–administrator interactions, how school curriculum and classroom pedagogies are incomplete, and how school policies and regulations end up marginalizing different bodies.[22] Stereotyping and labeling of South Asian youth and Tamil youth with the *gang* label and *Paki* as racist name-calling may be the most blatant forms of racism. But the familiar cries of a lack of curricular sophistication; absence of Black, First Nations/Ab-original, and other minority teachers; and the differential treatment of school subjects are all laced with racial undertones.

Zine clearly points to the importance of our schools dealing with the sacred and secular split in the educational system, as well as the daily tensions between religion and sexuality.[23] There are also concerns of racism and Is-lamophobia, and the misrepresentation of Islam in school curricula (e.g., world religion classes). Furthermore, the pervasiveness of gendered Islamo-phobia and the politics of veiling point to how negative stereotypes constitute violence to bodies in the post–September 11, 2001, context.[24] South and Southeast Asian students have to navigate around the split personality or double-culture syndrome while conforming to the competing demands of home and school. The resulting tension is that youths develop a double persona. An Anglicized name at school, taking off of the hijab, and being the good culturally and religiously observant kid at home reflect this tension.[25] There is also the ongoing difficulty in maintaining a religious lifestyle in secular schools where there is dating, alcohol, and drugs.

A lot has been written on South Asian students and the model minority syndrome.[26] There are the parental and community expectations to do well in the hard sciences as opposed to social science. Youths may be encouraged at home to be medical doctors or go into physical sciences as opposed to the arts and social sciences. This places tremendous pressure on the Asian youth for the fear of not meeting such expectations. Consequently, South Asian youth facing problems may be reluctant to ask for help at school. Among Somali and other African youth, language and accent discrimination is a significant issue. ESL labeling is common sometimes just because of differences in ac-cents, that is, not speaking English according to the "proper" standards.[27]

Sixth, I will be remiss if no mention is made of the zero tolerance policy and the Safe School Act that are leading to suspensions and expulsions of minoritized bodies from school. For these youth the policy raises the question of fairness and educational access. We know that a number of immigrant youth in Ontario are unable to attend school, even though the Education Act says they are entitled to do so, because their parents lack the proper immi-gration documentation. However, the most contentious issue for many of these communities is the zero tolerance policy and the suspension and ex-pulsion of students deemed to engage in violent behavior. Local communities and parent groups are calling on schools to revisit these policies and practices and also look at the root causes of school violence while bringing a compre-hensive understanding to "violence."[28] School boards that claim financial hardships when called upon to implement antiracist/equity changes and initiatives still find the money to hire expensive lawyers to keep some youth out of school! It is not difficult to understand why some parents are asking: What is the school's responsibility? Is it to act as the police or to educate young people? Many of the students who are expelled or suspended are students of color, especially Black and Aboriginal youth and males, and are left to languish during their suspension. Personally it is an eye opener to see the school boards spending precious limited funds to hire lawyers in a bid to expel students. Minority parents are at an extreme disadvantage when having to mount legal challenges to such expulsions. We need to question these types of legal action against students and their families and the misuse of financial resources.[29]

WHAT CAN BE DONE?

The foregoing highlights significant challenges that must be addressed to create healthy sustainable schooling environments for all learners. It requires the different stakeholders in our school system to come together to search for effective ways to address ensuing problems. In this endeavor the learner's responsibilities are paramount. The right to an education comes with responsibilities. Education means cultivating respect for the knowledge and the experiences of one's peers, parents, elders, and community. Education for collective empowerment means we allow learning to impact daily lives. It also means providing a service to the wider community. Academic success can only be enriched by such appreciation of community work and service.

But how do schools prepare students to take on these responsibilities? I believe that the idea of having a critical inquisitive mind means that a learner must be prepared to challenge the teacher, ask critical questions about schooling, and use received knowledge to work for social and political change. In the context of this chapter, I am speaking of the why, how, and when of the exclusions or omissions, negations, and devaluations of experiences and histories in the curriculum, texts, instruction, and classroom pedagogies. Learning for diversity means that we insist that teaching be about the complete history of ideas and events that have shaped and continue to shape human growth and development. A school curriculum must reflect every learner's experience, history, culture, and social reality.

In truth, teachers and school administrators have a special obligation in recognizing and responding to diversity and difference in schools; however, there are two crucial points of which I believe we must be mindful. The first relates to the necessity of making a distinction between the concept of schooling and that of education. Schooling should not be considered education in and of itself. In point of fact, formal institutionalized schooling structures and practices have created a split with education. If we view education as a process that entails varied options, strategies, and multiple ways of knowing and thinking through which students come to engage with and understand their world, then we can see how institutionalized discursive and material schooling practices that insist on a formalized monocultural and homogenized understanding of the world can inscribe and reproduce in students a sense of disengagement and alienation, negating and devaluing the embodied knowledges of difference that all students bring to their learning environment. As a consequence, such formal schooling practices run the risk of despiritualizing our youth through the enforcement of normalizing routines that effectively coerce students into amputating their differences. Thus the conceptualization and measure of success in the increasing marketization of education that constructs student bodies as mere commodities for the so-called global economy becomes predicated on the degree to which students are willing—or able—to physically, emotionally, and psychologically negate their differences to pass for what is, in effect, an enforced culturally explicit construction of normalcy.[30] What we have then, given that all students represent myriad differences, and therefore all students are thus wounded to varying degrees, is in fact the imposition of systemic and institutionalized miseducation.

This leads me to the second critical point that I want to address, that of difference. Actually a great deal is spoken about difference in Euro-Canadian schooling contexts and yet either it is conceptualized in the mainstream multicultural discourse of saris, samosas, and steelbands that treats difference as an essence and an exotic add-on to the European norm, or it is viewed as a problem in which sameness and the stress on commonality is the preferred solution. Both intersect with each other to sustain and reproduce dominating social relations of power. In the former, difference is conceptualized in authentic, essentialized, exoticized, culturalist terms and is positioned as independent of other social experiences, such as race, class, gender, disability, and sexuality;[31] thus it is presented and understood as a form of signification that is removed from political, social, and historical or contemporary struggles and constraints.[32] In the latter, where difference is viewed as a site of conflict and contestation, the discourse of sameness ignores (and denies) both the racialized asymmetrical power relations in which the politics of difference are inscribed and the implication of social materiality embedded within such relations.[33]

Difference is more than simply a site of individual contestation. In Western social systems and institutionalized contexts and arenas (such as education), difference—its conceptualization and the ways in which it is engaged in systemic binary oppositional hierarchical terms—mediates through knowledge production and hegemonic discursive and material practices the asymmetrical relations of power that determine to a great extent the (dis)engagement, alienation, well-being, spiritual health, and happiness of all our students, including the communities of difference from which they emerge. As Audre Lorde long ago observed, Western European history has indoctrinated us to perceive "human differences in simplistic opposition to each other: dominant/subordinate, good/bad, up/down, superior/inferior [valid/invalid, legitimate/illegitimate, civilized/uncivilized] with always the psychic impregnation of the most desired and valued coming first followed by the inferiorized."[34]

Some of the critical pedagogical questions that we must ask ourselves in our engagements with difference and diversity in the contexts of schooling and education revolve around the need for deeper conceptual clarity that is complex, multicentered, and liberating. We must ask ourselves, for example, who gets to define difference? Whose articulations are taken up and produced as legitimate and valid conceptualizations and enunciations? Whom do such articulations and knowledges serve? At the same time, even while we ask such questions, we must be mindful of the need to work through the lens of curriculum as cultural practice so as to acknowledge, engage, and (re)position difference and diversity as sources of embodied resistance, agency, and transformative knowledge—thereby challenging the epistemic violence of Western cultural knowledge as it relates to the material exigencies of racialized and marginalized subjects and communities. Teaching is not just about affecting knowledge. It is about a preparedness to learn and unlearn. A teacher must allow students, parents, families, and guardians to teach. As informal educators our students, parents, families, and guardians have knowledge to share with us. Many of our students speak to us from their lived experiences and the challenges they encounter in their daily lives. But do our classroom pedagogies always acknowledge this? For example, as I have suggested, it is important to openly and sincerely talk and teach about race and difference. Racism and social inequality must be acknowledged and dealt with. As educators we can begin a genuine dialogue for change by first admitting to the conceptual flaws of a color-blind approach to schooling.

By the same token we cannot downplay the role of parents, community workers, and Elders in the struggle to recognize and respond to difference and diversity. Parents, guardians, community workers, and elders are equal and willing partners in the provision of education to youth because it is realized that education is too important to be left in the hands of schools alone. By becoming sounding boards as youth deal with the pressures of schooling and social maturation, parents and community elders are playing their roles in enhancing learning. There are other ways to enrich learning outcomes. By developing the crucial ability to use the teachable moments in the homes, parents can assist in youth learning. As we begin to define parental involvement broadly to include parents, communities, and Elders, these participants become sounding boards, creating conditions to assist youth learning and challenging schools to meet their responsibility to a diverse body politic. Education can make a profound impact in the lives of the learners.

CONCLUSION

Antiracism is about changing current processes of schooling and educational delivery. In concluding this discussion, I offer some directions to future educational practices for addressing difference and diversity in schooling. We need alternative educational outlets that create and nurture supportive environments for all students. For example, to deal with issues of racial minority youth disaffection and disengagement from the mainstream school system we need to promote alternative and healthy schools that provide inclusive learning environments. Some of these may well be outside the mainstream school system. Schools and local communities can work in partnerships to create supportive environments for students who have faced problems with the school system. It is important for our educational institutions to support students' grassroots organizing and advocacy around equity in the curriculum. Specifically, educators can support students' organizing around race, diversity, and equity issues. Usually what is missing in progressive antiracist work is institutional support. We must always be searching for educational innovations, programs that seek the collaboration of educators, parents, communities, students, and other community groups and associations, programs that offer a popular education approach for students to be able to integrate issues of work, learning, and the labor force with diversity and equity concerns.

To win the confidence of local communities so that schools can truly contribute to addressing social inequities, there must be effective outreach targeting minority communities in particular.

Such community outreach may include support for establishing resource centers and recreational facilities in socioeconomically disadvantaged neighborhoods. After-school programs for culture and heritage education, indigenous language education, and community forums and workshops are useful in conscientizing learners on the issues of race, difference, and power. There must be concrete efforts to support curricular initiatives and development that promote curriculum rewrites to ensure questions of race and oppression are addressed.

We need diverse staff representation in our schools if we are serious about addressing the question of difference and power. These bodies are crucial in linking identity to schooling and knowledge production. Their presence helps ensure learners of a sense of caring and acknowledgment, that all peoples have something to contribute to the educational process. The physical representation of different bodies can assist in establishing a link between educational theory and practice around equity and diversity issues. This representation addresses questions of power and knowledge and the importance of grounding school knowledge in daily lived experiences of learners.

The challenges are enormous but with political will, institutional commitment, and support they can be overcome. It is vital for us to work with a philosophy of hope in antiracist politics by recognizing our possibilities and limitations. In conclusion, I want to paraphrase Adrienne Rich and assert that the working-class racialized youth in our school systems today are not there to receive an education, they are there to reclaim their education.[35] These youth see themselves as active and creative subjects and not simply youth to be acted on. Educators must assist learners in their endeavors and make learning and education possible for these youth. Together, we must assist these students as they challenge any attempts to dominate the past, contaminate the present, and steal their future. Breaking out of the increasingly gated-community mentality of education, new, empowered, and community-based visions of education must be given voice and operationalized. In opening these proverbial gates, the circle of educational inclusion is widened to more voices, more meaningful participation, and the potential for societal gains.

NOTES

1. Christine Sleeter, "How White Teachers Construct Race," in C. McCarthy and W. Crichlow (eds.), *Race, Identity and Representation in Education* (New York: Routledge, 1993), 157–171.

2. M. Omi and H. Winant, "On the Theoretical Concept of Race," in C. McCarthy and W. Crichlow (eds.), *Race, Identity and Representation in Education* (New York: Routledge, 1993), 3–10.

3. Jewell Smith, "In Search of John Ogbu." Paper presented at the annual meeting of the American Educational Research Association (AERA), San Francisco, CA, April 11, 1995.

4. A. Memmi, *The Colonizer and the Colonized* (Boston: Beacon Press, 1969).

5. A. Cesaire, *Discourse on Colonialism* (New York: Monthly Review Press, 1972).

6. R. Miles, *Racism* (London: Tavistock, 1989); R. Miles, *Racism after "Race Relations"* (London: Routledge, 1993); P. Li, "Race and Ethnicity," in P. Li (ed.), *Race and Ethnic Relations in Canada* (Toronto: Oxford University Press, 1990), 3–17.

7. E. Lawson, *Notes on Racialization and Racialized Subjects* (Toronto: Department of Sociology and Equity Studies, Ontario Institute for Studies in Education of the University of Toronto, 2004).

8. G. J. S. Dei, "Rethinking the Role of Indigenous Knowledges in the Academy," *International Journal of Inclusive Education* 4, no. 2 (2000): 111–132.

9. G. J. S. Dei, "Introduction—Mapping the Terrain: Towards a New Politics of Resistance," in G. J. S. Dei and A. Kempf (eds.), *Anti-Colonialism and Education: The Politics of Resistance* (Rotterdam: Sense Publishers), 1–24.

10. P. Howard, personal communication, 2004.

11. Joe L. Kincheloe and Shirley R. Steinberg, "Addressing the Crisis of Whiteness: Reconfiguring White Identity in a Pedagogy of Whiteness," in J. L. Kincheloe, S. R. Steinberg, N. M Rodriguez, and R. E. Chennault (eds.), *White Reign: Deploying Whiteness in America* (New York: St Martin's Press, 1998), 3–29.

12. G. J. S. Dei, L. Holmes, J. Mazzuca, E. McIsaac, and R. Campbell, *Push Out or Drop Out? The Dynamics of Black/African-Canadian Students Disengagement from School* (Toronto: Ontario Ministry of Education and Training, 1995); G. J. S. Dei, E. McIsaac, J. Mazzuca, and J. Zine, *Reconstructing Dropouts: Understanding the Dynamics of Black Students Disengagement from School* (Toronto: University of Toronto Press, 1997); K. Brathwaite and C. James, *Educating African-Canadians* (Toronto: John Lorimer, 1996); C. James, *Seeing Ourselves: Exploring Race, Ethnicity and Culture* (Toronto: Thompson Educational Publishing, 1995).

13. Canadian Alliance of Black Educators, *Sharing the Challenge, I, II, III: A Focus on Black High School Students* (Toronto: Canadian Alliance of Black Educators, 1992); Black Educators Working Group (BEWG), *Submission to the Ontario Royal Commission on Learning* (Toronto: BEWG, 1993); C. James, *Making It* (Oakville, ON: Mosaic Press, 1990); C. E. James, "What Students Are Saying about African Studies Courses in High School," *Our Schools/Our Selves* 47 (1996): 130–145; V. D'Oyley and C. James, *Re/visioning: Canadian Perspectives on the Education of Africans in the Late 20th Century* (Toronto: Captus Press, 1998); P. Solomon, *Black Resistance in High School: Forging a Separatist Culture* (Albany: State University of New York Press, 1992).

14. G. J. S. Dei and S. Razack (eds.), *Inclusive Schooling: An Inventory of Contemporary Practices Designed to Meet the Challenges of a Diverse Student Body* (Toronto: Ministry of Education and Training, 1995); K. Dehli, *Parent Activism and School Reform in Toronto* (Toronto: Ontario Institute for Studies in Education, 1994).

15. G. J. S. Dei, "The Challenge of Promoting Inclusive Education in Ontario Schools." Paper presented at the mayor's forum on Youth and Community Safety, University of Toronto, Scarborough Campus, June 18, 2004. Available online at www.tdsb.on.ca. Accessed September 1, 2005.

16. Ontario Human Rights Commission (OHRC), *Paying the Price: The Human Cost of Racial Profiling Report* (Toronto: OHRC, 2003); M. J. Brown, *In Their Own Voices: African-Canadians in the Greater Toronto Area Share Experiences of Police Profiling* (Toronto: African-Canadian Coalition on Racial Profiling, 2004).

17. J. Zine, "Staying on the 'Straight Path': A Critical Ethnography of Islamic Schooling in Ontario," doctoral dissertation, Department of Sociology and Equity Studies, Ontario Institute for Studies in Education, University of Toronto, 2004.

18. P. H. Collins, *Black Feminist Thought: Knowledge, Conscientiousness and the Politics of Empowerment* (Boston: Unwin Hyman, 1990).

19. Kincheloe and Steinberg, "Addressing the Crisis of Whiteness."

20. G. J. S. Dei and L. Karumanchery, "School Reforms in Ontario: The 'Marketization' of Education and the Resulting Silence on Equity," *Alberta Journal of Educational Research* 45, no. 2 (1999): 111–131; R. Hatcher, "Social Justice and the Politics of School Effectiveness and Improvement," *Race, Ethnicity and Education* 1, no. 2 (1998): 267–289.

21. B. D. Tatum, "Talking about Race, Learning about Racism: The Application of Racial Identity Development Theory in the Classroom," *Harvard Educational Review* 62, no. 1 (1992): 1–24.

22. Dei, McIsaac, Mazzuca, and Zine, *Reconstructing Dropouts*; J. Zine, "Staying on the 'Straight Path' "; C. E. James and A. Shadd, *Talking about Identity: Encounters in Race, Ethnicity and Language* (Toronto: Between the Lines Press, 2001); Brown, *In Their Own Voices.*

23. Zine, "Redefining Resistance"; J. Zine, "Muslim Youth in Canadian Schools: Education and the Politics of Religious Identity," *Anthropology and Education Quarterly* 32, no. 4 (2001): 399–423.

24. J. Zine, "Staying on the 'Straight Path' "; J. Zine, "Dealing with September 12: The Challenge of Anti-Islamaphobia Education," *Orbit* 33, no. 3 (2004): 39–41.

25. Zine, "Muslim Youth in Canadian Schools"; Zine, "Redefining Resistance."

26. A. Brah, "Re-Framing Europe: En-gendered Racisms, Ethnicities and Nationalisms in Contemporary Western Europe," *Feminist Review* 45 (1993): 9–28; A. Brah, "Difference, Diversity and Differentiation" in J. Donald and A. Rattansi (eds.), *Race, Culture and Difference* (London: Sage, 1999), 126–145; S. Razack, "The Perils of Talking about Culture: Schooling Research in South and East Asian Students," *Race, Gender and Class* 2, no. 3 (1995): 67–82.

27. G. J. S. Dei and M. Lordan, "Language, Linguistic Discrimination, and Polyvocality: A Dialogue of Possibilities—Bringing Languages into Discussions of Discrimination and Racism," in Z. Amin and G. Dei(eds.), *Language, Race and the Poetics of Anti-racism* (forthcoming).

28. C. G. Roman, *Schools, Neighbourhoods and Violence: Crime within the Daily Routines of Youth* (Lanham, MD: Lexington Books, 2004).

29. E. Lawson, personal communication, 2004.

30. S. Doyle-Wood, "Defining Difference in Canadian Schooling Contexts," in G. J. S. Dei, N. Amin, and A. Abdi (eds.), *Social Difference and Schooling in Canada—Pedagogical Challenges* (forthcoming).

31. Brah, "Difference, Diversity and Differentiation."

32. P. McLaren, "White Terror and Oppositional Agency: Towards a Critical Multiculturalism," in D. T. Goldberg (ed.), *Multiculturalism: A Critical Reader* (Oxford: Blackwell, 1997), 45–74.

33. S. Doyle-Wood, "Passing for Black? The Epistemology of Passing: Re-Reckoning and Old Trope," in A. Asgharzadeh, E. Lawson, and A. Wahab(eds.), *Diasporic Ruptures: Transnationalism, Globalization and Identity Discourses* (forthcoming).

34. A. Lorde, *Sister Outsider: Essays and Speeches* (Berkley: Crossing Press, 1984), 114.

35. A. Rich, *On Lies, Secrets and Silence* (New York: Norton, 1979).

3

Against Racism and Irrationalism: Toward an Integrated Movement of Class Struggle in Schools and Out

Rich Gibson

> There are two times for making money, one on the up-building of a country, and the other in its destruction.
>
> —Rhett Butler, *Gone with the Wind*

> We had been dealing with, had been made and mangled by, another machinery altogether. It had never been in our interest to overthrow it. It had been necessary to make the machinery work for our benefit and the possibility of its doing so had been so to speak, built in.
>
> —James Baldwin, *Nobody Knows My Name*

> In most cases it is not enough for revolution that the lower classes should not want to live in the old way. It is also necessary that the upper classes should be unable to rule and govern in the old way.
>
> —Vladimir Lenin, "May Day Action by the Revolutionary Proletariat" (1913)

THE SOCIAL CONTEXT OF RACISM AND EDUCATION

I assume my audience has some grasp of the venomous nature of racism and the existence of segregation and, to one degree or another, acknowledge and oppose it. Others, please stop here.

This chapter is especially directed toward education workers, students, parents, and community people who hope to oppose racism and schooling for inequality but avoid consciously addressing the common origins of racism and school inequality, their impetus, and the future. These honest people therefore cannot or do not create properly reasoned paths to overcome systematic injustice.

Unable to locate racism and unjust education historically—that is, unable to abstract the role of racism and schooling within the whole of the world's social system, capitalism, as it develops—liberal analysts and agents for change are unable to see how it is people might be able to unravel why things are as they are, locate themselves as change agents, and act. They mystify capitalism, tamper with its parts, and misdirect change strategies while empowering inequitable schooling and racism, perhaps in new forms. Treating repeated and necessary social tendencies as flukes, focusing myopically on what is seen as aberrations in society, liberalism clinically expunges the reasoned, passionate rage requisite to transcend inequality.

I assume, as well, that the reader knows something about the depth of racist oppression (shorter life spans, incarceration, massive unemployment, constant danger and surveillance, the double life of the oppressed) and that schools are segregated as much as they were in 1954. The methods of teaching and the substance of the curricula are segregated.[1]

I assume the reader is aware that we live in an era of crises—the internationalization of not trade but permanent war economies, each eyeing the other for a slim advantage in the relentless search for markets, raw materials, and labor. Dominant ideas, flowing from elites, and resistant ideas, flowing from the oppressed, compete in this context, the former usually overriding the latter. This is the backdrop of educational work today.

I assume the reader is somewhat aware the No Child Left Behind (NCLB) act, the result of twenty-five years of maneuvering by elites—including the leaders of both major teachers' unions—is a method of social control to regulate what children know and how they come to know it while making the division of society by class and race seem not political but scientific. That this is going on is clear enough and proved in depth elsewhere. At issue to me is: Why and what to do, or not do?

My message is simple: School workers do not have to be missionaries for the ideology of capitalism or its sword and shield (racism), although taking the chance to transcend our current conditions is risky business. The risk is worth it; it gives meaning to the privilege of time on the planet. There is urgency to my message. Inside a powerful nation promising perpetual war to the world in the midst of rising inequality, segregation, racism, imperialism, and nationalism, time is short.

Herein, I ask radical, to-the-root questions and try to answer them:

1. What is capitalism? What is racism? Why have school?
2. What is the relationship of capitalism, schools, and racism?
3. What is the liberal, or postmodern, answer to capitalism, racism, and schooling?
4. What has been done in the past?
5. What can school workers, individually and collectively, do now?

Capitalism is the world system, the whole. It is dynamic; incomplete; a system in constant flux, upending community, trust, and every aspect of daily life; and offering the narrowest edge to each participant (subject) and throngs of examples of what happens to miscreants born without capital, especially those of color. Recognizing capital as the whole is key to getting at its parts and to social change.

The concept of totality makes it possible to override notions of interests, advantages, or beliefs (sentiments) when applied to the question of racism. White people as a whole have more opportunities and live in less danger than Black people in the United States, and at the same time, it is true that some White people, if they choose to find ways to overcome their advantages of Whiteness, can to one degree or another split what is a thin advantage from a belief system—even when that sentiment must run counter to a powerful view that racism is correct.

With a concept of totality, one can also adopt a reasoned utopian vision of what could be, fashioned from what is.

White privilege is no myth. It appears as a 250 percent better chance to survive at birth, inherited wealth, softened surveillance, more mobility, better medical care, and the blithe acceptance of the face in the mirror as normal. But the focus on White privilege ignores the human and social loss that these petty bribes offer. Too often, the blaming stance of White privilege compels appeals to guilt—hardly a stable motivator for change—and excuses dead-end separatism. Moralizing and separatism, each of the two hands, form blinders over the chance to see a larger picture, that is, life beyond capitalism where all would gain from all.

Historian and sociologist Ted Allen says White people lose, not win, from racism.[2] Paralleling his argument but not overlaying it, it may be that White people in the United States gain momentarily from racist activity. But in the long run, even in less than a lifetime, it is clear that White people lose from racism and gain advantages from antiracist action. In schools for example, it was the racism of a mostly White and suburban workforce that allowed city (Black and Hispanic) school systems to be assaulted first by curricula regulations, harsh measures applied to high-stakes test results, and subsequent school closings and layoffs. An injury to one, though, only preceded an injury to all, as the same measures were applied to suburban districts later.

So a vision of the whole—which offers the possibility of a world that has transcended the limits of capital and gone beyond divide-and-rule methods into a world where all win from all—then sets up the possibility of rightly locating specific struggles against racism, that is, the necessity of taking leadership from Black teachers, students, and parents who are going to be hurt first and worst by attacks on schooling and life.

Capitalism is not the highest stage of human development. Things change, sometimes because of technological advances, sometimes because of the connection of ideas and strife.

Capitalism is the nest of schools and racism today. Each flows into the other, but home base is capital itself. Reluctance to name the capitalist system may come from honest misanalysis, timidity, opportunism, a wise assessment of one's ability to survive, or ignorance. The social relations capital demands must be identified to grapple with the problems of education and racism, as capital routinely changes and updates racism and its domination of education, often behind a cloak woven of claims to democracy, freedom, and equality.

The same social relations that create racism outside schools also create racism inside schools. The crux of the matter is altering those social conditions, outside and in. Class struggle, the relentless battles that capital requires, as well as action to overcome the deadly results of racism is the combat zone of schooling. Class struggle is the air for educators and organizers.

Racism is a practical and pedagogical problem. Neither theory nor social practice alone can eclipse it. As Jean Anyon has famously said, "doing school reform without doing social and economic reform is like washing the air on one side of a screen door; it just won't work."[3] The challenge is to locate education and racism within the whole of society and to see what each of us, individually and collectively, can do to transform it. Where are we and how might we act? And, after all, just who is "we?"

Capitalist society is rooted in the irrational exploitation of people by other people, the many by the few. Capitalism and socialism (capitalism with a benevolent party in charge) are failed systems that no longer make sense, offering the world endless war and inequality.

Still, capitalism has a litany of dodges—some based on the facts of its advances in science and political life, others in cultural spectacles—and its promise that anyone can make it if they just participate, as in the lottery slogan, "Someone must win: why not you?" You participate. They profit. Daily life within capital's walls, the struggle to survive and the immediate experiences capital offers, disguises its role by appearing to privatize daily life, isolating people and their problems when all human life is truly social. Most of the problems of daily life inside an authoritarian system divided by the violence inherent in the split of rich and poor can be traced back to the economy, though the tracing can be complex, convoluted, and not necessarily a straight line—a broad tendency.

The revolutions capital fomented in science, technology, communications, production, distribution, and exchange—and in advanced areas public education—offer the possibility for a united world, where everyone could live reasonably well in ecological harmony. In this sense, capitalism has socialized the world.

The production of capital itself also thrusts everyone apart into a desperate search for work, profits, cheap labor, raw materials, and markets, or they risk living with idleness, the chief occupation of the third world. United in fact, masses of people are divided by irrational, senseless, forces of nation, religion, race, sex, and gender required by the world economic system: capitalism. What truly divides people is social class. This does not equate the rest with illusion; it calls to question the necessity of irrationalism. Within this study of real yet unreasonable life, there is a way out beyond capital.[4]

Public education follows capital's path: It is hardly public or educational. Public schooling exists, but it is in fact tax-supported schooling segregated by class and race, as are the curricula and methods of teaching: unity and separation at the same time. Corporations that demand tax breaks and shift the tax burden onto the working class use the public schools as a massive free daycare system, warehousing children.

There is no single public education system in the United States; there are five or six: premedicine and law, preteacher and social worker, pre–skilled worker, prelaborer, premilitary, preprison. The truly rich and truly poor opt out of public education; the rich attend private academies, the poor drop out early. Each system of schooling is divided by class, then race. In a decaying economy offering few meaningful jobs with health benefits attached, teachers are tasked to tamp down the kids' expectations, making a lower horizon normal.

The substance of education overrides its methods. To the point, it is good that people learn to read in public school, but literacy and humane character have only coincidence in common. The perverse unity of form and substance in much of schooling is demonstrated in the lies taught to kids using methods that obscure the intellectual processes that can reveal lies.[5] This is the main thrust of capitalist education.

WHAT IS RACISM? THE LIMITS OF LIBERALISM

Racism is a set of ideas, connected to power, that treats external appearances (skin color, hair texture, facial features, eye color, language, etc.) as fundamental differences that cannot be changed and is transferred by inheritance (blood), making the object of racism less than human: ready for extermination. Racism is distinct from bigotry. A Christian bigot may well allow a Jew to convert. A racist would not.

Race itself is a myth, counter to biological fact. People are far more alike than different. Intermingling mostly with pleasure over 100,000 years ruined the racist science of distinguishing levels of intelligence, or humanity, by tracking race-based gene banks. Nevertheless, fear of a malignant gene leads to an influential series of fantasies about sexuality that permeate most societies. Rapes become a form of political revenge.

The mythology of race is a powerful reality, a key divide-and-conquer tool used with extraordinary success by elites everywhere. Coupled with continued wage differentials between people of color and Whites, racism is profitable.[6]

There is nothing necessarily logical about racist thinking, except to understand it as a method of domination. One method of domination is to convince the oppressed that domination does not exist. As Baldwin put it, "there are no workers, only candidates for the boss's daughter."[7]

Religious irrationalism (bigotry) has shifted in its prejudices over time, depending on historical circumstances, potential threats or rewards, desire, and the thinnest forms of perception. Religious and ethnic tolerance can dissolve fast; the former Yugoslavia is a good example. Similarly, racism tricked itself into believing, for example, that Native American women were potential wives, whereas Indian men were to be exterminated.

Starting from a defective premise, racism makes no rational sense until it is connected to power. The pope in the Vatican during the Nazi era was willing to, at the very least, allow the German fascists to exterminate the Jews, whereas his cardinals in Italy (a society which enjoyed a long history of integration of Jews and Christians and secularism—as well as a fairly large communist movement) frequently sheltered Jews, openly dismissed German exterminationist anti-Semitism as absurd. The key for the pope was defeating communism, routinely linked to Judaism.[8]

Racism is a relatively new irrational idea. When and why the idea of race, rather than tribe, nation, religion, language, and so on became consequential is a matter of dispute among historians. Some, like Theodore Allen and Alexander Saxton (addressing the nineteenth century), trace racism to the origins of capitalist expansion and early imperialism. Others suggest that racism rises up from religious irrationalism—Spanish conquistadors saw indigenous people more as heathens than as an inferior race and typically considered converts potential partners.[9]

Georg Lukacs warned about irrationalism in this way:

> Now irrationalism always begins with this (necessary, irrevocable, but always relative) discrepancy between the intellectual reflection and the objective original. The source of the discrepancy lies in the fact that the tasks directly presented to thought in a given instance, as long as they are still tasks, still unresolved problems, appear in a form which at first gives the impression that thought, the forming of concepts, breaks down in the face of reality, that the reality confronting thought represents an area beyond reason (the rationality of the category system of the conceptual method used so far). . . . Hegel . . . analyzed a . . . real road to a resolution of these difficulties. . . . What if (however) a virtue is made of . . . the inability to comprehend the world intellectually? That if a virtue is made of this necessity and the inability to comprehend the world intellectually is presented as a 'higher perception as faith, intuition, and so on? Clearly this problem will crop up at every stage of knowledge and social development, i.e., each time that social evolution and hence science and philosophy are forced to make a leap forward in order to answer the real questions arising. . . . It is not chiefly intellectual and philosophical considerations which decide a thinker's choice between the old and the new, but class allegiance . . . (which is often) halted at the threshold of knowledge and turned round and fled in the opposite direction.[10]

We never know all there is to know about anything. The movement in knowledge from what appears to be to a greater understanding of what actually is (appearance to essence) is a perpetual process. At base, if it is true that things change (and it is), it follows that our experiments on reality will always give results that trail behind the changes in that reality.

To decide that the gap between what is known and what is not known is holy, and to turn around and worship that gap—and those who will interpret it—is a very dangerous move. All forms of irrationalism—mysticism, religion, racism, ethnic rivalry—are inherently intolerant and at the same time, improvable.

They talk funny, smell bad, eat strange food, are ugly, different, cannot do the job, deserve to be where they are, are sexually potent, seductive, large, lazy but mule-like, are tricky but stupid, hold all the wealth or are inherently poor, listen to lousy music, worship an evil god, want to get into your family's precious gene bank, and so on. Nobody on Earth has failed to encounter racism or to be part of it. Racism envelops the world.

White supremacy is the most common, but hardly the only type of racism. Japanese expansionist racism made the massacres in China and Indonesia during World War II possible. White racism coupled with nationalism made the U.S. internment of Japanese people possible as well.[11]

It is possible for a few members of a dominated group to both benefit and suffer from racism: the corrupt mayor of Detroit, Kwame Kilpatrick, looting the public coffers for private gain; or the prime minister of Grenada, Keith Mitchell, lording over a fleet of SUVs while holding the last prisoners of the cold war, the Grenada Seventeen, in a seventeenth-century jail since 1983—long after the United States–imposed sentences have been served. Both Mitchell and Kilpatrick suffer from racism. They are, after all, Black. At the same time, they use their positions mainly for personal gain. They live contradictory lives as oppressors and the oppressed, but the primary aspect of that contradiction is their role as oppressors.[12] Teachers in schools can oppress children, their role being a matter of choice. They are, after all, what they do.

Racism can be directly tied to the economic interests of people who are not elites. Germans moved into the vacated homes of Jews forced into the ghettos, as did Poles. Small businesspeople as well as major grocery chains profited from the Japanese internment of World War II.[13] Racist wars or imprisonment can mean jobs for contractors, laborers, and guards. Teachers in White, wealthy school districts have routinely done nothing while their colleagues and children in poor districts have suffered the collapse of their school system with cuts in everything from low-cost lunches to wages and benefits.

Millions of people in the world today live in poverty and have neither education nor hope. Although education is no guarantee of enlightenment (educated German elites were, proportionally, far more likely to be fascists), a combination of no education, poverty, and hopelessness can quickly turn people to irrational explanations of their circumstances and ways to solve them: religion, nationalism, racism, pogroms, or war.[14]

Ethnicity is a similar but not equivalent idea. Ethnicity also confuses matters of likeness and difference and sometimes tracks inheritance (through blood or property), but the borders of ethnicity can take many forms, such as geography, language, culture, and so forth, in each instance claiming commonality along any line but class. No one thinks of the working class as an ethnic group—even though, for example, a teacher in the United States and a teacher in the United Kingdom have more in common with each other than they do with George Bush or Tony Blair. The mythology of ethnicity is sufficiently close to the lore of racism that, for the sake of brevity, I only address the latter.

Racism, like every form of irrationalism, is a fatal idea, so it is never merely an idea. But it is not an idea that occurs to people at birth. Racism is learned, and within a society divided into rich and poor but ruled by the rich, learning is often a method of deception. Such is the nature of capitalist schools where, as often as not, teachers willingly or unwillingly teach lies to children, using methods of constructing knowledge that make decoding lies nearly impossible.[15]

As the world's wars intensified in the late twentieth and early twenty-first centuries, the vast majority of teachers in the United States and their unions allowed themselves to be motivated mostly by racism, cowardice, ignorance, and opportunism. Leaders of school worker unions, the American Federation of Teachers and the National Education Association, allied themselves with corporate interests like the U.S. Chamber of Commerce and the Business Roundtable and the bipartisan actions of the U.S. government in support of anti–working-class, racist curricula regulations and high-stakes testing—all cloaked in talk about the national interest. It was rare to see rank-and-file teachers mounting any notable resistance, although pockets of opposition did appear—as in the Detroit teacher wildcat strike of 1999.[16]

At some point, history judges people by what they do. As teachers' wages and benefits are connected to test results, it may be that there will be more resistance, but school workers' acquiescence to date only contributes to the growing gap between rich and poor, Black and White, in the United States so far. Judgment is still out on the school workforce, but time is not limitless.

Hitler's Germany had to construct exterminationist, racist anti-Semitism. First Judaism, a religion, had to be set up as a matter of race, in the blood. Elaborate systems were created to track down Jewish blood. At the same time, Jews had to be seen as subspecies, a lower race (though worrisomely mighty), and hence a threat to the human gene bank. This required even more propaganda. It followed that the German Aryans had to eliminate the threat to humanity, so they set about it (and sought to conquer the world) with the support of a sizable section, perhaps a vast majority, of the population of what may have been the most literate and cultured society of its time—especially the educated and gentry classes.[17]

Teachers in Germany, overwhelmingly, did not resist fascism. Indeed, most were early volunteers in the Nazi Party. By 1937, 97 percent of the teaching force were Nazis, and Jews were thrown out of the profession with barely a whimper from their colleagues.[18] In Italy, there was some resistance from teachers and religious instructors. However, fascista volunteers dominated the teaching force there, too, almost totally by 1934.[19] In Germany teachers watched their Jewish colleagues become segregated, then exterminated. Although that horror of fascism is hard to imagine, so is the day-to-day school life in which, for example, teachers deliberately demanded that Jewish elementary children join other kids in milk and snack lines, then as the Jewish kids approached with empty cups raised, the teachers told them, "Run along, Jewess, next please." This went on day after day.[20]

German anti-Semites had considerable support from research that traced genetic bases for intelligence conducted in the United States, particularly at prestigious California universities where the knowledge produced was used to sterilize thousands of women and the research used to buttress fascist thinking. California scientists believed they could define intelligence, link it to genes, and improve human genetics by stamping out poisoned inheritances. German scientists used the U.S. research as a defense during the Nuremberg trials. Once the decision that some identifiable group is less than human is made, the last step of the irrational turn, the killing, is sure to follow.[21] This demonstrates the direct link of education, racism, violence, and death.

In the United States, racism seems obvious to those with the conscious lens to notice it. Geographic racism is sometimes easy to see, as the notorious 8 Mile Road divider in Detroit. Racism sometimes goes nearly unnoticed, as is the wall at the Mexican border in San Diego—San Diegans routinely insist on the diverse nature of their community. But wealthy San Diego, where less than 15 percent of the population can afford to buy a home, keeps its poor in Mexico, letting them in and out according to the need for cheap labor.

As noted, racism can offer privileges to members of a majority, or dominant, caste. Over time, those privileges can become invisible to all but the victims and the conscious profiteers. In one San Diego County elementary school I visited, the assembled teachers put it quite clearly: "We don't have a problem with racism here; we're all White." This is racism reified.

When pulled over by a state trooper, most White male youth need not worry about being murdered. White women rarely worry about being trailed by store detectives or about being White—which most see as simply their normal state of being. Black people must be conscious of Blackness, as a matter of life and death. White people live much longer than Black people. White people get better hospital treatment, live in less polluted areas, and suffer less stress, whereas centuries of slavery still lay heavily on the Black population. White people inherit much more wealth, getting a running start. Imperialist adventures, such as the U.S. invasions of Vietnam, Grenada, and the Middle East, are commonly fabricated with racist overtones. Conrad's "exterminate all the brutes,"[22] still plays well today, as does the missionary view of setting out to repair inferior societies (common among educators as well). On the other side of the coin, employers who systematically segregate workforces and pit one group against another can lay no claim to innocence.[23]

Good schools are usually seen today as segregated schools with higher test scores. Segregated schools are not necessarily better for White people than people of color. Segregated White schools do typically have more books, supplies, lower class size, and so on, whereas schools serving Black children are denied heat, light, playgrounds, libraries, and so forth. But the main lesson of segregated schooling is segregation: in service only to elites, hurting most kids—Black, White, and brown.

All masters want to replace the mind of the slaves with the mind of the master. When achieved, that consciousness is the victory of Taylorism—one of the reasons for house slaves—and the history of most religions. Refusing to participate in the process—that is, a sit-down strike, or teaching other slaves to read a compass, or leaving the priesthood—all that can be terrifying to those who have enjoyed the occasional smile of the master. In the relationship of the haves and have-nots, no one is innocent. Teachers teeter on this balance beam, choosing moment to moment whose interests they serve. But like victims of racism, however, educators do not necessarily see the system of domination racism serves, just as many prisoners cannot see beyond the walls.

Standardized curricula and textbooks seek to interrupt the teacher–student relationship, creating a publisher (profiteer)–consumer relationship, and, in the case of poorly educated or submissive students and teachers, publishers find eager victims.

Walls of domination are constructed by an absence of analysis of the workings of history, of class struggle. Racism is not merely a set of bad ideas that float about, incidentally passed from generation to generation. Racism is a material force that has a history, a coming to being over time, a present, and a future. Connected to divide-and-rule profitability, racism is joined to many forms of the accumulation of capital: Those who start with more capital usually live a bit better. Each instance is specific, however, and Whiteness and large hope chests do not necessarily connect.

Racism makes war palatable. The struggle for cheap labor, markets, and raw materials make war necessary. Degrading the enemy to the level of a nonhuman makes murder considerably easier. The language of racism sets up the possibility of seeing another human as an animal. Gook. Frog. Raghead. Gerry. Jap. Greaser. Camel rider. Slant. Infidel. Even with the traditional marine training choral response, "Kill! Kill! Kill!," killing is somewhat less heartfelt, more tolerable, when any respect for the humanity of the enemy is eliminated.

Blindness on the part of those who witlessly enjoy modest privileges makes sense of Hegel's thought: The truth of the master is in the slave.[24] Those at the short end of the stick often have the best understanding of the whole of domination. But people with petty privileges can wake up to the overriding domination and unite with oppressed minorities for thorough social change. Historically, communists, socialists, and anarchists have taken the lead in this struggle because they have, to one degree or another, recognized the relationship of exploitation and racism and joined out of solidarity, not evangelizing.[25]

The real minority group is those who hold wealth, but they have little concern about their minority status and prefer it is not noticed. To the contrary, the international majority group, poor and working people, rarely recognize their real status as people who could overturn their circumstances. Although history is largely the result of their struggles, truly international outbursts against oppression are relatively rare. Even so, mass integrated movements like the early stages of the civil rights movement, the Industrial Workers of the World at the turn of the twentieth century, and the Congress for Industrial Organization in the 1930s, or the not-so-mass but turning-point raid of John Brown before the Civil War have been key to society and social change. It is equally clear that racist divisions in social movements were useful to elites—an Achilles heel of the working-class unions or the movement against the war in Vietnam. At issue, in these cases, are class and class-consciousness, including antiracist consciousness, that does not necessarily develop, but that can develop and grow deepened by theory, as a long view of history demonstrates.

Because elites depend on racism, and as every exploitive relationship is a form of violence, it follows that racism will not be overcome solely through education for caring, diversity, or love—nor even history. The U.S. Civil War, the Armenian genocide, the Nazi Holocaust, the U.S. war on Vietnam, the Rwanda genocide—all witness the willingness of elites to kill millions of people to retain their privileges. Racism will only be overcome through mass integrated struggles directed to its source. Even so, consciousness—what people know, and how they come to know it—is a vital political and pedagogical question. Absent consciousness, there is no learning from struggles that are likely to occur—must occur—because people throughout the world are now positioned so that they must fight to live and love.

Separatist movements like the Nation of Islam, Marcus Garvey, and others have not been mass movements and have not been successful, perhaps because most members of minority groups realize that separatism creates the conditions for extermination. The Black nationalist claims of the past, even coming from self-described Marxists, now seem almost quaint. Although it is clear that Black people in the United States will necessarily lead resistance, as they must at some point fight to live, it is equally clear that Black revolutionary power alone, or the election of Black mayors, will not succeed.[26] Uprisings like the 1992 Los Angeles riots demonstrate that even spontaneous insurgency can be integrated.

Trendy postmodernist pretexts for nation/culture/sex/gender-based identity groups, in which the narrowest interest is elevated to a pivotal role, follow the same path, disconnecting social change from history and the future (suggesting that this moment is utterly new, and completely encapsulated). Postmodernists, divorcing the past, present, and future and disengaging class struggle from the processes of the world, become unintelligible (so their prolix writing often cannot be read), or they insist that the crux of the matter is an individual identity, splitting the dialectic of likeness and difference, leaving current antiwar protest movements, for example, fragmented and ineffective.[27]

Racism does have a psychology and is part of the construction of the identity of, probably, everyone. Psychology—character analysis—is often taken apart from the infinitely complex interacting causes of all events. This view "captures a particularly impoverished shadow of the actual social relations in the world, concerning itself only with the projections."[28] Psychology is part of the story of racism but not the whole of it. Identity formation and class structure create and re-create each other and, because nothing comes from nothing, demands to pinpoint an exact origin will probably go unmet. Economic and psychological formation is congruent. Addressing the part without seeing the bigger picture, the individual within the whole of social relations, leads to blind canyons of resistance.[29] It is not sufficient to fight racism inside one's mind, nor even inside many minds. It is collective action that can offer the lessons to show the way to overcome racism and the control of capital.

As a part of identity, a form of profit, a divide-and-conquer tool, an extension of irrationalism that makes supremacy and inferiority seem natural or sets up a particular group as an example to others for just how bad things might get, racism is a method of class rule. The key form of oppression (sexism, ableism, nationalism, agism, etc.) may switch or intermix from moment to moment under changing social conditions, but the crux of the issue is class domination, formed from the struggle for cheap labor, raw materials, markets, and sheer power: capitalism.

Racism will live long after what I think will be mass struggles to overturn the rule of capital and place society in the hands of the masses of people, probably proving that ideology can exert its own forms of power, but there is no getting rid of racism without recognizing its importance to capital's personifications.

When racism becomes so pervasive that it goes unnoticed by many people, it helps elites deny the continued existence of overarching master–slave relationships. Defeating racism is essential to any social movement for equality and justice, just as is discovering and taking leadership from minority group members, whose understanding of oppression may be more profound. This is not to say that criticism comes to an end, or that people think with their skin and deserve elevated treatment because of it. It is simply to say, if nothing else, that it will take a mass integrated movement with minority leadership directed at the rule of capital itself to overcome the crises we face now: Within a world united more than ever by systems of exchange, production, technology, and transportation, there is an international war of the rich on the poor, intensified inequality, deepening segregation of all aspects of life, witless nationalism, and an explosion of evangelical irrationalism.

To miss this point, or to ignore it, leads masses of people up dangerous avenues, my next key argument. There is nothing magical in daily life or even the resistance that workers must mount to survive that reveals the role of class rule in society or what to do about it. The deepest failure of socialism, the failure to forge a mass of class-conscious people who could defend what they had won, demonstrates this point rather clearly. Grasping class rule as a matter of reality and seeking to transform it in ways beyond missionaryism, is a matter of social action, imagination, and teaching, addressed next.

Twentieth-century history suggests that only leftists (communists, socialists, anarchists) with their view of transforming the whole of capitalist relations have consistently fought racism, in every form, as was true in Germany, Austria, China, South Africa, Vietnam, Eastern Europe, and the United States. To say their positions were always wise—never tainted with opportunism, nationalism, or subservience (as in the Communist Party USA's eagerness to take direction from the Soviet Union)—or that they were fully successful is not the case. But it is correct to say that they fought back consistently, and their organizations made their resistance powerful.[30]

Ignoring (or denying, or labeling as reductionist) the interplay of race and class—one influencing and rebounding back on the other from moment to moment, a slippery relationship that can change with circumstances— is common among sociologists, multiculturalists, and postmodernists. From this error comes many others, like identifying the nation as an area of overarching commonality (the "salad bowl" having replaced the "melting pot"; pluralism under prolix banners as a substitute for integrated class struggle) and therefore relying on the nation-state (government) and its ideological premises to re-solve problems of domination, when the state and its ideology exists to enforce domination.[31] It follows that mass resistance is outside the scope of those who refuse to see the interaction of race and class, and this myopia causes them to not only misperceive the processes of the world but offer faulty compasses for leading change. They seek to resolve questions of race and class by ignoring class. They disarm those who follow them into the hands of elites.

Nationalism is the idea that we are all in this together, probably through coincidence of geography or ethnic accident. Nationalism implies difference, even superiority. Rising inequality everywhere graphically demonstrates that we are not all in this together in one nation—not in the courts, not at work, not at the ballot box, nor in the schools. What rightly divides the world is social class. The false belief that everyone in a given geographic location has something unaccountable unifying them (and thus setting them apart from others) has been every bit as popular as racism, and sometimes stands well above it. Racism and nationalism appear together so often, they can be con-sidered twins. But multiculturalists and others typically rely on nationalism to figure ways out of the issue of racism, an impossible twist that because of rising inequality, will only strengthen those who profit from the racist divide.[32]

Class rule and racism will not be defeated by education alone, though antiracists must turn to education as a way to solve the problem.

Racism, in limited ways, may have existed prior to the rule of capital, under feudalism, but capitalist science gave racism its pretense today. Capi-talism requires racism. Hence, antiracist educational action attacks the Achilles heel of capitalism.

Racism is now mediated through the system of capital, as form of ir-rationalism, and as a material force, chronic among masses of people ad-dicted by daily experience as workers and consumers to a color-coded war of all on all. Individual and institutional racism buttress one another, their impact set by power. Individual racists with no capital or organization have little impact. Organized racists, such as the Ku Klux Klan or similar gangs or institutional racists who reject affirmative action, have power and influence.

Institutional (corporate) racists can make use of individual and organized racists.

Like racism, education has existed to one degree or another for centuries, much of it rising out of churches and religious education. As capitalism advanced, so did its schools, resulting in the slightly varying forms of education in the world today, each mainly using teachers as missionaries for capital in its church: school.

Capitalist schooling as a mystifier and church schooling is good metaphor. Under capital, private property is simply assumed, its origins never interrogated, just as gods are proved by faith. In church, faith is rooted in love but is usually overmatched by fear of hell. Labor under capital is supposedly free, although all work within the system is coercive, under surveillance—work or starve. In schools, learning to build curiosity is replaced by learning for the test, and later, just as labor under capital becomes the resentment of labor, the resentment of learning becomes a bedrock of life. Capitalist schools and church schooling are designed to convince participants, rightly or wrongly, that they have an interest in eternalizing their systems.

The suspension of criticism is a centerpiece of capitalism, its schools, and the church. Questioning that goes to the root of issues, like, "Why are some people so rich, and others so poor?" or "Why must we pay someone to interpret God for us?" or "How do we know God is not evil?" are rarely posed in schools or church.

The nineteenth-century Native American schools, churches, and government created in the name of civilization and fairness—really hubris and greed (the toxicity of benevolence)—demonstrate the relationship of capital and mysticism. Church pedagogical kidnaping of Native American youth in the United States followed an illuminating path: send the troops and seize the land; send the missionaries (teachers) to civilize the kids' institutionally aberrant behavior using carrot-and-stick methods and curricula to reform their identities and demolish their substandard culture; and win over a few of the brighter ones and turn them back on what was once their people. Sometimes the Native American kids ran away, burned their schools, or died. Some resisted. Many fit in. The parallels to the education of working-class kids today are striking.[33]

Capitalism and racism reverberate back and forth on one another. Each is rooted in exploitation, alienation, the battle for surplus value, commodity fetishism, reification, the state, and the human psyche formed within this context, particularly within the authoritarian family. Work, the family, humane interactions, and intellectualism are now disintegrating to one degree or another—liquefying. These aspects of capitalism are described briefly later in to set the stage to discuss racism and education.

IMPERIAL EXPLOITATION, RACISM, AND SCHOOL

Exploitation and Violence

Value is created by human labor. Most value is possessed by people who did not produce it. Possession in this form means violence. The system of capital, subordinating humane desires for freedom and creativity, necessitates exploitation. Some own, others do not. Those who own typically seek to do the thinking and expect others to dig, a division of mental and manual labor. Those who do the work do not hold the reins.

The earliest significant forms of capital were won through imperialist robbery.[34] The surpluses of capital made available from invasions, slavery, and forced labor created accumulations that could be reinvested in machines, factories, and so on. Racism helped make forced labor and mass murder acceptable, civilizing the savages.

Capital, like religion, must expand or die. Microsoft eats Netscape, despite antimonopoly laws. Packard, Hudson, Studebaker, Kmart, even Chrysler (now owned by Daimler) no longer exist. Capitalists war with other capitalists. To exploit labor and compete, capital needs violence.

The twentieth century promises of the end of the cold war, peace and prosperity, could not stand. Capitalism means war, as its hundreds of years of rule demonstrates. Those who hold capital require nation-based armies to protect themselves from other capitalists and the people who work for them. Capital, though, which cares nothing about who rides it, knows no borders and operates nationally and internationally at the same time (as the battles over the Chinese purchase of U.S. oil companies demonstrates). Although capital operates internationally, its personifications, bound by their own history, cannot.

Ownership, codified by law and sheer force, means that the few are able to expropriate much of the value created by the many. This value, called *surplus value* by Marx, can be called *profits*—the amount beyond that spent to re-create the working class, to maintain and produce equipment, taxes, and so on—kept by the owner. Surplus value is the giant sucking pump of capital that moves the whole system. Capital's great secrets are its shrouded existence and surplus value.[35]

In capital's intrinsically master-and-slave relationship, a victory of the master is to convince the slave that slavery is freedom, that labor is justly rewarded, that there is no master–slave relationship at all. Or slaves might be convinced they have an interest in maintaining slim privileges within a system that has been so successful with equating a dime with privilege. Capitalist education serves this purpose—forms of voluntary submission—while at the same time offering masses of students the tools and some information to think otherwise, if they can see beyond the walls. Capitalism must have nuclear physicists who do not worry about bombs, but many physicists do just that.

Exploitation compels alienation, the separation of people from people. Those who do not own significant amounts of capital (which can separate people dollar by dollar, color by color, shade by shade, sex by sex), oppose each other for a limited number of jobs. At the same time, these people form a multiracial class—workers, people who do not hold a lot of capital. Thus, workers and owners are classes pitted against each other and, taken uncritically, workers are pitted against workers and bosses are also pitted against bosses (because only those who grab the most surplus value win). History suggests that owners are far more likely than employees to recognize their commonality when faced with a united challenge.

Why Have School? Educators as Workers

Educators are, mostly, workers, although when they are called on to spend an average of $1,200 of their own money for school supplies each year, they are reminded of their professionalism.[36] There are 49 million children in public schools in the United States and more than 3.4 million teachers and school workers. The overwhelming majority of students are future workers or soldiers. Youth, not school workers, are the prime target of schooling, though the actions of school workers can be very influential and can send youth up better paths than to become targets.[37]

Capital's schools are huge markets that involve not only students and educators but tens of thousands of others. Consider the school buses, textbooks, lunches, grounds-keepers, architects, guard companies, test manufacturers, advertisers, and clothing manufacturers. School is a multibillion-dollar business, not a think tank distinct from the crude workings of the world. Follow the money.

The rule of business, profits, grinds on while simultaneously the problems of business arise—cheating, chicanery, and sexual exploitation of those who hold less power. Developers cheat on contracts, suppliers bait and switch supplies, and most of school work is done by women, whereas most of education's top bosses are men.

Because schools are home to developing sexuality yet are tasked with repressing sexuality through demands for splitting pleasure and reproduction (abstinence education), it follows that schools are also sensual places, where desire can overwhelm a geometry lesson. Repressed desire, the line from advertiser to purchaser, can underpin an obsequious personality or an authoritarian one. The lure of freedom, contradicted by habitually repressed yearning, shapes subjects who can dream of freedom but will not fight for it.[38]

School workers produce value in capital's markets. When educators and kids arrive in school, they confront a billion-dollar business, more powerful than unorganized kids and teachers. This is part of the answer to the critical question that is rarely asked: Why have school? Educators shape the next generation of workers and labor power, and they generate hope, real or false—a linchpin of social order.[39]

Hope, accumulated over generations of teachers' hard work, is the reason parents send their kids to school—to strangers. In addition to skill training and some restricted intellectual activity, schools also promote nationalism, warehouse kids (a huge free daycare system supplementing corporations that insist the main tax burden should be on the working class), and commercialize sports—schools' promise of hope is now more myth than reality. What hope exists comes from those rarities who swim against the tide. Government funds come primarily from the exploitation of other workers, and the valuable labor of school workers is exploited—that is, they are not paid for the full value of their labor—which is both ideological and practical, and they do not control the processes nor the products of their work.

Teachers do not set their own hours, wages, or working conditions. They do not control the curriculum or the pedagogical methods to be employed. Powerful corporate interests control textbook publishing, for example, and seek to replace the critical and human relationships of a particular teacher meeting a unique child in a classroom with the standardized curricula and techniques (policed by high-stakes examinations that measure little but race and class) that serve those who hold power. The less educators (workers) resist this subservient alienating relationship, the more they enrich both those who own and capitalism itself. So although teachers may think of themselves as more professionals than workers, they are more workers than professionals. The more they uncritically pursue surplus value, the less free and creative they are, and the more oppressed the kids are.[40]

Alienation

In schools, educators are alienated (separated, estranged) from students (grading, tests, class size), the curriculum (textbooks, regulated curricula), parents, administrators, and each other (competition for jobs and wages). Teachers are alienated from their own education and creativity as regimented curricula and tests replace the mind of the educator with the mind of the test-prep company, that is, the mind of capital. Counselors are replaced by test-score charts, and librarians by clerks (or the libraries are closed).

Kids, the focus or product of schools, are particularly alienated. They are segregated by capital's geography of money and power, by race, by tracking within schools, by ability and disability, and even in some public schools, by sex. They are set apart from school workers and administrators in a boss–worker relationship. Kids are distanced from meaningful struggles for what is true and its foundation, freedom, the day-to-day realities and significance of labor, democracy, equality, and sensuality as a source of responsible pleasure.

Although there are many kinds of segregated unpublic miseducation, depending mostly on the parental incomes on which the school feeds, the main message of school to most students is that learning itself is an alien, generally meaningless task. There is school work and real life. It is rare for capitalism—the role of social classes and where students and school workers are located in this system—to be discussed in schools. The questions, "Who are we?," "Who do *I* fit as part of *we*?," "Who shall we say is *we*, and them?," "Why are we here?," "Why should we do this?," "Who decides?," and "Who gains?" are often too dangerous to raise in schools. Much of public schooling is wasted time—soldiering, getting through the day to get to the next day—work-life preparation.

Racist alienation is structured into the history of public schools. In the United States, more than 90 percent of the teaching force is White and self-described as middle class, facing a child population that is now mostly poor kids of color. Race and class set not only school boundaries but the structures of the teachers' unions, organized mostly along occupational lines—mostly White teachers and degreed workers in one unit, other support personnel in other units. Because they do not pay dues—capitalist unions' bottom line—students and parents do not vote in and are rarely invited to education union meetings, though students and parents are key to organizing power for school workers.

Racism in education appears in the curriculum (textbooks and tests), discipline and graduation rates, the differing facilities like school buildings, supplies, and libraries, overcrowding and noise, language and cultural clashes between White middle-class educators and kids and parents of color, administrators' willingness to demonstrate and use force, the seizure of entire city (read: "of color") school systems by state or corporate interests, and the No Child Left Behind act, which uses high-stakes tests (designed to deepen regulation of what children are taught, and the ways they are taught) that truly measure little more than class and race and divide kids along those lines, falsely using science as capital's sword and shield.

Commodity Fetishism

Capitalism propelled, in part, by the sale of commodities to realize surplus value causes, over time, both workers and the employer classes to relate more to things than they do to other people. Money appears to beget money, machines seem to create value. A worker's daily life, indeed the activity that sets up nearly all other of her life interactions, is measured by a boss in terms of added value.

When scientific forms of management are successfully employed, measuring and regulating each worker's every movement, labor seems to vanish, as do top bosses. Teachers' good judgement about a particular kid gets replaced by scripted curricula, tests, and standardized measurements for ability or disability. Educators are supervised by a growing body of overseers holding clipboards and charts, making sure all are on task, that is, within bounds. Some schools script so carefully, overseers expect to walk into any classroom at any time and rightly predict the activity.

The script or the test becomes the purpose of school, not human interactions in an authentic struggle for what is true. The regulated curricula and tests grow into fetishes that rule people, rather than the inverse. Test scores become real estate values. The human potential of children is shoved aside as educators are ordered to cheat on tests, drive out likely low-scorers, target kids on the cusp of passing, and abandon creativity.

Commodity fetishism causes people to measure self-worth by merchandise, especially the chief commodity, money, which in many instances becomes an item of worship. Businesses no longer focus on making, say, steel for use, but on making money for profits. Schools (where the prime commodity is also money) do not concentrate on authentic learning but on test scores as measures of human value. At the same time, as self-discipline and motivation is overwhelmed by extrinsic punish and reward systems, history—the discipline that helps people discover who they are, why they are there, that things change, and gives hints for what to do—is erased from the curricula, untested. Social studies teachers then demand tests, not so much to resurrect history but because No Test = No Job.[41]

People who must sell their labor and their lives become commodities themselves and often view themselves and their own children that way, as do their employers. People begin to see what are really relations between people as relations between things (every human relationship mainly an economic one).

In schools, children have been routinely commodified, sold to companies like McGraw-Hill (textbooks) and Coca-Cola. This process has accelerated in the past decade. In schools that serve poor and working-class communities, commodification grows severe as kids are sold to Channel One, Nike, and others to gain vital school supplies, whereas schools serving wealthier parents can count on the inequitable distribution of taxes and private donations to offer a wide range of opportunities from swimming pools to art classes. The message to impecunious kids of color sitting in bad school facilities with no libraries: You are worth less.

Commodity fetishism creates an inverted world: The more you have, the more you are. In schools, the higher the test scores, the better the school. The inversion: The higher the test score, the more rich, White, and yet subservient you are. The more you have, the more you are controlled by it.

Reification

Human relations among people disguised as the relations between things become so habitual that it seems natural. Things people produce govern peoples' lives. Natural laws, really inventions of people, replace real analytical abilities in U.S. curricula. The economy's invisible hand is credited with doing this or that, unquestioned as to whose economy is doing what to whom. Supply and demand, or scarcity and choice, are seen as the core of economics rather than seeing economics as the story of the social relations people create over time in their struggle with nature to produce and reproduce life, or in political science, discussing democracy as if it had nothing to do with social inequality. All of these devices strip people of their own ability to locate themselves within the changing nature of history, to abstract their social positions and see the commonalities of what appear to be individual problems but are truly social problems, and hence to exert control over their own lives.

Normalcy in capitalist countries is really fabricated assent to exploitation masked as liberty: hegemony. Racist segregation is routinely posed as a matter of choice. High-stakes testing is conditioned into the culture, seen as the key to educational assessment, when all the data say that multiple forms of assessment are necessary for validity. As fetishes, test scores are good examples of reification in school. Curricula standardization and high-stakes test results are used as proof for false promises to make schooling more equitable, when in fact they are simply harsher measures for social control. Test scores are worshiped uncritically, influencing peoples' live far beyond their real value, affecting real estate values, for example. The uncritical view of capital's processes as normalcy is reification.

Crises, Resistance, Change, Racism, and Schools

Marx's analysis said that the workings of capital above are riddled with crises, feed on them.[42] These crises are interrelated, but to take them in parts:

   a. Overproduction: Because over time capital uses technology, speed-up, wage cuts, and so on to drive down wages and raise the levels of surplus value, at a certain point, the mass of workers can no longer afford to buy the products they produce.
   b. Declining rate of profits: Because labor creates all value and at the same time employers must invest heavily in technological improvements to keep ahead of competitors, value stored up in the means of production comes to outweigh value in what Marx called variable (or more profitable) capital, that is, the workers. So although the workers become impoverished by overproduction, the bosses are driven toward other ways to increase surplus value beyond technological advances. Rising inequality appears in schools in the form of hungry kids, collapsed families, the lack of books and supplies, and attacks on teacher health care, benefits and retirement funds.
   c. War: Every continent is now either the home of a war or sending participants to a war, and it has been like this for more than 100 years. That should be proof enough of the capital = war axiom. Nationalist war (not class war) marches directly into classrooms, into the curricula.
   d. Change: The multitude of crises may lead to social change. World War I gave birth to the Russian revolution, World War II to the Chinese revolution. Revolutions are usually made by the young.

At a certain point in capitalism's development, finance and monopoly capital (banking interests with big fish always eating little fish, etc.) dominate even manufacturing capital. Facing similar pressures of the earliest capitalists, financiers must seek new markets, cheap labor, and raw materials at a frantic pace, a tempo that the centrality of money and technology makes possible and necessary.

Capital has always accumulated land, resources, and surplus labor from all over the world. Today's intensified imperialism, typified now by oil wars, was born within and along with nations and relies on national armies for a good part of its strength; the battle for resources frequently becomes imperialist war (as in World War I, Vietnam, Iraq, etc.) between nations, each ruling class claiming ethical high ground. Marx said workers in imperialist armies "do not fight their enemies, but the enemies of their enemies."[43]

Imperialist wars were the logical and necessary culmination of capitalist development. Although wars were an indication of the weaknesses of capitalists (and would lead to revolutions as happened later in the Soviet Union and China), capital does not die because of crises but thrives in the destruction. Still, the processes of capitalism, of which war is a part, also draw people together in unprecedented ways, offering them intellectual and material possibilities to live in new ways, if they so choose.

Crises do not produce or sustain real change. Human critical consciousness, the falsely proclaimed product of education, is the only factor that animates and preserves fundamental social change.

Love, work, knowledge (the struggle for what is true), and the struggle for freedom, equality, and creativity are the motivating forces of history, the heart of resistance and revolution. People resist because they must to live. From this daily struggle, in the midst of crises, real change can be won.

Schools, like any workplace, are disputed territory where people resist in struggles to be more creative, knowledgeable, free, connected with others, and better paid. For example, it is cheaper to expand class size in schools rather than hire enough teachers so an ideal number of about twelve kids would be in each class. School workers have historically resisted the expansion of class size and tried to reduce it for decades, just as the struggle for the shorter work week typifies the history of the working class.

Resistance to capital's crises and wars can reasonably be expected to come first from the people who arrived in life shortchanged (without capital, poor people of color), and it is fair to say that the wisdom of poor people of color, seen by most academics as an object to be repaired, is likely to be deeper than those whose inheritance is hubris.

Resistance, however, is not necessarily transformation (a complete overcoming). Resistance can merely re-create oppression in new ways. In schools, kids can resist by refusing to learn anything at all, rejecting the struggle for knowledge, joining racist gangs, choosing self-destruction. They fail to see that authentic education is revolutionary: The struggle for what is true. Teachers can win class size limits for a few, as California schools limited kindergarten through grade three class size. But, over time, this victory simply created a mass divide in the work force, when the struggle for caps on all of kindergarten through grade twelve was abandoned by the unions.

Education, always simultaneously individual and social, presupposes change—quantities of work turn into qualitative difference, as in many forms of literacy practice forging a literate person. At issue remains what it is that people need to know and, significantly, how do they need to come to know it to get beyond capital, or "How might working people break out of what is really a vast company store, an international casino?" Ideas and pedagogy would seem to be a key product of schools—as would a full examination of the role of racism as a prop for injustice.

Government, the State, and Schooling

Marx viewed the state and government as directly tied to the system of production in which it was born. Feudal estates and serfdom gave rise to kings and queens, whereas mass production and finance capital gave rise to bourgeoisie democracy; but each system of rule (government rooted in inequality) was or is mainly a weapon in the hands of the powerful, not a neutral force seeking justice for all, though the state can be used by the powerful to appear to resolve crises that pose a common problem.[44]

Schools are governmental institutions, subject to rule. Other state institutions are somewhat easier to decode. The military is clearly a hierarchical weapon of the powerful, as are the police and the tax system. The welfare system exists to regulate, not truly provide for, poor people (and why are there poor people?). The prisons are full of the poor.

Today's schools are, above all, capitalist schools. They are not, as comfortable postmodernists have claimed, semiautonomous space or relatively autonomous areas. The only thing that is semiautonomous today is capital itself, rushing beyond conscious human control—the broom the sorcerer's apprentice must chase.[45] Capital's schools serve, mostly, capital's interests, while at the same time, opposition occurs, as it does in any workplace.

This contradiction becomes graphic. It is no longer true that education will move one up in society because the general trajectory is down. But a critical education can save your life, perhaps keep you out of a war.[46] It is capital's state, the government, that must sustain apartheid conditions in U.S. schools.

Class Consciousness

Class consciousness is the awareness that one is

part of a social group that, through common work activity at the same time reproduces a social system and others in it who do not have the same interests regarding that system, and who do not participate in it in the same manner . . . it is an orientation toward political action . . . an awareness of others, of those who are similar and those who are different with regard to their long-term interests, and an awareness of the social structure that makes their differences real.[47]

Class consciousness implies antiracism and anticapitalism, as well as a vision of a better future against which today's actions can be tested. This is not to simply reduce every question of race, sex, religion, or ethnicity immediately to greed and profits, but it is to say that the war for surplus value has, at the end of the day, decisive influence in setting up all the social relations of capital.

Capital's schools, racism, nationalism, sexism, and religion all disguise social problems, problems of class, as well as problems of individual people, competing races and nations, or fate. That is, capital's schools are designed, above all, to create a veneer of limited knowledge, but to wipe out class consciousness. To date, this is succeeding.

Class consciousness has been seen as

a. a logical and necessary result of the advance of productive forces—that is, when the world is industrialized, people will become class conscious;[48]
b. an awareness of the whole picture of capital through the daily bitter experiences that capital must offer the working class and the intervention of an advanced party;[49]
c. an offering to working people from organized intellectuals and dedicated activists, especially as crises arise;[50]
d. workers' spontaneous response to their collective, persistent problems, because work is always alienating;[51] and
e. the natural product of intellectuals produced by the working class itself, organic intellectuals whose ideas can be more easily accepted and grasped.[52]

None of these formulas has worked well. Class consciousness, then, is a pedagogical and practical problem that has not been resolved; it plagues the working classes of the world as crises of capital—inequality, imperialist war, rising irrationalism, international bankruptcies, militarism, and so on—making the current situation especially menacing and urgent.

The crux of the pedagogical issue goes beyond transcending racist alienation and defeating exploitation. At the heart of the question is the view that people can overcome the master–slave relationship consciously, yet not re-create it at a new level to forge a new society, a caring community, from the rubble of the old.

THINKING THROUGH CAPITAL, EDUCATION, AND RACISM

Capital's segregated racist schools miseducate people about how to think, the processes of knowledge won through centuries of struggle. Although the scientific method is taught in schools, it is taught in the absence of (a) abstraction—that is, what is the historical location of this, who gains, and so on?—and (b) examination of external and internal contradictions—that is, how does school relate to society, and how do issues of exploitation, alienation, commodity fetishism, reification, and change appear in school?

Few teachers I have witnessed offer "this is how I think about this, my philosophy," because they simply have never had the chance to wonder about it. School knowledge is metaphysical. One subject is unrelated to another—mathematics without history, art without mathematics, race apart from class. In school, change is always distant, of the past, and incremental, not revolutionary. Above all, students are rarely taught that they themselves are historians and makers of history—not the objects of others but collective subjects of their own designs.[53]

Kids are seldom taught ways to abstract from their immediate circumstances to conduct investigations of the contradictions in their own lives: What limits me? Why am I encouraged to see social problems as individual problems, and so forth? Schooling miseducates most people to become victims of history rather than to look at a globe and think, "This is ours; how shall we choose to interact with it?"

Designed to wipe out historical understanding, NCLB—supported by both major political parties, the U.S. Chambers of Commerce, the Business Roundtable, and the major teacher unions—is a good example of the role of the state as an enforcer of alienated, commodified, reified schooling leading to crises in education.[54]

Teachers, mistrained in many colleges of education that value pedagogical methods over curricular substance (i.e., not seeing the two as a relationship but promoting a one-sided view), do not learn to search for the bigger picture, to abstract, either. Without abstracting beyond education and racism, the question, "How do education, school workers, and racism fit and function in our world today?" is only partially answered, and therefore only partially addressed.[55] Once abstraction is established, however, we can begin to examine its processes and how it might change.

Capital's miseducated people who cannot locate themselves as makers of history rely on others to create and preserve social change; the artifice of priests. This obliterates the possibility of a mass, informed movement of people dedicated for action on the side of reason, democracy, and equality against racism. People can make their own histories, "become the heroes of their own life," if they can grasp the circumstances that surround them.[56] Those who cannot grasp the whole of the social processes, capital, have no North Star. Clearly this is a pedagogical challenge.

Capitalist schools are profoundly hierarchical, and growing more so. The hierarchies can be seen in pay scales, the relationship of geography and power (who has the most space and the most desirable space?), class- and race-tracking kids, the deep split between teachers and support workers, and the differing ways that parents and kids are treated depending on their power or income.

Habituation to hierarchy deepens subservience. Even oppositionists seek to mimic their bosses, to become like them not overcome them—union hacks or Black mayors. The last century demonstrates that even profound changes in the productive forces of society and violent shifts in the ownership of production do not necessarily create the class consciousness that is vital to make and preserve social change.

NCLB will and has led to resistance, some coming from officials who feel it is underfunded, some from resisters who oppose its central goals—divide and rule. As schools are reconstituted, closed, privatized, made small, and so on, youth and school workers in poor communities will fight back, especially as war bangs louder on the schoolroom door. It is the task of educators to make sense of that resistance, to see that it is pedagogical resistance, a school better than school.

In sum, race, class, and schools within the system of capital are all designed to reinvigorate capitalism unless an organized conscious effort can be built to criticize and overturn it. Now, within a criticism of a study of racism, we will see how education workers, students, and community people are positioned to change the world.

REFORMERS AS REACTIONARIES

Misleading the Struggle for Truth against Racism

Though the United States's greatest historian—a young W. E. B. Du-Bois—is often approvingly quoted, "The problem of the twentieth century is the color line," in fact, the problem of the ages is the linkage of irrationalism—the witting or unwitting suspension of critique—to exploitation (of labor, oil, places to buy and sell, the profits of deception) and power. Du-Bois, a Marxist, recognized this in saying that the way to liberation was through "systematic investigation," overcoming ignorance.[57]

Investigation absent action, however, is mere library work. Social practice is key, but social practice can just re-create more and more of the same practice. At some point, when life and curiosity cause a significant problem to be posed, imagination—usually won through self-actualized freedom—must leap ahead of what is toward what might be. People must learn to fight for a way to live in which they themselves have never lived. It is possible to choose a united, caring world and make decisions about how to get there. The alternative is decades of barbarism. Curiosity, imagination, and freedom should be the bedrocks of schooling, even in the restrictive, militarized atmosphere of education today.

The transition to a communal world, "renewal," as James Baldwin called it, is theoretical and practical; a matter of thought, life, death, and love. Abolitionist John Brown rightly saw that "moral suasion" alone would never create social change, but he also recognized that once a problem—racism and slavery—had been posed, "a settlement of this question, that must come up for settlement sooner than you think."[58]

More often than not, it is civil strife built up over time—active resistance—that calls attention to the need for a settlement. Timothy Tyson, speaking about an uprising against racism in the South, puts it this way: "[They] ... did not even consider altering the racial caste system until rocks began to fly and buildings began to burn."[59]

Brown, who was reconciled with his death by his actions in life, preceded Baldwin: "One must *earn* one's death by confronting the conundrum of life." Renewal comes with danger. All that appears to be constant must be made transitory, from the processes of today's economy to the challenges of daily life.[60] In sum, what we do counts.

Schools and racism are inextricably linked to capitalism and violence. Whereas each of us must struggle for our daily bread, schools claim to offer an opportunity to study what is, systematically, to learn and imagine what might be. To a degree, settled by power, schools can be held to that promise. This study of real material conditions requires freedom, which means a fight with those whose interests are tied to oppression and ignorance. That fight will be severe and engaged within specific circumstances, each of us determining how we may make the greatest contribution over time. There will be a fight. Connecting reason to power has always been dangerous, as Galileo learned. At issue is what form it will take, how the mass of people can learn from the past, and who wins.

Beyond that, I pose three questions to those who struggle for social justice: (1) how can we educators keep our integrity and survive? (2) what is it that people need to know, and how must we come to know it, to lead reasonably free, caring, connected lives? and (3) why is it that it is so easy to turn so many people into instruments of their own oppression? I don't suggest I can fully answer those questions, but I offer them to stimulate a greater understanding of what follows.

The Centrality of School

School workers in North America are well positioned to make social change. In the twenty-first century, schools, not industrial workplaces, are the focal points of social life. School work cannot be outsourced, although it can be degraded. The industrial working class, typically seen as the motor of change, has been decimated. Their jobs have gone first to the South, then farther south to Mexico, and now to China. Along the way, industrial workers, misled by their unions, became habituated to making concessions to their employers, and both industrial and teacher union leaders declared their loyalty to the bosses, partners in production.[61]

Educators are slightly better off than most working people today. Most educators have health benefits. But school workers' fates are directly tied to the children they teach, whose fates are, above all else, determined by birthright. This is especially true as wages and working conditions are tied to kids' test scores, which reflect little more than social economic status.[62] Even though modest privileges set most teachers apart from the industrial working class and many students, teachers typically carry picket signs saying, "I don't want to strike, but I will," that is, they resist because they have to resist. Youth in school will have to resist as well to fend off the draft and military recruiters, to sever the noose of test results for graduation, and even to get books. Teachers' struggles are quite likely to trail behind the struggles of poor and working-class kids and parents, especially people of color who have historically led the way because they must act first to live.

Surely the promise and reality of school is contradictory. Schools declare they work with ideas, critical thinking, and children. Hence, school work is somewhat different from most jobs where critique is undesirable, and widgets are the purpose of the work. Educators have a little more freedom than most workers, although freedom is rapidly vanishing under a wave of standardization and high-stakes testing. Regimentation is designed to strip the learning processes of connectedness (math from writing, science from history); fragment learning; coerce school workers, students, and parents; and regulate what is known and how people come to know it. High-stakes testing is a form of child abuse, violence, which lies behind all activity of the government, such as truancy laws: come here or get arrested. Whether or not educational workers continue to conduct this abuse without resistance is a test of their own analytical powers, ethics, and courage; a test of what was probably an early promise to themselves.

Schools serve capital's governments' own inhuman needs: profits, mindless workers and soldiers, and people who do not ask, "Why are things as they are?" Most teachers cannot announce themselves as serious agents of real change, but they can demonstrate the processes of struggling for what is true, even if they cannot openly pronounce it.

To reiterate, schools, mirroring and reproducing life in the United States, are more segregated than they were in 1954, before the *Brown v. Board of Education* decision. Therefore, teaching to overcome racism in the United States today is complex. Inside a segregated box, it is hard to see out.[63] Research may or may not help.

Whitewashing Class: An Academic Outlook on Racism

To illustrate the academic research, I refer to *Whitewashing Race: The Myth of a Color-Blind Society*, edited by seven of the most prominent intellectuals in academia today, professors in prestigious universities, sociologists, educators, economists, and winners of awards.[64] I choose this text because of its quality, its superior reportage of clear research, its freshness, its passionate striving to attack racism, because its outlook is shared by many educators, and because of the illustrative stance of the writers.

The authors of *Whitewashing Race* graphically address a position that pervades liberal academia, a stance I suggest is, despite the power of its analysis, wrong. Taken piece by piece (with my critique) they say:

1. *We live in an inequitable society.* Racism is so pervasive that most people do not see it, as fish are unaware of the water. But, the authors say, a lot of research has been produced that denies racist inequality, posing Black

people as failures of merit and, beyond that, set up for failure by affirmative action programs. The authors believe that conservatives now claim there is no significant level of racism in the United States; the country has achieved a color-blind state and therefore programs like affirmative action, welfare, and entitlements not only operate inside a fiction, they actually work against White people who bear no blame for the past. Those conservatives are the target of the text, posed as a new threat.

Denial of racist inequality is akin to supporting White supremacy. Our academics argue, "White perspective is not the product of skin color but of culture and experience...the perspective of the namers, the holders of 'natural privilege,' and invisible power."[65]

Although the notion of White perspective has to be seen as a problem when taken apart from class perspective, there is of course nothing new about racist positions, all going back to the first race-tagged slave. Nevertheless, on the other side of the coin, it is common, even today, to look back into history and seek to judge people of the past using the standards of the past, and to conclude, for example, about Abraham Lincoln's, or Thomas Jefferson's racism that "the society was so steeped in racism, well, who knew?" The slaves knew. That is who knew.

Scientific, academic racism is not new. Bought and paid scientists at work for domination have, for more than a century, fabricated a litany of reasons for White supremacy from bad genes to bad culture, single-family homes, incompetent languages, innate illiteracy, profligacy, and so on. We can, now, simply follow the money.[66] And in each instance, it makes sense to witness how the money flows to and from institutions of society and the demands of a capitalist economy, the exploitation of alienated labor in which working people do not control the process or products of their work and enrich their enemies at the same time. The authors of *Whitewashing Race* are not willing to take that final, logical, italicized step and say the unprintable word: capitalism.

Enforcement of racist social inequality, say the authors, has taken a variety of paths: the sharpening segregation of Black people in the cities, disinvestment in the cities coupled with economic incentives available to Whites to leave urban areas, segregated and unequal education, the systematic imprisonment of Black people accelerated in recent decades, the eradication of civil rights laws and antiracist employment protection backed by calls for color-blind legality, and the erosion of voting rights and political equality.

2. *We live within a system of unequal schooling. Whitewashing Race* buttresses the case with an examination of school inequality in defense of public education—attacking what they see as an effort by elites to eliminate public schools. They go at positions taken by the authors of the notorious

The Bell Curve: "A substantial difference in cognitive ability distributions separates whites from blacks. . . . Latino and black immigrants are . . . putting some downward pressure on the distribution of intelligence."[67]

The writers also address the more contemporary *America in Black and White*, which insists that it is an advantage to be a minority person in the color-blind United States, that affirmative action (which the *The Bell Curve* also suggests will never work—bad Black genes laying it to ruin) is, in fact, a form of discrimination that disadvantages White people.[68] In sum, the goals of the civil rights movement are won. Now color-coded affirmative action creates a mass injustice. Proof for these scientists is high-stakes standardized test scores, which writers of *Whitewashing Race* largely also accept as a worthy instrument.

Whitewashing Race counters conservative attacks on public schools with a brief history of systematic racism in the United States: slavery, the continued segregation of schools, the impoverishment of inner-city schools via shifts in the tax structure and lack of funding, and the political geography of segregation.

Although it appears the authors would understand that it is not possible to do school reform without doing economic and social reform in society, *Whitewashing Race* insists that the way to fix racist school conditions is through, "enforcing clearly defined state standards organized to achieve learning levels necessary for black students to attend four year colleges . . . raise expectations in low-income schools."[69]

On one hand, the state and government, which were active partners with the rich and the processes of capitalism and the changes in the tax structure, for example, are seen as a solution to the problems they helped create. On the other hand, the authors cannot see the use of capital's state standards as a method to gain greater control over what is taught and how in public schooling. Indeed, the very notion of public schooling, which is neither public (segregated along lines of class and race) nor especially educative (promoting racism, nationalism, and militarism, while denying the role of class in society) is never seen as a social problem in itself.[70]

School rebellions by teachers, students, and community people have taken a variety of forms in the last decade. Teachers in Tijuana seized their schools using tactics of the worldwide sit-down strikes of the 1930s.[71] In Detroit in 1999, a wildcat teachers' strike, with mass student and community support, was motivated by "books, supplies, and lower class size." Students have walked out of schools en masse, protesting issues from bad food to high-stakes tests to the current wars. The academic authors note none of this and clearly have no interest in supporting or fomenting it, nor do they keep an eye on the poorest of the poor and their resistance and budding social movements, who resist because they have to resist but whose resistance could be informed by educators who have had the privilege of time to form a broader view, to abstract.

3. *Black people are jailed more often than Whites.* Black people have long been imprisoned far out of proportion to White people, but the acceleration of this process since the 1980s is remarkable. The conservative ruse is to declare the criminal justice system now holds no bias and, therefore, something untold must be amiss among Black people.

Whitewashing Race shows that, in every step of the system—beginning with the role of an impoverished birthright; color-coded employment practices; biased juvenile authorities; the role of the police, the judge, and the law; meeting the bondsperson; not being able to buy the lawyer or bribe the judge or prosecutor—racist discrimination guides the way.

Whitewashing Race goes well past much liberal analysis, which Aldoph Reed Jr. assailed in *The Nation* a decade ago: "We can trace Murray's [*The Bell Curve*] legitimacy directly to the spinelessness, opportunism and racial bad faith of the liberals in the social policy establishment. . . . Most of those objecting to Herrnstein and Murray's racism . . . embrace positions that are almost indistinguishable, except for the resort to biology."[72] Accepting the validity of IQ testing, liberals have offered a variety of excuses: single-parent families, "lack of prenatal care . . . no breast-feeding, not enough mental stimulation for infants." It is a false quarrel— liberals and conservatives operating from a common starting point.[73]

Whitewashing Race upgrades the debate with an examination of the processes showing "that discriminatory outcomes can be produced by actions that appear bureaucratically neutral or color-blind," countering the notion, "that crime and poverty are not linked."[74] But although *Whitewashing Race* is willing to connect criminality and the economy, the authors do not tie together crime and capitalism, the crime noted by Proudhon: "Property is robbery."[75] Thus, the radical to-the-root question is not "Why do people steal?" But more to the point: "Why do impoverished people not steal more?" This radicalism is absent in *Whitewashing Race*, and, therefore, the authors are left with urging a "more serious and creative [solution] . . . of a legacy of discrimination and disinvestment in black communities."[76]

This will not happen in the absence of social strife, and even then most reform efforts would seek to restore the rule of capital, veiled by a host of investigatory committees, research bodies, and welfare programs, all backed up by the force of the economy (those involved in uprisings will be fired) and the armed forces and police.[77]

4. *Civil rights laws have been nearly eliminated.* Today, we hear echoes of the nineteenth century, "Whites . . . maintained privileges by law, by conscious acts of discrimination, and by acts of violence."[78] Economic inequality[79] or "white accumulation and black disaccumulation," plays an important role in legal affairs.[80]

But, really, so what? In *Whitewashing Race*, Anatole France's famous homily, "The law, in its majestic equality, forbids the rich as well as the poor to sleep under bridges, to beg in the streets, and to steal bread," is only tangentially taken up. Nor is the tsunami of Reagan/Bush/Clinton/Bush–appointed judges, one to the right of the next, filling the courts now, discouraging even the most crusading lawyers from litigation. "Discrimination and . . . systematic disinvestment," as causes for continuing a racist legal system dances around the point: the relationship of government and capitalism.[81]

5. *Voting rights laws run parallel to civil rights laws.* The result of a mass violent uprising in the Civil War, and a somewhat more peaceful uprising in the 1960s, voting rights laws, like all law, simply reflect political reality. Authors in *Whitewashing Race* recognize that voting rights minus economic opportunity and jobs are not sufficient to win justice, but the authors believe the vote was a key goal, and victory, of the civil rights movement: the Voting Rights Act of 1965.[82]

In fact, voting rights were, early on, a secondary goal of the civil rights movement. At issue initially were jobs and education. Foundations encouraged a shift toward voting rights as the movement gained strength, and the movement leaders shifted their attention to the ballot box.[83]

That aside, *Whitewashing Race* does recognize that electoral power goes in two directions: to those who have people and to those who have money.[84] Politicians want groups of voters and donations. Recent electoral campaigns demonstrate that groups of voters in the United States can be narrowly parsed out, from evangelical Christians and antiabortionists, working down to the most base of interests to: "What's in it for me?" Moreover, the color-blind claim of conservative electoral analyses really just masks a hidden majority rank.

The authors fail to note, though, that money buys votes, corrupts ballot counts, and rules the courts, that is, runs the show. Those who have the cash make the rules. The authors are clear, however: If a ballot count was conducted along lines that the vote has demonstrated in the most recent national elections, racists would win.

Whitewashing Race helps prove this case by demonstrating that there are clear voting lines between Black people and White people—more distinct than between, say, Democrats and Republicans—on questions of welfare, inequality, public health, and so forth. There is discernible race conscious-ness in the United States.

So what is to be done? The gap between what is and what ought to be is filled with dreams, "a set of principles," in *Whitewashing Race*: Tax the rich. Promote diversity. Raise the minimum wage. Invest in public projects.[85] Create a fund for reparations for past injustices. Reestablish civil rights and voting rights laws more fairly, that is, change the law. Improve schools by transforming teacher seniority rights, the standardization of the curricula and teaching methods, and so on. Why should this be done? Because we all lose from racism, the nationalist's solution.[86] The authors close with a quote from James Baldwin, "make American what America must become," or we will all lose.[87]

Baldwin was wrong on that. Most of us will lose, and surely those who stand with their feet on the necks of others cannot move, but they do live longer, have more constitutional rights, don't go to jail, and go to better schools where what is a lie to a working-class kid is not a lie to a wealthy scion.

The blind spots in *Whitewashing Race*, as in most liberal views of the sources and efforts to overcome racism in school and elsewhere, are:

1. A failure to grasp that the state and government are not neutral observers seeking justice over time, but weapons of class violence for those in power, and, from another angle, elites are rarely if ever so overwhelmed by goodwill or evidence of suffering and injustice that they pick their own pockets and wipe out the basis of their mastery;
2. Struggles to get the state to battle racism in schools and elsewhere mean that energy will be expended in cul-de-sacs, and when there is success, it is the success of missionaries, not the ineradicable organized social movement of conscious people required to sustain any kind of change;
3. In this case, that to turn to the standardization of the curricula, for ex-ample, is to necessarily accept the twin maneuver of ruling elites all over the Western world, the Taylorization of schooling noosed by high-stakes standardized testing designed to deepen the segregation of schooling, veiled by bogus scientific measurement (the true measures being race, class, and willingness to be subservient);
4. The liberal movement disguises class domination and impoverishes po-tential poor and working-class movements to counter it;
5. A belief that research, discourse, and voting—state-sponsored education as opposed to direct organized action—will somehow make social change;
6. An appeal to liberal elites when it has been liberal elites from Johnson to Carter to Clinton who initiated the war on Vietnam, wiped out mental health facilities, and eradicated the welfare system; and

7. A failure to locate the urgency of this historical moment, a profound crisis of international imperialism in which the United States is no longer a power on the rise but a desperate player clearly willing to "exterminate all the brutes," to maintain its dominion.

In sum, although research, voting, appeals to conscience, and so on are hardly harmful, they will not produce a mass movement of conscious people who can make and preserve change.

John Brown wanted social life, "to be organized on a less selfish basis, for while material interests gained something by the deification of pure self-ishness, men and women lost much by it . . . all great reforms . . . were based on broad, generous, self-sacrificing principles."[88] He understood that the struggle from what is to what ought to be which was his dedication, went beyond the missionary sense of benevolence to real self-sacrifice, in solidarity, not benevolence.

WHAT TO DO, REALLY?

Radical critique of capitalist schooling and racism must be connected with the daily life of school workers, parents, and community people and, simultaneously, affixed to the curious passion that is assassinated by most schooling. Unleashing inquisitive enthusiasm in students and educators requires freedom—always an issue settled by power.

In schools, power is won by uniting students, parents, and community people in addressing common problems and demonstrating their common sources. Unity makes resistance possible. Although many battles will be lost, as in the fights against high-stakes testing and regimented curricula, winning is better defined as assisting more and more people to be critically class conscious, so they can carry the struggle.

Overturning capital is a reasonable, rational, long-term goal but a process that will involve a great deal of destruction. Promises made by radicals in the past, promises of a quick shift to better material lives, will probably be impossible to keep. Life will not, for most people, quickly get better, particularly not as we stand at the threshold of an area of fascist barbarism.[89]

It follows that if change is going to happen, it is going to take a long time. The perseverance necessary to motivate people over that gulf between what is and what should be cannot be built on a vision of more goods and merchandise. It can be built, though, on a promise for a meaningful life as a resister, a revolutionary now, and a system of ethics that is drawn from a view of where we want to go.

Those ethics, involving inclusion, antiracism, antisexism, action-orientation, radical critique, internationalism, democracy, equality, and deep comradeship are drawn from thousands of years of history, not from a thunderclap. Ethics do not stand outside of material circumstances to be applied mechanically but creatively from a careful examination of things as they are and how they might change. And with an eye on the future, education must address human needs, desires, and dreams.

Capital, racism, and schools are of a piece today, one aiding the other. In this context, adults are likely to trail kids in social action, but adults can set the stage and the goals for kids, then learn from them.

It follows that the charge to every ethical education worker, kid, parent, and community worker is to recognize the limits set by capital and to see how, in daily life, we can go beyond them.

Close friendships over time are inherently radical today, in an era of disposable people. Close friendships make possible the reintroduction of joy into schools.

Remembering the pervasiveness of racism, and determining to notice and fight its appearances in one way or another, every day, connects theory and action. Integrate the playground, the teachers' lounge, or the cafeteria. Investigate the process of capital, from reintroducing labor as a central force in history. At the other end of capital's circuits, examine commodity prices and the geographies of power by measuring, comparing, and contrasting, playgrounds.

Organize field trips for poor kids and rich kids to exchange schools. Teach the hows and whys of having a demonstration using any example from history: the Boston Tea Party to the Boxer Rebellion, to the Paris Commune, to the civil rights or antiwar movements. We can teach that things change, that quantitative change can become qualitative change, that each of us can understand and transform the world. Restore the role of theory to schooling, in the real struggle to gain and test knowledge in the material world. Fight for the freedom to teach to a genuine connection of a unique student in a special community meeting a particular educator.

Justice, however, demands organization. New truly revolutionary organization is desperately needed—beyond reformist, divisive, nationalist, racist unionism, beyond the reformers of the past, beyond socialism. Transitional organizations may form the path of social practice that guides the way.

In schools, which I have argued are now the central organizing points of class struggle in the Americas, organization needs to unite school workers, all school workers, parents, community people, and others not only to maximize power but to split off the opportunism and individualism that propels nearly all of academic life and go beyond schools to initiate work in the military, on the docks, and in the remaining factories. Within this, adults will need to learn from kids, White people take leadership from people of color, men take criticism from women, all sharing the joys and burdens of ethical transformation, personal and social.

It is now nearly impossible for people to openly lead truly radical organizations and stay employed, get tenure, and so on. This means that some people will need to be professional organizer-researchers, others will need to be able to join anonymously. Whatever the case, it is clear that to meet a historically well-organized, armed, ruthless opposition that holds all the powers of violence of the state, a revolutionary force must be developed that not only sets itself in opposition to capital but raises its fist as well for equality, community, all for one and one for all.

In the United States, the only school-based organization that has had the courage to name capitalism, consistently link racism and capitalism, examine the present with an eye on the future, and organize against capital through research and action has been the Rouge Forum.[90] Other school resister groups have entered the fray, like the people behind *Substance* edited by George Schmidt in Chicago (www.substancenews.com), and many individual researchers (like Ohanian and Emery) have contributed to the struggle. In England, the Cole-Hill group and the *Journal for Critical Policy Studies* have played parallel roles.[91]

There is clear disagreement over the goals of the members of all these transitory groups. Some seek to preserve public schooling in its ideal form. Others want to make schooling ungovernable. Others still seek to foment enough strife to abolish capital's schools and create opposition freedom schools, as did the African National Congress in South Africa for nearly a decade. This debate goes directly back to the heart of the questions: Why have school? Why does racism persist? The debaters must hear Rhett Butler, quoted in the introduction but summarized by Jay Gould, "I can buy one half of the working class to kill the other half."[92]

Eventually, the many will not be ruled by the few. Social justice and reason will prevail, but not soon. In the interim, a reasonably sane life contributing to the common good can be won through revolutionary action and theory.

NOTES

1. G. Orfield and S. Yun, *The Resegregation of Schools* (Cambridge, MA: Harvard Civil Rights Project, 1999). Available online at www.civilrightsproject.harvard.edu/research/deseg/Resegregation_American_Schools99.pdf. Accessed April 26, 2005.

2. T. Allen, *The Invention of the White Race* (New York: Verso, 1994).

3. J. Anyon, *Ghetto Schooling* (New York: Teachers College Press, 1997), xv.

4. I. Meszaros, *Beyond Capital: Toward a Theory of Transition* (Monthly Review Press, 1995).

5. J. Loewen, *Lies My Teacher Told Me* (New York: New Press, 1995).

6. R. Kochher, *The Wealth of Hispanic Households* (Washington, DC: Pew Hispanic Center, 2004). Available online at pewhispanic.org/reports/report.php? ReportID=34.

7. J. Baldwin, *Nobody Knows My Name* (New York: Dell Press, 1961), 88.

8. J. Weiss, *Ideology of Death* (New York: Ivan Dee, 1997); J. Weiss, *The Politics of Hate* (New York: Ivan Dee, 2002).

9. George M. Fredrickson, *Racism: A Short History* (Princeton, NJ: Princeton University Press), 6.

10. G. Lukács, *Destruction of Reason* (Atlantic Highlands, NJ: Humanities Press, 1952), 100.

11. G. Myers, *History of Bigotry in the United States* (New York: Capricorn Books, 1960).

12. J. Elrick and J. Schaeffer, "Mayor Charged Bahamas Trip," *Detroit Free Press* (June 16, 2005). Available online at www.freep.com/news/locway/kilp16e_2; R. Gibson, "The Grenada 17: Last Prisoners of the Cold War are Black," *Counterpunch* (June 5/6, 2004). Available online at www.counterpunch.org/gibson06052004.html.

13. Weiss, *Ideology of Death*, 187.

14. Ibid., 227.

15. Loewen, *Lies My Teacher Told Me*.

16. R. Gibson, "NEA-AFL-CIO? No," *Cultural Logic* 2, no. 1 (1999). Available online at eserver.org/clogic/2_1/gibson.html.

17. Weiss, *Ideology of Death*; D. Goldhagen, *Hitler's Willing Executioners: Ordinary Germans and the Holocaust* (New York: Vintage, 1997).

18. E. Mann, *School for Barbarians* (New York: Modern Age Books, 1938), 51.

19. Minio Paluello, *Education in Fascist Italy* (London: Oxford University Press, 1946).

20. Mann, *School for Barbarians*, 103.

21. B. Mehler, "Eliminating the Inferior: American and Nazi Sterilization Programs," *Science for the People* (November–December 1987): 14–18; S. Kuhl, *The Nazi Connection, Eugenics, American Racism, and German Nationalism* (New York: Oxford University Press, 1994); Weiss, *Ideology of Death*.

22. Joseph Conrad, *Heart of Darkness* (New York: Penguin, 1995) 84.

23. C. Leduff, "Racism in the Slaughterhouse," *New York Times Online* (June 16, 2000). Available online at www.nytimes.com/library/national/race/061600leduff_meat.html.

24. G. W. F. Hegel, *Phenomenology of Spirit* (New York: Oxford University Press, 1979).

25. R. Kelley, *Hammer and the Hoe* (Chapel Hill: University of North Carolina Press, 1990); Weiss, *Ideology of Death*.

26. J. Boggs, *Racism and the Class Struggle* (New York: Monthly Review Press, 1970), 180.

27. Ernst Breisach, *On the Future of History: The Postmodernist Challenge and Its Aftermath* (Chicago: University of Chicago Press, 2003).

28. R. Levins and R. Lewontin, *The Dialectical Biologist* (Cambridge, MA: Harvard University Press, 1985), 271.

29. W. Reich, *The Mass Psychology of Fascism,* 3rd ed. (New York: Farrar, Straus and Giroux, 1980).

30. Kelley, *Hammer and the Hoe*; Weiss, *Ideology of Death.*

31. V. I. Lenin, *State and Revolution* (Beijing: China Publications, 1965).

32. F. Perlman, *The Continuing Appeal of Nationalism* (Detroit: Black and Red Press, 1970).

33. D. W. Adams, *Education for Extinction* (Lawrence: University of Kansas Press, 1997).

34. Perlman, *The Continuing Appeal of Nationalism.*

35. Meszaros, *Beyond Capital,* 422.

36. Stephen Krashen, "The Hard Work Hypothesis: Is Doing Your Homework Enough to Overcome the Effects of Poverty?" *Multicultural Education* 12, no. 4 (2005): 16–19. Available online at www.sdkrashen.com/articles/hardwork/index.html.

37. National Coalition for Education Statistics at a glance. Available online at nces.ed.gov/programs/digest/d03.

38. E. Fromm, *The Fear of Freedom* (London: Kegan, 1942).

39. D. Singer, *Prelude to Revolution, France in May 1968* (Cambridge, MA: South End Press, 1970).

40. K. Emery and S. Ohanian, *Why Is Corporate America Bashing Public Schools?* (Portsmouth, NH: Heinemann, 2004).

41. See David McCollough, author of *1776*, in a question and answer session at the Amercian Historical Association meeting, History Channel, July 2, 2005.

42. Karl Marx and Frederick Engels, *The Communist Manifesto* (Chicago: Haymarket, 2005).

43. See chapter 1 of K. Marx and F. Engels, *Communist Manifesto.* Available online at www.marxists.org/archive/marx/works/1848/communist_manifesto/ch01.htm.

44. Meszaros, *Beyond Capital,* 60.

45. R. Miliband, *Marxism and Politics* (New York: Oxford University Press, 1977), 73–75.

46. "Meritocracy in America, Even Higher Society Is Harder to Attain," *Economist* (December 29, 2004). Available online at www.economist.com/world/na/displayStory.cfm?story_id=3518560.

47. Ron Eyerman, *False Consciousness and Ideology in Marxist Theory* (Atlantic Highlands, NJ: Humanities Press, 1981): 282–298.

48. See, for example, the work of Karl Kautsky, Kautsky Internet Archive, www.marxist.org/Kautsky/index.htm.

49. Georg Lukács, *History and Class Consciousness* (Cambridge, MA: MIT Press, 1972).

50. V. I. Lenin, *State and Revolution* (Beijing: China Publications, 1965).

51. M. Glaberman, "Workers Make Their Own Reality," Available online at www.rohan.sdsu.edu/%7Ergibson/workersreality.htm.

52. Antonio Gramsci, *Selections from the Prison Notebooks* (London: Lawrence and Wishart, 1971).

53. Bertell Ollman, *Dance of the Dialectic* (Chicago: University of Illinois Press, 2003), 63.

54. McCullough, AHA convention, 2005.

55. Ollman, *Dance of the Dialectic.*

56. C. Dickens, *David Copperfield* (London: Oxford University Press, 1987), 1.

57. W. E. B. DuBois, *The Souls of Black Folk* (New York: Fawcett Books, 1953), vii, 23.

58. W. E. B. DuBois, *John Brown* (New York: International Publishers, 1962), 349–350.

59. T. Tyson, *Blood Don't Sign My Name* (New York: Crown Publishers, 2004), 79.

60. Baldwin, *Nobody Knows My Name*, 92; DuBois, *John Brown*, 349–350, 368.

61. Gibson, "NEA-AFL-CIO? No."

62. Krashen, "The Hard Work Hypothesis."

63. D. Fears, "Schools More Segregated Than Ever," *Washington Post* (July 16, 2001). Available online at www.washingtonpost.com/ac2/wp_dyn?pagename=article&node=&contentId=A11185_2001Jul17.

64. M. Brown et al. (eds.), *Whitewashing Race: The Myth of a Color-Blind Society* (Berkeley: University of California Press, 2003).

65. Ibid., 59, 228.

66. W. Tucker, *The Funding of Scientific Racism* (Chicago: University of Illinois Press, 2002).

67. C. Murray and R. Herrnstein, *The Bell Curve: Intelligence and Class Structure in American Life* (New York: Free Press, 1994), 315, 360–361.

68. S. Thernstrom and A. Thernstrom, *American in Black and White* (New York: Simon and Schuster, 1999).

69. Brown et al., *Whitewashing Race*, 245.

70. R. Gibson, "Outfoxing the Destruction of Wisdom," *Theory and Research in Education* 29, no. 2 (2001): 308–329. Available online at www.pipeline.com/~rgibson/Outfoxing.htm.

71. A. Cearly, "Tijuana Teachers Lead Sit-down," *San Diego Union Tribune* (April 5, 2001). Available online at www.pipeline.com/~rgibson/sitin.htm.

72. A. Reed, "The Bell Curve," *Nation* 259, no. 18 (November 28, 1994): 654–662

73. 73. Ibid.

74. Brown et al., *Whitewashing Race*, 138, 154.

75. P. J. Proudhon, *What Is Property*, chapter 1, (undated). Available online at dhm.best.vwh.net/archives/proudhon_1toc.html.

76. Brown et al., *Whitewashing Race*, 160.

77. R. Cloward and F. Piven, *Regulating the Poor* (New York: Vintage, 1993).

78. Brown et al., *Whitewashing Race*, 163.

79. Never clearly delineated in *Whitewashing Race*, the role of class is unmentioned other than a brief glimpse on p. 228.

80. Brown et al., *Whitewashing Race*, 163.

81. Ibid., 160.

82. Ibid., 165.

83. R. Moses, *Radical Equations: Civil Rights from Mississippi to the Algebra Project* (New York: Beacon Press, 2002).

84. S. Alinsky, *Saul Alinsky Biography* (undated). Available online: saul_alinsky.biography.ms.

85. Brown et al., *Whitewashing Race*, 229.

86. Ibid.

87. Ibid., 251.

88. DuBois, *John Brown*, 171–172.

89. C. Johnson, "The US Is Becoming a Fascist Society," NPR interview, July 12, 2004.

90. See Web site www.RougeForum.org

91. G. Rikowski and R. Gibson, "An E-Dialogue," (2004). Available online at www.pipeline.com/%7Erougeforum/RikowskiGibsonDialogueFinal.htm.

92. B. Gross, *Friendly Fascism, the New Face of Power in America* (Cambridge, MA: South End Press, 1980)

4

Rethinking Particularity: Individualist Perspectives on Race and Multiculturalism

John F. Welsh

> Every State is bound to treat free men as cogs in a machine. And this is precisely what it should not do; hence, the State must perish.
> —Hegel, *Erstes Systemprogramm des Deutschen Idealismus*, 1796

RACE AND RACISM IN THEORY AND SOCIETY

The young Hegel's appraisal of the treatment of people by the state was dead-on accurate, but his prediction about the future of the state reflects the basic problem with idealist thought: Predicting that something must happen does not necessarily mean that it will. His enthusiasm for a world based on individual liberty was prompted by the profound changes occurring as part of the French and American Revolutions, but it was soon eclipsed by the growth and extension of state power as the central organizing principle of modern national societies. The political philosophy of the mature Hegel assigned the state a pivotal role in society. Today, state power penetrates every facet of human existence and has replaced civil society as the space where human development occurs. Thus human experience has become remarkably standardized, undoubtedly a consequence of the global extension of state power and capitalist exchange relations. As statist political structures and corporate organizational models penetrate and dominate every corner of the globe and every realm of human activity, state capitalism is totalized as a world system. The dialectic between the state and Hegel's free subject is an important issue in this social formation, but it is also important to understand how this antagonism affects the knowledge process and other societal dynamics.[1]

Race and *racism* are concepts and phenomena that have undergone important social transformations as the state capitalist social system evolved into a global totality. One of the most important transformations of race and ethnic group relations in higher education in the United States is that multiculturalism has been elevated to the status of an ideé fixe as educational organizations attempt to adapt to the vagaries of state capitalism.[2] In higher education in North America, contemporary conceptions of race and racism are framed through the interpretive lens of multiculturalism. Although it is difficult to identify the central texts that outline its components, *multiculturalism* is broadly understood as a body of ideas that enables colleges and universities to overcome forms of prejudice, discrimination, violence, and stratification based on race and ethnicity in their academic, student, and staffing policies. Today, where is the strategic plan, or the recruitment viewbook, or the commencement speech that does not assign multiculturalism a prominent place in the pantheon of institutional priorities? Diversity seems to refer to a desired set of conditions at institutions, whereas multiculturalism is an ideology, agenda, and political practice that is thought to be the singular tool that educational organizations need to eliminate racism and transform race relations in higher education in North America.[3]

Despite the nearly universal and uncritical elevation of multiculturalism in higher education as the only theoretical alternative to racist ideology, there are conflicts and contradictions in the multiculturalist view of the world and its agenda for managing crises in higher education and the society beyond it. First, the concept of *racism*, like elitism and sexism, is used in policy discourse in the higher education community as a pejorative catchall that supposedly describes and explains an infinite array of attitudes, behaviors, and facts that are thought to be unfortunate from the viewpoint of those using the term. The word is frequently used to stigmatize and discredit individuals and groups who run afoul of diversity elites who have the ability to define and control behavior within the academy. The term connotes much and denotes little.[4]

Second, the term *race* itself is far from conceptually clear in the policy discourse about higher learning in North America. Among the many subtleties in the term, there is a clear tendency toward the conceptualization and study of race and racism as trans-human facts with an ultimate reality that is fixed and not amenable to human control. This tendency is associated with those theorists and analysts who argue that race is a persistent universal feature of educational organizations. Race is conceived as either physical or biological substrata to human existence that exist and operate independently of human thought and social practice in society, its institutions, and its organizations.[5]

The approach that reifies race and racial stratification is diametrically opposed to the idea that race is a socially constructed, humanly experienced reality that may vary spatially and historically. Race and racism are social constructions and mechanisms through which human activities and experiences may or may not be organized. For humans and because of humans, the ultimate reality of race and racism are what humans create and live. Race and racism exist as sociocultural constructs, which are created, communicated, and known through symbols that are supported by political power. Both are measured through socially produced cultural artifacts. Although race may be thought to constitute a biological substratum to human experience, it is important to understand that even the biological and physical realities of race enter the realms of human activity and experience only as they are identified and made meaningful through symbolic interaction. The biological and physical realities of race do not speak or act for themselves. They become real and meaningful in human experience only because they are defined as such by human beings interacting in a symbolic environment that is frequently characterized by conflict, violence, and contradiction. The multiculturalist conception of the reality or permanence of race is opposed by the notion that both race and racism must be understood from a dialectical and humanist standpoint.[6]

A philosophically adequate concept and theory of the transformation of race relations cannot conceive of race or racism as external, trans-human facts that are somehow autonomous from social and cultural life, nor can it adequately study race with an interest in discovering any ultimate nature apart from human thought and practice. The philosophical externalization and objectification of race as a feature of social life serves the cultural and material interests of societal and academic elites, but it frustrates the visioning and achievement of a global totality free of domination and stratification based on race, ethnicity, and other social categories. To the extent that multiculturalism reifies race and racial stratification as universal features of social life, it proffers a flawed concept of social relations and social transformation. An alternative interpretation of the persistence of racism is that the problem is not that the forces of discrimination are so strong but that the philosophy of change is so weak. If the societal and educational goal is to construct and promote a society free of domination, a multiculturalist critique is insufficient.

An important root of the multiculturalist agenda in higher education is the effort to promote academic life, student life, and staffing programs intended to broaden access and participation in colleges and universities. The student rebellions of the 1960s were especially important in the creation and expansion of identity-based studies and programs in higher education that appear under an evolving array of monikers, such as African American and Pan-African studies; Latino, Chicano, and Hispanic studies; and women's studies. However, the multiculturalist transformation of the college curriculum has been supplemented and supported by other institutional policies and practices that are also intended to broaden participation and achievement of disenfranchised groups in higher education, such as (1) racial and ethnic quotas and preferences in admissions; (2) programs in financial aid that target specific racial and ethnic groups; (3) hate speech codes that seek to prohibit defamatory and hurtful speech, as well as speech that is thought to lead to violence; and (4) preferential recruiting, hiring, and compensation practices of faculty and staff that seek to achieve statistical equality in staffing and compensation.[7]

In higher education in North America at the beginning of the twenty-first century, the study of racism and opposition to it are organizationally segregated into administrative support offices, institutional policies, and academic programs grounded in particular racial and ethnic identities. It is important to question whether colleges and universities in North America are optimally organized and led to contribute to the struggle against prejudice and discrimination in higher education and outside of it. The central issue is whether concepts and theories of race and racism are intended to be management strategies for the balkanized university, or are they intended to constitute a philosophy of human liberation from racism and other forms of domination? It is an important organizational contradiction in higher education that the major intellectual and administrative expressions of opposition to racism are focused on particular manifestations rather than universal critiques of it at a time in human history when economic, communications, and political systems are forming a global totality. The important questions for students of race and racism today are: What does the formation of a world system imply for the dialectics of human liberation? Is the multiculturalist agenda, which elevates particularist concepts and lines of inquiry, sufficient, or do we need to search for universalist concepts and lines of inquiry?

The implications for free inquiry and human liberation posed by elevation of multiculturalism as absolute truth in higher education are profound. The purpose of this chapter is to offer a critique of multiculturalism in the curriculum, organization, and administration of higher education as an ideé fixe or a reification that frustrates an optimal understanding of racism and human freedom. Multiculturalism is a mirror image, or the negative recognition, of racism, not its theoretical transcendence. This is an important point of critique because higher education both reflects and shapes the knowledge process in the larger society.

This chapter specifically addresses two questions about the philosophy and purpose of multiculturalism in higher education: (1) What are the basic points of critique of multiculturalism as process and ideology in higher education? (2) What are some theoretical alternatives to multiculturalism that critique racism but provide an individualist vision of social relations? The chapter critiques the collectivist, relativist, exclusionist, statist, and determinist elements of multiculturalism. It suggests that concepts promoting the universal importance of human freedom, not race nor the particularistic concepts associated with multiculturalism, should become the central category in discourse about curricular, organizational, and administrative change in higher education.

MULTICULTURALISM AS PROCESS AND IDEOLOGY IN HIGHER EDUCATION

The concept of racism in critical educational thought historically entailed the notion that universal cultural, economic, social, political, and psychological dynamics undergird the identification and subjugation of people based on biological, cultural, or linguistic categories. Thus despite the particular manifestations of racism, which vary by time and space, critical inquiry initially explored the basic or generalized principles that contributed to our social self-knowledge of forms of prejudice, discrimination, and violence based on biology, culture, and language. Indeed, an important argument of those who have offered empirical, theoretical, or conceptual critiques of racism is that an understanding of the broad, generalized, or universal dynamics of racism is central to social progress, justice, and the transformation of society into a form that better serves human purposes. Hence the cultural and historical understanding of any one particular manifestation of racist social relations may not be sufficient to overcome even that one expression of racism. Whatever the contributions of particular studies of race and ethnicity, the telos of critical inquiry should also include a contribution to a generalized understanding of race and ethnicity and a universal philosophy of human freedom. It is very doubtful that multiculturalist ideology fulfills this vision.[8]

This section elaborates on this point by discussing five dimensions of multiculturalism in the curriculum, organization, and administration of higher education. Taken together, these five dimensions of multiculturalism help define it as an ideology and a process in higher education. This section argues that multiculturalism offers a flawed philosophical stance on race, knowledge, and social relations. Multiculturalism is not the philosophical transcendence of racism, only its negative recognition.

Collectivism

One of the fundamental elements of racist thought is that it is a collectivist, not individualist, ideology because it promotes the idea that the collective attributions of racial, ethnic, and linguistic groups matter more than the character and behaviors of individuals in public policy and cultural symbols. Racism defines and proscribes human identity and behavior in collective constructs rooted in biological, cultural, or linguistic phenomena. Furthermore, racist thought attempts, through its advocates, to affect or determine public policy through the seizure of political power to impose a regime of social relations that actualizes racist thought. The self-fulfilling component of racist thought is not left to chance; instead, racist political activists seek to ensure that their definition of the situation is made real through the levers of the state.

As the mirror image of racism, multiculturalism is also a collectivist, not individualist, ideology in that it promotes collective notions of victimization and the idea that collective action is the only viable or conceivable response to racism. Similar to racism, multiculturalism promotes in area- and identity-based studies the idea that human identity and action must be reduced to collective constructs rooted in biological, cultural, or linguistic phenomena. Of course, multiculturalist ideology interprets historical process and social facts from a partisan perspective; it is always on the side of those it defines as victims and views the knowledge process as a moment in the liberation of the victims. However, the experience of the victim and the liberation of the victim are always understood in terms of collective experiences and needs. Multiculturalist ideology has not demonstrated why collective experiences and needs must take precedence over individual experiences and needs. At a minimum, it is questionable whether the collectivism of racism can be effectively challenged by the collectivism of multiculturalism. Multiculturalism is also an ideology that promotes the subjugation of individuals to the collectivity and, thus, entails all of the social, cultural, and political problems associated with collectivism. What sort of liberation is it when individuals are emancipated from one collectivist ideology only to be subjugated to another? Perhaps ideologies and behaviors that promote individualism are more optimal responses to collectivist notions and movements that promote or reinforce racial superiority.

Relativism

Originally based in the philosophical precept that racial groups should not be viewed as superior or inferior, multiculturalism sought to promote inclusiveness and tolerance in higher education through the idea that there is a type of cultural equality, or at least the idea that no one society, culture, or linguistic group can be demonstrated to be superior to others. In its nascent form, the multiculturalist critique of racism simply built on top of the cultural relativist notion of the early Western ethnographers and anthropologists, who were concerned that the cultural filter of the Western nations would be used to interpret discoveries about preliterate societies. However, the cultural relativism of the multiculturalist critique of the curriculum in higher education has been transformed into an attack on Western culture and concepts, placing race and racism at the center of its analysis. In the higher education curriculum, especially in the humanities, social sciences, and education, those theories, ideas, and scholarly studies that attempt to recenter discourse on social relations on other concepts have been nearly universally condemned in higher education as racist or chauvinist. Many institutions in North America, in fact, have adopted policies that identify philosophical, ideological, or curricular challenges to the relativism of multiculturalism as hate speech and elevate multiculturalism as the final statement on race, ethnicity, and social relations in higher education.

Multiculturalism is a relativist ideology in that it promotes the notion that one culture or one cultural element cannot be shown or understood to be superior to another, and that each culture should be understood in its own context. Although the multiculturalist philosophy of change includes a number of analytic dimensions and appears to be applicable to a wide array of social and cultural issues in higher education, at base, it entails a relativist notion that one society, culture, or group cannot and should not judge or evaluate another society, culture, or group by its own standards or frame of reference.[9]

Of course, the intent of the relativism of multiculturalist ideology is to establish an epistemological equality among races, cultures, and linguistic groups so that all groups or cultures will be tolerated, at least in the abstract. At first blush, it seems curious, however, that the tolerance of multiculturalism requires institutional policies and coercion for its promotion. Shouldn't cultural tolerance need little more than the good intentions of well-meaning people for its realization? No, because cultural relativism is a self-contradictory concept. In a relativist world, no societal goal or value can be demonstrated to be better than another. Hence, following the logic of cultural relativism, racist and multiculturalist thought must both be understood in their cultural context; multiculturalism cannot be demonstrated to be superior to other ideas in any ultimate way. As it enters the world of political practice, multiculturalism must be imposed by political and institutional policy because it cannot make a case for itself in the realm of free discourse and open inquiry.

Statism

Racism is a statist ideology in that it requires political authority, power, law, and public policy to enforce the domination and subjugation of racial, ethnic, and linguistic groups. Multiculturalism is also a statist ideology in that it looks to the state, public, and institutional policy and enforcement mechanisms to ameliorate, rectify, or eliminate forms of prejudice, discrimination, and violence. Multiculturalism's vision for responding to coercion against disadvantaged social groups is the acquisition of state power and the application of its coercive resources to assist them.

Multiculturalism assumes that the same authority and power structures that were once used to dominate and subjugate people can and should be used to emancipate them. Certainly, the effectiveness of the use of state power to emancipate subjugated social groups can be questioned, but it is also important to note that multiculturalist ideology does nothing to challenge the relationship between the state and other social institutions, nor does it challenge the power of the state over the individual. It assumes that the state is a neutral social structure that can be used to implement any social or educational policy. The political challenge for multiculturalists is either to seize the state apparatus or to influence it so that the state sufficiently responds to their social and cultural agenda. Multiculturalism is a statist ideology because it looks to the state for the solution of all critical social problems; it reinforces state power.[10]

Exclusionism

Racism and multiculturalism are also exclusionist ideologies that particularize human experiences, worth, values, and needs. Both undermine common bonds among people and both negate the notion that political, ethical, and educational systems should operate on the basis of the application of universal principles.[11]

Racism particularizes by defending and promoting the philosophy and practice of differentiating and separating people for the purposes of domination and subjugation based on race, ethnicity, or linguistic group. It elevates some groups above others. It argues that social desiderata should be distributed based on racial, cultural, or linguistic identity. Multiculturalism particularizes by defending and promoting the philosophy and practice of differentiating and separating people for the purpose of subjugating them to the authority of political, cultural, and educational elites, who are presumed to promote ideas and public policies oriented toward the emancipation of disadvantaged racial, cultural, and linguistic groups.

Staffing practices, scholarship programs, and identity-based studies that aim at the social, cultural, and political promotion of specific groups are exclusionist practices legitimated by multiculturalist ideology. Financial aid programs targeted at African American students, though intended to help improve access to higher education, are preferential practices that exclude Hispanic, Native American, and Asian American students. Hiring practices targeted at Hispanic workers are preferential practices that exclude African American and Asian American workers. Preferential programs of all types function to separate groups and engender intergroup conflict. They are based on the assumption that the structures of prejudice, discrimination, and violence directed against racial, ethnic, and linguistic groups are fundamentally different and, thus, require particular programs and policies for their amelioration. Preferential practices have been effectively and appropriately criticized by a variety of political interests as new forms of discrimination. To the extent that multiculturalism promotes the elevation of some groups at the expense of others, it is an enemy of human liberation. At the very minimum, it eschews discourse on the universal meaning of human liberation.

Determinism

Racism is a determinist ideology that promotes the idea that race, culture, and linguistic identity structure the thought, proclivities, ability, and achievements of individuals. Racism is a destructive ideology for many reasons. Perhaps its determinist element is the most important among these because it negates the ability of human beings to freely pursue their interests and to cultivate their talents. Racist social regimes implement limitations on human freedom through laws, policies, and cultural symbols that derogate individuals, deny opportunities, and exact official violence against persons to punish challenges and promote fear and helplessness against the regime.

Significantly, multiculturalism elevates culture to a determinant, not just mediating, role in the structuring of human thought, behavior, and experience. The more important culture's role in shaping thought and behavior, the more significant multiculturalism is as an ideology that interprets racial and ethnic phenomena. The less significant culture's role in shaping thought and behavior, the less significant multiculturalism is in challenging forms of prejudice, discrimination, and violence. The multiculturalist agenda, therefore, must assign culture a determining role in individual behavior and the social construction of reality. Multiculturalism, like racism, carries with it all of the problems of determinist ideology. Most significantly, it either excises notions of individual freedom, spontaneity, and autonomy from social and political discourse or subordinates them to other values and goals. What sort of emancipation does multiculturalism really offer if it elevates culture to a determinant status and reduces human individuals to passive receptacles of the political, social, and cultural dictates of the regime?[12]

THE DIALECTICS OF LIBERTY IN THEORY AND SOCIETY

The particularization of the curriculum, organization, and administration of colleges and universities into identity-based programs obviates dialogue on universals. The curriculum, organization, and administration of higher education must be transformed to promote liberty as a universal human right and need. The philosophical precepts of both racism and multiculturalism contradict efforts to create organizations and a society that are more responsive to the human need for freedom and to knowledge processes that enhance self-knowledge and self-determination.

It seems important to challenge the collectivist, relativist, exclusionist, statist, and determinist elements of multiculturalism but to also acknowledge and respond to the type of world that is evolving. Efforts to change organizations and society, as well as our sense of who we are, should be focused more toward the future than toward the past. The peculiar temporal orientation of multiculturalism appears to contradict the need to build a better future because the tribalism of the human past cannot be reconciled with the globalism and cultural homogenization that is evolving in our world today.

Although globalism entails many significant problems for human beings and the planet they live on, it may also provide new opportunities for self-knowledge and social change. Foremost among these, discussions of human universals now have more of a social, cultural, and economic foundation than they ever did in the past. Because of the evolution of the world system, it may now be possible to infuse into the curricula philosophical orientations that are focused on the articulation of universal principles addressed to human freedom. It is difficult to find support for this notion among the traditional left-wing perspectives in both the study of higher education and its administration and governance. The leftist analysis of higher education, including multiculturalism, liberalism, critical theory, and socialism, has not been strong in its critique of the state or in the promulgation of the universality of human freedom. Because the critique of political power and the state is central to the critique of both multiculturalism and racism, it is important to search for emancipatory dimensions in those philosophical traditions that have centered their analysis on human freedom and the critique of the state and political power. This means that we must look beyond the traditional formulations of the left, center, and right to promote the idea of freedom as a universal. As a means of injecting new ideas into discourse on race and ethnicity in higher education, this section discusses four individualist philosophical positions and their relevance to curricular, organizational, and administrative theory in higher education.

Objectivism

Ayn Rand articulated an individualist, procapitalist philosophy she called *Objectivism* in her novels and many essays. She initially articulated her philosophy in the form of heroes in her best-selling novels *The Fountainhead* and *Atlas Shrugged*. She later expressed her philosophy in nonfiction form. She has been taken much more seriously in academia in recent decades. However, her ideas have not been widely infused or confronted in educational or social science literature. There is at least one academic journal devoted to studies about her novels and philosophy. Important critical academic analyses of her work have emerged in recent years. Rand initially resisted commentary on racism because she believed that the left dominated discourse on race. However, she eventually articulated a critique of racism that evolved from her ethics and politics.[13] Her philosophy entails a critique of both racism and multiculturalism that her followers subsequently extended to the contemporary philosophical, educational, and political environment.

The primary theme of Rand's Objectivism is that any philosophy should define the abstract and universal principles by which human beings must think and act if they are to live the life proper to humans. The basic elements of objectivism are summarized in her thoughts on the nature of objective reality, epistemology, ethics, and politics. She strongly rejected any belief in the supernatural and any claim that individuals or groups create their own separate reality. Her Objectivist ontology was primarily directed against religion, mysticism, and any other ideology that militated against human beings living on Earth. Objectivism rejects any notion that faith and feelings are viable means of understanding ourselves and our world and any form of determinism or belief that people are victims of forces beyond their control. Furthermore, it rejects skepticism, or any view that knowledge is impossible, and dualism, or any view that reality can be divided into the knowable and the unknowable.

Although her social ontology may be criticized for minimizing the constitutive role that humans play in the construction of reality, it is important to understand that Rand was a fervent atheist and tireless critic of religious and philosophical fetishisms that mystify human freedom and responsibility. Her insistence that human beings are fully competent to know themselves and their world is a type of humanism that is based on the idea that reason is the conceptual faculty that identifies and integrates the raw data provided by senses. Because reason is humanity's only means of acquiring knowledge, the primary standard for judging values and behavior is living as human beings, or life or survival as rational beings. Rationality is humanity's basic virtue, and each person is conceived in Rand's philosophy as a totality, or to use her terminology, each individual is an end in himself or herself. Thus she rejects any form of altruism or ideology that morality is based on living for others, society, or public purposes.

Objectivist ethical principles form the basis of its social ontology and politics in that no individual or group has the right to initiate physical force against others because no one has the right to seek value or any form of desiderata from others. People have the right to use force only in self-defense and only against those who initiate its use. People must interact with each other giving value for value through voluntary mutual consent. The only social system that bars the use of physical force from human social relationships is laissez-faire capitalism, which is based on the recognition of individual rights, including property rights. The only proper role of the state is to protect individual rights, or to protect people from those who initiate the use of physical force. Thus Rand rejected any form of collectivism, such as fascism or socialism, as well as the idea of the mixed economy or welfare state that is expected to regulate the economy and redistribute wealth.

Rand's vision of laissez-faire capitalism was radically different from the state capitalism or mixed economy that exists in our world. For Rand, capitalism was an unknown ideal that was frustrated by religious mysticism, altruistic ethics, and the intrusion of the state in modern economies. Rand offered a sharp critique of racism as a brutal form of collectivism and opposed multiculturalism as irrational and unethical. In her view, the mixed economy of the welfare state or state capitalism produced a predatory state that imposes an altruistic ideology that legitimates the sacrifice of individual rights to public purposes and appropriates social and economic value created by individuals for use by the state. The mixed economy of modern state capitalism not only entails a state that preys on individuals and groups, it fragments society by setting individuals and groups against each other because of the arbitrary and unearned redistribution of social desiderata. As the arbiter of social worth and desiderata, the state engenders conflict among groups who receive privileges conferred by the state and those who are victims of the state's decision making. Multiculturalism is a form of predatory statism that requires the sacrifice of the autonomy, property, and resources of some individuals for the benefit of others. Objectivism opposes multiculturalist ideology for its negation of the values of individuality and rationality and promotion of the sacrifice of individuals and their rights to the state.

Libertarianism

Libertarianism emerged as a movement and political force in the early 1970s in the United States through the confluence of disaffected paleo-conservatives and antiwar, antidraft new leftists who sought an alternative to leftist and conservative approaches to the conflicts and crises of the 1960s and early 1970s. In 2005, the Libertarian Party in the United States claimed to be the largest third party in the county with over 200,000 members and over 600 elected officials who identify themselves as members of the party.

Although many of the early libertarians in the United States owe much of their philosophical development to Ayn Rand, the arrogance, theatricality, and cult-like environment of Objectivism suggested to many in the 1970s and 1980s that a separate movement and political party was needed to advance the goals of individualist, procapitalist, and antistatist activists in the United States. Rand remained an important thinker and source of inspiration for many libertarians, but the limited government philosophies of John Locke and Thomas Jefferson and the laissez-faire economic philosophies of Adam Smith, Fredrick A. Hayek, and Ludwig von Mises emerged as the classic statements on society, economy, and politics for the emerging libertarian movement in the United States.[14]

Arguably the most significant statement published during the formative phase of libertarianism in the United States was Robert Nozick's *Anarchy, State, and Utopia*.[15] Nozick's political philosophy is a classic statement on libertarianism because it seeks to identify the legitimate philosophical foundations of the state while also articulating the limits of state power grounded in a theory of individual rights. Nozick is not an anarchist because he is searching for a justification and role for the state, but he seeks a middle ground somewhere between anarchy and the state. He settles on the concept of the minimal state as a framework for utopia. Within this framework he explores a number of topics that have considerable relevance for racism and the restructuring of race relations, including concepts of justice, equality, opportunity, and self-esteem.

Following his precursors in classical liberalism, Nozick bases his theory of the minimal state on an atomistic view of the individual and society. He observes that individuals lead separate lives and concludes that it is wrong to sacrifice one person for the sake of another or for the sake of some public purpose. Nozick's thesis of self-ownership states that one individual cannot be a resource for another unless there is a voluntary agreement. Furthermore, the state cannot legitimately force an individual to suffer some sort of loss or disadvantage just so another will benefit. Only the individual has the right to determine what happens to his or her life, liberty, and body. For Nozick, individual rights are absolute and paramount in that they trump all other considerations of need, justice, and happiness. Individual rights comprise the totality of the political vision of libertarianism. The key thesis of self-ownership is that, except for punishment or self-defense, the only things that others may do to an individual are those to which she or he voluntarily consents. Each individual must be protected by a sphere of rights, into which neither other individuals nor the institutions of society may intrude. By recognizing the right to noninterference we respect the separateness of the lives of individuals.

Nozick was not the first to articulate this thesis of self-ownership; it appears to be included in the political theories of Thomas Hobbes, John Locke, John Stuart Mill, and Rand. However, with the possible exception of the writings of Max Stirner, Nozick is unique in the emphasis he places on self-ownership. His thesis of self-ownership, however, constitutes one of the two elements of his theory of the minimal state. The second element is his view of property rights. For Nozick, property rights also fall within the protected sphere of individual rights. Where individuals have a justified right to property, this right is as comprehensive and sacrosanct as the right to life, liberty, and body. No individual or societal institution can legitimately interfere with an individual's property without their consent, even for the sake of public purposes or a presumed greater good. Contrary to those who argue that legitimate property rights are based on need or merit, Nozick argues that entitlement is key. Individuals may be entitled to legitimate ownership of property (1) if it has been justly transferred from others; (2) in certain circumstances, if it has been appropriated in an unowned form from nature; or (3) if its transfer rectifies past injustices.

Nozick's view of the absolute right to life, liberty, and property form the basic principles of the minimal state. The state is justified in as much as it protects people against force, fraud, and theft and enforces contracts between people. Its only legitimate role is to safeguard the rights of individuals; those actions or programs of the state that go beyond this function violate the rights of individuals. Thus efforts by governments to protect citizens against internal and external aggression would appear to be legitimate under Nozick's formulation, but those efforts to provide public services—to take care of those who cannot care for themselves and supervise the lives of individuals—are not legitimate governmental activities. To drive home the point about the appropriate role of the minimal state, Nozick argued that people do not have rights to welfare assistance and the state has no business assisting the poor.

Nozick's political philosophy carries with it clear messages regarding race and multiculturalism in higher education. To begin with, his theory of individual rights and entitlement theory of justice provide strong critiques of racism and the domination and exploitation of racial, ethnic, and linguistic groups. It is also clear that any effort by the state to promote discrimination or to encourage the appropriation of life, liberty, and property of individuals from marginalized groups is illegitimate. However, it is also clear that the minimal state has a very limited role in responding to racism. His minimalist utopia prohibits any official form of racism and the differential or preferential treatment of people to provide equality of opportunity or outcomes. There is one important exception to this point in Nozick's philosophy: His entitlement theory of justice provides an opening to transfer property to rectify past injustices. His view of property rights appears to justify the redistribution of social desiderata to rebalance or correct past discrimination. Because it is clear that Nozick views racism as the violence of some individuals against others, there is some basis in his thought for the reparations perspective in the multiculturalist agenda, not to achieve equality in social desiderata through public policy but to repair past injustices through the courts.

Much of Nozick's philosophical perspective has been interpreted in a practical, political context by the Libertarian Party in the United States. In his book on libertarianism, David Boaz argues that racism and individualism clearly clash.[16] He argues that in American history the libertarian and individualist dimensions of the American Revolution gave rise to the abolitionist movement and served as an important philosophical and inspirational sources of the civil rights movement. In concert with Nozick, Boaz is also very critical of government-sponsored racism as well as efforts by the state to achieve some sort of racial parity in hiring and the distribution of other social desiderata. In concert with Rand, Boaz is concerned about the social fragmentation generated by the state. He argues that public and institutional policies that provide privileges for one group, inevitably generate intergroup hostility and discrimination against others. Boaz describes situations where one minority group will complain that another minority group is benefiting too much from preferential policies.

Thus the platform of the U.S. Libertarian Party notes that discrimination imposed by government has caused many social and educational problems and that antidiscrimination laws generate the same problems. Libertarians argue that individual rights should not be denied, abridged, or enhanced at the expense of other people's rights by laws at any level of government based on sex, wealth, race, color, creed, age, national origin, personal habits, political preference, or sexual orientation. They support repealing any law that imposes discrimination by government. Libertarians do not advocate for either public or private discrimination because both are anti-individualist, but they do not support laws or public policies that attempt to ban or rectify private discrimination.[17]

Anarcho-Capitalism

Another important tendency in modern individualist thought has been articulated by academic economists as a less moderate and more uncompromising critique of the state. It also places greater reliance on natural law and the free market to structure human relationships. Murray Rothbard and David Friedman are probably the best known expositors of a position known as "anarcho-capitalism" and offer the most forceful opposition between market and power as competing principles in social organization. In their view, the state operates on the basis of coercion; the market operates on the basis of voluntary agreement.[18]

Unlike the left-oriented anarchists, anarcho-capitalists generally place little or no value on equality, believing that inequalities along all dimensions, including income and wealth, are perfectly legitimate as the natural consequence of human freedom—if they are not artificially created by the state.

For the anarcho-capitalists, much of racism is generated by the state or becomes patterned behavior in social institutions supported by the state. Thus the anarcho-capitalists advocate a critique of racism that is similar to that offered by the objectivists and the libertarians: Racism is a collectivist ideology promulgated by governments that have an interest in patterned social inequalities. It is important to understand that anarcho-capitalism emerged out of the modern American libertarian movement, and understand their position as a more consistent, albeit radical, version of the antistatist elements of Objectivism and libertarianism.

The libertarians who argue for a minimal state maintain that government should be limited to the protection of individuals and their private property against physical invasion; accordingly, they favor a government limited to supplying police, courts, a legal code, and national defense. This normative position on the power of the state is similar to laissez-faire economic theory, according to which private property and unregulated competition generally lead to both an efficient allocation of resources and a high rate of economic progress. The difference between the anarcho-capitalists and the objectivists and libertarians is the promotion of the free market as the societal mechanism to provide the internal and external defense of individual liberty. Both Rothbard and Freidman argue that the state can be abolished because these defensive functions can be turned over to the free market. Anarcho-capitalism argues that police services can be sold by freely competitive firms, that a court system would emerge to peacefully arbitrate disputes between firms, and that a sensible legal code could be developed through custom, precedent, and contract. Rothbard argues that a great deal of modern law, such as the Anglo-American common law, originated not in legislatures but from the decentralized rulings of judges.

Rothbard and Freidman praise the increasing reliance on private security guards, gated communities, arbitration and mediation, and other market-based defensive and legal services assumed to be the sole province of a governmental monopoly. Market alternatives to government services would take over all legitimate security and public services. Market structures might involve individuals or groups subscribing to one of a large number of competing police services; these police services would then set up contracts or networks for peacefully handling disputes between members of each others' agencies. Alternately, police services might be bundled with housing services, just as landlords often bundle water and power with rental housing and gardening and security are today provided to residents in gated communities and apartment complexes. The underlying idea is that contrary to popular belief, private police would have strong incentives to be peaceful and respect individual rights. Failure to peacefully arbitrate will yield to jointly destructive warfare, which is bad for profits.

Both Rothbard and Friedman argued that higher education should be fully privatized for many reasons. Their arguments suggest that privatized colleges and universities will likely be diverse and responsive to all racial and ethnic groups because these firms will want to ensure their long-term profitability. Unlike left-anarchists, anarcho-capitalists believe in the punishment of criminals and suggest that racially motivated crimes and forms of discrimination can be controlled through market mechanisms. Traditional punishment might be meted out after a conviction by a neutral arbitrator, or a system of monetary restitution might exist instead. Convicted criminals would owe their victims compensation and would be forced to work until the debt was paid off. The anarcho-capitalist position emphasizes a restitutionalist, not retributionist, perspective on crime and social control.

Anarcho-capitalism has many critics on the left and the right. The central criticism offered by socialist, liberals, conservatives, and libertarians is that it is unlikely that market processes can effectively provide for the security of people and their property. When this point is interpreted in the realm of race relations, the argument is that critics lack confidence that the anarcho-capitalist utopia will provide individuals from minority or marginalized groups with the safety and autonomy the need to pursue their own interests and promote their own prosperity. However, the anarcho-capitalist position allows individuals to organize to provide for their own protection or to sell protective services to others. For many critics of anarcho-capitalism, the lack of a state or any entity to provide for the public good makes it difficult to understand how social justice or even equality of opportunity can be made social realities.

Individualist Anarchism

The appearance of libertarian and anarcho-capitalist perspectives in the 1970s directed some focus on the variety and richness of anarchist ideas that date back at least to the writings of William Godwin at the end of the eighteenth century. The majority of anarchists throughout the nineteenth and twentieth centuries advocated a left-oriented ideology that was critical of both capitalism and the state socialism of Marx and his followers but still oriented toward collective ownership of productive property. Individualists in Europe and the United States articulated an anarchist perspective that, although critical of the state and capitalism, nevertheless defended private property and voluntary, market-based relationships. The individualist variant

of anarchism was sharply critical of all forms of domination, including hor-
izontal forms of control that may emerge from nongovernmental dynamics, such as public opinion and morality. Individualists sought not a stateless
form of communism but a more radical social form that enabled each individual to pursue his or her own interests and not infringing on those of
others. Individualist anarchism had roots in the abolitionist movement in
the United States and promoted critiques of both government and capitalism
for their oppression and degradation of individuals. The American individualist anarchists were particularly ardent critics of racism but did not argue
that individuals must be sacrificed to a collectivist state. Contemporary individualist anarchists are critical of capitalism and the social production of
poverty, but they do not envision liberation as a stateless version of communism. They differ from the Objectivists and libertarians in that they seek
the full abolition of the state, not just a scaling back of the state to a minimal form. They are similar to Objectivists and libertarians, however, in that
they believe in the application of universal principles supporting individual
liberty.[19]

Max Stirner, a contemporary and acquaintance of Marx and Engels, was
arguably the most important individualist anarchist thinker because of the
very forceful case for individualism stated in his book *The Ego and Its Own*.[20]
Rand, Nozick, Rothbard, and Friedman all base their individualism on an
empiricist epistemology and an atomistic social ontology. Most libertarian
writers who trace the historical roots of their thought typically identify
natural law and social contract theory as intellectual antecedents. Stirner's
work, however, is rooted in Hegelianism; Stirner's epistemology is clearly
dialectical and his ontology is defined by struggle and conflict of complex
social and ideological forces. Significantly, *The Ego and Its Own* has a pattern
that is very similar to Hegel's *Phenomenology of Spirit*.[21] Stirner's egoism
emerges out of the conflict between materialism and idealism. The main
triad in his dialectical formulation is materialist—idealist—egoist. Stirner
viewed idealism as the negation of materialism, but believed that Hegel,
Feuerbach, Marx, and Engels created new oppressive ideologies because they
attempted to subject thought to abstractions such as "spirit," "man," and
"history." He called Marx and Engels the last idealists and believed that
socialist thought was particularly pernicious because its abstractions were a
worldly sort.

Stirner's philosophy begins with the collapse of idealist thought and the
need for a higher presupposition, which is his dialectical egoism. For Stirner,
the key to human freedom is the realization that interests and needs are as
unique as the person. It is up to individuals to discover what and who they

are. There is no moral or ideological reference point outside the values chosen by the individual or the unique one. Individuals are thus defined by their willed or chosen relations, which constitute their property. The notion of property, or Eigentum, applies to social relationships as well as material possessions. Identity and community are both based on willed relationships. The union of egoists is Stirner's concept of a willed relationship, which is continuously renewed by all who support it through acts of will. The "union of egoists" requires that all parties participate through conscious egoism. Ultimately, the most important relationship in the union of egoists is my relationship to myself. Stirner argues that the dialectical egoist sees self as a subject of all of his or her valuing relationships. My relationship to myself is a creative nothingness in which I meet myself as a subject and appropriate and consume myself as my own. Stirner's individualist anarchism entails a profound critique of state, race, and culture as spooks or abstractions to be dissolved into a union of egoists in which subjects freely choose their identities, needs, and goals.

American writers Benjamin R. Tucker and Lysander Spooner developed some of the themes initially articulated by Stirner, but also integrated many of the ideas of Pierre-Joseph Proudhon, Herbert Spencer, William Greene, and Josiah Warren into a broader statement of individualist anarchism. Tucker is known not only through his own writings but also by editing and publishing the periodical *Liberty*, which became the main venue of Stirnerite egoism in the United States. Tucker was an abolitionist and expressed a sharp disdain for religiously based legislation or constraints on what he called *noninvasive behaviors*. He articulated his vision of individualist anarchism through editorials in *Liberty* that were later compiled into a collection called *Instead of a Book by a Man Too Busy to Write One*.[22]

Tucker's focus during the late nineteenth and early twentieth centuries was to explain how the state's economic control of commerce could occur and what impacts it had on individuals and society. Unlike the objectivists, libertarians, and anarcho-capitalists, he believed that interest and profit were forms of exploitation. Although interest and profit were not direct examples of coercion, they were artificially supported by the state-sponsored banking monopoly, which is maintained by coercion. Tucker believed that any state-supported interest and profit were forms of usury and the basis of the oppression of laborers, minorities, and women. Tucker's economically focused individualist anarchism interpreted the oppression and poverty of workers and other marginalized groups as the result of four monopolies maintained by governments: (1) the money monopoly, or the state's power to determine and control legitimate currency on the basis of trade and commerce; (2) the land monopoly, or the power of the state to determine legitimate access, ownership, and control of nature; (3) tariffs, or the power to artificially set prices and control exchange; and (4) patents, or the power to determine ownership of knowledge and intellect. From Tucker's perspective, racial domination is generated by the state's control of economic activity at very fundamental levels. State power produces monopolies that conspire against free trade and the ability of individuals to define and pursue their own interests.

Liberty was not just the main literary vehicle for Stirner's ideas and Tucker's economics. It was also an important journal for the publication of American individualist thought based on natural law theory. This strand of political thought was closely associated with legal theorist Lysander Spooner. The Stirnerite egoists differed from the natural law anarchists on the notion of an individual's right to be free from coercion. They believed that natural laws were superstitions and rejected moral philosophy in its entirety. In the view of Stirner and the egoists, freedom is not based in natural right but as a pragmatic compromise where each egoist pursues self-interest. The natural law position espoused by Spooner basically viewed government as the enemy of the freedoms individuals enjoyed in nature. Spooner was also an abolitionist, entrepreneur, and activist who fought state-sponsored discrimination against the poor, which usually appeared in the form of constraints on commerce that protect the rich from competition from the poor.

Spooner's most important contribution to individualist anarchist theory was called *No Treason: The Constitution of No Authority*, which argued that the U.S. Constitution has no legal or political authority over anyone because no one has signed it.[23] In the absence of any evidence of consent, the Constitution has no basis as a legal document. For Spooner and other individualist anarchists, consent or voluntary agreement is essential to any type of contract or social relationship. The idea of an implied social contract as the foundation of political authority is particularly abhorrent to an individualist anarchist because it deprives individuals of the opportunity to choose. Although the dialectical egoists and the natural law anarchists differ in the terminology and their views about the source of freedom, they are united in their criticism of any form of coerced relationship in any group or organization.

RACISM AND THE INDIVIDUALIST ALTERNATIVE

The critique of the state and the ideologies that legitimate state power, coupled with Hegel's vision of the free subject as the goal of philosophy and society, provide a powerful vantage point to interpret contemporary educational issues and managerial ideologies. Critique and opposition to racism cannot be reduced to the multiculturalist understanding of racism without inflicting serious damage to the interest in human freedom. Our understanding of race and ethnicity does not need to be reduced to a single choice of racism or multiculturalism.

Multiculturalism is not a philosophy of liberation. Instead, it is a managerial ideology that reinforces existing authority structures and negates individuality. It is important to uncouple the critique of racism and the multiculturalist agenda. Multiculturalism is a form of collectivism that reduces individuals to racial and ethnic categories defined by the government. It promotes determinism in science, society, and educational policy. It is a dogma that constrains discourse and thought. It promotes coercion and militates against individualist values of voluntary consent, personal responsibility, and self-reliance. Although multiculturalism seeks to promote equality and tolerance, it offers very little in the way of a vision for a future of higher education that optimizes opportunities for the cultivation of individual human talent. There are at least four individualist philosophies that, whatever their shortcomings, offer perspectives on knowledge, social relations, and complex organization that entail both a critique of racism and the false promise of an externally mediated multiculturalist utopia. Individualist theories provide an important alternative body of knowledge that can be a source of inspiration and critique as we consider the future of race and higher education.

NOTES

1. A classic statement on the formation of state capitalism is Raya Dunayevskaya, *Marxism and Freedom: From 1776 until Today* (New York: Bookman Associates, 1958). Outstanding discussions of the development of the capitalist world system are found in Immanuel Wallerstein, *World Inequality* (Boston: Black Rose Books, 1996) and Fernand Braudel, *The Structures of Everyday Life: The Limits of the Possible* (Berkeley: University of California Press, 1992), *The Wheels of Commerce* (Berkeley: University of California Press, 1992), and *The Perspective of the World* (Berkeley: University of California Press, 1992). The classic statement of how thought is becoming increasingly standardized is Herbert Marcuse, *One-Dimensional Man: Studies in the Ideology of Advanced Industrial Society* (Boston: Beacon Press, 1964).

2. For a sampler of multicultural ideology applied to contemporary issues in higher education, see Benjamin Bowser, Terry Jones, and Gale Auletta Young, *Toward the Multicultural University* (Westport, CT: Praeger, 1995) and Patricia Gurin, Jeffrey Lehman, and Earl Lewis, *Defending Diversity: Affirmative Action at the University of Michigan* (Ann Arbor: University of Michigan Press, 2004). An important

multiculturalist statement on the college curriculum is found in Martha Nussbaum, *Cultivating Humanity: A Classical Defense of Reform in Liberal Education* (Cambridge, MA: Harvard University Press, 1997).

3. A good discussion of the infusion of multicultural concepts into the college curriculum is found in Marilyn Lutzer, *Multiculturalism in the College Curriculum: A Handbook of Strategies and Resources for Faculty* (Westport, CT: Greenwood, 1995). Good critiques of the multicultural curriculum are found in David Bromwich, *Politics by Other Means: Higher Education and Group Thinking* (New Haven, CT: Yale University Press, 1992) and Lynn Cheney, *Telling the Truth: Why Our Culture and Our Country Have Stopped Making Sense—And What We Can Do about It* (New York: Simon and Schuster, 1995).

4. Tammy Bruce, *The New Thought Police: Inside the Left's Assault on Free Speech and Free Minds* (Roseville, CA: Prima, 2001) and Tammy Bruce, *The Death of Right and Wrong: Exposing the Left's Assault on Our Culture and Values* (Roseville, CA: Prima, 2003). Also see Cheney, *Telling the Truth*, and Diane Ravitch, *The Language Police: How Pressure Groups Restrict What Students Learn* (New York: Knopf, 2003).

5. A good multiculturalist discussion of the perspective that race is always a factor in social life is Stella Nkomo, "Race in Organizations," in Christopher Brown (ed.), *Organization and Governance in Higher Education* (Boston: Pearson Custom Publishing, 2000), 417–435. For broader discussions of the same race is real viewpoint, also see Cornel West, *Race Matters* (Boston: Beacon Press, 1993). For treatments of the same issue that search for the biological or physical roots of racial differences, and which have different political conclusions from Nkomo and West, see Vincent Savich and Frank Miele, *Race: The Reality of Human Differences* (Boulder, CO: Westview Press, 2004); J. Phillippe Rushton, *Race, Evolution and Behavior: A Life History Perspective* (Port Huron, MI: Charles Darwin Research Institute, 2000); Jared Taylor and George McDaniel, *A Race against Time: Racial Heresies for the 21st Century* (Oakton, VA: New City Foundation, 2003); and Steven Gregory and Roger Sajek, *Race* (New Brunswick, NJ: Rutgers University Press, 1994).

6. Karl Marx developed a dialectical, humanist, and constructivist view of racism in his early essay "On the Jewish Question," which is included in *Writings of the Young Marx on Philosophy and Society* (New York: Doubleday, 1983). Jean-Paul Sartre did the same in *Anti-Semite and Jew* (New York: Shocken Books, 1965). Also see Frantz Fanon, *Black Skins, White Masks* (New York: Grove Press, 1967) for a similar view. Although their politics are vastly different, Dinesh D'Souza and Peter Wood provide arguments that race and diversity are constructed relationships: Dinesh D'Souza, *The End of Racism* (New York: Free Press, 1995) and Peter Wood, *Diversity: The Invention of a Concept* (San Francisco: Encounter Books, 2003).

7. For multiculturalist discussions of this point, see Ruth Sidel, *Battling Bias: The Struggle for Identity and Community on College Campuses* (New York: Penguin Books, 1994); William Tierney, *Building Communities of Difference: Higher Education in the Twenty-First Century* (Westport, CT: Bergin and Garvey, 1993); and William Tierney, "Cultural Politics and the Curriculum in Postsecondary Education," in Lisa Lattuca, Jennifer Grant Haworth, and Clifton Conrad (eds.), *College and University Curriculum* (Boston: Pearson Custom Publishing, 2002), 25–35. Cautionary perspectives are offered by Stephan Thernstrom and Abigail Thernstrom, *America in Black and White: One Nation, Indivisible* (New York: Simon and Schuster, 1997);

Stephan Thernstrom and Abigail Thernstrom, *No Excuses: Closing the Racial Gap in Learning* (New York: Simon and Schuster, 2003); and J. Harvie Wilkinson, *One Nation Indivisible: How Ethnic Separatism Threatens America* (New York: Addison Wesley Longman, 1997).

8. For a left-oriented discussion of this point, see Douglas Kellner, "A Marcuse Renaissance?" in John Borkina and Timothy Lukes (eds.), *Marcuse: From the New Left to the Next Left* (Lawrence: University of Kansas Press, 1994). More conservative perspectives are presented in Roger Kimball, *Tenured Radicals: How Politics Has Corrupted Our Higher Education* (New York: Harper and Row, 1990) and Sandra Stotsky, *Losing Our Language: How Multicultural Classroom Instruction Is Undermining Our Children's Ability to Read, Write and Reason* (New York: Free Press, 1999). A classic but very controversial statement on this point is Allan Bloom, *The Closing of the American Mind: How Higher Education Has Failed Democracy and Impoverished the Souls of Today's Students* (New York: Simon and Schuster, 1987).

9. See Cheney, *Telling the Truth* and Bruce, *The New Thought Police*. For great discussions about this point placed in an historical context, see Peter Collier and David Horowitz, *Second Thoughts about the Sixties* (New York: Summit Books, 1990) and Richard J. Ellis, *The Dark Side of the Left: Illiberal Egalitarianism in America* (Lawrence: University of Kansas Press, 1998). These books demonstrate that the multicultural left in the United States has been consistently authoritarian in its approach to politics and culture.

10. See Ravitch, *The Language Police*; Bruce, *The New Thought Police*; and Collier and Horowitz, *Second Thoughts about the Sixties*.

11. This is an important point that will be developed in later sections of this chapter, but see Wilkinson, *One Nation Indivisible*.

12. A very curious expression of this point appeared in the recent controversy over the comments that comedian Bill Cosby made about the Black underclass in the United States. Cosby essentially said that there needs to be some accountability of individuals and families for the social disorganization experienced by far too many African Americans. Cosby's comments were savaged by Eric Michael Dyson, *Is Bill Cosby Right, or Has the Black Middle Class Lost its Mind?* (New York: Basic Civitas Books, 2005). The basic issue is, to what extent are individuals in the Black underclass responsible for changing their life experiences? Dyson argues a determinist perspective, arguing that the Black underclass are victims of culture. Cosby appears to have argued that there is some opportunity for the Black underclass to affect its own future.

13. Ayn Rand, *Fountainhead* (New York: Signet, 1996), *Atlas Shrugged* (New York: Signet, 1996), *Capitalism: The Unknown Ideal* (New York: Signet 1986), and *The Virtue of Selfishness: A New Concept of Egoism* (New York: Signet, 1989). For an excellent academic treatment that focuses on Rand's radicalism, see Chris Matthew Sciabarra, *Ayn Rand: The Russian Radical* (University Park: Pennsylvania State University Press, 1995).

14. David Boaz, *Libertarianism: A Primer* (New York: Free Press, 1997).

15. Robert Nozick, *Anarchy, State, and Utopia* (New York: Basic Books, 1974).

16. Boaz, *Libertarianism*, 98–102.

17. The platform of the Libertarian Party can be retrieved online at www.lp.org.

18. The basic elements of Rothbard's ideas are found in Murray Rothbard, *For a New Liberty: The Libertarian Manifesto* (San Francisco: Fox and Wilkes, 1978). Friedman's anarcho-capitalism is described in David Friedman, *The Machinery of Freedom: A Guide to Radical Capitalism* (Chicago: Open Court, 1973). For a discussion of Rothbard's specific ideas on higher education, see Murray Rothbard, *Education: Free and Compulsory* (Auburn, AL: Ludwig von Mises Institute, 1999). For outstanding discussions of anarcho-capitalism, especially the work of Rothbard, see Chris Matthew Sciabarra, *Total Freedom: Toward a Dialectical Libertarianism* (University Park: Pennsylvania State University Press, 2000) and Justin Raimondo, *An Enemy of the State: The Life of Murray Rothbard* (Amherst, NY: Prometheus Books, 2000).

19. Still the best historical overview of anarchism up to the 1960s is George Woodcock, *Anarchism: A History of Libertarian Ideas and Movements* (Cleveland, OH: World Publishing, 1962). However, Woodcock's book is extremely weak in its discussion of individualist anarchism. See John Henry Mackay, *The Anarchists: A Picture of Civilization at the Close of the Nineteenth Century* (Brooklyn, NY: Autonomedia, 1999) for a fictionalized confrontation between communist and individualist anarchists. In addition to the novel, this volume includes a series of essays that discuss individualist anarchism and Mackay's ideas applied to the context of the twenty-first century.

20. Max Stirner, *The Ego and Its Own* (Cambridge: Cambridge University Press, 1995). The best academic treatment of Stirner in English is R. W. K. Patterson, *The Nihilistic Egoist Max Stirner* (Oxford: Oxford University Press, 1971).

21. G. W. F. Hegel, *Phenomenology of Spirit* (Oxford: Oxford University Press, 1977).

22. Benjamin R. Tucker, *Instead of a Book by a Man Too Busy to Write One* (New York: Haskell House, 1969). The best intellectual history of individualist anarchism in the United States, including both Tucker and Spooner, is James J. Martin, *Men against the State: The Expositors of Individualist Anarchism in American, 1827–1908* (Colorado Springs, CO: Ralph Myles, 1970).

23. Lysander Spooner, *No Treason: The Constitution of No Authority* (Larkspur, CO: Pine Tree Press, 1966).

II

RACISM AND ANTIRACISM IN SCHOOLS

5

High-Stakes Testing, Nationally and in the South: Disparate Impact, Opportunity to Learn, and Current Legal Protections

Jay P. Heubert

INTRODUCTION

This chapter focuses on *high-stakes tests*, defined here as tests that states and school districts use in deciding whether individual students will receive high school diplomas or be promoted to the next grade. It places the South's graduation- and promotion-test programs into the context of such testing nationally. It also considers how federal law, including the No Child Left Behind act of 2001 (NCLB) and the Individuals with Disabilities Education Act of 1997 (IDEA), both of which emphasize system accountability (for states, school districts, and schools), may influence state and district assessment programs that instead have high stakes for individual students.

Large-scale assessment, including testing for high-stakes purposes, has changed in important ways since the minimum competency test (MCT) programs of the 1970s and 1980s. First, most current tests embody much higher

This chapter was previously published in *School Resegregation: Must the South Turn Back?* edited by John Charles Boger and Gary Orfield. Copyright © 2005 by the University of North Carolina Press. Used by permission of the publisher.

The author is grateful to the Carnegie Scholars Program of the Carnegie Corporation of New York, which supported this research, and to Erica Frankenberg and Rebecca High, who provided first-rate research and editorial support. The views expressed are the author's.

academic standards. Second, due chiefly to changes in federal law, including NCLB and IDEA, many more low achievers, especially students with disabilities and English-language learners (ELLs) are now included among those tested. Third, although state graduation testing has increased somewhat, state- and district-level promotion testing has grown rapidly.

Other important changes are less widely recognized. For example, recent changes in federal law have weakened important civil rights protections, even in situations where students of color, students with disabilities, and ELLs fail high-stakes tests at rates far higher than in the 1970s and 1980s. Also, legal standards developed in older cases involving MCTs, though useful, do not take into account the current standards movement, which, in seeking to educate all students to high standards, places heavy new demands on assessments, schools, and students. The results are (1) a changed legal climate in which to evaluate current graduation tests and promotion tests, and (2) a more complex educational context that educators and researchers may need to help courts understand that may call for refinement in the standards developed decades ago in MCT cases.

The sections to follow (1) describe the current nature and scope of graduation and promotion testing in the United States, both of which are particularly prevalent in the Southern states; (2) examine empirical evidence on the current disparate effects of such testing on minority students, students with disabilities, and ELLs; (3) consider varied evidence now available about whether states, school districts, and schools are teaching all students the kinds of knowledge and skills they need to pass high-stakes tests; and (4) examine the current status of federal law concerning high-stakes testing, pointing out changes in the law, limitations in the law's current treatment of high-stakes tests, and shortcomings in existing mechanisms for enforcing broadly accepted norms of appropriate test use.

THE NATURE AND EXTENT OF HIGH-STAKES TESTING IN THE UNITED STATES

The Extent of Graduation Testing

As part of the back to the basics movement in the 1970s and early 1980s, seventeen states adopted MCTs, which students had to pass to receive standard high school diplomas, even if they had completed satisfactorily all other requirements for graduation.

In the past five years, the number of states with graduation tests remained fairly constant at eighteen, rising to nineteen in spring 2003.[1] Graduation testing has always been especially popular in the Southern states; this was true in the early days of MCT and remains so today: Eleven of the current nineteen graduation-test states are defined in the census as "southern states."[2] Nationally, about five more states are now planning to adopt graduation tests between now and 2008.[3] As will be discussed, however, there are factors that may lead states to reconsider or postpone such requirements.

Equally important is the changing nature of large-scale assessments. Although earlier exit tests focused on minimum competencies, more than two-thirds of the current tests embody standards at the tenth-grade level or higher,[4] and an increasing number reflect world-class standards such as those embodied in the National Assessment of Educational Progress (NAEP), a highly regarded assessment administered nationally to representative samples of students. This trend reflects the emphasis in the standards movement and state and federal laws on helping all students reach high standards of achievement.

There is little debate over the desirability of teaching students high-level knowledge and skills; higher expectations and improved instruction lead to improved achievement.[5] At the same time, where standards are high and large numbers of students start out at low achievement levels, the gaps in teaching and learning that must be closed are greater than where standards reflect only basic skills. The gaps are greatest in schools where instruction is weak and resources are inadequate, conditions that are common in many Southern states and, more generally, in schools serving large numbers of low-achieving students.

As discussed later, student failure rates on newer, more demanding exit tests are much higher, more persistent, and more persistently disparate for different groups than on MCTs, where failure rates and group disparities typically declined quickly to low levels. Even after initial test implementation, there are graduation tests that some groups fail at rates of well over 50 percent.

In recent years, at least two states have withdrawn exit exam requirements and four have postponed them; others have lowered passing scores or allowed students to substitute scores on other tests for graduation purposes.[6]

Several factors seem to be involved. One is the continuing evidence of high and disparate failure rates, which raises educational questions as well as political ones. In 2003, for example, California postponed until 2006 the date by which students would have to pass a state graduation exam to receive a standard diploma. The state Board of Education acted in the face of predicted statewide diploma-denial rates of about 20 percent; evidence of far higher failure rates for African American students, Latino students, ELLs, and students with disabilities; and indications that many students were not yet being taught the knowledge and skills that the graduation tests measure.[7] Similarly, in 2003, when 13,000 Florida students failed that state's graduation test, the state allowed students to substitute scores from the SAT, ACT, and other standardized tests, and granted waivers to some students with disabilities.[8]

Declining state revenues, currently a serious problem in almost every stateincluding those in the South, is a second factor that could slow the growth of graduation testing.[9] The budget situation may also explain the apparent decline in the number of states providing special funding to help low-achieving students meet state test standards.[10]

Last but not least, Georgia and North Carolina have both postponed implementation of new versions of their graduation exams out of concern that the tests may not conform to the requirements of NCLB.

Two other developments have affected the scope of high-stakes testing: the rapid growth of promotion testing and the inclusion of students with disabilities and ELLs in large-scale assessments, some of them high-stakes tests.

The Extent of Promotion Testing

Promotion testing has grown very rapidly in response to concerns about social promotion. In 2001, seventeen states (including nine in the South) required or planned to require students to pass standardized tests as a condition of grade-to-grade promotion, compared with six in 1999. Of these, thirteen (including Florida, Louisiana, Mississippi, North Carolina, South Carolina, Texas, and Virginia) administered promotion tests at both the elementary and middle-school levels or planned to do so.[11]

Students of color are likelier than White students to live in states that administer graduation tests[12] and promotion tests.[13] In addition, many urban school districts, including the District of Columbia, New York City, Boston, and Chicago, have adopted promotion test policies even where states have not. Thus many of the nation's minority students and immigrant students— and increasing numbers of all students—must pass promotion tests.

NCLB, which requires end-of-year testing for students in grades three through eight as of 2005–2006, also seems to be fueling further growth in promotion testing. Neither NCLB nor any other federal statute requires promotion testing or any other kind of high-stakes testing. But North Carolina is already using for promotion purposes the new tests that NCLB mandates, and other states that administer promotion tests will probably do likewise.

Students with Disabilities, ELLs, and High-Stakes Testing

Since 1994, federal laws have required states and school districts to include students with disabilities and ELLs in their large-scale assessments, report disaggregated scores for these and other groups, and give all students access to high-quality instruction.[14] Many such students had previously been exempted from testing.[15]

This chapter deals less with system accountability than with tests that have high-stakes consequences for individual students, and on this question federal laws are silent. Thus NCLB and IDEA require system accountability but leave states and school districts to decide whether students with disabilities or ELLs who fail such tests will be subject to individual high-stakes consequences such as retention or denial of a standard diploma.[16]

This decision is a complex one, and states have approached it differently. Some authorize Individual Education Plan (IEP) teams to decide individually whether a student with disabilities who fails a promotion test will be promoted anyway. In other states, promotion test requirements apply fully to students with disabilities. States differ in similar ways on graduation testing.

In some states, students who fail state exit tests are eligible for alternative diplomas or certificates. Some, such as IEP diplomas, are available only to students with disabilities, though others, such as certificates of completion or attendance, may also be available to other students. Unfortunately, there is little research on the value of such certificates and alternate, nonstandard diplomas in terms of a student's future opportunities for education or employment. The only alternative certificate on which extensive research exists is the General Equivalency Diploma (GED), and evidence suggests that GED holders are more like high school dropouts than like the holders of standard diplomas in terms of future educational and employment opportunities.[17] Students with disabilities who do not receive standard diplomas have a right to special education and related services until the age of twenty-one or twenty-two.[18] Policy makers should therefore proceed cautiously with alternatives to standard diplomas.

FROM MINIMUM COMPETENCIES TO WORLD-CLASS STANDARDS: PASS RATES, DISPARATE IMPACT, AND OTHER EFFECTS OF HIGH-STAKES TESTING

A central objective of standards-based education reform is "to improve learning for students who have done poorly in the past" and to "reduce inequality in educational achievement" by helping all students reach high standards.[19] Indeed, many believe that "current versions of standards-based reforms will have their greatest impact on children at the bottom of the achievement distribution."[20]

Some believe that standards-based reform will benefit low-achieving students especially; as attorney William Taylor writes, "when schools and districts are held accountable for the achievement of all students, the means are at hand to force them to improve the quality of schooling provided for previously neglected students."[21] Taylor speaks here of system accountability. There is broad agreement that accountability for improved educational achievement should be both (1) widely shared,[22] and (2) based on school performance.[23]

Though "accountability for adults is in its infancy,"[24] accountability is expanding for individual students, who are increasingly subject to the serious and well-documented harms associated with being retained in grade or denied standard high school diplomas. In our society, for example, not having a standard high school diploma is associated with much lower income, diminished opportunities for employment and further education, higher risk of criminal incarceration, and greater likelihood of dysfunction in family life.[25] There are concerns that low-achieving students, including many minority students, students with disabilities, and ELLs—who typically rely heavily on their schools for academic knowledge—may be failing increasingly demanding high-stakes tests because their schools do not yet expose them to the knowledge and skills that students need to pass the tests.[26]

What is known, then, about the pass rates and group disparities on high-stakes tests? This section compares empirical evidence for early MCTs and current tests that embody higher standards.

State Pass Rates and Disparate Impact

Even on basic skills tests, minority students, students with disabilities, and ELLs typically fail at higher rates than other students, especially at first. For example, 20 percent of African American students (compared with 2 percent of White students) initially failed Florida's MCT.[27] And although most students with disabilities and ELLs were exempted from early exit tests, those who were tested failed at higher rates.

For a variety of reasons, failure rates typically decline among all groups in the years after a new graduation test is introduced.[28] This was true of early MCTs; within a few years, failure rates declined substantially for all groups.[29]

This pattern—high initial failure rates that decline over time—apparently holds true for graduation tests adopted more recently, but with important qualifications. First, where high-stakes tests embody demanding standards, initial failure rates are much higher than for earlier tests. Second, group disparities on high-standards tests are typically quite high—well beyond the requirements for showing disparate impact under federal law. A test is considered to have adverse impact when a statistical analysis shows that one group's pass rate is significantly lower than another's,[30] or when one group's pass rate is less than four-fifths of another's.[31] Third, both failure rates and group disparities on high-standards tests typically decline more slowly. The following discussion illustrates how failure rates and group differences can change as tests become more demanding.

Texas's graduation test, the Texas Assessment of Academic Skills (TAAS), is set at the seventh- or eighth-grade level, higher than earlier MCTs but lower than current standards in most states.[32] Texas reports that pass rates of African Americans and Latinos roughly doubled between 1994 and 1998, and that the gap in failure rates between Whites, African Americans, and Latinos narrowed considerably during that time—conclusions that scholars have since questioned.[33] Texas's data for 1998 nonetheless show continuing disparities: cumulative failure rates of 17.6 percent for African American students, 17.4 percent for Hispanic students, and 6.7 percent for White students.[34] Thus even on fairly low-level exit tests, failure rates for African Americans and Hispanics remain higher in Texas than was true for early basic skills exit tests, and a court found that TAAS has adverse impact.[35]

The same pattern is evident in Florida, where the Florida Comprehensive Assessment Test was introduced in 1998. Pass rates for all groups have increased over time. As noted earlier, however, when the graduation-test requirement took effect in spring 2003 some 13,000 seniors were denied standard diplomas. These included about 5.2 percent of White seniors, 19.1 percent of African Americans, and 11.9 percent of Latinos.[36]

Moreover, these statistics for Texas and Florida understate minority failure rates and group discrepancies because they do not account for students who were not tested because they had dropped out, been retained in grade, or been excluded improperly from the test-taking population—all categories in which minority students, students with disabilities, and ELLs are disproportionately represented.[37]

California's English and mathematics exit tests, first administered in spring 2001, reflect ninth-grade standards.[38] According to data from the California Department of Education, through May 2002—the most recent administration for which the state posts data on the rates at which groups passed both tests needed for graduation—failure rates for students in the class of 2004 were far higher than those of the early basic skills tests: only 48 percent of all test-takers had passed both tests, and for African Americans, Hispanics, students with disabilities, and ELLs, pass rates were far lower. Among African Americans and Hispanics, 28 percent and 30 percent, respectively, had passed both tests, compared with 65 percent of Whites. Students with disabilities and ELLs had passed both tests at far lower rates: 13 percent and 19 percent, respectively.[39] Spring 2003 data for the class of 2004 show improved subtest pass rates for all groups,[40] but faced with the prospect of denying diplomas to more than 20 percent of all students in spring 2004, the state postponed until 2006 the date by which students must pass both tests to receive standard high-school diplomas.

Failure rates are typically highest on exit exams that embody world-class standards, such as those of NAEP assessments. About 38 percent of all students would fail tests that reflect such world-class standards, and failure rates would be about twice as high for minority students.[41] Careful multistate studies show students with disabilities failing various state tests at rates 30 to 40 percentage points higher than for other students.[42]

In Massachusetts, where current world-class examinations were introduced in 1999 and the graduation-test requirement took effect in spring 2003, pass rates for the class of 2003 increased between 2001 and 2003:

- As tenth-graders in 2001, 71 percent of White students had passed both tests needed for graduation, compared with 18 percent of African American students, 14 percent of Hispanic students, and 9 percent of ELLs. Thirty percent of students with disabilities passed compared with 61 percent of nondisabled students.[43]
- By spring 2003, the following percentages of twelfth-graders had passed both tests needed for graduation: 97 percent of Whites, 86 percent of African Americans, 83 percent of Hispanics, 82 percent of ELLs, 80 percent of students with disabilities, and 97 percent of nondisabled students.[44]

These are substantial gains. At the same time, five years after initial test implementation these data show high and disproportionate failure rates for students of color, ELLs, and students with disabilities. Moreover, because the reported pass rates are for seniors, they do not take into account members of the 2003 cohort who, due to dropout, retention, and other factors, had not reached twelfth grade by spring 2003. Calculations by Anne Wheelock of Boston College suggest that graduation rates would be much lower if they accounted for nearly 17,000 additional students who were part of the 2003 cohort as ninth-graders but not as twelfth-graders four years later.[45]

New York received national publicity when it reported that nearly twice as many students with disabilities passed the state's new Regents English Exam in academic year 1998–1999 as had taken the exam two years earlier.[46] This information is factually correct, but the state's own pass-rate data suggest somewhat less dramatic changes. Between academic years 1997–1998 and 1999–2000, the percentages of twelfth-grade students with disabilities who passed New York's Regents English Exam increased from 5.1 percent to 8.0 percent.[47] In other words, the percentages of twelfth-graders who had *not* passed the Regents English Exam declined from 94.9 percent to 92.0 percent over two years—and these figures exclude dropouts, students previously retained, or students absent on test day; Koretz and Hamilton estimate that only about half the students with disabilities were present for a Regents English Exam administration they studied.[48]

These data, although limited, suggest that where high-stakes tests embody higher content and performance standards, (1) initial failure rates are higher than for earlier tests, (2) group disparities are typically quite high and legally disparate, and (3) both failure rates and group disparities typically decline more slowly than for earlier MCTs.

Evaluating State Pass-Rate Data

State data on high-stakes tests understate low achievement and group disparities, for two reasons. First, NAEP data, which researchers consider more reliable than state test reports, consistently show much less gain in student performance than do state test results. This was true during the 1980s—when most states reported sharply increased student achievement even as aggregate NAEP data showed little or no gain—and it remains true today.

As many states report higher pass rates on more demanding graduation tests, national NAEP results for 2000 show that the math achievement of twelfth-graders has declined since 1996, with significantly more students in the below basic category and significantly fewer students demonstrating basic mastery.[49] Although NAEP scores have improved for fourth- and eighth-grade students, nationally and especially in some states, twelfth-graders are likelier to be affected by state graduation test policies.

A study of the Texas achievement gap is noteworthy.[50] A court there placed heavy emphasis on state data showing that the achievement gap between White, African American, and Latino students had closed dramatically between 1994 and 1998 on the TAAS.[51] Using NAEP data, however, Klein and colleagues showed that the achievement gap between White students and other groups in Texas had actually *increased* slightly during this period. For Robert Linn, this evidence "raises serious questions about the trustworthiness of the TAAS result for making inferences about improvements in achievement in Texas or about the relative size of the gains for different segments of the student population."[52]

National NAEP math results for 2000 also suggest a widening racial achievement gap among thirteen- and seventeen-year-olds.[53] The racial gap is widening most at higher performance levels, an obvious concern as more states' tests emphasize high-level skills.[54] NAEP does not yet include enough students with disabilities (or ELLs) in its samples to provide meaningful state-level performance scores for these groups, but future NAEP results should help assess state data that suggests improvements for these groups.

Second, as discussed earlier, the meaning of state pass-rate data depends on what proportion of all students took the test. Apparently good news—that 100 percent of eleventh-graders passed a graduation test, for example—means something quite different if three-fourths of all students dropped out before eleventh grade, or if many students with disabilities or ELLs did not take the test. Because the standards movement is concerned with all students, an assessment of the disproportionate impact of high-stakes testing should consider the many individuals who do not take such tests with other students their age.

As noted earlier, state test data rarely include information on dropouts, students previously retained in grade, students improperly exempted or excluded from testing, or students absent on test days. Even NAEP results do not account for these students. At the grade levels where states administer exit tests, however, these students often represent a substantial portion of the cohort. If these students were included in the denominator when states calculated pass rates, those rates would be much lower, especially for minority students, students with disabilities, and ELLs.

A closely related question is whether exit testing or promotion testing causes increased dropout rates or retention in grade. The effects of graduation testing are debated. Walt Haney argues that the Texas graduation test does increase retention and dropout, especially for African Americans and Hispanics, although Martin Carnoy and colleagues claim that high retention and dropout rates for these groups are not due to TAAS.[55] A 2001 California survey indicates that 80 percent of principals and 61 percent of teachers in the state believe that graduation tests there will have "a strongly negative or negative impact on student dropout rates," and that 55 percent of principals and 32 percent of teachers think the tests will have "a strongly negative or negative impact on student retention rates."[56] The most carefully designed national longitudinal study of high school students to date—students who were eighth-graders in 1988 and seniors in 1992—finds no general relationship between basic skills graduation tests and dropout rates, but concludes that students in the lowest quintile are "25% more likely to drop out of high school than comparable peers in non-test states."[57]

There is less debate about failing promotion tests. Decades of research show that students required to repeat a grade are much worse off than similar low-performing students who are instead promoted to the next grade. A committee of the National Research Council (NRC) found that low-performing elementary and secondary school students who are held back—as compared with equally weak students who are promoted—do less well academically, are much worse off socially, and are far likelier to drop out.[58] Other studies conclude that retention in grade is the single strongest predictor of which students will drop out.[59] The evidence on simple retention in grade is so compelling that a committee of the NRC concluded that it constitutes inappropriate test use for states or school districts to use test scores for this purpose.[60]

Thus, unless schools rely on early intervention rather than retention to reduce the number of low achievers, the proliferation of promotion testing is likely to increase, perhaps significantly, the numbers of minority students, students with disabilities, and ELLs who suffer the serious economic, educational, and other harms associated with dropping out. And, as noted earlier, NCLB will probably lead to more promotion testing even though it does not require it. It would be unfortunate—and hardly evidence of success—if states, school districts, or schools achieved high graduation test pass rates because large numbers of low achievers had already left school and were no longer among the test-takers.

EVIDENCE THAT STUDENTS ARE BEING TAUGHT THE REQUISITE KNOWLEDGE AND SKILLS

The standards movement rests on the premise that virtually all students can reach high levels of achievement if they receive high-quality curriculum and instruction. This premise rests, in turn, on dramatic recent research findings in such areas as brain development, early childhood education, and effective pedagogy. In three federal statutes,[61] Congress has accepted this premise and the research supporting it.

Standards on the appropriate use of high-stakes tests are consistent with the standards movement's central premise. Under applicable legal standards and psychometric norms, states may administer tests that all students must pass as a condition of receiving standard high school diplomas—*if* states and schools first give students an adequate opportunity to acquire the knowledge and skills that such tests measure. Courts have ruled for two decades that graduation tests must be a fair measure of what students have been taught.[62] The measurement profession, the NRC, and the American Educational Research Association (AERA) all say that results of large-scale tests may be used in making individual promotion or graduation decisions only *after* students have had an adequate opportunity to acquire the knowledge and skills that such tests measure. These standards apply to all students, including ELLs and students with disabilities. This prior opportunity to learn requirement does not apply to the use of student test information to improve schools.

It is far harder today than in the MCT days to ensure that all students have had a meaningful opportunity to learn the knowledge and skills that tests measure. Standards have gotten much higher and they now apply to many more low-achieving students, who start out behind and often must also overcome barriers related to disability, English proficiency, or poverty. Moreover, the school districts and schools that serve large numbers of needy students often must operate with less money and fewer certified teachers than other school districts and schools, even though NCLB requires that all eligible students be taught by teachers who are certified in the subjects they teach.

Criteria by Which to Evaluate "Opportunity to Learn"

There are different types of evidence by which to determine whether students are being taught the knowledge and skills that tests measure.

Perhaps the most straightforward approach is to examine actual indicators of student achievement, such as test scores and grades. As Lauress Wise and his colleagues suggest in evaluating California test results, "the best evidence that a school system is providing its students adequate opportunity to learn the required material is whether most students do, in fact, learn the material."[63] And even if most students are learning well, there are usually subgroups whose achievement is low and who may not have received an adequate opportunity to learn. Indeed, what is adequate opportunity to learn for some students may be inadequate for others.

A second broad approach that federal law employs is to see whether states have met system accountability standards that are intended to gauge how well schools are serving different kinds of students and ensure that states and school districts set high standards for all students.

A third broad approach focuses on whether states have adopted demanding content and performance standards; on whether curriculum, instruction, and large-scale assessments are properly aligned with those standards; and on whether schools and teachers possess the capacity to deliver high-quality instruction to all students. This approach is based on the logic of the standards movement, under which improved capacity and alignment are the principal means to improved student achievement.[64] It is also a requirement of NCLB.

Evidence that Schools Are Teaching Students the Knowledge and Skills that Tests Measure

There is research evidence that achievement, especially for younger students, has improved in some states and schools. There is also evidence, however, that many schools are not yet giving all students an opportunity to acquire the knowledge and skills they need to pass increasingly demanding high-stakes tests.

Consider state pass-rate data of the kind already discussed. Although pass rates continue to rise, there are many states, especially those with more demanding exit tests, that continue to show failure rates for minority students, students with disabilities, and ELLs that are disproportionate and unacceptably high. If virtually all children can learn to high standards, such high failure rates must be due at least partly to insufficient high-quality instruction.

In terms of state compliance with current federal system accountability requirements, the good news is that more states meet current federal system accountability requirements than before.[65] Despite the requirements of NCLB and IDEA, many states do not yet include all students with disabilities or ELLs in their assessment systems, and many do not yet disaggregate achievement information properly for various student populations.[66] Without such data, states and school districts lack basic information about how well low-achieving groups are performing and how they might be served more effectively. Such information is a precondition to improved achievement.

And what is the evidence that curriculum and instruction are aligned with high-stakes assessments? Eva Baker and Robert Linn describe alignment as "the linchpin of standards-based accountability systems" and express the view that "in many parts of the country . . . alignment is weak."[67] There is evidence that such alignment is increasing[68] but also evidence that alignment—and the improved capacity that alignment requires—are still more aspiration than reality in many schools.

Empirical research supports such expressions of concern. One line of research, by Andrew Porter, John Smithson, and others, studies eleven states and finds only modest overlap between a state's tests and what teachers in that state say they teach. For example, in fourth-grade mathematics, reports from five states showed overlaps ranging from a high of 45 percent to a low of 23 percent; in eighth-grade mathematics, reports from six states showed overlaps ranging from a high of 35 percent to a low of 5 percent.[69] In other subjects overlap was comparable or even lower. Other studies find low overlap and "instructional content . . . not very well aligned with . . . the state test."[70]

Despite limitations, these studies suggest that many states and schools have not yet reached the point where they are teaching students all or even most of what state tests measure. This is a serious problem where tests are used to make high-stakes decisions about individual students, as is true in some states Porter and Smithson studied. In such circumstances, close alignment should precede the use of test scores for high-stakes purposes.

Alignment is closely linked with capacity. According to Richard Elmore, "the work of turning a school around entails improving the knowledge and skills of teachers—changing their knowledge of content and how to teach it— and helping them to understand where their students are in their academic development." In many places, the necessary investments have yet to be made: "Low-performing schools, and the people who work in them, don't know what to do. If they did, they would be doing it already. . . . Without substantial investments in capacity, [the increased pressure of test-based accountability] is likely to aggravate the existing inequalities between low-performing and high-performing schools and students."[71]

Indeed, a central objective of education reform efforts since at least the 1950s has been to attract strong teachers to schools that serve large numbers of low-achieving students. Reversing traditional teacher mobility patterns, in which experienced, well-regarded teachers gravitate toward wealthier suburban schools, "is a necessary condition for standards-based reform to improve educational outcomes for children of color."[72] However, according to Richard Murnane and Frank Levy, as well as Helen Ladd,[73] current standards and accountability mechanisms may already be increasing the incentives for marketable teachers to avoid or leave schools with high proportions of low-achieving students.

There are also long-standing problems of alignment and capacity between general education and programs for students with disabilities or ELLs, both of which also serve large minority populations. For example, although some studies document real progress in reducing barriers between general education and special education,[74] others raise serious concerns. Case studies at high schools in three states found that many special education teachers "lacked guidance about how to align IEPs with the standards," that they were "by and large . . . not involved in school-wide discussions about standards," that special education teachers "tended to use the IEPs rather than the standards as a guide for instruction," that "most IEPs were not aligned with the standards," and that many special education and general education teachers "tended to have a 'wait and see' attitude about exposing students with disabilities to and engaging them in standards-based instruction."[75]

Taken together, such studies suggest improvement coupled with major continuing problems of capacity and alignment. State test-score data, studies of system accountability under federal law, state-specific studies of alignment, and studies of standards-based reform for students with disabilities all indicate that many schools are not yet teaching students the full range of subject matter and skills that high-stakes tests measure. It therefore seems problematic that so many states and school districts are already administering or moving forward with high-stakes graduation or promotion tests.

FEDERAL LAW ON HIGH-STAKES TESTING

Under what circumstances will the federal government or other entities intervene where some student groups fail high-stakes tests at substantially higher rates than other students, or where there is evidence that states and schools do not yet teach students the knowledge and skills that graduation or promotion tests measure?[76]

Despite clear "opportunity to learn" language in the standards of the measurement profession, covering both promotion tests and graduation tests,[77] the measurement profession itself will not intervene. There is no mechanism by which the testing profession investigates complaints or enforces its own standards.[78] Thus legal action may be the likeliest mechanism for challenging inappropriate use of high-stakes tests.

Legal protections, however, may be less extensive than many educators, parents, and students think. In 2001, the Supreme Court held that private individuals could no longer bring disparate impact cases under Title VI of the Civil Rights Act of 1964, the federal civil rights statute that most strongly protects minority groups and ELLs. Similarly, most graduation test cases were decided in the days of minimum competency testing and suggest a judicial reluctance to probe deeply whether schools are actually teaching what exit tests measure. And in the relatively few cases involving promotion test policies, courts have tended to assume that students benefit from retention in grade and have no legal interest in avoiding it.

Changed conditions in education argue for more sensitive judicial inquiry. Even if it were appropriate to assume that most schools taught students basic skills, recent research suggests that there are problems in assuming that all students are being taught the knowledge and skills that current high-standards exit tests measure, especially as students with disabilities and ELLs increasingly take part and researchers document continuing problems of alignment and school capacity. Similarly, court opinions on promotion testing do not refer to strong research on grade retention's harmful effects.

It may be possible to resolve concerns over high-stakes testing through the policy process. But if judges are to play a role in protecting equality of opportunity, they will need help from educators, researchers, and lawyers in understanding the current policy context, the current educational realities, and the complex issues surrounding high-stakes testing.

Disparate Impact Claims

Since the early 1970s, most cases alleging discrimination in education have been brought under federal civil rights statutes and the regulations that accompany them. The regulations forbid federal fund recipients from engaging in policies or practices that, although not overtly discriminatory, produce disparate impact and have the effect of discriminating—unless the defendant can show that the policies or practices advance a substantial, legitimate objective.

Thus, in *Lau v. Nichols* (1974), a case brought by parents of children who had recently arrived from China, the Supreme Court ruled that San Francisco's failure to make any provision for the students' language needs had the effect of discriminating against them, in violation of Title VI regulations. Similarly, when private citizens challenged the Texas graduation test, the court explored whether TAAS had a disproportionate, adverse impact on African American and Hispanic students. Concluding that it did, the court nonetheless ruled for Texas because the court accepted the state's asserted justifications: that TAAS provided a uniform, objective standard for high school diplomas in Texas, and group disparities were being reduced.

In 2001, however, in *Alexander v. Sandoval*, the Supreme Court ruled five to four that only the federal government and not private individuals may invoke the Title VI regulations that allow disparate impact claims.[79] If *Sandoval* had been decided thirty years ago, hundreds of discrimination cases—many successful—could never have been brought, including the famous *Lau* case and the Title VI part of the 2000 TAAS case. Since *Sandoval*, numerous discrimination cases have been dismissed.

What can private individuals do? They can file complaints with the Department of Education or Department of Justice, which is still authorized to bring disparate impact cases, administratively or in court. In the current climate, however, these agencies are probably less likely than private individuals to challenge testing programs.

Private individuals can also file their own lawsuits, but they must prove that educational policies or practices having adverse impact were motivated at least partly by intent to discriminate. This standard is very hard to meet, and intent claims have consistently been rejected in cases challenging exit tests. Thus, unless Congress overrules *Sandoval*, which is unlikely in the present climate, this decision substantially reduces the likelihood of successful discrimination cases against high-stakes testing programs.

Graduation Testing and Opportunity to Learn

Relying on due-process provisions in the U.S. Constitution, federal courts have ruled that students have a legally protected "property interest" in receiving standard high school diplomas if they have completed their other graduation requirements. Where this property interest exists, courts then examine (1) whether students received sufficient advance notice of the exit test requirements, and (2) whether the exit test is a fair measure of what students have actually been taught.

In the early graduation test cases, which involved basic skills tests, most courts did not inquire deeply into whether students were being taught the requisite knowledge and skills. In *Anderson v. Banks*, where a school official acknowledged that there had been no effort to determine whether students were being taught what the district's exit test measured, the court ruled without discussion that the district could rectify the situation within two years, given the availability of remedial programs and multiple test-taking opportunities.[80] In *Debra P. v. Turlington* (1983), a statewide case in Florida, the court concluded after four years had passed that the test was a fair measure of what students were taught based on (1) evidence that the test measured skills included in the state curriculum, (2) a survey showing that most teachers considered the skills ones they should teach, and (3) evidence that teachers were actually teaching the requisite knowledge and skills in Florida's classrooms.

It would be problematic today, however, for judges to assume that the gaps could be closed so quickly when the gaps are often far greater, when historically excluded groups are increasingly included in high-stakes testing, when numerous indicators show that many states are not yet providing adequate opportunities for student to learn the knowledge and skills they need, and when profound capacity problems have been well defined and documented. And though courts are usually inclined to defer to educators' judgments, some high-stakes testing programs appear to lack a firm foundation in educational research or practice. As Richard Elmore points out, "State policies require proficiency levels for grade promotion and graduation for students . . . without any empirical evidence or any defensible theory about how much it is feasible to expect students to learn over a given period of time or what types of instruction have to be in place in order for students to meet expected rates of improvement."[81] These are matters that call for careful scrutiny.

It is therefore noteworthy that two recent court decisions, both involving students with disabilities, did not explore more thoroughly the issues surrounding whether students had been taught what a state exit test measures.

Rene v. Reed arose in Indiana, which announced in 1997 that most learning-disabled (LD) students would have to pass the state's exit exam in spring 2000 to receive standard diplomas.[82] Previously, students with disabilities had received diplomas if they met their IEP requirements, which often did not track the state standards. In spring 2000, over 1,000 LD students failed the test. The students sued in state court, arguing that their IEPs had not been modified in time for them to learn the knowledge and skills on the graduation test, particularly since they had been behind in 1997. The state argued that students had had sufficient time to prepare in light of remedial programs, opportunities to retake the exam, and the option to remain in school for further instruction after the senior year.

Although recognizing Indiana's legal duty to test only what students had been taught, the judge found it implausible that the LD students had not been exposed to the subjects on the exit test. In reaching this conclusion, the opinion showed little evidence that the court had considered the difficulty of the exit test, students' prior achievement levels, or whether schools had the capacity to provide students with the instruction they needed. The court encouraged students to remain in school after the senior year to receive additional instruction and retake the test.[83]

In California, students with disabilities filed a lawsuit challenging the state exit test, which was first administered in spring 2001 and that at the time, all students in the class of 2004 needed to pass to graduate.[84] (As already noted, California subsequently extended this deadline until spring 2006.) Before the trial began, the students sought a preliminary injunction, an emergency court order, on several matters that they said could not wait until after the trial. One claim was that students with disabilities would not have sufficient time before spring 2004 to learn what the exit test measures.

In February 2002, the court issued detailed orders on issues of testing accommodations and alternative assessments. The court declined, however, to act immediately on the opportunity to learn claim, saying only that "the present state of the evidence does not reveal an asymmetry between what students are taught and [the exit test]."[85]

Because only 10.3 percent of all students with disabilities who took both state tests in spring 2001 passed,[86] there does appear to have been some evidence of asymmetry between what students had been taught and what the exit test then required them to know by spring 2004. The Court of Appeals for the Ninth Circuit was therefore correct when it affirmed this decision, not because there was no asymmetry but because possible delays in the 2004 deadline made the claim premature.[87]

More thorough consideration of opportunity to learn issues would not be without precedent. Early cases held that students with disabilities, like their nondisabled peers, could be denied standard high school diplomas if they failed exit exams—as long as they had received sufficient advance notice and they had already been taught the knowledge and skills that the exam measured.[88] These courts also recognized that students with disabilities would probably need more time than other students to master the requisite knowledge, both because some "learn at a slower rate than regular division students"[89] and because students whose IEPs did not yet reflect the content of the state exit test would have to be taught a substantially different curriculum before they could be expected to pass the state test.

In other words, these courts saw even in the early 1980s that for students with disabilities, opportunity to learn issues could be complex, requiring an inquiry into how far behind students were at the outset, what measures would be needed to align IEPs and instruction with state standards and tests, and how much time these students would need to master the requisite knowledge and skill once schools were equipped to provide the necessary instruction. Similar logic would apply to ELLs and low–socioeconomic status (SES) students, who must also acquire increasingly high-level knowledge and skill whileovercoming different barriers and whose schools often have limited capacity to provide high-quality instruction to these students.

Promotion Testing and Opportunity to Learn

According to the standards of the testing profession, promotion tests (like graduation tests) should cover only the "content and skills that students have had an opportunity to learn."[90] The AERA agrees,[91] as does the Department of Education's Office for Civil Rights.[92]

Nonetheless, most courts that have evaluated promotion tests under the Constitution's due-process clause have taken a different view. As already noted, the due-process claims recognized in *Debra P.* and other cases rest on the view that students have a property interest in receiving a high school diploma. Without this property interest, students would have no claim to remedies such as advance notice of testing or a test that measures only what students have actually been taught.

There have been few reported federal cases involving promotion test policies, and in each the court has upheld promotion testing. Two related rationales emerge. First, courts have drawn a distinction between graduation testing and promotion testing, declining to recognize a property interest in being promoted. As one federal appeals court said about a classroom-based promotion test, "We conclude that *Debra P.* is distinguishable and hold that plaintiffs had no property right [that would justify judicial intervention]."[93] The decision rested, in part, on the court's view that retention in grade is beneficial for low achievers: "A program of retention for students who do not perform satisfactory work is both acceptable and desirable."[94] A more recent decision used similar language in upholding a statewide retention test policy: "[The policy] is designed to help the retained students: a student who is not promoted is given what is, in effect, a remedial year which should allow the student to catch up on the skills that he is lacking and perform better in the future."[95]

Such views are understandable, particularly considering the bipartisan calls to end social promotion. As previously discussed, however, there is powerful social science evidence on the harmful effects of retention. It shows that students who are retained—compared with similar low-performing students who are promoted—are likely to have lower academic achievement, impaired social development, and a much greater likelihood of dropping out.[96] Moreover, some critics of social promotion are equally critical of retention in grade, finding early intervention strategies preferable to both.

Courts presented with this research might conclude that a student does have a property interest in avoiding retention. A student's interest in avoiding retention is certainly greater than the interest in avoiding a short-term suspension from school, in which courts have long recognized a property interest. If such a property interest in avoiding retention were recognized, presumably students would also have a right to advance notice and a test that measures only what they have been taught.

At present, however, students probably cannot count on courts to support them in opportunity to learn cases involving promotion tests.

CONCLUSION

Evidence presented here shows that minority students, students with disabilities, and ELLs are failing some state tests, especially those that reflect high standards, at rates higher than 50 percent; disparate impact often declines slowly; and failure rates would be higher if states took into account students who have dropped out, been retained, or been excluded improperly from testing. This chapter also presents powerful evidence from leading scholars that many students are not yet being taught the knowledge and skills that current high-stakes tests measure.

Low-achieving students need high-quality instruction more than anyone else, and there is little question that data from large-scale assessments, if used properly, can help improve instruction, hold schools accountable for improved achievement, and identify and address students' learning needs. It is a tragedy that so many of these students have been ill-served by their schools for so long, and it will be a welcome change when states and schools aspire to educate all students to high standards.

At the same time, where demanding tests have high stakes for individual students, minority students, students with disabilities, ELLs, and low-SES students are at heightened risk of suffering the serious, well-documented harms associated with grade retention and denial of high school diplomas. It would be a great loss if high-stakes testing policies operated to deny diplomas to large numbers of these students or subject them to the serious harms of retention. It would be unfortunate if states and schools used high-stakes tests in ways that punished students for not knowing what their schools had never taught them.

Principles of law and measurement hold that high-stakes tests should only measure what students have already been taught, and there should be ways of ensuring that high-stakes tests are used properly.

But the measurement profession does not enforce its own rules of appropriate test use, and the law is limited in the protections it affords. The

Supreme Court has closed off for now the chief route by which individuals have challenged educational policies and practices that have adverse impact by race, national origin, and language. Federal courts have thus far been unsympathetic to lawsuits challenging promotion testing, perhaps because they are unfamiliar with powerful research, now widely accepted, on the negative effects of grade retention.

In reviewing future legal challenges, courts will have to evaluate circumstances markedly different from those associated with early minimum competency tests. Fortunately, much more is understood today about the human and social consequences of inappropriate test use, about what school improvement requires, and about how educators can help all students acquire high-level knowledge and skills. Educators and researchers who understand these complex issues well can help judges as they attempt to apply and modify legal precedents and principles in light of dramatically changed educational objectives and of realities that have been slower to change.

NOTES

1. Keith Gayler, Naomi Chudowsky, Nancy Kober, and Madlene Hamilton, *State High School Exit Exams Put to the Test* (Washington, DC: Center on Education Policy, 2003).

2. Ibid. The eleven Southern states with exit exams in 2003 were Alabama, Florida, Georgia, Louisiana, Maryland, Mississippi, North Carolina, South Carolina, Tennessee, Texas, and Virginia.

3. Ibid.

4. American Federation of Teachers, *Making Standards Matter 2001: A 50-State Report on Efforts to Implement a Standards System* (Washington, DC: American Federation of Teachers, 2001).

5. No Child Left Behind Act of 2001, Public Law 107–110, January 8, 2002; Richard F. Elmore, *Building a New Structure for School Leadership* (Washington, DC: Albert Shanker Institute, 2000); Individuals with Disabilities Education Act, 20 U.S.C. section 1401 et. seq. (1997).

6. Gayler et al., *State High School Exit Exams*.

7. Lauress Wise, D. E. Sipes, Carolyn DeMeyer Harris, Carol E. George, J. Patrick Ford, and Shaobang Sun, *Independent Evaluation of the California High School Exit Examination (CAHSEE): Analysis of the 2001 Administration* (Sacramento: California Department of Education, 2002).

8. Gayler et al., *State High School Exit Exams*.

9. John Gehring, "States Open Fiscal Year on Shaky Ground," *Education Week* (August 6, 2003): 24, 29; Mary Ann Zehr, "Once 'Sacred,' School Aid Falls Prey to Budget Cuts, NCSL Report Finds," *Education Week* (May 7, 2003): 22.

10. American Federation of Teachers, "Making Standards Matter 2001."

11. Ibid.

12. Gayler et al., *State High School Exit Exams.*

13. Sean F. Reardon, "Eighth-Grade Minimum Competency Testing and Early High School Dropout Patterns," paper presented at the annual meeting of the American Educational Research Association, New York, NY, April 1996.

14. Individuals with Disabilities Education Act; Improving America's Schools Act, 20 U.S.C. sections 6301 et seq. (1994).

15. Martha Thurlow, "Biting the Bullet: Including Special Needs Students in Accountability Systems," in Susan H. Fuhrman and Richard F. Elmore (eds.), *Redesigning Accountability Systems for Education* (New York: Teachers College Press, 2004), 115–137.

16. Jay Heubert, "Disability, Race, and High-Stakes Testing of Students," in Daniel J. Losen and Gary Orfield (eds.), *Racial Inequity in Special Education* (Cambridge, MA: Harvard Education Publishing Group, 2002), 123–152.

17. Alexandra Beatty, Ulric Neisser, William T. Trent, and Jay P. Heubert (eds.), *Understanding Dropouts: Statistics, Strategies, and High-Stakes Testing* (Washington, DC: National Academies Press, 2001).

18. Individuals with Disabilities Education Act.

19. Eva Baker and Robert Linn, "Validity Issues for Accountability Systems," in Susan H. Fuhrman and Richard F. Elmore (eds.), *Redesigning Accountability Systems for Education* (New York: Teachers College Press, 2004).

20. Richard Murnane and Frank Levy, "Will Standards-Based Reforms Improve the Education of Children of Color?" *National Tax Journal* 54, no. 2 (2001): 401.

21. William Taylor, "Standards, Tests, and Civil Rights," *Education Week* (November 20, 2000): 56.

22. Jay Heubert and Robert M. Hauser, *High Stakes: Testing for Tracking, Promotion, and Graduation* (Washington, DC: National Academy Press, 1999).

23. No Child Left Behind Act of 2001, 107–110; Richard F. Elmore and Robert Rothman, *Testing, Teaching, and Learning: A Guide for States and School Districts* (Washington, DC: National Academy Press, 1999).

24. Susan Fuhrman, M. Goertz, and M. Duffy, "Slow Down, You Move Too Fast: The Politics of Changing High Stakes Accountability Policies for Students," in Susan H. Fuhrman and Richard F. Elmore (eds.), *Redesigning Accountability Systems for Education* (New York: Teachers College Press, 2004), 245–273.

25. Heubert and Hauser, *High Stakes.*

26. Richard F. Elmore, "The Problem of Stakes in Performance-Based Accountability Systems," in Susan H. Fuhrman and Richard F. Elmore (eds.), *Redesigning Accountability Systems for Education* (New York: Teachers College Press, 2004), 275–296.

27. *Debra P. v. Turlington,* 474 F. Supp. 244 (M.D. Fla. 1979); aff'd in part and rev'd in part, 644 F.2d 397 (5th Cir. 1981); rem'd, 564 F. Supp. 177 (M.D. Fla. 1983); aff'd, 730 F.2d 1405 (11th Cir. 1984).

28. Robert Linn, "Assessments and Accountability," *Educational Researcher* 29, no. 2 (2000): 4–16.

29. Brian A. Jacob, "Getting Tough? The Impact of High School Graduation Exams," *Educational Evaluation and Policy Analysis* 23, no. 3 (2001): 99–122.

30. Office for Civil Rights, *The Use of Tests When Making High-Stakes Decisions for Students: A Resource Guide for Educators and Policymakers* (Washington, DC: U.S. Department of Education, 2000).

31. *G.I. Forum v. Texas Education Agency*, 87 F. Supp. 2d 667 (W.D. Tex. 2000).

32. P. Schrag, "Too Good to Be True," *American Prospect* 4, no. 11 (2000): 46.

33. Stephen P. Klein, Laura S. Hamilton, Daniel F. McCaffrey, and Brian M. Stecher, *What Do Test Scores in Texas Tell Us?* (Santa Monica, CA: RAND, 2000); Robert Linn, *The Design and Evaluation of Educational Assessment and Accountability Systems* (Los Angeles: National Center for Research on Evaluation, Standards, and Student Testing, University of California, 2001).

34. Gary Natriello and Aaron Pallas, "The Development and Impact of High-Stakes Testing," in Gary Orfield and Mindy L. Kornhaber (eds.), *Raising Standards or Raising Barriers: Inequality and High-stakes Testing in Public Education* (New York: Century Foundation, 2001), 19–38.

35. *G.I. Forum v. Texas Education Agency.*

36. Florida Dept. of Education, *School Diploma, Certificate, and GED Report*, October 2003.

37. Natriello and Pallas, "The Development and Impact of High-Stakes Testing."

38. Fuhrman et al., "Slow Down, You Move Too Fast."

39. California Dept. of Education, *Class of 2004: Estimated Overall Cumulative Passing Rates for the California High School Exit Examination (CAHSEE), March 2001 through May 2002* (May 2002).

40. Wise et al., *Independent Evaluation.*

41. Linn, "Assessments and Accountability."

42. James E. Ysseldyke, Martha Thurlow, Karen L. Langenfeld, J. Ruth Nelson, Ellen Teelucksingh, and Allison Seyfarth, *Educational Results for Students with Disabilities: What Do the Data Tell Us?* (Minneapolis, MN: National Center on Educational Outcomes, 1998); Martha Thurlow, J. Ruth Nelson, Ellen Teelucksingh, and James E. Ysseldyke, *Where's Waldo: A Third Search for Students with Disabilities in State Accountability Reports* (Minneapolis, MN: National Center on Educational Outcomes, 2000).

43. Massachusetts Department of Education, *Spring 2001 MCAS Tests: State Results by Race/Ethnicity and Student Status* (Boston: Massachusetts Department of Education, 2001); I am grateful to Jeffrey Nellhaus, Mass. Dept. of Education, who graciously provided data on students with disabilities and ELLs.

44. Massachusetts Department of Education, *Progress Report on Students Attaining the Competency Determination Statewide and by District: Classes of 2003 and 2004* (Boston: Massachusetts Department of Education, 2003).

45. Using state enrollment figures, Wheelock estimates an overall on-time graduation rate of 73.3 percent rather than the state's reported 95 percent, and the following on-time graduation rates for different groups: for Whites, 78.1 percent rather than the state's reported 97 percent; for African Americans, 60.9 percent rather than 86 percent; for Latinos, 46.2 percent rather than 83 percent. (Anne Wheelock, e-mail communication to Heubert, October 6, 2003.) How important a role the graduation test plays in such attrition is the subject of debate.

46. Bess Keller, "More New York Special Education Students Passing State Tests," *Education Week* (April 12, 2000): 33.

47. New York Department of Education, Office of Vocational and Educational Services for Students with Disabilities, *2000 Pocket Book of Goals and Results for Individuals with Disabilities* (Albany: New York Department of Education, 2000);

New York Department of Education, Office of Vocational and Educational Services for Students with Disabilities, *2002 Pocket Book of Goals and Results for Individuals with Disabilities* (Albany: New York Department of Education, 2001).

48. Daniel Koretz and Laura Hamilton, *The Performance of Students with Disabilities on New York's Revised Regents Examination in English* (Los Angeles: National Center for Research on Evaluation, Standards, and Student Testing, University of California, 2001).

49. "NAEP achievement," *Education Week* 20, no. 45 (August 8, 2001): 24.

50. Klein et al., *What Do Test Scores in Texas Tell Us?*

51. *G.I. Forum v. Texas Education Agency.*

52. Linn, *The Design and Evaluation of Educational Assessment and Accountability Systems*, 28.

53. National Center for Education Statistics, *The Condition of Education 2001* (Washington, DC: National Center for Education Statistics, 2001).

54. Jaekyung Lee, "Racial and Ethnic Achievement Gap Trends: Reversing the Progress toward Equity?" *Educational Researcher* 31, no. 1 (2002): 3–12.

55. Murnane and Levy, "Will Standards-Based Reforms Improve the Education of Children of Color?"

56. Wise et al., *Independent Evaluation*, 45.

57. Jacob, "Getting Tough?" 116.

58. Robert M. Hauser, "Should We End Social Promotion? Truth and Consequences," in Gary Orfield and Mindy L. Kornhaber (eds.), *Raising Standards or Raising Barriers? Inequality and High-Stakes Testing in Public Education* (New York: Century Fund, 2001), 151–178; Heubert and Hauser, *High Stakes.*

59. Pete Goldschmidt and Jia Wang, "When Can Schools Affect Dropout Behavior? A Longitudinal Multilevel Analysis," *American Educational Research Journal* 36, no. 5 (1999): 715–738; Dean Lillard and Phillip DeCicca, "Higher Standards, More Dropouts? Evidence within and across Time," *Economics of Education Review* 20, no. 5 (2001): 459–474.

60. Heubert and Hauser, *High Stakes.*

61. Improving America's Schools Act; Individuals with Disabilities Education Act; No Child Left Behind Act.

62. *Debra P. v. Turlington*; *G.I. Forum v. Texas Education Agency.*

63. Wise et al., *Independent Evaluation*, 93 (emphasis in original).

64. Susan H. Fuhrman, "Conclusion," in Susan H. Fuhrman (ed.), *From the Capitol to the Classroom: Standards-Based Reform in the States* (Chicago: University of Chicago Press, National Society for the Study of Education, 2001), 263–278.

65. Thurlow, "Biting the Bullet."

66. Citizens' Commission on Civil Rights, *Closing the Deal: A Preliminary Report on State Compliance with Final Assessment and Accountability Requirements under the Improving America's Schools Act of 1994* (Washington, DC: Citizens' Commission on Civil Rights, 2001); E. Robelin, "States Sluggish on Execution of 1994 ESEA," *Education Week* (November 28, 2001): 1, 26, 27; Michael Cohen, *Review of State Assessment Systems for Title I.* Memorandum to Chief State School Officers from the Assistant Secretary for Elementary and Secondary Education, U.S. Department of Education (January 19, 2001).

67. Baker and Linn, "Alignment," 1–3.

68. Eva Baker and Robert Linn, "Alignment: Policy Goals, Policy Strategies, and Policy Outcomes," *CRESST Line* (Winter 2000): 1–3.

69. Andrew C. Porter and John L. Smithson, "Alignment of State Testing Programs, NAEP, and Reports of Teacher Practice in Grades 4 and 8," paper presented at the annual meeting of the American Educational Research Association, New Orleans, LA, April 2000.

70. Rolf K. Blank, Andrew Porter, and John Smithson, *New Tools for Analyzing Teaching, Curriculum, and Standards in Mathematics and Science: Results from Survey of Enacted Curriculum Project Final Report* (Washington, DC: Council of Chief State School Officers, 2001).

71. Richard F. Elmore, "Unwarranted Intrusion," *Education Next* (Palo Alto, CA: Hoover Institution, 2002). Available online at www.educationnext.org/20021/ 30.html. Accessed August 1, 2005.

72. Murnane and Levy, "Will Standards-Based Reforms Improve the Education of Children of Color?" 411.

73. Ibid.; Helen Ladd, "Briefing for the U.S. Civil Rights Commission." paper delivered at a hearing of the U.S. Commission on Civil Rights, Charlotte, NC, February 6, 2003.

74. Margaret J. McLaughlin, *Reform for Every Learner: Teachers' Views on Standards and Students with Disabilities* (Alexandria, VA: Center for Policy Research on the Impact of General and Special Education Reform, 2000).

75. Don Dailey, Kathy Zantal-Wiener, and Virginia Roach, *Reforming High School Learning: The Effect of the Standards Movement on Secondary Students with Disabilities* (Alexandria, VA: Center for Policy Research on the Impact of General and Special Education Reform, 2000).

76. Other legal issues, although important, are beyond the scope of this chapter.

77. American Education Research Association, *AERA Position Statement Concerning High-stakes Testing in Pre-K-12 Education* (Washington, DC: AERA, 2000). Available online at www.aera.net.about/policy/stakes.htm. Accessed August 1, 2005; AERA, American Psychological Association (APA), and National Council on Measurement in Education (NCME), *Standards for Educational and Psychological Testing.* (Washington, DC: AERA, APA, and NCME, 1999).

78. Heubert and Hauser, *High Stakes.*

79. *Alexander v. Sandoval,* 532 U.S. 275 (2001).

80. *Anderson v. Banks,* 540 F. Supp. 472 (S.D. Ga. 1981).

81. Elmore, "The Problem of Stakes."

82. *Rene v. Reed,* 751 N.E.2d 736 (Ind. App. 2001).

83. Because this litigation involved a request for a preliminary injunction—a court order issued *before* a full hearing in court—the Indiana courts could still reach a different result after trial, though that is unlikely given the strong language in which the courts rejected students' due-process claims. An Indiana appeals court affirmed the decision.

84. *Chapman v. California Department of Education,* No C. 01-01780 CRB, Preliminary Injunction (N.D. Cal. February 21, 2002).

85. Ibid., 9.

86. Wise et al., *Independent Evaluation.*

87. *Smiley v. California Dept. of Education*, U.S. App. LEXIS 26516 (9th Cir. Dec. 19, 2002).

88. *Brookhart v. Illinois State Board of Education*, 697 F. 2d 179 (7th Cir. 1983); *Board of Education v. Ambach*, 436 N.Y.S.2d 564 (N.Y. 1981).

89. *Brookhart v. Illinois State Board of Education*, 187.

90. AERA, APA, and NCME, *Standards for Educational and Psychological Testing*, 146.

91. AERA, *AERA Position Statement*.

92. Office for Civil Rights, *The Use of Tests*, 20.

93. *Bester v. Tuscaloosa Bd. of Education*, 722 F.2d 1514 (11th Cir. 1984).

94. Ibid, 7.

95. *Erik V. v. Causby*, 977 F. Supp. 384 (E.D.N.C. 1997). Another circuit court, apparently in an unpublished opinion, recently rejected due-process claims in connection with a Louisiana state promotion test; Brian Thevenot, "Students Who Fail LEAP Can Be Held Back," *Times-Picayune* (September 18, 2001): 1.

96. Hauser, "Should We End Social Promotion?"; Heubert and Hauser, *High Stakes*.

Whole Schooling As a Framework for Antiracist Education

Michael Peterson

INTRODUCTION

How do we create schools that are not, by their nature, racist? Perhaps we must begin by asking the question a different way: "How can we create schools that value diverse voices, experiences, abilities, and cultures and support diverse children in their learning and growth?" It is this latter question that a growing network of individuals and schools around the world associated with the Whole Schooling Consortium have been exploring since its inception in 1997. Expressing the question this way has advantages and some dangers. On one hand, the advantage is that it seeks to identify positive theories, practices, and solutions rather than getting lost in the complexities and hurt of the problem. Problems provide a backdrop but are not the point of focus. On the other hand, there is always the potential when

This chapter is based on an adaptation of the following three documents: Michael Peterson, *Whole Schooling: Six Principles for Effective Schooling* (Detroit, MI: Whole Schooling Consortium, 2005). Available online at www.wholeschooling.net; Michael Peterson, "Whole Schooling: An Inclusive Framework for School Renewal and Professional Inquiry," paper presented at the Inclusive and Supportive Education Conference, Glasgow, Scotland, 2005; and Michael Peterson, "Inclusive School Renewal," paper presented at the Annual Conference of the Association for Supervision and Curriculum Development, 2005.

using positive language of simply using this as a screen to ignore difficult and painful realities.

Part of the difficulty in developing proactive answers to this question is its complexity and the tendency to focus dialogue in schools around two themes—curriculum and instruction, or what is taught and how. These are huge areas of endeavor. However, they ignore an equally important foundation—the social and emotional underpinnings of the culture of the school as it impacts directly on the experiences and sensed welfare of children. Of course, antiracism work seeks directly to address this need. But the need to address racism is embedded in and connected to many other issues of social and emotional support that include

- Identification and labeling of children as having disabilities, being gifted, or at risk
- Segregating such children from the larger school population
- Marginalizing students for a wide range of reasons—sexual preference, personality, social skills, race, culture, disability, and more
- Intolerance and periodic cruelty by adults to children who may be struggling

To seek to address racism without simultaneously building a culture of support for all children is difficult, if not impossible. This chapter, therefore, describes an approach to envisioning a school that is effective for all children, a framework called *whole schooling*. Toward this end, I start with a discussion of the purpose of schooling that must provide the foundation for any consideration of how schools should be. I then discuss principles and practices for both ineffective and effective schools for all children—principles and practices that provide a foundation to counteract racism and build support and respect for all children.

THE PURPOSE OF SCHOOLING

Somehow most people think they know the purpose of schools—to help children learn and grow. All who discuss the purpose of schools affirm this goal of personal development. However, when the question is asked: "to what end?" and, furthermore, when you ask, "how do you know if you are successful?," very different answers emerge. Two primary opposing views exist. Some believe the purpose should center on *citizenship*, helping children develop their own capacity for success in life and becoming effective citizens for democracy—individuals who have skills, attitudes, and knowledge to be productive community members, leaders, parents, and workers. This stands in sharp contrast to those who believe the ultimate purpose of schools is to create workers who can meet the standards of industry. The problem is that most people when asked this question will agree that we should be educating children to be citizens and to become the people that they can be. However, in practice, present systems of standardized testing work directly against these outcomes, narrowing the focus and curriculum of schools.

In the United States, the oft-stated purpose of schools, embedded in federal legislation and found in most mission statements of school systems, is to create thinking citizens who can make decisions and effectively engage in multiple adult roles—community leader, parent, worker. If this is so, research demonstrates clearly that classroom practice must systematically and explicitly provide students the opportunity to make choices, solve problems among a group, develop consensus, and deal with conflict. In such classrooms, students of great differences can all have an effective voice, students are motivated to learn as they develop a sense of ownership of a classroom community, and students are allowed and taught how to use power in their personal lives. Particularly for students with many life challenges who may have little control in their home lives, giving students power and control in the classroom can both prevent problematic behaviors and promote higher levels of learning.[1]

PERSONAL BEST LEARNING

This brings us, then, to thinking about how learning is structured and how we go about deciding the question: "Was schooling effective?" Three different approaches are described in table 6-1. The traditional model of schooling posits that we teach all students the same content in the same way. We expect some to do well and some to fail and consider this the problem of the student, not of the educator. This approach has been problematic in that some students do not learn well and there are no expectations that it will be otherwise. This has been particularly problematic related to students of color and low-income students.

More recently, throughout the world, standards-based reform has established a new approach purportedly to address the problems of the traditional model. In this approach, all minimal standards of performance are set, typically as a score on a standardized test, that all students are expected

Table 6-1   Differing Approaches to Learning Goals and Evaluation of Schools

Same Teaching for All *Accept different outcomes*	Same Standard for All *Expect same outcomes for all*	Personal Best Learning *Expect different outcomes based on individualized excellence*
Develop curriculum strands across subjects guiding curriculum content.	Establish expectations of academic facts and knowledge for every age and grade level organized around traditional academic subjects—reading, writing, math, social studies, and science.	Develop outcome goals for students that reflect the overall purpose of schools—citizenship, academic skills, social-emotional abilities, and character. Develop strands for curriculum content across and linking subjects
Provide the same instruction for all students.	Expect students to achieve these standards regardless of ability, background, or prior knowledge.	Expect students to make ongoing growth and progress, starting with present understanding and deepening and widening.
Assessment is based on the ability of the school to provide equal educational experiences to all students.	All students will take a standardized test as a measure of identified skills and content knowledge.	All students will be assessed to determine individual progress. Schoolwide reporting systems may be developed to reflect this.

to achieve despite their differing ability levels. In this system, a student who is considered highly gifted and a student with a cognitive disability are expected to achieve at the same level. Schools, then, are evaluated based on their ability to achieve such equal outcomes for all students. The problems of this model, however, are substantial. Having one standard for all ensures that some students, the most capable, learn beneath their capacity and other students, even though they work hard and learn a great deal, will be considered failures.

Whole schooling posits a more effective model than either of these: personal best learning. In this model, we expect all students to achieve at their personal best level and for ongoing instruction to recognize where students are and engage them in learning using multiple modalities, approaches, and supports to move to the next level. In this scenario, a student would be considered successful if he or she were making progress and meeting learning goals. We would have very different expectations of highly gifted students and students with cognitive disabilities in, say, American history class though they may be working on similar content in that class. In this scheme, we would evaluate schools based on (a) their ability to create instructional environments that support personal best and just right learning challenges without segregating students by ability, race, culture, language, or other variables, and (b) the achievement of higher learning outcomes appropriate for each student.

Why is personal best learning important for antiracist education? Both the traditional and standards-based reform models have distinctly negative impacts on students of various races and cultures, particularly when there is an interaction between socioeconomic status and race. The standards-based movement, with its emphasis on standardized testing in selected curriculum areas is being shown to deemphasize a focus on the whole child and the importance of building a social-emotional foundation in the culture of the school. A personalized, multilevel approach to learning has the potential to strengthen an appreciation of diversity on many dimensions, thus strengthening the celebration rather than the functional punishment of various forms of diversity.

CREATING SCHOOL CULTURES THAT SUPPORT HIGH LEARNING FOR ALL

How can schools be designed to help create high levels of learning among students that increase individual opportunity? How can schools help children become citizens for democracy, providing social, business, and community leadership to develop innovations and solve important problems. We must pay very close attention to what helps and what hurts in reaching these important ends.

Many schools, particularly those that serve working-class and lower-income children, use practices that ensure that many children fail and are left behind. It is as if such schools systemically and explicitly developed a school *deform* plan, to use the language of James Kauffman.[2] What are the principles that guide practices of such schools? They are listed in the left column in table 6-2.

These practices work together to create conditions that hamper the learning process. Once such cultures become embedded, they are difficult to

Table 6-2   Contrasting Principles of Ineffective and Effective Schools for Diverse
            Children

Principles of Schools Designed to Leave Many Children Behind	Whole Schooling Principles: Supporting All Children in Learning Well Together
1. Demand compliance and obedience *of staff and students.*	1. Empower citizens for democracy.
2. Segregate, track, and ability group.	2. Include all in learning well together.
3. Teach to the middle using one *size fits all instruction.*	3. Provide authentic multilevel instruction.
4. Create a culture of pressure, tension, and competition.	4. Build community.
5. Isolate adults and ensure professional turf.	5. Support learning.
6. Parents and school staff blame one another.	6. Partner with parents and the community.

change. But change can and must occur if we are to meet the promise to our children and create future citizen leaders for our communities. What are the principles that describe a school culture that supports high levels of learning for all? They are listed in the right column in table 6-2.

After several years of work, I have collaborated with colleagues to develop six principles that represent a simple but comprehensive synthesis of scientific research on practices designed to maximize learning at high levels. Each of these principles is interactive and mutually reinforcing. These six principles of whole schooling establish a culture and set of practices in schools and classrooms that promote learning and growth. We know that for learning to occur, children must feel safe, accepted, a sense of belonging, and cared for. Including heterogeneous students in classes together is a critical component as is the practice of democracy—systematic sharing of power within the school and classroom. Support to teachers and students and partnering with parents and the community help fill out the picture of social, emotional, physical, and cognitive support needed for high levels of achievement. Although the language of school focuses primarily on instruction and the academic subjects of school—reading, writing, math, science, and more—without attention to these foundation building blocks, learning will falter. These relationships are illustrated in figure 6-1. Following, I describe in greater detail how ineffective and effective principles play out in schools and classrooms.

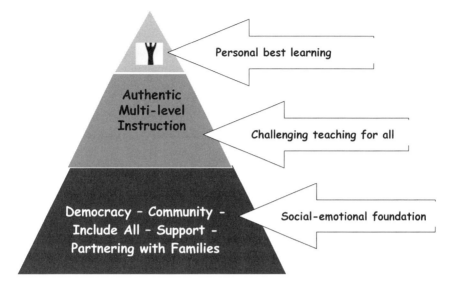

Figure 6-1   Whole Schooling Pyramid of Support for Learning

BUILDING THE SOCIAL AND EMOTIONAL FOUNDATION

Building Community

Too many schools in both low-income urban areas and high-income suburbs become places of competition, social sorting, and ranking. Some schools actually institutionalize such dynamics by listing test scores in rank order of all students in the school. The growth of zero tolerance policies, particularly in low-income urban schools, contributes to this dynamic. In an effort to create safe schools, such policies may become methods of expressing intolerance for and lack of concern with students who demonstrate behavioral challenges. Such school cultures minimize attention to helping students learn skills to deal with internal feelings of anger and hurt and interpersonal conflict.[3]

What is needed instead is a schoolwide focus on building a sense of community and care, using multiple strategies to assist students in providing help to one another and positive behavioral support strategies based on an ongoing commitment to challenging students when difficulties occur. In his testimony to Congress, Sugai listed a number of basic features of systematic support for ensuring appropriate behavior in schools.[4] Two of these were integration of academic and behavioral support for all students:

- The application of evidence-based behavioral practices and systems promotes academic engagement and achievement, and the use of empirically supported instructional practices and systems promotes displays of prosocial student behavior and creates safe classroom and school settings.
- All students in a school should have access to positive, preventive, structured, and ongoing opportunities to learn, practice, and be acknowledged for displays of prosocial schoolwide and individual social skills.

If schools are to work for all, students must receive instruction and support in social, emotional, and behavioral learning to support academic growth. For such individual learning to occur, a true community of learners is necessary to provide a context and environment in which such learning is part of the day-to-day, minute-to-minute experience.

Brain research has clearly documented the importance for learning of a sense of emotional safety and support. As Caine and Caine state, for effective learning to occur students must experience a "relaxed state of alertness."[5] Alertness is promoted by instruction that is engaging and at the level of the learner, and a relaxed state occurs when a student feels a sense of belonging in the group, caring by the teacher, acceptance by other students, and a lack of anger, tension, competition, or humiliation. Numerous concrete strategies have been documented that have shown substantial impact on a sense of community in the classroom and subsequent impacts on learning.[6] In a classroom and school that systemically builds a community of learners many behavioral problems are prevented.

Horrocks, both an academic and a classroom teacher, stated that

classroom community is built through developing a sense of shared history by creating opportunities for shared experiences. It is about the basic things:

- Shared story time
- Collaborative writing
- Singing with your group
- Field trips
- Watching a slide show of the activities your class did this week
- Establishing routines at the beginning and end of the day and week
- Enlisting students help in the managing of the class
- Shared decision-making
- Future planning

- Initiating reflective discussions
- Celebrating accomplishments
- Three before me
- Kids helping kids before depending on service relationships
- Developing buddy systems and critical friends and learning pods
- Kids undertake the rituals of welcoming and bidding farewell.[7]

In such a school, behavior problems are much less frequent. Children feel cared for, have choices, and do not feel constrained, yet are intentionally taught responsibility in the process. However, many students with high needs continue to challenge teachers. Positive behavioral support strategies have proven valuable in helping such students develop alternative means for having their needs met.[8] Rather than viewing children as needing to be controlled, teachers understand that all behavior communicates a message. When a child acts out, this is his or her way of telling staff about something they need. The challenge is to help figure out what that need is and help them learn alternative strategies for meeting it. Glasser described five needs of human beings that can provide a way to understand children: (1) survival, (2) love and belonging, (3) power, (4) fun, and (5) freedom. Most often, schools ignore many of these needs and actually create behavior problems in their attempt to thwart children having these needs met.[9]

Schools that have successfully supported children with behavioral, emotional, and life challenges have developed numerous strategies for assisting support such students. Most critical is a several step process based on a functional assessment of behavior—discerning the underlying needs a particular behavior is expressing and developing strategies to help the child have this need met in more proactive and socially responsive ways.

School staff can do other things to deal with problematic behavior in a positive way. Some of these include

- Dialoguing and joint planning with the parents
- Creating a room where the child can go, under supervision, when he needs a break to deal with emotional stress. This can be the library, a support room, or a more private location in the class, like under the teacher's desk.
- Building social support for the child. Get a circle of support together of classmates who together plan with the child and teacher how to provide help and support.
- Doing a "meeting needs audit" of the total school to determine how well the school is meeting the five needs identified by Glasser for children in the building; developing a range of activities that may address discrepancies.

Empowering Citizens for Democracy

It is well documented that in too many schools serving low-income children, a culture of staff anger toward both children and parents is often pervasive. Low expectations, difficulties with behavior management, and problems with parental connections all contribute to problems in learning and effective relationships among, children, and school staff. In such cultures, the tendency is to use approaches that attempt to highly regulate and control the behavior of students in the school.[10] For example, in such schools students are expected to sit quietly at their desks and work and raise their hands to make simple movements in the class; in elementary school, students are marched in regulated lines from class to class; in high schools, security guards check students coming into school and periodically make sweeps and searches of lockers looking for prohibited items.

The result is that in these schools democratic processes where students and staff alike have a sense of input, control, and choice in their daily routines is limited or virtually nonexistent.[11] A cycle of control and challenge is born that dramatically reduces learning about responsibility and citizenship, increases anger and the need of students to challenge what they see as repressive authority, and sets in place emotions and tensions that reduce learning.[12]

Such schools tend to have higher referral rates for special education, as segregation and exclusion are added as tools of control.[13] In schools across socioeconomic spectrums, however, the norm of segregated special education classes is to limit also opportunities for choice, control, and power in the classroom with similar outcomes as in low-income schools. While the tone is one of beneficence and care rather than repression, student initiative is often similarly impaired.

A school that seeks to prepare children to be citizens in a democracy must embed the living and modeling of democracy. This occurs at the three levels of interactions and decision making among (1) school staff, (2) parents and the local community, and (3) children and educators in classrooms. Although children experience this primarily in the classroom itself, it is difficult to establish democratic classroom instruction when shared decision making and a sense of community are not present among adult staff in the school and between educators, parents, and community members. In such a context, however, children starting at the youngest ages may be afforded numerous opportunities for learning the substantive skills of democracy. These include but are not limited to

- Helping students understand their individual and collective rights and responsibilities
- Creating class meetings
- Writing class agreements
- Formulating a class code of conduct
- Recognizing that everyone belongs to a culture group—multicultural education is for all because diversity makes us better
- Emphasizing individual responsibility for removing barriers that marginalize
- Cultivating the skills of problem solving and conflict resolution[14]

Including All in Learning Together

Segregation and isolation create many problems for many students in schools. Low-income minority students in urban areas are at higher risk for referral for special education, and alternative schools are used for an increasing number of students who are considered have behavioral problems and are socially maladjusted. The President's Commission on Excellence in Special Education found substantive problems with the segregation of students with disabilities. One key finding was stated as follows:

> This Commission . . . is deeply concerned that many children with severe disabilities, including those children with autism or emotional disturbance, are relegated to segregated educational settings simply because of their disability. Despite decades of successful inclusion of children with disabilities in regular schools . . . , there are children with disabilities who are still segregated simply because their disability creates difficulties in providing integrated educational experiences. [15]

The commission further directly stressed educating all students within general education settings, including those with severe disabilities.

> Major Recommendation 3: Consider children with disabilities as general education children first: Special education and general education are treated as separate systems, but in fact share responsibility for the child with disabilities. In instruction, the systems must work together to provide effective teaching and ensure that those with additional needs benefit from strong teaching and instructional methods that should be offered to a child through general education.[16]

Overrepresentation of students of color in special education has been relatedly recognized as a critical issue, a factor crucial in urban areas. Losen and Orfield's recently edited book clearly describes these patterns.[17] Black students are three times as likely to be labeled as having mental retardation and twice as likely to be labeled emotionally disturbed as White students, although far fewer such students are identified as gifted and talented than expected. Research shows that being served in special education does not lead to improved outcomes, and minority students are more likely than White students to be served in segregated educational settings.[18]

For high levels of learning to occur for all students, developing inclusive classrooms is necessary, not optional. The literature is clear that for students with and without disabilities, integrated and inclusive classes are associated with higher levels of academic achievement.[19] Orfield and Gordon note that for students to become effective leaders in a multicultural society, schooling must provide opportunities to engage students with diverse racial, ethnic, and ability characteristics.[20] The sense of community and social safety promoted in inclusive classes as well as respect for diverse abilities and characteristics provide an emotional foundation that allows brain functioning at the highest levels, preventing the downward shifts when fear and rejection are prevalent. Diversity represented in inclusive classrooms provides a stimulus and challenge to deep thinking that occurs less in segregated classes.[21]

The school and staff together make a commitment that all students should be welcomed into the school and that teachers and other staff will work to have inclusive classes, heterogeneously grouped where students who are gifted through severely disabled learn, play, and work together. For this to occur and become part of the culture of the school, the total staff must be committed to this as a value for children; be able to articulate the reasons for their belief; be willing to defend this practice against detractors; and be willing to struggle, learn, and seek answers when it doesn't seem to be working for a particular child.

In most schools, this will mean shifting special education, gifted, at-risk, and other students from separate classes into general education; identifying the students who are presently in separate special education, gifted, or other schools who would typically attend the school and invite them back; and redesigning the role of specialists to provide support for inclusive teaching.

Collaboration and Support for Learning

If schools are to be successful, a professional community of support among teachers is necessary as well. Typically, teaching is an isolated and isolating profession. This is particularly problematic when teachers are dealing with children with many life challenges. If teachers do not have support in the class or forums for dialogue, communication, sharing, and problem solving, it is all too easy for frustrations to develop and students with high needs to become targets.[22] In many urban schools, as is the case in most schools in the Detroit area, specialized resources are used for special classes and schools or pull-out resource rooms, further isolating students and providing general education teachers little help and assistance, thus contributing to these problematic dynamics.[23]

In a school committed to high levels of learning for all students, research has shown that specialists and support staff develop an effective, collaborative, transdisciplinary support system for teachers, students, and families. Such schools use specialized school and community resources (special education, Title I, gifted education) to strengthen the general education classroom, developing support teams to assist with academic, social, and medical needs.[24]

Supporting teachers in working with students at multiple ability levels or have emotional and social challenges in their lives is critical. This is particularly important as the shift toward building an inclusive culture in the school is occurring. Teachers who are used to trying to teach at only one level have difficulty figuring out how to teach at multiple levels. Even teachers who do this well sometimes don't know that they do or what is multilevel and what is not.

A range of specialists are available to most schools to deal with special needs and problems of children—social workers, special education teachers, bilingual teachers, psychologists, nurses, occupational therapists, speech therapists, and others. In a traditional school, most of these people work on their own with limited consultation with others and pull children out of class for various services. In an effective school, however, specialists work to support the general education classroom teacher. Furthermore, they work as a *team*.

Special education teachers play an important role in an inclusive school. How this role develops, however, can vary dramatically depending on philosophy and purpose. Three key roles and strategies are emerging out of research related to in-class special education support by teachers and aides.[25]

Adapting curriculum around the needs of individual students. In this approach, curriculum or instructional practice are not questioned. The problem is assumed to reside in the child. Nevertheless, accommodations are made for individual needs collaboratively between support personnel and general education teachers. These might include different worksheets, less work, or more time to do work.

Teacher needs. In this approach, a support teacher provides assistance to the classroom teacher in strengthening or areas of relative need in the teacher's repertoire. This might include helping the teacher learn skills in literacy or science by developing a lesson and teaching it.

Authentic, multilevel instructional design. Here the support teacher and general education teacher work together to design lessons that engage children at multiple levels.

As schools provide effective support for learning, this would be implemented in a range of ways. Student support teams often meet weekly to talk about children with special problems and needs and brainstorm together how to deal with the issue. General education teachers and specialists have scheduled planning times at least every two weeks to develop plans on teaching together and address concerns of specific children. Special education teachers and other support staff, such as gifted and reading specialists, would be assigned to several rooms where they collaborate with teachers. When we observe the room we would see the teacher, paraprofessionals, or other specialists (such as speech or occupational therapists) working with all the students in the class while ensuring that the students with special needs were receiving the help they need. The special education and general education teacher would work together with each taking responsibility for all students. In such a school implementing effective practices, we would not see a paraprofessional at the back of the class with a student with a disability or sitting constantly with a student with a disability clearly working only with him, students in ability groups working with the special education teacher, or a student with special needs separated from the rest of the class.[26]

Partnership with Families and Community Resources

In too many schools, substantial tension and poor relationships exist between parents and the school. Educators blame parents for their lack of interest in their children. Parents blame teachers for not helping their children learn. Epstein and others have documented the critical importance of developing partnerships with parents.[27] These same dynamics often play out with parents of students with disabilities across socioeconomic groups.[28] The lack of instruction at multiple levels and commitment of educators to helping students with emotional and behavioral challenges, as well as the tendency to be critical and refer students to segregated special education programs, all contribute to conflict and alienation between educators and parents of students with disabilities.

Effective schools recognize the need to develop multiple strategies to reach out to parents, bringing them into the life of the school and the classroom in meaningful ways, listening to their input regarding their children, and developing collaborative instructional and support strategies. All this begins, of course, with simply welcoming all children into the class. Further partnerships are needed in an effective school that link with community resources, on one hand, and use the resources and learning activities of the school, on the other hand, to strengthen the local community.[29]

Parents of children with special needs have typically gone through much with their children. In traditional schools, these parents receive much negative feedback from the school. Their children are rejected and sent away to special education classes or separate schools.

In effective schools, educators immediately invite their children into inclusive classes. They meet with and listen carefully to what parents have to tell us about their children, seeking to understand the child's gifts, strengths, and needs, strategies that work, and interests of the child from the parent. Teachers work to welcome all children into their classes and communicate to parents that they want the input of the family to help the teacher know about the child.

AUTHENTIC, MULTILEVEL LEARNING FOR PERSONAL BEST LEARNING

Much instruction in schools, particularly those that serve low-income students, is unengaging, rote, and unauthentic with little recognition of or place for differences in abilities and learning styles. Haberman described what he called the *pedagogy of poverty* used in too many urban classrooms with low-income children and contrasted this with good teaching, strategies that included involvement

> with issues they regard as vital concerns, . . . involved with explanations of human differences, . . . helped to see major concepts, big ideas, and general principles and are not merely engaged in the pursuit of isolated facts, . . . applying ideals such as fairness, equity, or justice to their world, . . . actively involved in heterogeneous groups, . . . involved in redoing, polishing, or perfecting their work, involved in reflecting on their own lives and how they have come to believe and feel as they do. [30]

These themes reflect the broader summary by Zemelman, Daniels, and Hyde in their cross-discipline analysis of best practice standards for teaching and learning of the major national professional educational organizations.[31]

These recommendations called for less rote learning, memorization of skills, and lecture and more active involvement in authentic learning projects in heterogeneous groups in which democratic leadership was both promoted and explicitly taught. Moreover, the President's Commission on Excellence in Special Education found that "while recent research has begun to determine critical factors in instruction, more high-quality research is needed on instructional variables that improve achievement by students with disabilities."[32]

Furthermore, in virtually every classroom, there is a broad range of abilities and learning styles among the students, ranging from a minimum of three grade levels to as many as seven to eight in schools serving different socioeconomic groups. Yet instruction in the pedagogy of poverty so well described by Haberman typically insists that all students be at "grade level," thus ignoring the needs of a substantial number of students functioning both below and above that level. Instruction that is multilevel, allowing all students—from those with severe mental retardation to students who are highly gifted—to be challenged at their own level of ability and provided proper supports, scaffolds, and attention to their individualized learning styles.

Students with labels ranging from highly gifted to severely cognitively impaired bring a very wide range of abilities to classrooms. Although traditional practice has promoted segregating and sorting students by presumed ability levels, the literature is clear that heterogeneous grouping within and across classes promotes higher levels of learning for all involved. For inclusive classrooms to function effectively, however, teachers must shift from monolithic, one-level instruction to instruction intentionally designed for students with differing ability levels to learn together well. A growing literature is developing regarding such authentic, multilevel, and differentiated instruction that documents instructional strategies.[33]

Schools are typically structured along grade levels and teach using standardized materials as if all children in a particular grade were at the same level. The reality, however, is that any class, whether attempting to be inclusive or not, contains children functioning three to six grade levels apart.

Effective schools, and the teachers and staff within them, embrace this diversity of culture, language, and ability and make it part of the design of instruction. Rather than designing instruction around a narrow span of abilities, whole-schooling teachers design their instruction by intentionally pulling from the voices, culture, and experience of students and allowing them to work at their own just right level of ability challenge. The idea, however, is not to make it easier for those kids who aren't at grade level. Rather, effective teachers

- Ground curriculum in the interaction of "personal experiences from children's lives" and "culturally grounded stories, songs, and" other "ways of expressing community values and beliefs,"[34] community issues and needs, and the mandated curriculum of the state or school district
- Use issues and problems to ground learning in authentic challenges using interdisciplinary themes, problem-based learning, writing for real audiences, and other strategies
- Design lessons so students may be challenged at multiple levels of ability without being separated into special classes of ability groups
- Challenge students at their own level (zone of proximal development)
- Provide support and scaffolding so children can push ahead to their own next level of learning
- Use authentic teaching strategies that engage children in learning via activities that relate to their lives at home and in the community and connect to the real world
- Engage the multiple intelligences and learning styles of children so that multiple pathways for learning and demonstrating achievement are available
- Involve students in collaborative pair or group work where they draw on each other's strengths

Schools where teachers teach in this way have few children whose needs are not met. However, since staff members are constantly learning, never getting it quite right all the time, there will often be children for whom teaching is not working. The staff members then figure a range of adaptations to the curriculum, paying attention to what works and how this might be incorporated next time into an overall teaching strategy.

BUILDING A WHOLE SCHOOL: HIGH LEARNING AND COMMUNITY FOR ALL

Since 1997, I have worked in numerous urban schools engaging them in using these principles to guide school improvement. Next, I describe some of the methods by which school staff can use the six principles of whole schooling (see table 6-2) to engage in dialogue and planning for meaningful school improvement.[35]

Key Questions

Central is the agreement of the staff that the six principles provide a valuable and needed set of goals for the school. If this is true, then stakeholders may consider the degree to which the school as a whole, as well as individual classrooms, are based on the six principles and develop strategies for improvement. Following are examples of key questions to address.

1. *Empowering in a democracy.* To what degree are multiple constituencies involved in making significant school decisions? How are students involved? Do students have multiple opportunities for daily decision-making, choices, and involvement in resolution of conflicts?
2. *Including all.* Are all students in general education classes? Where are students who would typically come to this school who are not present? How might the school connect its students to other students with diverse characteristics (important for schools without racial or ethnic diversity)?
3. *Providing authentic multilevel instruction.* To what degree are instructional strategies used to help students with very differing ability levels learn well together? Are there teachers who are using exemplary strategies? How might they assist other teachers? What assistance does the school staff need in learning multi-level instruction?
4. *Building community.* Does a sense of community pervade the school among staff, parents, children? How might the school strengthen community? Is there a commitment to children with social-emotional problems? Is positive behavioral support integrated into practice?
5. *Supporting learning.* Are staff members used to support students in general education? Do they work as a team for the entire school? Do they help design of authentic, multi-level instruction, building community, and using positive behavioral supports in the classroom?
6. *Partnering with families and the community.* To what degree do parents feel a partnership with parents, particularly parents of students with great challenges? To what degree are the talents of parents and the local community used to strengthen learning?

Team Self-Assessment and Action Planning

Several tools are available that may be used by teams or the entire school staff in conducting a self-assessment and engaging in action planning. These include

- *Whole Schooling: Strengths and Needs of Your School.* This is an open-ended questionnaire organized according to the six principles of whole schooling. This tool asks individuals to describe strengths and needs related to each principle and suggest ideas for change and improvement strategies. When these are completed, the narrative comments can be compiled and organized by each principle.

- *Whole Schooling: Self-Assessment and Action Planning Guide.* This tool lists school-wide and classroom practices that one would expect to see if a principle is being followed and those one would hope not to see for each principle. The respondent identifies practices used in the school from the total lists. The tool suggests exemplary and problematic practices that can be used as a menu of problems and possibilities.
- *Whole Schooling Self-Assessment Rating Scale.* A variety of items intended to reflect exemplary practice are listed for each principle. The respondent rates the school, or individual classroom, using a 5-point Likert scale where 1 is low and 5 is high.

Assessments using these tools may focus school-wide, on individual classrooms, or clustered by teams. For example, the third-grade teachers or the science department in a high school may conduct a team assessment. The school improvement team may look at these data and use them as the basis for a strategic action plan. Similarly, individual teachers and school teams may utilize the information to understand strengths, areas of need, and develop strategies for improvement.

School Capacity and Assets

School improvement must build on strengths of staff, parents, students, and the community. Any school possesses a wealth of resources. This simple open-ended tool is used to capture capacities and assets of the total staff and parents in the school. The tool asks individuals to list and briefly describe assets they have related to each of the six principles of whole schooling that they would be willing to share with others. This information is then compiled and put into a resource directory for the school. It can become a tool for person-to-person connections, a source of resources for staff development, and a way of building increased appreciation among all involved.

Study/Action Teams based on the Six Principles of Whole Schooling

As the school identifies areas of need, study/action teams may be developed. These might be organized based on the six principles of whole schooling or subdivisions of these principles. For example, a school might be particularly concerned with both math and literacy instruction. They may organize a team designed to help improve "authentic, multi-level instruction" in each of these areas. The school should carefully consider, however, developing working groups that address the social-emotional foundations for learning—including all, building community (along with positive behavioral supports), supporting learning, and partnering with families and the community. This is particularly important since these areas often receive too little attention. Study/action teams may collect data related to the issue they are investigating, read materials together, discuss implications for practice, go to a conference or school site visits together, identify new strategies to try with students, and engage in reflective dialogue about daily practice, all aimed at creating positive change.

CONCLUSION

We know so much now about how children learn, about how to build a community, how to help children with significant emotional and behavioral challenges. But the challenges and problems are also many. We hope that we will work together to move beyond repression, punishment, rejection, boredom, and isolation to create schools that lead to communities which are empowering, democratic, inclusive, engaging, all based on a sense of community, partnership, support, and care.

NOTES

1. Michael W. Apple, *Democratic Schools* (Alexandria, VA: Association for Supervision and Curriculum Development, 1995); Celia Oyler, *Making Room for All Students: Sharing Teacher Authority in Room 104* (New York: Teachers College Press, 1996).

2. J. Kauffman, *Education Deform* (Lanham, MD: Scarecrow Press, 2002).

3. William Ayers, B. Dohrn, and R. Ayers, *Zero Tolerance: Resisting the Drive for Punishment in Our Schools* (New York: The New Press, 2001); L. Lantieri and J. Patti, *Waging Peace in Our Schools* (Boston: Beacon Press, 1996).

4. G. M. Sugai, "School-wide Positive Behavior Supports: Achieving and Sustaining Effective Learning Environments for All Students," testimony submitted to the Committee on Health, Education, Labor, and Pensions, Washington, DC, April 21, 2002. Quotation on p. 7.

5. R. N. Caine and G. Caine, *Making Connections: Teaching and the Human Brain* (Alexandria, VA: Association for Supervision and Curriculum Development, 1991).

6. Thomas Sergiovanni, *Building Community in Our Schools.* (San Francisco: Jossey-Bass, 1994); Michael Peterson and M. Hittie, *Inclusive Teaching: Creating Effective Schools for All Learners* (Boston: Allyn and Bacon, 2002); J. S. Thousand, R. A. Villa, and A. I. Nevin, *Creativity and Collaborative Learning: A Practical Guide to Empowering Students and Teachers* (Baltimore, MD: Paul H. Brookes, 1994).

7. Chris Horrocks, "Community and Democracy in Schools," paper presented at Douglas College, Vancouver, British Columbia, March 16, 2005.

8. Lantieri and Patti, *Waging Peace in our Schools*; Sugai, "School-wide Positive Behavior Supports."

9. William Glasser, *The Quality School: Managing Students without Coercion* (New York: Harper Perennial, 1992.)

10. A. Koshewa, *Discipline and Democracy: Teachers on Trial* (Portsmouth, NH: Heinemann, 1999).

11. Jean Anyon, *Ghetto Schooling: A Political Economy of Urban Educational Reform* (New York: Teachers College Press, 1997).

12. Apple, *Democratic Schools*; Caine and Caine, *Making Connections*.

13. E. Fierros and J. Conroy, "Double Jeopardy: An Exploration of Restrictiveness and Race in Special Education," in D. Losen and G. Orfield (eds.), *Racial Inequity in Special Education* (Cambridge, MA: Harvard Education Publishing Group, 2002), 43–62.

14. Horrocks, "Community and Democracy in Schools."

15. President's Commission of Excellence in Special Education, *A New Era: Revitalizing Special Education for Children and Their Families* (Jessup, MD: U.S. Department of Education, Education Publications Center, 2002).

16. Ibid.

17. D. Losen and G. Orfield (eds.), *Racial Inequity in Special Education* (Cambridge, MA: Harvard Education Publishing Group, 2002).

18. Fierros and Conroy, "Double Jeopardy."

19. E. T. Baker, M. C. Wang, and H. J. Walberg, "The Effects of Inclusion on Learning," *Educational Leadership* 52, no. 4 (1994): 33–35; C. Moore, D. Gilbreath, and F. Maiuri, *Educating Students with Disabilities in General Education Classrooms: A Summary of the Research* (Eugene: Western Regional Resource Center, University of Oregon, 1998); Peterson and Hittie, *Inclusive Teaching*.

20. G. Orfield with N. Gordon, *Schools More Separate: Consequences of a Decade of Resegregation.* (Cambridge, MA: Civil Rights Project, Harvard University, 2001).

21. M. McLaughlin and M. Rouse, *Special Education and School Reform in the United States and Britain* (New York: Routledge, 2000).

22. J. Evans, I. Lunt, K. Wedell, and A. Dyson, *Collaborating for Effectiveness: Empowering Schools to Be Inclusive* (Philadelphia: Open University Press, 1999); L. Idol, *Creating Collaborative and Inclusive Schools* (Austin, TX: Eitell Press,1997); D. Johnson, *Critical Issue: Enhancing Learning through Multiage Grouping* (Naperville, IL: North Central Regional Educational Laboratory, 1998); C. Walther-Thomas, L. Korinek, V. McLaughlin, and B. Toler Williams, *Collaboration for Inclusive Education: Developing Successful Programs* (Boston: Allyn and Bacon, 2000).

23. Detroit Public Schools, *Effectiveness and Efficiency Report* (Detroit: Detroit Public Schools, 2002).

24. Evans, Lunt, Wedell and Dyson, "Collaborating for Effectiveness"; Idol, *Creating Collaborative and Inclusive Schools*; Walther-Thomas et al., *Collaboration for Inclusive Education.*

25. Michael Peterson, L. Tamor, H. Feen, and M. Silagy, *Learning Well Together: Lessons about Connecting Inclusive Education to Whole School Improvement*, Whole Schooling Research Project Final Report (Detroit, MI: Whole Schooling Consortium, Wayne State University, 2002).

26. Ibid.

27. J. Epstein, "Theory to Practice: School and Family Partnerships Lead to School Improvement," in C. Fagnano and B. Werber (eds.) *School, Family, and Community Interaction: A View from the Firing Lines* (San Francisco: Westview Press, 1994), 39–54.

28. C. Fagnano and B. Werber (eds.), *School, Family, and Community Interaction: A View from the Firing Lines* (San Francisco: Westview Press, 1994); V. Hildebrand, L. Phenice, M. Gray, and R. Hines, *Knowing and Serving Diverse Families* (Columbus, OH: Merrill, 2000); D. Taylor, *Many Families; Many Literacies* (Portsmouth, NH: Heinemann, 1997).

29. Fagnano and Werber, *School, Family, and Community Interaction*; Hildebrand et al. *Knowing and Serving Diverse Families*; Taylor, *Many Families; Many Literacies.*

30. Martin Haberman, "The Pedagogy of Poverty versus Good Teaching," *ENC Online*. Available online at equity.enc.org/equity/eqtyres/erg/111376/1376.htm. Accessed April 11, 2005.

31. S. Zemelman, H. Daniels, and A. Hyde, *Best Practice: New Standards for Teaching and Learning in America's Schools* (Portsmouth, NH: Heinemann, 1988).

32. President's Commission, *A New Era.*

33. T. Armstrong, *Multiple Intelligences in the Classroom* (Alexandria, VA: Association for Supervision and Curriculum Development, 1994); Peterson et al., *Learning Well Together*; C. Tomlinson, *The Differentiated Classroom: Responding to the Needs of All Learners* (Alexandria, VA: Association for Supervision and Curriculum Development, 1999).

34. Valerie O. Pang, *Multicultural Education: A Caring-Centered, Reflective Approach* (New York: McGraw-Hill, 2005).

35. Michael Peterson, *Whole Schooling: Ways School Staff Can Use the Six Principles for School Improvement* (Detroit, MI: Whole Schooling Consortium, 2003). Available online at www.wholeschooling.net.

7

Antiracist Education in Majority White Schools

Christine Sleeter and Linda Turner Bynoe

INTRODUCTION

White youth, particularly those from privileged backgrounds, are socialized to believe that because they are hard-working, smart, and hold high values, they ought to become the leaders—the wealthiest and most privileged people in the world. When this does not transpire, many are bewildered and resentful and fearfully blame others for their failure. All youth, however, when socialized to accept the humanity of others, are better able to be humbled and love themselves.[1]

To produce caring citizens who are critical thinkers and are knowledgeable, confident, and articulate, educators, parents, and community leaders must first show that youth from all walks of life matter. Riane Eisler states, "If we prepare today's children to meet the unprecedented challenges they face, if we help them begin to lay the foundations for a partnership rather than a dominator world, tomorrow's children will have the potential to create a new era of human evolution."[2] This chapter discusses why antiracist education is important to this larger endeavor and offers some insights and suggestions for developing it in majority White schools.

WHAT WE MEAN BY ANTIRACIST EDUCATION

Understanding antiracist education requires understanding institutional racism. Many people, particularly Whites, have such a sketchy understanding of racism that they misinterpret and then dismiss antiracist education as being antiacademic or anti-American. For example, in 2005 a widely publicized dispute challenged an antiracist math curriculum in Massachusetts. Many objections to it revealed lack of understanding about racism. In a news report, one observer referred to antiracism as "talking about culture," another commented that children should learn the basics first, and yet another saw antiracism as combating prejudice at the expense of teaching.[3] These objections conceived of racism as interpersonal attitudes only and assumed schooling and its curriculum to be generally neutral and fair to everyone. Critics saw antiracism, then, as an unnecessary addition that politicized schooling and reduced its academic focus.

Although antiracism addresses prejudice, it also addresses a much broader, more fundamental system of institutions, including schools that operate in ways that routinely benefit White people more than people of color. Paul Kivel defined institutional racism as "the institutionalization of social injustice based on skin color, other physical characteristics, and cultural and religious difference. White racism is the uneven and unfair distribution of power, privilege, and material goods favoring white people."[4] Institutionalized practices are so routine and taken for granted, however, that they appear normal, particularly to Whites. Most White people grow up learning that it is not polite to talk about racism. As a result, Whites can become very well educated but at the same time remain ignorant of institutional racism and then resist attempts to challenge or dismantle it.

Examples of institutional racism in majority White schools include offering better and more challenging teaching for White children than children of color; using tracking, special education, and gifted programs to allocate qualitatively different instruction to students; and teaching a curriculum that reflects White perspectives to the exclusion of perspectives of diverse communities of color. Antiracist education is "an action-oriented strategy for institutional, systemic change to address racism and the interlocking systems of social oppression."[5] It includes dismantling institutional racism within schools and school systems, as well as examining how racist systems are maintained in the wider society, the roles of individuals in maintaining them, and how racism can be challenged.

Antiracist educators advocate breaking down racism through collaboration between White people and communities that are usually excluded from decision making, particularly communities of color.[6] To do this, Whites need to learn how institutional racism works and how White people benefit from it. Whites should confront personal as well as institutionalized beliefs that minimize constructive and meaningful cross-racial and cross-cultural dialogue, decision making, and action.[7]

WHY IS ANTIRACIST EDUCATION IMPORTANT IN MAJORITY WHITE SCHOOLS?

We now illustrate why antiracist education is important in majority White schools with reference to reactions of our own students when they encounter it at the university level. California State University, Monterey Bay, is a nontraditional institution that emphasizes multicultural education for a pluralistic society and promotes a quintessential social justice paradigm. The expansion of students at universities who are women, people of color, and other previously disenfranchised and marginalized segments of the population requires a renewed philosophy of education and socialization. This trend toward socially just, antiracist teaching in higher education is the archetype to reshape academic systems. University education provides students complex social experiences that involve both ideas and emotions. When university students are exposed to new pedagogies and voices and encouraged to go beyond their private interests, develop a sense of civic and social responsibility, and discover how they, as individuals, contribute to the larger community of which they are a part, they respond in various ways.[8]

Many students—both White and of color—when initially exposed to a pluralistic, antiracist curriculum in which centuries of falsehood and defamation are scrutinized and the whole human experience is explored, regret and resent the banality of their kindergarten through grade twelve education. Some students feel that their education manipulated information and used propaganda, miseducation, lies, and denial to distort the reality of the total human experience, leaving them ignorant of what was and is true about their community and society. Instead of being socialized as children to view cultures in relation to the human experience as collaborative efforts among groups and as groups of unique citizens who have different relationships to power, they were taught to classify cultures as "ancient or modern, technologically developed or underdeveloped, Eastern or Western, religious or secular, capitalists or communist."[9] Students are not taught to include various historical perspectives or value the relationship created through historical events.

For example, some students learned that Columbus discovered America by sailing three ships, meeting with indigenous people, sharing gifts, and returning to Europe the victor. Most students questioned neither the sanitized version of the tale nor the political process of exclusion. Ira Shor suggests that students are taught to have an intransitive consciousness when they learn to accept and celebrate the status quo.[10] A White male university student stated, "I really felt like I had been cheated out of a proper education when I found out for myself all of the true stories in American history. I was taught to be a conformist and therefore I believed everything my teachers said. They wasted my time; I have to deconstruct twelve years of instruction." A Black female university student stated about her public education, "For years I was embarrassed and in denial of my African heritage. The depiction of African people in videos was one of poverty and ignorance, not of a nation of people whose history is rich in traditions, education and wealth. My ignorance robbed me of pride in my heritage and self-confidence and deprived other students a better understanding of black Americans." These remarks indicate that university students who experience antiracist curriculum arise from the traditional teachings to a semitransitive consciousness that permits them to believe in cause and effect.

No education system is politically neutral. School life fosters conformity, placing extreme pressure on all students to think, behave, and view life from the same Eurocentric perspective. Many of our schools strive to produce obedient citizens who are socially controlled, not critical thinkers who are prepared to enhance the society. Yet the result of producing critically conscious people is to transform the mysterious events of the past to an understanding of and participation for liberation.[11] An education system that builds within its curriculum "critical consciousness or critical transitivity allows people to make broad connections between single problems and the larger social system. The critically conscious individual connects personal and social domains when studying or acting on any problem or subject matter."[12]

The call to build systems that recognize critical thinking, cultural diversity, multiple worldviews, unjust use of power, and the concomitant demand that there be a transformation in our classrooms in how and what we teach has been a necessary revolution to a corrupt and dying academy.[13] But building just and inclusive systems is not easy and does not come naturally, particularly when students have been socialized to accept the status quo. Some teachers willing to take the risk of making their teaching practices a site of resistance may lack strategies to deal with antagonisms, student frustration, and refusal to relearn through multicultural, antiracist education. Without new strategies, such teachers often revert to traditional pedagogies.

In her essay "On Race and Voice: Challenges for Liberation Education in the 1990s," Chandra Mohanty writes,

> Resistance that is random and isolated is clearly not as effective as that which is mobilized through systemic politicized practices of teaching and learning. Uncovering and reclaiming subjugated knowledge is one way to lay claims to alternative histories. But these knowledges need to be understood and defined pedagogically, as questions of strategy and practice as well as of scholarship, in order to transform educational institutions radically.[14]

The benefits of antiracist education to students, schools, and society are worth the risks and challenges. Many White university students, as they come to recognize the reality of diversity and injustices of racism, feel they are ill prepared to work and live with diverse ethnicities, cultures, and races within our society or to succeed as culturally competent people in this country.

Trends in desegregation and resegregation over the last one-third century in the United States illustrate effects of cross-cultural incompetence. According to Frankenberg, Lee, and Orfield, "Whites are the most segregated group in education institutions, attending schools that are on average, 80 percent white. This causes most children to experience separate societies and schools."[15] School segregation intensified throughout the 1980s and 1990s as White flight increased with the onset of three major Supreme Court decisions authorizing a return to segregated neighborhood schools. White students who live in homogeneous communities, are educated in the traditional Western paradigms, and remain within an isolated geographic location may find it difficult to achieve their career aspirations and or life goals because of cross-cultural incompetence. Those who want to broaden their exposure and go away to college to advance their global careers are fearful that they are unprepared to compete internationally and collaborate with other ethnic groups as partners.

For example, in response to the passing of Proposition 209 (Affirmative Action) in California in August 1997, UC Berkeley's Boalt School of Law announced that none of the fifteen African American students admitted decided to enroll, which Herma Hill Kay, dean of the Law School, called "a total wipeout." One student who had deferred admission from the previous year became the only African American in the first-year class of 270 students.[16] Several White students became alarmed by this announcement, concerned that they were denied the opportunity to interact with and learn from and about African Americans. These future lawyers were astute enough to understand the importance of preparing to work with African Americans as clients and colleagues in the near future. With the movement throughout the United States toward gentrification (also called urban renewal, the process by which developers buy into a poor community and fix it up, thus increasing property values and making it unaffordable for the old residents to continue to live in their homes), will urban areas become more segregated and White?

The remainder of this chapter addresses building antiracist education in majority White settings. After offering a conceptual framework that can guide educational planning, we suggest several factors, with examples, that we believe should be part of antiracist education.

RACE, RACISM, AND WHITE IDENTITY DEVELOPMENT

A theory of racial identity development, coupled with research on antiracist work in schools, can guide planning. According to Janet Helms, "the term 'racial identity' actually refers to a sense of group or collective identity based on one's perception that he or she shares a common racial heritage with a particular racial group."[17] Children learn to see race as well as other differences before they enter school. By third grade, children have learned a good deal from the world around them and are beginning to act out their place in the social order accordingly.[18] Whites and people of color experience racial identity differently because they experience racism differently. Coming to understand and challenge racism entails reworking one's own conception of self, which makes it a difficult and long-term process.[19] Racial identity development theory posits stages of people's experience as they move from seeing unequal race relations as normal to working actively for racial justice and equality.

People at the stage of conformity and passive acceptance tacitly accept racism, assuming the racial order to be normal. They believe and have internalized racial stereotypes that justify why Whites tend to be better off than people of color, such as tending to score higher on tests, attaining higher levels of education, or tending to live in more affluent neighborhoods. Whites at this stage take White perspectives for granted, as the norm and believe White people are generally hard-working and fair. They deny the existence of discrimination, usually giving it little thought or assuming it to be a thing of the past. Students of color at this stage also tacitly accept racial inequality and their own subordinate status. Although most parents of color try to instill in their children a positive sense of self, as children encounter media, prejudice, and Eurocentric schools, they learn how they are seen by the dominant society and often internalize negative images. Schools that do nothing to address racism perpetuate and teach conformity and passive acceptance. For example, seeing mainly Whites in college-bound tracks, and learning mainly accomplishments of White people in history, science, and literature confirms students' self-understandings that fit within a racial hierarchy.

In majority White settings, challenging conformity and passive acceptance is like getting fish to see water,[20] but with the added difficulty of getting Whites to recognize how racism benefits Whites. Helms called the stage of initial recognition of racism as disintegration for Whites and dissonance for people of color. For many Whites, a combination of socialization and lacking personal contact with people of color limits access to other points of view or experiences. Learning about racism, especially as one becomes older, can be immensely painful, prompting feelings of anger and guilt. Lacking an understanding of the historical development of institutional racism, White people frequently interpret racism as individual prejudice only. As a result, many Whites resist questioning racism because they believe that doing so would confirm themselves as biased bad people. Working- or lower-class Whites, particularly, lacking power and having relatively few social advantages, resist seeing themselves as oppressors.[21] Students of color in majority White settings who are learning to advance according to rules of the mainstream and who define success based on White identity may also resist initially. Helms terms the process of confronting racism as one of dissonance for people of color, who do experience discrimination repeatedly and mainly need to analyze what those experiences mean. Helping students and teachers through disintegration and dissonance involves teaching about institutional racism, its intersection with the class structure, and how racism can be challenged.

People of color and Whites experience continued racial identity development quite differently, which implies that schools should plan for different forms of support. Whites generally cope with the pain of disintegration either by continuing to learn or by reverting back to earlier perspectives, called *reintegration*. Some Whites become hostile toward people of color, particularly if they do not see a constructive place for themselves and their realities in antiracism; others simply drift back to indifference. *Pseudoindependence* refers to Whites continuing to learn about racism, but mainly at an intellectual level and often by trying to adopt a colorized identity, for example, using Black English or wearing non-White ethnic symbols of identity. But as David

Gillborn found in a case study of two British schools working with antiracism, schools are often ill-equipped to help White students construct an alternative identity. White students seeing students of color celebrating a historically submerged sense of place and culture can feel left out.[22] Immersion refers to seeking out and learning about alternative antiracist White identities through role models, autobiographies, or histories. We give examples later in this chapter.

For students of color, immersion involves constructing a new identity that affirms the power, strength, resilience, and beauty of oneself and one's community. This usually involves plunging into the study of one's community from an insider's point of view. Ultimately, this is a very healthy and healing growth process, although it may be initially accompanied by anger toward the dominant society, particularly the older the student is and the longer she or he has lived at a stage of conformity. As one gains knowledge of the history of oppression one's community has endured and strategies used to survive oppression, one gains a new respect for the community. A challenge to majority White settings is providing students of color with safe space for this work.

Ultimately, if people internalize reworked, antiracist identities, they reach a stage of active commitment, which entails a long-term commitment to take on the work of struggling for social justice. People at the stage of active commitment can collaborate productively with others of diverse backgrounds to rework social systems so that they support everyone. Developing multiracial teams to work on school or community social justice issues help develop students' antiracist identities.

BUILDING ANTIRACIST EDUCATION IN MAJORITY WHITE SCHOOLS

Antiracist education in majority White schools must include restructuring the curriculum, policies, and relationships among local community and parents and nearby communities. To this end, we make recommendations regarding expectations, curriculum, and the teacher, providing antiracist White role models, bridging communities using electronic tools, and involving parents and the wider community.

Eliminating Institutionalized Low Expectations

Researchers consistently find expectations of many teachers to vary according to student race and class background. Often teachers see students who are White and Asian, as well as students of middle- or upper-class backgrounds, as more teachable than students who are Black or Latino or who come from lower-class backgrounds. Commonly low expectations rest on teachers' beliefs about extent to which parents value education.[23] Far too often, however, such beliefs are based on inaccurate assumptions rather than direct communication with parents. Most parents of color see schooling as essential to their children's upward mobility. Parents may avoid coming into the school for a variety of reasons, but at the same time count on teachers to offer their children a strong curriculum grounded in high expectations.

Tracking and special education commonly trap students of color into low expectations and lower levels of learning. For example, the Education Commission for the States reported that

American Indian students are consistently represented in disproportionately large numbers in the LD [learning disabilities] category. And more than twice the number of Black students (2.6%) are identified as mentally retarded when compared with White students (1.2%). In fact, some studies show that African-American children are almost three times more likely to be labeled "mentally retarded" than their White counterparts.[24]

At the same time, classes for gifted students are disproportionately White.

Although people often view tracking as meeting students' instructional needs, for the most part students in lower tracks (who are usually disproportionately students of color) do not receive curriculum that is designed to catch them up; furthermore, lower-track class work is often boring. Many students who are placed in lower-track classes and special education actually do better in upper-level courses that are more challenging and interesting. One research study found both high-achieving and low-achieving students more likely to *fail* lower-level than upper-level courses and *do better* in upper-level courses.[25]

Research consistently shows that students from communities that have been historically underserved can achieve when the teachers and school believe they can and take responsibility to make it happen.[26] Rather than attributing student achievement to family background, teachers who succeed with students from historically underserved communities build relationships with students and parents as well as they can and seek various ways to ensure that students get academic support. For example, to institutionalize academic achievement for all of its students, Rockville Centre School District in New York, a majority White district with a significant proportion of students of color, has been leveling up over the past ten years. All of its high school students are served in heterogeneous upper-track classes. Test results show increases among both traditionally low and high achievers and a marked closing of the racial achievement gap.[27]

Antiracist education must abolish deficiency-oriented thinking about students of color that is used to justify underteaching. In majority White schools, if African American, Latino, or Native American students are over-represented in remedial and lower-track classes and underrepresented in measures of high achievement, dismantling racism must mean dismantling systems and beliefs that perpetuate these disparities.

Curriculum

An antiracist curriculum teaches young people about how racism works and how people—including White people—can challenge it. This kind of curriculum also helps students learn to question beliefs that support racism, see the common humanity people share, and imagine how they can work on behalf of justice.

For example, consider how high school students learned to critically evaluate key ideas surrounding race and difference. The monogenetic theory proposes that all humans are descended from a single pair of ancestors and supports the theory that race is a social construction. Cheikh Anta Diop, an Egyptologist and linguist, and John P. Myers, a sociologist who studied the scientific and biological conception of race,[28] determined that race is a meaningless concept. The monogenetic theory expects students to see similarities among all people in appearance, reactions, emotions, problems, values, and goals through their daily trials and tribulations, interactions, and relationships. Contrarily, the polygenetic theory (popularized in the United States) suggests that races are distinct and separate from one another. If the polygenetic theory is believed, questions regarding biological similarities could be a subject for dialogue. For example: All humans can marry and procreate with each other, exchange blood and organs, and have virtually the same DNA.

While facilitating a summer leadership workshop for diverse high school students, monogenetic and polygenetic theories were introduced. Students demonstrated interest in the topic, yet were confused about what to believe. Homework assignments required students to talk with their parents and other family members about their understanding of both theories. The outcomes were amazing; students challenged their parents with information read in books, from videos shown in class, and stories told in the Bible. The family dialogues varied from long discussions about beliefs to emphatic and absolute confirmation of one theory or the other to suggesting that they learn more about the topics. Each student had information to share about his or her parents' reaction and knowledge. Posing theoretical questions about humanity to students and indirectly to their parents provides a way of connecting students to the ideas of their humanity, the humanism of other ethnic groups, the myths about humanity, and the social construction of difference.

Writing autobiography and biography provides students an opportunity to differentiate diverse human traits and the historical constructions of human difference. For example, Kailin has her predominantly White college students write a racial cultural autobiography in which they reflect on a variety of dimensions of their lives in five-year segments, such as their growing awareness of race and racism, events that affected them significantly, or how family, friends, books, and movies affected them. She then guides students in reflecting on their own lives in the context of the lives of other students and in the context of struggles around race and racism historically in the broader society. Through this process, she works to help students develop a sense of themselves as part of a larger history and as potentially as part of ongoing struggles for justice.[29] Dillard has college students share their life stories through creative autobiographies that blend the arts with storytelling and sharing. After examining their own lives, students can then read biographies of people whose racial and cultural background differ from their own, looking for common themes that people share across boundaries of difference.[30]

Autobiography can be a particularly powerful tool for learning. We have observed students research their family tree, interview grandparents, and identify ancestors who were slave owners. In the process, they learned to express how the privileged heritage escalated their socioeconomic status over others in the class. Some students reach an epiphany and confess to their responsibility to resolving social inequities. Acknowledgment of one's heritage permits students to question power and privilege, and the distribution of wealth. It is imperative that students are not blamed or made to feel ashamed of their heritage. Their ability to dialogue with their families about their family's history is as important as knowing that they are not personally responsible for their family's deeds or the horrors perpetrated against many people throughout U.S. history. In these discussions students learn to assess oppression and guard against the traps of paternalism and models of domination.

Biography and autobiography can be used across a range of age levels. For example, Collins pointed out that although urban African American families often face appalling circumstances, a treasure trove of young adult literature by and about African Americans presents a much more complex, rich, and human picture than is usually presented in the media. Such biographies help expand the dreams of children of color and expand the views White students have about communities of color.[31] Biographies of others are probably of most benefit when read alongside one's own autobiography and those of one's peers, because it is through personal writing that everyday life issues, hopes, dreams, struggles, and cares are made real.

An antiracist curriculum helps young people understand not only what has happened in society but also why and what can be done about it. There is research evidence that a curriculum organized through an antiracist approach makes a stronger impact on students than curriculum that includes diversity but excludes information about racism. Curricula that include diverse people and simply label groups or group members (for example, pointing out the race, ethnicity, or gender of historical figures) draw students' attention to group markers and differences, inadvertently inviting stereotyping. Students see differences, but without help interpreting what differences do and do not mean, students fall back on stereotypes and misinformation they have learned elsewhere.[32] However, a teacher can also include information about racism that explains why events happened, or how race has been used unjustly and what might be done to address racism. Doing so appears to have a measurably positive impact on racial attitudes of both children of color and White children toward fairness and people of color. For example, students responded much more positively to a lesson about African American baseball player Jackie Robinson when it was contextualized with information about racism in the history of baseball than when Robinson's race was pointed out without that contextualization.[33] Young people know that society faces problems; antiracist curricula provide information about why problems exist, as well as examples of steps taken toward building fairness.

Media imagery, particularly mainstream media, reinforce the idea of difference as exotic, scary, or unbridgeable. Carlos Cortés described the media as part of an ongoing societal curriculum that bombards young people, often with imagery that is much more powerful than what they encounter in school. In the media curriculum, certain images and themes circulate repeatedly, such as people from the Middle East being cast as terrorists, African Americans being cast as criminals, or contemporary Native Americans showing up mainly in relation to gambling and casinos.[34] In majority White schools, media images may well account for most of what young people know about people other than themselves.

With the expediency of technology teachers can use the media, videos, TV, DVDs, and film as tools for cultural criticism and a means to deconstruct productions that are designed to promote and reinforce domination and privilege. Music videos can be a key component for doing this. Music videos are accessible and influential to all youth, including White students who attend predominantly White schools. Young people of all cultures connect with music videos, and many White youth construct themselves as social beings through the mediation of images seen in them. Images of hip-hop culture inspire youth's dress, banter, and attitudes. Focusing on popular culture has been one of the main ways teachers address the cultural gap between people of power, privilege, and discrimination.[35] Through examining music videos, youth can identify the common culture they share across racial and ethnic communities, issues that are of particular concern to some communities more than others; youth can also examine how the music industry at times reproduces racist practices (for example, when White artists get credit for creations of artists of color) and at other times challenges racism (for example, when multiracial groups of artists take political stands on issues of justice).

Many courses in higher education ask students to think critically and dialogue about how popular art is advertised, reviewed and disseminated as it affects artists of color, awakening their awareness of the processes of commodification.[36] It is the exercise of dialogue, according to Freire, "that allows students to talk to each other mutually. Students can learn what they know and don't know, and then use their knowledge to learn more as well as to solve observed problems. Dialogue is a capacity and inclination of human beings to reflect together on the meaning of their experience and their knowledge."[37] Students of all ages (from five to fifty) can bring their experiences and awareness of music videos, as well as other aspects of popular culture, to dialogue with peers on various subjects endemic to their shared goals.

White youth across this country are floundering for insights and strategies in the hope of surviving and progressing in this highly competitive world in which multicultural perspectives challenge and stereotype their being. Young White people, like all youth, are looking for a renewed spirituality and liberation from the narrow perspectives of their segregated communities. Young people are naturally curious about life and want to understand the shared sensibilities of humanity that transcend race, ethnicity, and class. As other racial and ethnic groups remain a mystery, curiosity expands until youth develop the fear and negativity exemplified by the media. However, if exposed to the other groups in ways that bring an awareness of common humanity, young people may learn to relate to diversity in ways that transform them to appreciate their positionality, heritage, spirituality, and the talents, histories, and perspectives of others.

Teaching with Enthusiasm and Integrity

Teachers who are able to make an impact on White students bring enthusiasm, knowledge, and integrity to the work of antiracist teaching. They are able to approach antiracism as interesting and worth working on, connected to an ethic of fairness and justice. Furthermore, they have a sufficiently strong sense of their own racial identity that they are able to keep going when they encounter resistance, which may come from other adults more than from students.

For example, in a description of her own thirty-year journey becoming a White antiracist teacher, Dale Weiss briefly described her ongoing process of learning about race, racism, and White privilege, pointing out that a teacher is always still a learner.[38] Antiracist teachers in majority White schools are not themselves finished products who have worked out all of the answers and understand all of the issues. Rather, they are involved in their own continued learning of how the racial stratification system works on themselves as well as on others.

As a teacher, Weiss found herself educating not just her first-graders, but also other teachers, administrators, and parents. In fact, her majority White class of children was her most receptive learning audience. She commented, "My students seemed to have an innate sense of fairness and were eager to address such issues as how to make the world a better place. But most other staff members did not share my commitment to anti-bias teaching, especially on matters of race." Weiss believed, for example, that Black history should be taught all year long as part of the regular curriculum. She engaged her students in creating a video called "Black History as Seen through the Eyes of First Graders," which the students found highly interesting. Some of her fellow teachers, however, made disparaging comments about her work; for instance, one put a note in her mailbox that asked, "Do you also care about whether your students understand *white* history?"[39]

Reflecting on the racial identity development framework we presented earlier, an antiracist teacher is engaged in his or her own racial identity development, while at the same time working with students and other adults who are positioned in a wide range of racial identity development levels. Often children are the most receptive learners because of their concern for fairness and because they have absorbed far less racial baggage than adults.

It has been our experience that the most effective antiracist teachers are inspired, enthusiastic, knowledgeable, and empathetic toward others. For example, one of us has worked with a White English teacher in a majority White high school in California, who developed and taught a unit on immigration to address expressions of racism she had witnessed among students and develop students' sense of empathy. Before teaching the unit, she put considerable work into developing her own knowledge base. Although she is not an expert on immigration, she acquired enough background knowledge to guide her students and be clear about the kind of empathetic learning she was working to promote. When teaching the unit, her style was not to preach but to engage students in considering racial issues from someone else's point of view using readings, video, reflective writing, and discussion as teaching tools. Speaking about use of video with reference to one of the White male students, she remarked, "It seems like it engages them, it pulls them in, even if they don't want to be pulled in. And he doesn't want to be pulled in, and it's still, it sort of grabs him once in a while."[40] Consistently, when working with students, she conveys genuine interest in what they think, while at the same time persistently and gently probing their thinking. With peers, she does the same: In an inviting and low-key way, she names her position on issues, invites people to say what they think, asks questions, and listens but does not retreat.

Antiracist White Role Models

White youth need models of antiracist White people they can actually identify with. Engaging White students in antiracism can place them in the position of being the named oppressor, thus alienating them from dialogue and engagement,[41] which presents a pedagogical dilemma for antiracist educators who embrace a student-centered pedagogy.[42] To help White youth grapple with the immersion stage of racial identity development and construct identities that work against racism, they need to see antiracist people who are like themselves and model identities White students might become.

When White students read about John Brown for the first time, they are passionate and many commend the efforts to include White antiracist heroes in the curriculum. White students need to be reminded that many leaders in the world, including Martin Luther King Jr., welcomed White people as messengers for equity and justice for the mass population. Often White students are grateful for the video "Eyes on the Prize" in which many of King's marches are shown with young White people participating or crying as they stood in front of the Lincoln Memorial in Washington, DC, listening to the words of the "I Have a Dream" speech. In most communities there are White people who may not be well known but work as allies with communities of color every day. When White students meet such people, they often feel inspired, renewed, and empowered to work for justice. White students must be given absolution for their ancestors so that they can open their minds and hearts and participate in various communities without reinforcing systemic injustices and the stereotypical assumptions made against them.

Additionally, White students must see people of color in power roles. Students must see teachers of color in their schools to facilitate an understanding that schools are reflective of a social system. Teachers of color can enrich the learning process by sharing their cultural backgrounds through daily interaction and conversation. Schools should strive to be cultural environments in which different views and perspectives offer experiential opportunities for students to gain authentic perspectives.

Bridging Communities through Electronic Tools

Students of the twenty-first century are the prime targets for building learning communities through global telecommunications technology. Their ability to interact and communicate with people across diverse world nations enables intercultural exchanges of ideas. This means that students in majority White schools need not remained isolated from cross-racial contact and exchange of ideas. Communications that facilitate interactions among students whose backgrounds differ by socioeconomic status, ethnic background, nationality, or region of residence provide reflective experiences for all participating parties. Intercultural and international exchanges through the use of technology expand students' literacy skills, enhance their multicultural awareness, prepare them for a global economy, and improve their self-concept by improving their ability to communicate with people from other cultures.[43] Ideas for furthering technological communications in curriculum development are in abundance.

Many teachers are enthusiastically using technology to introduce the concept of learning community at all levels of education. Learning communities, as defined by Kowch and Schwier, "are quite simply, collections of individuals who are bound together by natural will and a set of shared ideas and ideals and who are engaged by influencing each other within a learning process."[44] Their discovery of conference calls, chat rooms, and e-mails address the need for teachers to understand the impact these tools bring to bridging communities to students isolated in rural America. We will illustrate this through two projects, one based on e-mail exchanges and another that coupled e-mail with a face-to-face exchange.

E-mails are used today at all levels of education to form cross-group communication by connecting students of neighboring schools, encourage youth to use technology, and improve literacy. For example, high school students in New York City's different boroughs have exchanged stories about their schools, families, and class assignments as part of the Smart Cities: New York Initiative.[45] The program is the first of many to use information technologies to improve education in New York schools. This simple but contemporary pedagogical framework helped create an appreciation of the diversity in their city.

It was found that some students had been isolated, ethnocentric, and unaware of the vast diversity of the city of New York. Though sharing proximity to different groups in neighboring communities, some affluent White youth in New York City lacked knowledge and interaction with Blacks and Hispanics in other communities, and as a result had feelings of threat and anxiety about outside communities. Some White students' knowledge of people of color was limited to their role of employer. Black and Hispanic workers, who performed daily activities in White people's homes and businesses, were from some of those other communities. Rarely did White youth venture out into Black or Hispanic communities and interact with the people. E-mail exchanges set up by teachers in different school communities helped improve communications among students from different communities. Teachers had to learn to monitor students' e-mails closely and carefully to avoid miscommunications replete with elitism and biases. This close scrutiny also taught teachers how to communicate with students and understand multiple perspectives as they observed and read their student's two-way e-mail communications.

Project I-57 was a large one-year Illinois State Board of Education grant-funded program. Its goal was to use technology to broaden students understanding and appreciation for different ethnic, class, cultural groups, and communities throughout Illinois. The project was funded to evaluate expected changes in students' understanding, knowledge, and attitudes about other groups who lived in three distinctively different areas of the state: Chicago (an urban area), the central area or farm belt, and southern Illinois.[46] "Originally the hypothesis was meant to lessen racial prejudice in the US and led to education solutions such as school desegregation and bussing of minorities."[47] However, teachers learned to consider intergroups' communication biases, prejudices, and misunderstandings. Sundberg found that students needed to be guided to be cooperative, form a common identity, be complimentary or positive, and encourage students to self-disclose and assist other students in their technology progress. In Project I-57 students had opportunities to visit schools outside of their own group. The main concern was the amount of e-mail contact prior to the face-to-face visit. All of the students wanted to visit the out-group's community and schools. Most of the attitudes toward their e-mail pals were positive. Students made statements such as: "They were good kids and I like them a lot," "I felt good talking to a friend that was miles away from me," and "I felt pretty close to the student I communicated with because they were very common with us." A number of students described the experience as exciting. It taught teachers to be more involved in the communications' processes and seek opportunities to connect with other students outside of their immediate sphere of teaching.[48]

Yet it is experiential learning opportunities that create a deeper comprehension and life-altering impressions. Project I-57 culminated with students visiting their e-mail pals' communities. The field trips afforded students firsthand observations, liberating dialogues, and experiences with the interconnected humanity of all people. Interacting and dialoguing with people from outside one's local ethnic group offers an opportunity to question heritages and histories that are interconnected, interdependent, and integrated with the history of White people. Citizens who are antiracist leaders, critical thinkers, and culturally competent activists with a sense of community responsibility and service have multiple perspectives to link to, such as models of cooperation, consideration, empathy, and collaboration.[49]

Parents and the Community

Community educators—parents, teachers, politicians, private industry leaders, professional and social movement organizations, and other adults who benefit from youth's education—must become actively involved in antiracist education of its youth.[50] Communities that share a commitment to society's needs or understand the values and needs of its members start to address the effects power and priorities have on the social, political, and economic structure of different groups. Although Americans are more segregated than acknowledged, rigid borders and boundaries no longer exist. More and more youth groups are determining through technology, athletics, and popular culture how entrenched society is in individualism, consumerism, and competition. Furthermore, the United States is developing subcommunities of divergent people, such as the youth prison population. That this population is predominately youth of color is more problematic. Even

White youth gangs are emerging as divergent subcultures at alarming rates in White communities across the country.

John Dewey[51] and W. E. B. DuBois[52] stated almost a century ago that the role of community is to socialize youth to be the next generation of teachers, entrepreneurs, and leaders of businesses, organizations, and political, social, and community activists. James Banks echoed this when he stated,

> Education and educators are compelled to link knowledge, social commitment and action, which is best implemented when students examine different types of knowledge in a democratic learning institution. Schools are the best avenues to bridge cultural knowledge with school knowledge. When school knowledge and cultural knowledge is linked students are better able to conceptualize their positions and to challenge assumptions, stereotypes and misconceptions and perceptions of their positions in communities and the world.[53]

Schools are the vanguard to building youth programs that undergird youth's social development and learning rather than simply optional activities or projects for public relations purposes. Youth programs should include cross-cultural community activities that allow families to get to know each other and raise the intellectual tone of society, teaching a positive regard for humanity and cross-cultural sophistication and understanding. The vision or mission of schools in this time of No Child Left Behind must change from an economic and testing focus to strategies that deconstruct systems of segregation and provide an excellent education for all children. School and community leaders, entrepreneurs, leaders of businesses, organizations, and political activists should want to develop partnerships that embrace youth's talents, values, and intellect as the future producers and consumers of the country. Isolating any group intellectually, economically, and politically fosters a danger for society. The new revolutionaries are those young citizens today of all ethnic groups who are disenfranchised, miseducated, and culturally inadequate. Bridging communities and exposing youth to the similarities and differences of humans can only regenerate a population of caring, concerned, and critically thinking people.

Schools and communities must have a vision that starts with the children and teaches them that humans are interdependent, interconnected, and integrated.[54] Developing learning communities requires the conscious effort to bring in parents as partners. Many schools are providing classes for parents to learn how to participate in school activities, teacher conferences, and fundraisers. Schools that are predominately White may need to educate parents about the purpose and importance of antiracist education.

Communication and the exchange of information are key components of the relationships between parents and schools. Parents must be able to comprehend the information provided and willing to engage with a program in the interests of their children. Schools must rely on a body of parents to bring in other community partners. Middle-class White parents are quick to support education. Career obligations can impinge on their ability to participate in extracurricular programs, but their ability to contribute materially is easier. They are the business, organization, political, and entrepreneurial leaders of the community. Parents' connections and contacts cross many neighboring and distant communities, and their effort is instrumental in establishing cross-cultural learning communities.

Throughout the country, learning community reform models are being implemented to build academically excellent, developmentally responsive, and socially equitable learning environments in low socioeconomic, ethnically homogeneous communities. Lake Middle School provides an example of how family involvement, health, and counseling services helped prepare students for the next grade.[55] The principal, Paula Reeves, had a vision: As an instructional leader she improved the school's literacy efforts through professional development and the infusion of reading and writing across the curriculum. As she described it, her ultimate vision "was to make the Lake School into a full-service school." In addition to academic and after school programs, she also established the Wellness Center at Lake in partnership with two large hospitals in the area. The Wellness Center provided free heath services to students, staff and other members of the community. [56]

This innovative project started by pairing teaching assistants (TAs) and teachers as teams, incorporating a hierarchy for teams throughout the district. The leadership team was composed of school leaders, teachers, and TAs. It engaged parents and community partners in the implementation process. The agenda of the teams was to improve pedagogy and student results. The leadership and teaching teams were expected to embrace change and participate in brainstorming to ensure efforts to academically improve students. The teams included community businesses that taught leadership workshops and technical classes and supported the school district through parent and community involvement.

This project was successful because of the shared goals of the teachers, parents, and community. The leadership had a vision and reached out to the community to fulfill the academic, physical, and social needs of the students. Through a change in teaching structure, classroom practices, and leadership teams, the partnership's results were concrete: "There was improvement in small learning communities, expanded special education inclusion, innovative instructional strategies, better programs for family involvement and health and counseling and improved preparation for higher school and beyond."[57]

Community learning centers are a way to educated students and socialize them as future citizens. With school legislation forming at various levels of government it is important to think about schools and the need of children and society as we continue to teach. With the help and support of a community, even the most intrusive legislation can be overcome.

CONCLUSION

White youth in the United States are socialized to accept their dominant status through educational systems that emphasize individual rewards, consumerism, and meritocracy. But the rapid pace of technological change and the geographic mobility of individuals frequently alter traditions and communities.[58] As the world becomes smaller and the United States more diverse with increasing global joint ventures, young people are naive if they think they will spend their lives with people who look, think, or speak like and have the same values as themselves. The urgency to create an education system that works for everyone is based in the need to eliminate building systems of miseducation and fear. Ideally, educational systems would ensure opportunities for ethnic and racial integration at all levels. Gary Orfield states: "Americans believe their children benefit from integrated education and segregation has not been an effective policy."[59]

Community advocates interested in encouraging community goals within modern environments must consciously support practices that generate new goals that are meaningful and supportive of relationships among a diverse population. The future success of young people as citizens of the world community is at risk without antiracist education and integrated educational experiences. Most critically, education in areas of isolation must address the importance of personal contact. We must explore ways to desegregate schools and housing policies to avoid massive resegregation of large sections of the inner cities and suburbs.[60] Youth in homogeneous White communities must have every opportunity to face, talk with, and experience other groups on an emotional level, particularly given the impact of the media on their education. A sanitized education is nonproductive for the future of our citizens. Teachers as well as students, parents, and community leaders must be courageous risk-taking prophets for the elimination of racism and intolerance and become the role models for future culturally competent citizens who will take us into the twenty-first century as a global community of caring and hope.

NOTES

1. Linda Bynoe, "Strategies for Teaching Caring and Empowerment: Drawing from African American, Mexican American, and Native American Traditions," in Riane Eisler and Ron Miller (eds.), *Educating for a Culture of Peace* (Portsmouth, NH: Heinemann, 2004), 189–204.

2. Riane Eisler, "Education for a Culture of Peace," in Riane Eisler and Ron Miller (eds.), *Educating for a Culture of Peace* (Portsmouth, NH: Heinemann, 2004), 23.

3. L. Porteus, "Anti-Racist Message in Mass. Math Class," *Fox News* (February 8, 2005). Available online at www.foxnews.com; accessed on February 10, 2005.

4. Paul Kivel, *Uprooting Racism: How White People Can Work for Racial Justice* (Philadelphia: New Society, 1996), 2.

5. George J. Sefa Dei, *Anti-Racism Education* (Halifax, NS: Fernwood, 1996), 25.

6. Dei, *Anti-Racism Education*; Enid Lee, *Letters to Marcia: A Teacher's Guide to Anti-Racist Education* (Toronto, ON: Cross Cultural Communication Centre, 1985).

7. Carl James, "Multiculturalism in the Canadian Context," in Carl A. Grant and Joy L. Lei (eds.), *Global Constructions of Multicultural Education* (Mahwah, NJ: Lawrence Erlbaum, 2001), 175–204; Enid Lee, Deborah Menkart, and Margo Oka-zawa-Rey (eds.), *Beyond Heroes and Holidays: A Practical Guide to K-12 Anti-Racist, Multicultural Education and Staff Development* (Washington, DC: Network of Educators on the Americas, 1998).

8. Ernest L. Boyer, *The Undergraduate Experience in America* (New York: Harper and Row, 1987), 61.

9. Eisler, "Education for a Culture of Peace," 20.

10. Ira Shor, *Empowering Education: Critical Teaching for Social Change* (Chicago: University of Chicago Press, 1992).

11. Ibid.

12. Ibid., 128.

13. Bell hooks, *Teaching to Transgress* (New York: Routledge, 1994).

14. Chandra Mohanty, as cited in hooks, *Teaching to Transgress*, 22

15. Erica Frankenberg, C. Lee, and Gary Orfield, *A Multiracial Society with Segregated Schools: Are We Losing the Dream? A Descriptive Report* (Cambridge, MA: Harvard Civil Rights Project, 2003).

16. Carl Gutierrez-Jones, *Affirmative Action News* (Santa Barbara: University of California,1997). Available online at aad.english.ucsb.edu/pages/news1997.html; accessed on March 15, 2005.

17. Janet E. Helms, *Black and White Racial Identity: Theory, Research, and Practice* (Westport, CT: Greenwood Press, 1990), 3.

18. Debra Van Ausdale and Joe R. Feagin, *The First R: How Children Learn Race and Racism* (Lanham, MD: Rowman and Littlefield, 2001).

19. Chalmer E. Thompson and Robert T. Carter (eds.), *Racial Identity Theory* (Mahwah, NJ: Lawrence Erlbaum, 1997).

20. Kelly E. Maxwell, "Deconstructing Whiteness: Discovering the Water," in Virginia Lea and Judy Helfand (eds.), *Identifying Race and Transforming Whiteness in the Classroom* (New York: Peter Lang, 2004), 153–168.

21. David Gillborn, "Student Roles and Perspectives in Antiracist Education: A Crisis of White Ethnicity?" *British Educational Research Journal* 22, no. 2 (1996): 165–179.

22. Ibid.

23. See, for example, J. M. Codjoe, "Fighting a Public Enemy of Black Academic Achievement—The Persistence of Racism and the Schooling Experiences of Black Students in Canada," *Race Ethnicity and Education* 4, no. 4 (2001): 343–375; P. Hauser-Cram, S. R. Sirin, and D. Stipek, "When Teachers' and Parents' Values Differ: Teachers' Ratings of Academic Competence in Children from Low-Income Families," *Journal of Educational Psychology* 95, no. 4 (2003); and Valerie O. Pang and V. A. Sablan, "Teacher Efficacy," in Mary E. Dilworth (ed.), *Being Responsive to Cultural Differences* (Washington, DC: Corwin Press, 1998), 39–58.

24. Education Commission of the States, "Addressing the Disproportionate Number of Minority Students in Special Education," *ECS State Notes* (2003). Available online at www.ecs.org/clearinghouse/48/90/4890.htm; accessed February 22, 2005.

25. "A New Core Curriculum for All," *Thinking K–16, A Publication of the Education Trust* 7, no. 1 (2003).

26. See, for example, Cheryl T. Desmond, *Shaping the Culture of Schooling: The Rise of Outcome-Based Education* (Albany: SUNY Press, 1996); John B. Diamond, A. Randolph, and James P. Spillane, "Teachers' Expectations and Sense of Responsibility for Student Learning: The Importance of Race, Class, and Organizational Habitus," *Anthropology and Education Quarterly* 35, no. 1 (2004): 75–98; Gloria Ladson-Billings, *The Dreamkeepers* (San Francisco: Jossey-Bass, 1994); Deborah Meier, "Can the Odds Be Changed?" *Phi Delta Kappan* 79, no. 5 (1998): 358; Theresa Perry, Claude Steele, and Asa Hilliard III, *Young, Gifted and Black* (Boston: Beacon Press, 2003); and Pedro Reyes, J. D. Scribner, and A. P. Scribner (eds.), *Lessons from High-Performing Hispanic Schools* (New York: Teachers College Press, 1999).

27. Carol C. Burris, J. Heubert, and Henry Levin, "Math Acceleration for All," *Educational Leadership* 61, no. 5 (2004): 68–71.

28. J. Myers, *Minority Voices: Linking Personal Ethnic History and the Sociological Imagination* (Boston: Rowan University, 2005).

29. Julie Kailin, *Antiracist Education* (Boulder: Rowman and Littlefield, 2002).

30. Cynthia B. Dillard, "From Lessons of Self to Lessons of Others: Exploring the Role of Autobiography in the Process of Multicultural Learning and Teaching," *Multicultural Education* 4, no. 2 (1996): 33–37.

31. C. J. Collins, "A Tool for Change: Young Adult Literature in the Lives of Young Adult African-Americans," *Library Trends* 41, no. 3 (1993): 378.

32. Rebecca S. Bigler, "The Use of Multicultural Curricula and Materials to Counter Racism in Children," *Journal of Social Issues* 55 (1999): 687–705; Rebecca S. Bigler, C. S. Brown, and M. Markell, "When Groups Are Not Created Equal: Effects of Group Status on the Formation of Intergroup Attitudes in Children," *Child Development* 72 (2001): 1151–1162.

33. Julie K. Milligan and Rebecca S. Bigler, "Addressing Race and Racism in the Classroom," in Gary Orfield and Erica Frankenburg (eds.), *Can We Make a Rainbow?*

From Segregation to Integration (Charlottesville: University of Virginia Press, in press).

34. Carlos Cortés, *The Children Are Watching: How the Media Teach about Diversity* (New York: Teachers College Press, 2000).

35. Bell hooks, *All about Love: New Visions, a Warm Affirmation that Love Is Possible* (New York: Harper Collins, 2000).

36. Hooks, *Teaching to Transgress.*

37. As noted by Shor, *Empowering Education*, 86.

38. Dale Weiss, "Confronting White Privilege," *Rethinking Schools* 16, no. 4 (2002).

39. Ibid.

40. Christine Sleeter, *Unstandardizing Knowledge: Multicultural Curriculum Design and the Standards Movement* (New York: Teachers College Press, 2005).

41. David Gillborn, *Racism and Anti-Racism in Real Schools* (Buckingham: Open University Press, 1995).

42. Audrey Thompson, "Entertaining Doubts: Enjoyment and Ambiguity in White, Antiracist Classrooms," in E. Mirochnik and D.C. Sherman (eds), *Passion and Pedagogy: Relation, Creation, and Transformation in Teaching* (New York: Peter Lang, 2002), 431–452.

43. Xiadong Lin and Charles Kinzer, *The Importance of Technology for Making Cultural Values Visible* (Columbus: Ohio State University, College of Education, 2003).

44. Eugene Kowch and Richard Schwier, "Building Learning Communities with Technology—A Descriptive Report" (Discussion Paper No. 150) (Saskatoon: National Congress on Rural Education, 1997), 2.

45. R. McClintock, *Smart Cities: New York. Electronic Education for the New Millennium.* An Educational Framework Prepared for the New York City Board of Education and its Taskforce on Teaching and Learning in Cyberspace, December 2000.

46. P. Sundberg, "Building Positive Attitudes among Geographically-Diverse Students: The Project I-57 Experience," paper presented at the National Educational Computing Conference, July 25–27, 201, Chicago, IL.

47. Ibid., 2.

48. Ibid., 15.

49. J. S. Mbiti, *African Religion and Philosophies* (New York: Anchor: 1970); Ronald Takaki, *A Different Mirror: A History Multicultural America* (Boston: Little, Brown, 1995).

50. Bynoe, "Strategies for Teaching Caring and Empowerment."

51. John Dewey, *The School and Society* (Chicago: University of Chicago Press, [1900] 1956).

52. W. E. B. DuBois, *The Education of Black People: Ten Critiques, 1906–1960* (New York: Monthly Review Press, 1973).

53. James A. Banks, *Teaching Strategies for Ethnic Studies*, 5th ed. (Boston: Allyn and Bacon, 1991).

54. Eisler, "Education for a Culture of Peace."

55. Pritah Goplan, *Michigan Middle Start Studies of Middle Start School Improvement, Lake Middle School: A Case Study* (New York: Academy for Educational Development, 2001).

56. Ibid., 6.

57. Ibid.

58. John Gardner, "Building Community," in Joseph Kahne (ed.), *Reframing Educational Policy: Democracy, Community, and the Individual* (New York: Teachers College Columbia University, 1990), 33.

59. Gary Orfield, *Schools, More Separate: Consequences of a Decade of Resegregation: A Descriptive Report* (Cambridge, MA: Harvard Civil Rights Project, 2001).

60. Ibid.

8

Toward a Critical Race Pedagogy

Marvin Lynn

INTRODUCTION

As we enter the new millennium, it appears that Africans in America have come to yet another educational crossroads. The ominous question that has been and continues to lurk in the recesses of our minds is "At what point will our children have access to quality education?" and even more important, as Carter G. Woodson reminds us, to what degree will schooling serve African Americans if it teaches them to respect and honor the cultures of others and not their own?[1] As is evident in the critical analysis of Woodson, there has always existed a response to the level of miseducation that Africans have been forced to endure in the United States. Woodson's earlier studies describe in detail the difficulties encountered by freed Africans during the antebellum period to establish schools and participate in the educational process.[2] Butchart rounds out the debate with his analysis of how and why schools were created for Blacks in the South during the Reconstruction period and immediately thereafter.[3] His conclusion: Africans were offered schools before they were offered housing and employment. Furthermore, he argues that schools for Africans, as they were conceptualized by White abolitionists, were

This chapter originally appeared in *Urban Education*, volume 33, number 5 (January 1999): 606–626 and is reprinted here with permission of Sage Publishers.

not created with the intent of being spiritually, emotionally, and intellectually emancipating. Rather they served as a way to maintain control over the minds of newly freed slaves. James Anderson makes a similar argument about the development of education for African Americans during this period.[4] Other African American scholars have continued the tradition of building sound arguments that outline the inadequacies of schooling along with its failure to properly educate the vast majority of African Americans.[5]

Other scholars have developed a corpus of research that elucidates and typifies the practices of African American humanist pedagogues committed to using transformative practices within the context of elementary and high school classrooms as a way to successfully educate African American students.[6] This research draws mainly from African-centered epistemological paradigms such as Afrocentric feminist thought,[7] which conjoins Afrocentricity[8] and feminist standpoint theory. Like womanist theory,[9] which is an expression of the voices of African descended women "committed to the survival and wholeness of an entire people, male and female,"[10] the Afrocentric feminist embraces an Afrocentric position that is grounded in history and the struggles of African peoples.[11] These theoretical precepts have created a strong foundation from which theories and research of African American teachers have originated.

AFRICAN AMERICAN TEACHERS

According to Michele Foster, much of the research on teachers and teaching has either excluded African American pedagogues from the dialogue or has portrayed them in such a negative light as to convince research consumers that they are "ill-suited to educating African-American pupils effectively."[12] Foster has effectively shaken up the White male–dominated positivistic discourse on teachers and teaching so that the practices, beliefs, and thoughts of African American teachers are more thoroughly taken into account in the research literature. Foster uses a grounded theory approach—a research methodology for developing theory that is grounded in evidence systematically gathered and analyzed—to explain the unique styles of African American teachers.

For Foster, African American teachers' pedagogy is characterized by three significant ideals: cultural solidarity, affiliation or kinship, and connectedness. African American teachers express cultural solidarity with their students by communicating with them in a style that is used within their communities. They express feelings of kinship and connectedness by remaining connected to and often living within the communities of their students. This also manifests itself in the way that they treat their students—often referring to them as their own.

As Theresa Perry and Lisa Delpit note, African American teachers also use certain African-centered principles of humanity, such as the ancient Egyptian principles of Maat, which are "righteousness, truth, honest, propriety, harmony, order and reciprocity," and the Nguzo Saba principles of Kwanzaa, which are "unity, self-determination, collective work and responsibility, co-operative economics, purpose, creativity, and faith" to guide their practice.[13] In earlier works, Delpit also talked about the importance of using a culture-centered paradigm with African American students.[14] And though her work doesn't exclusively explicate the practices of African Americans, Ladson-Billings also highlights the importance of building a pedagogical style that emphasizes culture while helping students gain an arsenal of skills.[15] Carol Lee, however, points out that African-centered or Afrocentric pedagogy that emphasizes the historical legacy of African Americans and our connection to Africa has been the cornerstone of the curricula of a number of Black independent institutions or kindergarten through grade eight schools started by African Americans.[16]

Other research on African American teachers has also articulated their perceptions of race and racism in the United States, highlighting the perceptivity of these teachers with regard to issues of social inequity.[17] There exists a necessary link to the research African womanist pedagogues.[18] These teachers are characterized as demonstrating the capacity and need to act as other mothers for their students while consistently providing positive reinforcement, promoting collective responsibility and sharing, teaching them to be responsible for their own learning, using Afrocentric womanist pedagogy as a basis for their curriculum, and encouraging the academic, intellectual, and cultural development of their students. Theories of African womanist pedagogy along with Afrocentric feminist epistemology, which undergird theories of African American pedagogy and practice, are especially significant because they are mulitidimensional in their focus and, as a result, create an interplay between interlocking and interconnected forms of oppression such as racism, sexism, and elitism. In this way, it requires that we think more deeply about how critical analyses of schooling can be connected to a wider discourse on the role the educational system plays in ensuring the maintenance of current social, political, and economic conditions in the United States.

CRITICAL RACE THEORY

Critical race theory (CRT) can also be used to undergird and theoretically ground research on African Americans teachers committed to social justice endeavors.[19] According to Matsuda et al., CRT is a counterdiscourse generated by legal scholars of color who sought to inject the issue of racial oppression into the debate about the law and society.[20] As Tate also indicates, this form of scholarship grew out of their lack of satisfaction with critical legal studies as well as their dogged commitment to creating and sustaining a politicized discourse that was by and about people of color.[21] Critical race scholars argue that CRT should be used as an analytic framework for addressing issues of social inequity, because it

1. Offers a sound and systematic critique the legal system in the United States
2. Recognizes the centrality of race and intransigence of racism in contemporary American society
3. Rejects West-European and modernist claims of neutrality, objectivity, rationality, and universality
4. Historicizes its analysis by relying heavily on the experiential, situated, and subjugated knowledge of people of color
5. Is interdisciplinary in its focus because of its roots in philosophical, historical, and sociological traditions such as postmodernism, Marxism, Black nationalism, and black feminist thought
6. Seeks to eliminate racial oppression in the United States by linking it to other forms of oppression, such as sexism and classism or elitism.[22]

BUILDING A CRITICAL RACE PARADIGM IN EDUCATION

Recently, a number of scholars in the field of education have applied critical race analyses to educational issues.[23] According to Daniel Solorzano and Tara Yosso, CRT in education is: "An interdisciplinary attempt to approach educational problems and questions from the perspectives of Women and Men of color." They further state that

Critical Race Theory in education is defined as a framework or set of basic perspectives, methods, and *pedagogy* that seeks to identify, analyze, and transform those structural, cultural, and interpersonal aspects of education that maintain the marginal position and subordination of [African American and Latino] students. Critical Race Theory asks such questions as: (1) What role do schools themselves, school processes, and school structures help maintain racial, ethnic, and gender subordination?[24]

They also argue that CRT can be used as a point from which to begin the dialogue about the possibilities for schools to engage in the transformation of society by putting forth the question: "Can schools help end racial, gender, and ethnic subordination?" Solorzano has created a theoretical starting point from which to begin thinking directly to the possibilities that lie in connecting CRT to a broader discourse on pedagogy, particularly the emancipatory teaching practices of people of color attempting to use such liberatory strategies as a vehicle for counteracting the devaluation of racially oppressed students. Other scholars talk more generally about how CRT can be used to deal with concerns in education.

Ladson-Billings argues that a CRT-driven analysis in education would necessarily focus on "curriculum, instruction, assessment, school funding, and desegregation as exemplars of the relationship that can exist between CRT and education," schools, and the larger society.[25] The major concern of a critical race analysis of education would be to look analytically at the failure of the educational system in the United States to properly educate the majority of culturally and racially subordinated students. Naturally, this theoretical paradigm could also be used as a way to address liberatory work and praxis occurring in schools. In other words, CRT appears to be a natural place for situating the study of critical African American teachers because it is an analytic discourse that explicitly addresses issues of racial, ethnic, and gender inequality in education.

TOWARD A CRITICAL RACE PEDAGOGY

Critical race theorists Reginald Leamon Robinson in "Teaching from the Margins: Race as Pedagogical Sub-Text" and Charles Lawrence III in his article "The Word and the River: Pedagogy as Scholarship as Struggle" both talk about the implications for using a CRT framework for teaching law.[26] Similarly, critical educational theorists bell hooks, Sandra Jackson and Jose Solis, Gloria Ladson-Billings, and Joyce King also write about the difficulties they face when attempting to proffer a racialized pedagogy on college campuses.[27] The tales told by each of these Black scholars are not dissimilar to those told to me when I interviewed several African American elementary and high school teachers about their experiences.

AN EXPLORATORY STUDY

To begin to test the hypothesis that African American teachers committed to social justice agendas would encounter resistance from school authorities and colleagues, I conducted a series of interviews of so-called progressive urban school teachers of color or educators who expressed a commitment to issues of social justice and had a fairly well-defined sense of political, social, and ethnic identity.[28] To be considered for the study, the teachers had to meet the following criteria:

- They had taught in schools that served a significant number of African American youth
- They had taught for at least one full year but not more than seven and
- They had expressed a commitment to issues of social justice and were involved in some kind of effort to operationalize these goals through their work with outside organizations.

The Interviews

I used a purposive sampling technique as opposed to a random sampling approach, which allowed me to carefully select those individuals based on the aforementioned criteria.[29] I usually engaged in one or two face-to-face informal interviews with persons before asking them to participate in the study. After selecting the participants, I ultimately interviewed twelve individuals: five former teachers, four persons who were currently teaching, and three persons who were teacher-credential candidates. All of the participants were either students at a large graduate teaching institution or were affiliated with the institution in some way, either through having attended the institution previously or spending time with others who were in the process of obtaining their degrees. Some of the individuals were persons with whom I attended evening classes. Others were part of activist educational organizations in New York City. At the time, I did not require that all participants be African American; however, the vast majority of them were. This had mostly to do with my involvement in the African American political organizations within and outside of the university. Because this chapter is an examination of African American teachers with at least one year of experience, I will not be using the data from the interviews with the teacher-credential candidates or the teachers who did not classify themselves as African American. As a result, the data from eight out of twelve of the original interviews will be used. Also, pseudonyms are used in place of the actual names of the participants. See table 8-1 for the demographic data.

The average participant was twenty-eight years old. Half of my subjects were men and half were women. The number of years of full-time teaching experience ranged from one to seven with most participants having taught

Table 8-1 Demographic Data on Participants

Name	Age	Sex	Years of Experience	Grade Level Taught	School Location
Betty Awari	28	F	7	K	Brooklyn
Shaun DeLasse	23	M	1	Third	West Harlem
Stewart Freeman	37	M	3	Third	Midtown Manhattan
Calvin Hodges	25	M	1	Fourth	West Harlem
Rena Summers	29	F	3	Fourth	West Harlem
Caldwell				High Schl.	
Washington	29	M	1	Engl.	Patterson, NJ
Debra White	25	F	3	K	Patterson, NJ
Yvette Williams	31	F	2	Third	Patterson, NJ

between one and three years. The teachers had two years and six months of teaching experience, on average. All of the participants taught in schools that could be considered urban. With the exception of one, all of them taught in public schools. Caldwell taught in a Catholic all-boys school located in inner-city Patterson, NJ.

As the U.S. Department of Education reports, the average teacher in the United States is a White female with ten to fifteen years of teaching experience. As I indicated in the criteria, it was not my desire to find a sample that would match the general population of teachers in New York City or in the United States. I sought to interview younger teachers of color because I felt that I might have more in common with them.

Methods

In all instances, I met with the participants individually and tape-recorded the conversations with their permission. I asked each participant to answer a set of open-ended questions about his or her experiences and perceptions of urban schools and society in general. As is common in ethnographic interviews, I asked a number of follow-up questions, which were specific to each individual teacher. My hope was that this protocol would unveil certain elements of the participants' beliefs, teaching experiences, and thoughts on schools and how they negotiated within them. I used the works of Wax and Bogdan and Biklen to construct an interview protocol.[30] The interviews varied in length from one to two hours.

TOWARD A CRITICAL RACE PEDAGOGY: THE REFLECTIONS
OF AFRICAN AMERICAN TEACHERS

Peter McLaren and Michael Dantley argue that Cornel West's articulation of the "African-American prophetic tradition" in religion "offers an empowering pedagogical alternative for leaders in education" and can ultimately be used, along with Stuart Hall's notions of racialized pedagogy, to build a "critical pedagogy of race."[31] This notion is derived via class racialist perspective, which is a neo-Marxist analysis of race and racism in late capitalist society.

In CRT, however, the reflections and life stories of people of color are used as a way to build theories about the nature of race and racism in the United States. More important, people of color have some expertise in this area because of their direct experiences with racism. So, instead of talking about a critical pedagogy of race that still privileges class over race, critical race theorists might use the phrase *critical race pedagogy* as a way to avoid confusion about the prioritizing of one axis of domination over another. Preliminarily, a critical race pedagogy could be defined as an approach to addressing issues of racial, ethnic, and gender subordination within education that entails an articulation of emancipatory pedagogical practices.

In this chapter, I attempt to build a critical race pedagogy from the ground up via reflections of African American practitioners and intellectuals who were strongly committed to ideals and principles outlined earlier. Based on the interview data, it would appear that critical race pedagogues are concerned with four general issues, each of which is outlined next.

The Endemic Nature of Racism in the United States

Debra, a former kindergarten teacher, spoke emphatically about the insidious nature of racism in American society. She commented, "[Racism] is just embedded in everything that's in America. One race is supposed to be inferior because of the history of slavery and the ideology has never left the mind-set. I think it permeates every aspect of society." Similar to the way in which critical race theorist Derrick Bell argues in *Faces at the Bottom of the Well*, she is arguing that race and racism are permanent fixtures that have been woven into the very fabric of our society.[32] Moreover, both are arguing that racism is not aberrant, that it is a normal and fixed part of the American social landscape. For Debra, this was also evident in the way that a White supremacist society constructs and demeans that which is Black. African-centered theorists such as Marimba Ani have also written extensively about the role that European formations have played in animalizing and debasing the humanity of Africans.[33]

Stuart, a third-grade teacher, also expressed his belief in the notion that the United States and its educational system operate under an egregiously racist regime. For him, this manifests itself in the schools through teachers' dysconscious racism and lack of respect for African American children. Joyce King defines *dysconscious racism* as "an uncritical habit of mind (including perceptions, attitudes, assumptions and beliefs)" that "justifies inequity and exploitation by accepting the existing order of things as given."[34] Because of this dysconscious racism Stuart felt very strongly that

> as an African-American male, me and my people are constantly the victims of a racist onslaught on a daily basis. I feel that ... well, I won't describe myself as endangered species like an African elephant but the situation of Black men in this country today is one of real concern. I feel myself as being at risk and to that extent I'm radical in the determination of my safety and existence. I want to survive and I want my people to survive.

Similarly, Betty commented that she was inspired to teach because of the general "miseducation of African youth" in the school systems in the United States. Her critique of schooling in the United States also includes ideas about racist practices of school officials who are unwilling to come to terms with the degree to which their hegemonic practices instill in African American youth a sense of failure. In another statement about the endemic nature of racism in the educational system, Betty tells of an experience with a White parent:

> When I taught kindergarten, it was ridiculous. This one parent came to me crying. It was the first week of school. The children's name tags were still warm on their hooks and she came to saying that she doesn't think I can teach and I said "why?" And she said that she wanted her child's first teacher to be an elderly Jewish woman who can love and nurture her child and she's very disappointed that I'm there. This was not what she pictured for her child. I told her, "Well, you could give it a month and if you still feel like pulling your child out, pull your child out." In the first four weeks of school, there were about six to eight meetings about me and seven children were pulled out of class by their parents. I mean, the parents had a big problem with [my] race. I'm young and I'm Black and they just couldn't handle it!

The Importance of Cultural Identity

Betty also commented in depth about the nature of Western European hegemony and the manner in which it has impacted the cultural lives of African peoples worldwide:

I think that we as a race have allowed the deteriorating, immoral, hedonistic practices of the European to not only invade our community, but dictate our ideology. I think segregation was the best thing for us because when we were segregated our families had identity. Our women had respect. Our churches had strength and our leaders were our leaders and we didn't allow anyone else to define them for us. We chose them. Now, we're in this rat race to be White, to fit into their world and in that way we allow them to define everything we are. We have no identity. In pockets, we do, as a community we don't.

She warns, as Gary Peller does, that integration on Eurocentric terms has not benefited African Americans.[35]

In the same vein, Calvin, a fourth-grade teacher, eschews a depoliticized form of multiculturalism, which in his view only serves to further instantiate Eurocentric practices and ideals. He argues that this discourse is especially dangerous for African American youth who have no "cultural foundation from which they can begin to view other cultures." Similarly, Shaun, a third-grade teacher, talks about the necessity of maintaining cultural integrity and specificity and encouraging these ideals within the schools. Yvette, a former third-grade teacher, talked more specifically about using curricular tools that "capture the experience" of her African American students. For this former teacher, this becomes vital to the success of African American students. Finally, Stewart, a third-grade teacher, expressed anxiety at what he feels is a serious cultural mismatch between teachers and their students. In his view, schools of education do far too little to promote the cultural education for mostly White teachers who are teaching primarily African American and Latino students.

The Necessary Interaction of Race, Class, and Gender

A number of pedagogues argued about the necessary intersection of class and race. Shaun pointed out the educational system in the United States caters to a White middle class and creates "an ever-increasingly segregationist, separate but unequal education for minorities." He elaborates on this idea when he says that White middle-class suburbanites "are able to use their economic resources to make their schools better" and leaving aside educational institutions which serve the urban poor. In the same manner, Rena, a former fourth-grade teacher indicates the extent to which she finds that much of the problem with African American access to education is related to poverty. Debra and Stewart both comment that the problem of racism in the United States is accompanied by the problem of poverty, and the Black poor are in most need of resources and a good sound education. These words resonate strongly with those of Kimberle Crenshaw, who argues that we must look at the intersections of class, race, and gender very closely.[36]

Practicing a Liberatory Pedagogy

The following comments are representative of teachers' reflections about their pedagogy. As I mentioned earlier, their perceptions of their liberatory pedagogy represent a wide range of ideas, perceptions, and beliefs about the best ways to educate African American students. Their comments are consistent with the research findings of those scholars mentioned previously. For these teachers, practicing a liberatory pedagogy involves (1) teaching children about the importance of African culture, (2) encouraging and supporting dialogue in the classroom, (3) engaging in daily self-affirmation exercises with students, and (4) actively and consistently resisting and challenging authorities who advocate practices that are hegemonic and counteremancipatory.

Teaching Children about Africa and the Importance of Culture.   Calvin talks extensively about building his students' knowledge base about Africa by staying "aware of issues pertaining to the African community worldwide." He talks about using his experiences as a way to augment the cultural understanding of his students. For example, he shares with his students photos of slave dungeons on the Ivory Coast that he calls *vestiges of slavery*. For him, this becomes a real way to connect cathartic experiences to the real lives of his students.

Encouraging Inquiry, Dialogue, and Participation in Their Classrooms.   Caldwell, a high school English teacher, talked about the necessity of teaching his students to think critically about what they read and write. His goal as a teacher is to teach his students to be "coconstructors of knowledge," which gives them control over their own learning. Calvin also talked about the need for his students to learn to "be very critical and aware of their surroundings, of everything they look at, and everything they come into contact with." For this educator, students must participate in the process of thinking critically about the world. They develop this critical consciousness through reflection and dialogue with each other and with the teacher. This approach is reminiscent of a Freirean approach to teaching, which is based on the belief that the all teaching and learning is political and that the role of the school and teacher is to politicize their students through active dialogical engagement.[37] Critical race theorists also believe in using this approach in their classrooms.[38]

Practicing Daily the Act of Self-Affirmation with Their Students.   Yvette talked also about the importance of engaging young African American students in exercises aimed at affirming their subjectivity and individuality. She comments, "We did self-affirmation exercises in the morning. They wrote, 'I am beautiful. I can succeed.'" For this teacher, those exercises helped her African Americans students begin the process of salvaging and reconstructing their cultural, emotional, and spiritual selves. As Afrocentric theorists argue, it empowered them by allowing them to move themselves and their history from center to margin.[39]

The Act of Resisting School Authorities.   Derrick Bell, in his book *Confronting Authority: Reflections of an Ardent Protester*, talks about the necessity of educators to challenge school administration on issues of equity and fairness.[40] Though this work is not considered part of the CRT canon, it is an important work that unlike the others, provides us with some insight into how this leading author and critical legal scholar chose to live his own life with regard to issues of social justice. Though, admittedly, this was not a theme consistent throughout all the interviews, one respondent (Caldwell) chose to speak about an experience in which he confronted the administration on an issue that he felt was of paramount importance to his students. He comments:

> [A student in my class] was diagnosed with dyslexia. I asked the principal for help. The principal asked me what grade he was receiving in my course and I told him that the child was receiving a "D." The principal said, "Well, he's passing," and I responded, "But only barely." He then responded by telling me that all kids can't be honors students. I interpreted this to mean that when we teach African American students, we must accept the notion of "necessary losses." I retorted by stating that I felt we had different educational philosophies and I walked out.

Though some might consider Caldwell's behavior unproductive and unnecessarily combative, he felt very strongly that he had gained a degree of respect from his superiors because they knew they could count on him tell them exactly what he was thinking about issues of justice and fairness. As Bell reminds us, we must learn from the legacy of our forebears who fought against insurmountable odds to demand that they be treated with dignity and respect. In his eyes, we can afford to do no less than that.

CONCLUSION AND SUMMARY

The goal of this chapter has been to present in some form, the research on African American teachers by situating it within the literature on African-centered critiques of schooling. I have also attempted to define succinctly CRT and then appropriate it, as others have done, to the study of education in general and the study of African American teachers in particular. As I have attempted to illustrate, a critical race analysis of the perceptions and reflections of critical African American teachers can lead to new ideas and new theoretical approaches such as critical race pedagogy.

This discourse is different from extant critical analyses of schooling because it is multidimensional in its focus—it can and should take into account all of the facets of our multilayered identities while arguing that race should be used as the primary unit of analysis in critical discussions of schooling in the United States. CRT has the unique capacity to argue for the uplifting of people of color without negating other important aspects of their identity, such as gender and class.

As Omi and Winant argue, the United States is and has always been a racialized state, and we cannot ignore this reality lest we belie the history of this nation entirely.[41] Not only does the development of a critical race pedagogy in education demand that we more thoroughly investigate the failure of our schools to adequately educate racially subordinate youth in the United States, it requires that we talk about solutions.

Finally, as we begin the new millennium with all of the problems of the "color line" still fully intact,[42] we will continue to be in desperate need of some direction and guidance as to how we can begin to build a democracy that acknowledges and incorporates all of its citizenry into the construction of a strong diversified unit. CRT couldn't have come at a better time!

NOTES

1. C. G. Woodson, *The Miseducation of the Negro* (Trenton: Africa World Press, 1993).

2. C. G. Woodson, *Education of the Negro Prior to 1861: A History of the Education of the Colored People in the United States from the Beginning of Slavery to the Civil War* (Washington, DC: Associated Publishers, 1968).

3. R. E. Butchart, "Educating for Freedom: Northern Whites and the Origins of Black Education in the South, 1862–1875" (Ph.D. diss., State University of New York–Binghamton, 1976).

4. J. Anderson, *The Education of Blacks in the South, 1860–1935* (Chapel Hill: University of North Carolina Press, 1988).

5. J. Kunjufu, *Countering the Conspiracy to Destroy Black Boys* (Chicago: African-American Images, 1985); J. Kunjufu, *Countering the Conspiracy to Destroy Black Boys*, vol. 2 (Chicago: African-American Images, 1986); C. Lee and D. T. Slaughter-Defoe, "Historical and Sociocultural Influences on African-American Education," in J. Banks and C. A. McGee Banks (eds.), *Handbook of Research on Multicultural Education* (New York: Macmillan, 1995), 348–371; M. J. Shujaa (ed.), *Too Much Schooling, Too Little Education: A Paradox of Black Life in White Societies* (Trenton: Africa World Press, 1994/1995).

6. See, for example, L. Delpit, "The Silenced Dialogue: Power and Pedagogy in Educating Other People's Children," in M. Fine and L. Weis (eds.), *Beyond Silenced Voices: Class, Race and Gender in the United States* (Albany: State University of New York Press, 1993), 119–142; M. Foster, *Black Teachers on Teaching* (New York: New Press, 1997); A. Henry, "African Canadian Women Teachers' Activism: Recreating Communities of Caring and Resistance," *Journal of Negro Education* 61, no. 3 (1992): 392–404; G. Ladson-Billings, *The DreamKeepers: Successful Teachers of African-American Children* (San Francisco: Jossey-Bass, 1994); T. Perry and L. Delpit (eds.), *The Real Ebonics Debate: Power, Language and the Education of African-American Children* (Boston: Beacon Press, 1998).

7. P. Hill Collins, *Black Feminist Thought: Knowlege, Consciousness, and the Politics of Empowerment. Perspectives on Gender*, vol. 2 (New York: Routledge, 1991).

8. M. L. Asante, *The Afrocentric Idea* (Philadelphia: Temple University Press, 1987); M. L. Asante, *Afrocentricity* (Trenton: Africa World Press, 1988/1996).

9. Alice Walker, *In Search of Our Mothers' Gardens: Womanist Prose* (New York: Harvest Books, 1983).

10. Walker, quoted in Henry, "African Canadian Women Teachers' Activism."

11. Collins, *Black Feminist Thought.*

12. M. Foster, "African American Teachers and Culturally Relevant Pedagogy," in J. Banks and C. A. McGee Banks (eds.), *Handbook of Research on Multicultural Education* (New York: Macmillan, 1995), 221.

13. Perry and Delpit, *The Real Ebonics Debate*, 106.

14. Delpit, "The Silenced Dialogue"; L. Delpit, *Other People's Children* (New York: New Press, 1996).

15. Ladson-Billings, *The DreamKeepers*; G. Ladson-Billings, "Toward a Theory of Culturally Relevant Teaching," *American Educational Research Journal* 32, no. 3 (1995): 465–491.

16. Carol Lee and D. T. Slaughter-DeFoe, "Historical and Sociocultural Influences on Africaqn-American Education," in J. A. Banks and C. A. McGee Banks (eds.), *Handbook of Research on Multicultural Education* (New York: Macmillan, 1995): 348–371.

17. M. Foster, "The Politics of Race: Through African-American Teachers' Eyes," *Journal of Education* 172, no. 3 (1990): 123–141.

18. Henry, "African Canadian Women Teachers' Activism."

19. K. Crenshaw, N. Gotanda, G. Peller, and K. Thomas (eds.), *Critical Race Theory: The Key Writings that Formed the Movement* (New York: New Press, 1995); R. Delgado (ed.), *Critical Race Theory: The Cutting Edge* (Philadelphia: Temple University Press, 1995).

20. M. Matsuda, C. Lawrence, R. Delgado, and K. Crenshaw, *Words that Wound: Critical Race Theory, Assaultive Speech, and the First Amendment* (Boulder, CO: Westview Press, 1993).

21. W. F. Tate IV, "Critical Race Theory and Education: History, Theory and Implications," in M. W. Apple (ed.), *Review of Research in Education* (Washington, DC: AERA, 1997), 195–247.

22. Matsuda et al., *Words That Wound*; D. Solorzano, "Images and Words That Wound: Critical Race Theory, Racial Stereotyping, and Teacher Education," *Teacher Education Quarterly*, 24 (1997): 5–19; Tate, "Critical Race Theory and Education."

23. G. Ladson-Billings, "Just What Is Critical Race Theory and What's It Doing in a *Nice* Field Like Education?," *International Journal of Qualitative Studies in Education* 11, no. 1 (1998): 7–24; G. Ladson-Billings (ed.), *Critical Race Theory Perspectives on the Social Studies* (Greenwich, CT: Information Age Publishers, 2003); D. Solorzano, "Critical Race Theory, Racial Microaggressions, and the Experiences of Chicana and Chicano Scholars," *International Journal of Qualitative Studies in Education* 11, no. 1 (1998): 7–24; D. Solorzano and O. Villalpando, "Critical Race Theory, Marginality, and the Experience of Minority Students in Higher Education," in C. Torres and T. Mitchell (eds.), *Emerging Issues in the Sociology of Education: Comparative Perspectives* (Albany: SUNY Press, 1998), 211–224; D. Solorzano and T. Yosso, "Toward a Critical Race Theory of Chicana and Chicano Education," in C. Tejada, C. Martinez, Z. Leonardo, and P. McLaren (eds.), *Demarcating the Border of Chicana(o)/Latina(o) Education* (Cresskill, NJ: Hampton Press, 2000), 35–65; Tate, "Critical Race Theory and Education."

24. Solorzano and Yosso, "Toward a Critical Race Theory of Chicana and Chicano Education," 45; emphasis added.

25. Ladson-Billings, "Just What Is Critical Race Theory?" 18.

26. R. Robinson, "Teaching from the Margins: Race as a Pedagogical Sub-Text," *Western New England Law Review* 19 (1997): 151–181; Charles Lawrence, "The Word and the River: Pedagogy as Scholarship and Struggle," *Southern California Law Review* 65 (1991): 2231–2298.

27. B. Hooks, "Transformative Pedagogy and Multiculturalism" in T. Perry and J. Frazier (eds.), *Freedom's Plow* (New York: Routledge, 1993), 91–97; S. Jackson and J. Solis (eds.), *Beyond Comfort Zones in Multiculturalism: Confronting the Politics of Privilege* (Westport, CT: Bergin and Garvey, 1995); Ladson-Billings, "Just What Is Critical Race Theory?"; J. E. King, "Culture-Centered Knowledge: Black Studies, Curriculum Transformation, and Social Action," in J. Banks and C. A. McGee Banks (eds.), *Handbook of Research on Multicultural Education* (New York: Macmillan, 1995), 265–290; also see chapter 12, this volume, by Luis Urrieta Jr. and Michelle Reidel.

28. Marvin Lynn, "Choosing Your Battles: Progressive Young Teachers of Color and Their Experiences in Urban Schools," paper presented at "Reclaiming Voice: Ethnographic Inquiry and Research in PostModern Age" conference, Los Angeles, CA, June 1997.

29. S. B. Merriam, *Case Study Research in Education: A Qualitative Approach* (San Francisco: Jossey-Bass, 1988).

30. R. Bogdan and S. K. Biklen, *Qualitative Research in Education: An Introduction to Theory and Methods* (Boston: Allyn and Bacon, 1982); R. Wax, *Doing Fieldwork: Warnings and Advice* (Chicago: University of Chicago Press, 1992).

31. P. McLaren and M. Dantley, "Leadership and a Critical Pedagogy of Race: Cornel West, Stuart Hall, and the Prophetic Tradition," *Journal of Negro Education* 59, no. 1 (1990): 39, 41.

32. D. Bell, *Faces at the Bottom of the Well: The Permanence of Racism* (New York: Basic Books, 1992).

33. M. Ani, *Yurugu: An African-Centered Critique of European Cultural Thought and Behavior* (Trenton, NJ: Africa World Press, 1994).

34. Joyce King, "Unfinished Business: Black Students' Alienation and Black Teachers' Pedagogy," in M. Foster (ed.), *Readings an Equal Education: Qualitative Investigations into Schools and Schooling* (New York: AMS Press), 273–309.

35. G. Peller, "Race Consciousness" *Duke Law Journal* 4, (1990): 758–847.

36. Crenshaw et al., *Critical Race Theory*.

37. P. Freire, *Pedagogy of the Oppressed* (New York: Continuum, 1970); P. Freire, *Education for Critical Consciousness* (New York: Seabury Press, 1973).

38. Robinson, "Teaching from the Margins."

39. Asante, *The Afrocentric Idea*; Asante, *Afrocentricity*.

40. D. Bell, *Confronting Authority: Reflections of an Ardent Protester* (Boston: Beacon Press, 1994).

41. M. Omi and H. Winant, *Racial Formation in the United States: From the 1960's to the 1990's*, 2nd ed. (New York: Routledge, 1994).

42. W. E. B. DuBois, *The Souls of Black Folk* (New York: New American Library, 1969).

III

PREPARING ANTIRACIST EDUCATORS

9

Diaspora Literacy and Consciousness in the Struggle against Miseducation in the Black Community

Joyce E. King

Evaluation of the Slaves that Arrived from Benguela [Kongo] on the . . . of April, 1738:

> Young Women and Children:
> Mama/Cambia, with child dying: 6$000
> Bissoa/Bivalla, with child walking 8$000
> . . .
> Banba/Caceyo, child dying 4$000
> Tembo/Cabeto 8$000
> . . .
> Quimano, no child—died on the path 3$000
> Banba/Sonbi, child at the breast—almost dead 3$000
> . . .
> Nhama, open sores on both legs $ 500

The author gratefully acknowledges the assistance of Professor Sterling Stuckey [S. Stuckey, *Slave Culture* (New York: Oxford University Press, 1987)], a University of California–Riverside historian, with the research on historical sources for this chapter. This research was supported by funds from the James Irvine Foundation grant to Santa Clara University's "Excellence through Diversity Initiative" when the author served on the faculty of that institution. The views expressed do not necessarily reflect those of the university or the sponsor. This chapter has been revised and updated with a new introduction; it originally appeared in *The Journal of Negro Education* 61, no. 3 (1992) and is published with permission. © 1992 Howard University.

Camia 5$000

Cahunda, no child—died in the bush 5$000

Sungo, small girl 2$000

Ullunga 6$000

Tembo, old woman 12$000

Singa, defects on the toes of both feet 3$000

Bienba/Sungu, child at the breast 7$000

Sanga/Bienba, child walking—dying 3$000

Child, name unknown as she is dying and cannot speak, male without value, and a small girl Callenbo, no value because she is dying... [Partial] Summary of an inventory of slaves turned over to the government in the aftermath of a military expedition against Caconda [Angola] in 1736...au-authenticated and described as a "just war."

—J. C. Miller, "The Slave Trade in the Congo and Angola"[1]

If you talk about the slave trade, for example, you have to point out that the slaves came over to the New World primarily because Africans enslaved them first or captured them in war and sold them to the Europeans. They weren't picked up by Europeans in the depths of Africa, they were brought by Africans and you have to say that [and] that the whites were the ones, of course, that traded for them and brought them here and found them extremely useful.

—Carl Degler[2]

INTRODUCTION

The transatlantic slave trade that caused the displacement and death of untold millions spanned nearly four centuries. Our understanding of this African holocaust comes not only from modern scholarship and its representation in school texts and children's books but from orature such as tales, narratives, and traditional music as well as fiction.[3] For example, Courlander's novel *The African* relates the ordeal of a Fon youth who is captured by soldiers near his village and sold into slavery by the king of Dahomey, who, in doing so, betrayed his own people.[4] This youngster survives the deadly Middle Passage to America where he grows into manhood. His eventual escape is possible in part because neither the Middle Passage nor slavery obliterated his cultural memory—including proverbs like the following, by which his people affirmed their humanity and taught him to apprehend the world: "Knowledge is another name for strength."[5]

This chapter focuses analytical attention on ideological representations of the Middle Passage and how slavery began, as depicted in classroom textbooks adopted by the state of California in the early 1990s. The clash that ensued in California over the adoption of these controversial textbooks foreshadowed ongoing struggles concerning what and how students are learning about the Black experience. In fact, generations of academic researchers, educators, and activists have been concerned about improving what is taught in school. Their concerns include biased content as well as information missing from the curriculum. Carter G. Woodson's *Miseducation of the Negro*, published in 1933, represents a well-known scholarly approach to this historical problem.[6] Woodson demonstrated how all students are negatively affected by curriculum distortions regarding the Black experience. New fields of study and educational practice have emerged since the 1960s to address these same concerns, including African American and Black studies, ethnic studies, women's studies, feminist studies, White studies, and multicultural education. Furthermore, myriad commissions and task forces have produced countless studies, reports, and recommendations (e.g., the "Curriculum of Inclusion"). In 1984 the National Association of Black School Educators issued "Saving the African American Child: A Report on Black Academic and Cultural Excellence."

Recent examples of legislation enacted to correct ongoing curriculum deficiencies include the Amistad Act (New Jersey), the Underground Railroad Project (New York), and a high school course in African American studies now required to graduate from Philadelphia public high schools. Attempts to legislate the inclusion of content specific to the African American experience have been obstructed by various factors—from political intransigence to limited teacher knowledge to the failure to understand the common human interests in curricula informed by African American or Black studies scholarship. In New Jersey, for instance, local education officials recently rejected the request of a parent's group (A Parent's Initiative for Every Child's Education—APIECE) for a Black history course to fulfill the requirements of the Amistad Act. In rejecting the parents' request, these officials reveal several erroneous assumptions: that Black history is necessarily exclusionary and a diversity in America course is not only sufficient to meet the provisions of the law but also that a multiethnic approach is the best way to infuse content regarding the African American experience into the existing curriculum. Another assumption is that this approach will meet the needs of all students. As usually happens in such debates, the question of the scholarly perspectives in which the curriculum content will be grounded is ignored.[7]

This chapter, though originally published in 1992, sheds light on the politics of knowledge underlying such struggles over curriculum content. In the clash that took place in California, state and national education officials and mainstream scholars proclaimed the adoption of the textbooks that were the focus of the controversy examined in this chapter as a victory for multiculturalism. In this chapter and in my interactions with parents and multicultural education specialists who participated in the inquiry I designed to explore this clash, I use the beginnings of the Middle Passage in the African context as a milieu de mémoire to decipher covert alienating perspectives in the textbooks in question. These texts seek to explain slavery, but by omitting or distorting certain cultural signs, they preclude forms of knowledge and perspectives that are enabled by diaspora literacy, which Busia describes as "an ability to read a variety of cultural signs of the lives of Africa's children at home and in the New World."[8] Following Sylvia Wynter's explication of Black studies as a deciphering practice, the present study is an attempt to construct a milieu de mémoire or alternative standpoint from which to recover both memory and history.[9] According to Wynter, Black studies is a new mode of inquiry that "seeks to decipher *what* the process of rhetorical mystification *does*... not what texts and their signifying practices *mean* but what they can be deciphered to *do*."[10] My intention herein is to decipher, as ideological forms, both the representations of modern historical scholarship in California's textbooks and the ways in which this scholarship has been justified as accurate and valid knowledge.

I write about these matters not as a historian or a learning or reading specialist but as a sociologist interested in the sociology of knowledge that functions as ideology. My use of the word *ideology* follows Giddens's explication and critical analysis of ideology as understood by Marx, Mannheim, and Habermas and as it concerns "what counts as a valid claim to knowledge" and "the critique of domination."[11] Related to this is a concern about the "social domination of ideas" and consciousness as well as the role of the intellectual in "partisan struggles of political life."[12]

BLACK STUDIES AS THE CRITIQUE OF IDEOLOGY

> It is normally in the interests of dominant groups if the existence of contradictions is denied or their real basis obscured.
> —Anthony Giddens, *Central Problems in Sociological Theory*[13]

Because traditional textbooks also preclude forms of ideology critique that consciousness—that is, critical comprehension of the essential nature of society, its myths, and one's own interests—requires, this chapter attempts to stimulate discussion about the role of Black studies as ideology critique in the struggle against what Woodson called the "mis-education of the Negro." It describes an exploratory case study of parent and educator responses to critical analyses of the textbook controversy and explores the practical use-fulness of an intellectual perspective for collective social action. Such efforts to seek theoretical validation in social practice[14] and make more of the social totality the object of study[15] are two of the guiding tenets of both dialectical social theory and the African American intellectual tradition.[16]

I used an exploratory case study approach to examine the responses and reactions of parents and educators to a Black studies ideology critique.[17] That critique included (a) my own analysis of the textbook controversy, (b) presentation of examples of textbook distortions, (c) discussion of Wynter's essay-critique of American textbooks,[18] and (d) viewing of a one-hour vi-deotaped lecture and discussion in which Wynter presents her Black studies "cultural model perspective."[19] Participants in the study heard a brief pre-sentation that included analyses and examples of the textbook controversy and textbook distortions similar to those presented in this chapter; addi-tionally, each received a viewer's guide to the videotape, which included a timeline, an outline of critical (generative) themes, vocabulary terms, and a list of the scholars Wynter cites in her videotaped discussion. I conducted two group discussion and interview meetings with eight Black parents of high school students (who met as a support group) and four Black multicultural education specialists. (A vice principal, three teachers, and five students were also at the parent group meeting.) Four parents and one of the educators also participated in thirty- to fifty-minute follow-up interviews to solicit their feedback regarding the presentation and the videotape.

By bringing the views of parents and educators into the discussion of textbooks and what they do, I have attempted to decipher the socially cons-tructed appearances of the controversy surrounding the textbook adoption in California. I wanted to know (1) the extent to which or whether Black parents and activist educators recognize what school curricula actually do; (2) if a Black studies ideology critique is of interest to these parents and educators; and (3) if such an intellectual perspective expresses what they think, feel, and experience with regard to the struggles for education in Black communities. How important to educators and the Black community at large is a sophisticated theoretical understanding of what Wynter calls the "rules" that "institute the social order" and its "regime of truth?"[20] Does it illuminate the social contradictions involved in education under conditions of racial domination? Is a theoretical approach helpful, for instance, in their real-world struggles again miseducation? Does it stimulate reflection, social analysis, or action?

THEORETICAL BACKGROUND: DIASPORA LITERACY
AND HUMAN CONSCIOUSNESS

> *Malcolm:* The greatest mistake of the movement has been trying to organize a
> sleeping people around specific goals. You have to wake people up first; then
> you'll get action.
> *Miss Nadle:* Wake them up to their exploitation?
> *Malcolm:* No, to their humanity, to their own worth, and to their heritage.
> —G. Breitman, *Malcolm X Speaks*[21]

As Busia explains, diaspora literacy, or knowledge of our story, of Black
people's "cultural dispossession," can start one on the "journey of self-
recognition and healing."[22] The sociohistory of school knowledge, however,
maintains a destructive consciousness of class, race, ethnicity, and personality
that constricts the human spirit and perpetuates violence and inhumanity.[23]
Given the traditional cultural hegemony, which enshrines dominant group
values and perspectives in school texts, and notwithstanding the strength to
be gained from cultural "rememory" or diaspora literacy, we Blacks can know
our story in ways that are partial and distorted.[24] Thus, we need a human
consciousness to complement what Kohl would call our "multiple narratives."[25]

   As a social relations construct, human consciousness is more dynam-
ically and transformatively inclusive than any single category of existence.
In comparison to class, race, or gender consciousness, for example, human
consciousness grasps the essential nature of society, including Black people's
multiple identities as well as the specific ways that racism and other -isms
work. As such, it requires the mediation of new categories of analysis in
nonsynchronous, mutually reinforcing race, class, or gender terms.[26] I do
not use this construct to privilege or obliterate specific forms of difference,
nor do I seek to rule out what McCarthy calls the collective-identity politics
people need to apprehend the world both in its particularity and "social
totality."[27] However, in departing from the way Marx theorized about class
consciousness per se,[28] I nonetheless want to use his theoretical insights to
suggest that human consciousness encompasses Eyerman's definition of class
consciousness as "a political and social awareness that grows out of a common experience; perceived common interests and shared self-knowledge and
self-definition."[29] As Eyerman continues, human consciousness also "implies an awareness of others, of those who are similar and those who are different with regard to their long-term interest, and an awareness of the social
structure that makes this difference real."[30]

Just as diaspora literacy enables us to repossess our story (including our cultural identity as Africa's children), human consciousness permits us to retrieve our humanity from distorted notions of the conceptual Blackness that is the alter ego of the socially constructed category of Whiteness.[31] This process of self-repossession and cultural recovery from alienation is the universal human interest in the Black struggle for authentic "self-knowing" and collective identity that, like Black studies, challenges the interests the dominant ideology conceals in myths about "we the people." For those Black people who do not "sleepwalk inside America's myths,"[32] alienation can bring the gift of this transcendent human consciousness. The alternative to self- and cultural alienation engendered by these myths is not just unconsciousness but "dysconsciousness"—one way ideological justification(s) of racial domination (that is, the status quo) shape(s) people's perceptions and ideas about themselves and society.[33] If diaspora literacy aids the recovery of self-knowledge and cultural memory, human consciousness is an achievement, a spiritual discovery that recovers authentic being from fragmented knowing, acting, and being.[34]

THE CONTEXT: THE CALIFORNIA TEXTBOOK CONTROVERSY

> Our ancestors did not wade through rivers of blood so that we might surrender the interpretation of their lives into the hands of others.
> —Vincent Harding, "The Vocation of the Black Scholar
> and the Struggles of the Black Community"[35]

The State Board of Education in California, a textbook adoption state, relies on an advisory body to recommend textbooks and other instructional materials for adoption that schools can buy with state funds. As a member of this advisory body, the California Curriculum Development and Supplemental Materials Commission from 1986 to 1990, I participated in the development of the California *History/Social Science Framework* and the 1990 history textbook adoption.[36] I publicly opposed this adoption because in my view the textbooks recommended contained "egregious racial stereotyping, inaccuracies, distortions, omissions, justifications and trivialization of unethical and inhumane social practices, including racial slavery."[37] In my letter to the commission I also stated that "as a result of these shortcomings, these books fail(ed) to meet the standards set by the *Framework* for cultural diversity, ethical literacy, historical accuracy, opportunities to examine controversial issues and to develop critical thinking and democratic social participation skills."[38] After several tense public hearings with armed guards present; unprecedented attendance that reflected a groundswell of public concern, opposition, and divided opinions; and a direct appeal from the Black Caucus of the state legislature to postpone the adoption decision, the Board of Education adopted one kindergarten through grade eight series and an additional eighth-grade history text.

The concerns I raised about the textbooks were the same ones that I raised in 1987 about the inclusion of diverse perspectives when early drafts of the *Framework* were circulated for public input and review. Even though the *Framework* writing committee incorporated some of the changes I suggested into the final version of the document, the textbooks ultimately selected following this curriculum guide mirrored its fundamental conceptual flaws and biases. Not surprisingly, none of the history textbooks reviewed, including those that were eventually adopted, received higher than moderate ratings for cultural diversity, one of the *Framework*'s seventeen characteristics for evaluating the texts.

This abbreviated account belies other developments that can only be briefly mentioned here. First, state Department of Education officials and the publisher of the textbook series launched a massive public relations campaign that shaped public opinion and distorted the issues surrounding this controversial adoption. The superintendent of Public Instruction, who was selected as Man of the Week by a major network, denounced critics of the texts on national and local TV shows. The media helped spread the dire warnings that critics of the textbooks would launch the society into tribal warfare if their criticisms prevailed. Second, there was an effort to virtually anoint these books as multicultural despite their moderate evaluations on this criterion. The books were repeatedly compared to existing texts rather than to the evaluation criteria. In addition, the state Department of Education, the curriculum commissioners, and the Board of Education held an unusual joint press conference in July 1990 to praise the recommended textbooks even before the board voted to adopt them in October 1990. This chronology does not address the third aspect: the longer-term politics involved in the displacement of social studies in the curriculum by the history-geography–centered focus of the California *Framework* and its incorporation into the effort to establish national curriculum standards and tests for this subject.

At the local level, with the state's official endorsement of the adopted textbooks as sufficiently multicultural, many hoped the controversy would disappear as schools were left with practically no choice but to buy these books. Thus there is the deeper crisis of democracy and the deskilling of teachers. Moreover, this imprimatur of state adoption made dialogue about the flaws in these texts difficult at the community level. Teachers and parents were often pitted against each other; however, although skilled and knowledgeable teachers can use even the worst texts and the *Framework* to inspire critical learning, teachers with the skill and the concern to do so are increasingly rare.[39] It is even less likely that teachers, especially those in predominantly White communities, will bother to question their texts or attempt to develop counterknowledge when using them.[40]

Sustained resistance to the texts was taken up by parents and school board members in at least five communities that refused to buy the books in California (Butte County, East Palo Alto [Ravenswood City Schools], Hayward, Oakland, and San Jose [Alum Rock]).[41] The Los Angeles Unified School District agreed to purchase the books on condition that the publisher supply specially written supplemental materials for teaching about specific racial and ethnic groups and cultural diversity. Over strong community opposition, the San Francisco and Berkeley school districts bought the books, but they relied on the supplementals as well. The desires of teachers prevailed in the latter instances. The controversy continued unabated as communities throughout the state and the nation circulated materials to support alternatives.[42] Among the many letters of support I received, the essay-critique by Stanford University's Sylvia Wynter, "America as a World," has proved most useful in the education and social action efforts the controversy has stimulated.[43]

Harding's admonition (cited at the beginning of this section) seems rather prophetic in hindsight. Indeed, subsequent and ongoing public criticism of school texts and curricula has recatalyzed Black America's struggle around education issues.[44] Not surprisingly, community activism and academic curriculum challenges have become targets of a specious backlash that appropriates a particular version of multiculturalism to ward off this challenge—as will be explained later.[45] Although strong opposition to California's controversial kindergarten through grade eight history textbooks failed to prevent their adoption in that state, wide exposure of the clash that took place over these books stimulated increased public reaction across the nation. Conferences were convened, alternative curricula were created, and legal actions for educational redress continue.

IDEOLOGY/DOMINATION/ALIENATION: THE CENTRAL CLASH OVER THE TEXTBOOKS

> The air everywhere around is poisoned with truncated tales of our origins.
> That is also part of the wreckage of our people.
> —Ayi Kwei Armah, *Two Thousand Seasons*[46]

In defending California's chosen history textbooks as accurate and in the way they characterized the clash over the textbooks, state officials and the textbook developers used their power and the media to conceal the real basis of the controversy.[47] The clash in California is about ideology, not ethnicity; it is about how curricula and school knowledge support dominating power relations through historical narratives that alienate Black students and other students of color. To protect their interests, the dominant groups who hold power in American society choose to portray this controversy as a threat to national unity, to "E Pluribus Unum" itself. Yet, their rationalizations merely serve to justify the way in which these adopted history texts marginalize and suppress the Black struggle for justice and human values in this country—a struggle that Harding claims, if presented with truthful integrity, might awaken more of the nation's newly arrived immigrants and native Whites, the downwardly mobile in particular, to America's myths.[48]

To recognize the major ways ideology operates in any society, Giddens suggests we look for the "modes in which *domination is concealed as domination*" and "power is harnessed to conceal sectional interests."[49] According to Giddens, ideology works in the following ways: (1) sectional interests are represented as universal, (2) societal contradictions are denied or transmuted, and (3) the present is naturalized or reified. Each of these aspects was evident in the California textbook controversy.

Particularistic Sectional Interests versus the Public's Democratic Interests

Throughout California's controversial textbook adoption process, state officials claimed that self-interested ethnic and religious groups objected to the textbooks simply because they wanted to impose their own personal knowing on the curriculum. The superintendent of Public Instruction, a self-described liberal Democrat, proclaimed: "These groups only want the bad side of our history told; they want a glorified version of *their* history in the books."[50] Thus in national and local media accounts and education articles, the educational bureaucracy and dominant powerful groups denied their own particularistic, sectional interests (and the social contradictions involved) and instead repeatedly accused ethnic and religious groups critical of the textbooks of being self-interested. This theme was frequently and derisively reduced to the notion of ethnic cheerleading. The California Curriculum Commission's *Textbook Adoption Recommendations* report, which it submitted to the California State Board of Education, even dismissed public opposition and scholarly criticisms of the books as mere filiopietism. In this, the official account of the controversy, "special interest groups" are reported to have mistakenly elevated—for the sake of "children's self-esteem"—their "ancestral" identities above the common interests of the proverbial "unum."[51] The state Board of Education decided that adopting the texts recommended by the commission would preserve this shared culture. Thus these officials used their power to validate their choices as being the "latest authoritative historical research" of "established" scholars whom they deemed ostensibly guided by the search for truth.[52]

Contradictions Denied and Racism Transmuted into Ethnic Conflict

Many educators and parents expressed concerns about the textbook treatment of issues related to racial injustice. (One textbook equates racism, for example, with ethnic or cultural prejudice.) Threatening slogans warning of balkanization and impending tribal warfare repeated by scholars and media commentators further distorted the central clash over the issue of perspective bias in the textbooks and transmuted it into a problem of ethnic conflict. Repeatedly, the question was asked: "Can't a White man write accurately and with sensitivity about the experiences of other groups?" The answer, of course, is yes; the issue, however, is the social interests of the perspective from which any scholar writes, regardless of ethnicity, gender, religion, and so on. Yet because the problem of scholarly perspective surrounding this controversy was adroitly denied and redefined in ethnic conflict terms, the books were verified as accurate, with a few minor changes, but with no change in the predominant intellectual perspective.

The Reification and Naturalization of the Immigrant Experience

California's changing demographics provided a most appropriate context for understanding how the traditional perspectives of the adopted American history textbooks concealed the domination of the nation's subordinated non-White groups. These texts presented assimilation and acculturation as the appropriate path to success for these populations by reifying the experiences of the diverse groups of European ethnics who came through Ellis Island to become Americans, thus making the immigrant experience a template for all other groups. Portraying this historical European immigration and assimilation as the quintessential American experience permitted these texts to define African Americans as "forced immigrants" who "came in chains," as though our coming to America was somehow analogous to their immigration. This narrative also allows for the description of Native Americans as the first immigrants, who came across the Bering Straits—notwithstanding the perspectives of indigenous Native Americans regarding their origins,[53] the colonizing motives of the earliest founding settlers, or the contradictory and troublesome presence of a captive African population in the "land of the free."[54] Even if we leave aside the meaning of the word *immigrant* as one who *chooses* to relocate, the idealized immigrant perspective distorts the historical continuity of African Americans, Native Americans, and the indigenous peoples now known as Chicanos, Hispanics, or Latinos, who did not come to America in search of material gain or freedom but were conquered by European American settlers.[55] Significantly, however, California's chosen textbooks invited Black, red, and brown people—and other non-White, non-European newcomers (Asians, for example)—to identify with the selective interpretation of the history of European American immigrants. Just as this immigrant (even if multicultural) national identity, in which ethnicity becomes an option, displaces racial identity in these (and other) American history texts, this ruling idea of the American unum leaves racial hierarchy unacknowledged and unchallenged.[56]

What does this reification of the Euro-immigrant past do? It naturalizes the particular social, political, and economic interests of dominant Whites by making the interests of newly arrived, non-White immigrants appear to be identical to theirs. Furthermore, it suppresses the identification of these groups with Black America's transformative aspirations and historic struggles for justice (or with those of indigenous peoples). Hamilton contends that this divide-and-rule strategy is a characteristic of the new unum politics in California.[57] As minorities become the majority there, manifestations of this strategy's effects are clearly evident in conflicts between non-White groups.

Clearly, this reified immigrant experience is inclusive and multicultural only if we are *all* immigrants. Precisely because this is not the case, the textbooks (and the California *Framework*) insist that the United States is a nation of immigrants. However, the leitmotif of the immigrant experience in America (and elsewhere) has been the appearance of individual opportunity for upward mobility and economic advancement, more so than the collective struggle for justice. For the descendants of indigenous peoples forced to leave and give up their lands, one political consequence of accepting this ideology is the forfeiture of any basis of collective claims for redress and justice. However, to identify with one's collective interests is not, as was charged, excessive veneration of one's ancestors (i.e., filiopietism), but a logical antidote to domination and alienation.[58]

THE CONSEQUENCES OF MISEQUATING THE MIDDLE PASSAGE WITH ELLIS ISLAND

> Everything is all messed up here with the black people, they forget everything they know.
>
> —Harold Courlander, *The African*[59]

Black students' ancestral origins are doubly tainted within the cultural model framework that naturalizes the immigrant experience: Not only did their ancestors come to this land as slaves, but the masses of Black folk still live in poverty. The reality of the African presence, then and now, contradicts the myth of America as a land of freedom, justice, and equality of opportunity for all individuals; yet the subtext of White immigrant identity, manipulatively linked increasingly with model minority immigrant success, inherently implies that Black people's failure is a failure to assimilate and acculturate. The immigrant bias in the textbooks obscures the contradictions occasioned by racial injustice and misequates the Middle Passage with Ellis Island, thus distorting the African diaspora experience and making it an anomaly rather than a paradox of the American reality.

To place themselves within the immigrant paradigm, Black students must construct an attenuated identity that can only originate with the degraded status of their enslaved African ancestors who arrived not by Ellis Island, that now-celebrated gateway to the land of our dreams, but by the horrors of the Middle Passage route.[60] Forcing this reified immigrant identity on Black students further stigmatizes the rupture between them and their ancestors, who did not choose to come to America.[61] Educators and parents are painfully aware that many Black students are traumatized and humiliated when reading about slavery or other topics concerning their ancestry. They often report that Black students do not want to discuss slavery or be identified with Africa,[62] and many admit that they lack the conceptual tools to intervene in this dangerous dynamic.[63] Moreover, there is generalized silence about it in disciplines and fields of pedagogical inquiry that might otherwise be of help to them.

What is at stake is not just that all students are expected to internalize the Euro-immigrant ideological perspective and identity insisted on in the approved textbooks. Nor is it just that questioning this assumption generated alarm and countercharges of disuniting racial separatism. Moreover, this ideological perspective, and school texts that endorse and promote it, obviate the need for any social analysis of the persistent racial inequity that already disunites America. Such textbooks cannot enable Black students or others to understand the root causes of the historical and contemporary injustices people continue to endure, nor can they prepare them to participate in the continuing struggle for social transformation. Notwithstanding, California's history curriculum *Framework*, these textbooks, and implicitly the politics justified therein, are being promoted as a model for the nation.[64]

MISREPRESENTING THE BEGINNINGS OF THE MIDDLE PASSAGE IN THE AFRICAN CONTEXT IN HISTORY TEXTBOOKS

> My pa tell me dat 'way back in slavery time—'way back in Africa—dere been a nigger.... He been de chief er he tribe, an' when dem white folks was ketchin' niggers for slavery, dat ole nigger nuse to entice 'em into trap. He'd get 'em on boat wey dem white folks could ketch 'em an' chain 'em. White folks nused to gee him money an' all kind er little thing, an' he'd betray 'em.
>
> —E. C. L. Adams, "The King Buzzard"[65]

The fictive tale of King Buzzard, an African leader whose spirit is condemned to wander in the swamps for betraying his own people, coincides with narrative recollections of the ways people were kidnapped, captured, and tricked (sometimes with red cloth, for example) onto ships bound for the Middle Passage.[66] This tale also reveals the moral judgment of those who were thus betrayed. On another level, it concurs with standard historical explanations.[67] However, as Rawley's work points out, the majority of slaves were not kidnapped: "Slaves were supplied to White traders by Africans, who procured their supplies by making war, consigning unfortunates for sale, and condemning criminals."[68] Does this suggest that Africans were less civilized and had less human feeling for one another than their European contemporaries had for each other? Was the transatlantic slave trade primarily African people's own fault? Whether or not these questions are ones historians seek to answer, they dominate the popular imagination and wreak havoc in the classroom.

The transatlantic slave trade went through several phases. However, it did not begin with local chiefs selling their own people to Europeans; before it ended, Europeans instigated and engaged in outright wars in Africa and made military alliances to capture their own prisoners of war for sale.[69] In addition to variations in the trade over time, the diversity among the African peoples involved is a factor of major significance that is generally overlooked. Indeed, as Wynter notes, there was no concept of Africans among these diverse peoples at that time; rather, the peoples of Africa identified with their lineage (family or kinship), clan, or descent group, and not with the continent.[70] Following Miller, she concludes that initially slavery could not have been a simple matter of "Africans selling Africans."[71] The historical and literary record is replete with details regarding specific cultural differences among the captives that were well known to the White traders, who likewise did not see themselves in pan-European terms before the advent of racial justifications of the slave trade.

Davidson stresses that greater inquiry into "the mind of the European and the conditions in Africa" is needed.[72] For example, though most textbooks acknowledge that slavery in Africa differed from plantation slavery in the Americas, they do not compare, as Davidson does, African slavery with European slavery, serfdom, and vassalship. Differing conceptions of slavery— that is, of the varieties of unfree labor, servitude, subjugation, and tribute among the diverse people of Africa *and Europe*—are not examined. The following textbook explanations of how the slave trade began in the Kongo in Africa show why such an analysis is needed and should be included, particularly in teacher education.

The seventh-grade textbook adopted by the state of California, *Across the Centuries*,[73] includes a section titled "Slaves, Guns and Civil War," which describes the friendly relations between the kings of the Kongo and Portugal. Their initial cordial and mutually respectful relations degenerated as the slave trade became a profitable business for the Portuguese. The text explains: "The Kongo had no gold" and slaves were "what the Portuguese wanted as payment" for the "luxury goods" (status symbols) the king of the Kongo (the Mani-Kongo Nzinga Mbemba) obtained from them. The lesson explains that the Kongolese king, pictured wearing his favorite imported boots, converted to Christianity and opposed the slave trade, though later he even decided to support it for reasons of wealth and power. One of his many letters to Portugal's rulers pleading for an end to slavery is excerpted in this chapter. The text describes the brutal actions and profit motives of the Portuguese who stopped at nothing to get slaves and treated them like beasts of burden in contrast with the different notion of slavery in Africa. Portuguese merchants, it relates, "destroyed Kongo's trade in goods and replaced it with trade in human beings" and encouraged civil wars among the Kongolese such that "villages staged raids against each other to capture slaves and sell them to the Portuguese."[74] The lesson concludes by emphasizing that the Kongolese (and other) rulers were trapped in a tangled web of trading slaves to get guns for protection from slave raiders.

Although this text's account is neither factually inaccurate nor totally wrong, what it omits or fails to examine closely makes it only half true.

It reinforces ethnocentric stereotypes, particularly with respect to judgments and conclusions students are expected to form.[75] Furthermore, indigenous cultural values associated with kingship, vassalship, and tribute in the African context are not examined, although the captioned illustration of the Kongolese king mentions such factors. The text focuses on the gifts and trade goods the king gives to and receives from the Portuguese, his governors, and subjects as proof of their loyalty or as tribute to his power and authority.[76] However, it neglects to explain that, within the traditional system of social relations in African societies, gift giving symbolizes and concretizes the communal values of mutual responsibility and reciprocity—not just political tribute.[77] Without an analysis of Kongolese conceptions of generosity associated with gift giving and trade that places this notion within its proper cultural context, students will be hard-pressed to understand or judge either the Kongolese people's behavior or their king's varying motives using the standards and viewpoints of that society. Moreover, the text implies that the king's desire for luxury goods on easy credit terms impelled him into slave trading with the Portuguese. Discussing the social value of these goods only as political currency in the king's self-interest is a limited focus for understanding the beginnings of the slave trade and the Middle Passage in the African context. Additionally, after pointing out that the Portuguese destroyed preexisting Kongolese trading practices, the text asks students to consider how the Kongo changed after the arrival of the Portuguese. What it fails to explore are the cultural values that were displaced by the so-called trade in human beings—cultural values that were replaced by those of the Portuguese. In this lies the possibility of appreciating the humanity of both groups as well as how people in each group came to violate their own cultural norms.

Wynter deciphers the cultural mode of rationality in the worlds of the enslavers in both Europe and Africa to discover the prescriptive rules of each social order that encoded, for example, moral and ethical justifications for slavery.[78] Thus what Wynter calls a cultural model perspective is needed to determine whether, from the standpoint of the Kongolese people themselves, the king's actions represent "an exceptional case of despotism found in every country" (as Martin Delaney once observed),[79] or social breakdown in contrast to earlier periods of Kongolese history when the power of kings was "qualified by tribal equality."[80]

Another missing element is a discussion of the role of lineage in Africa, for kinship affiliation determined one's status and identity in local communities or villages.[81] Without comprehending the significance of lineage and kinship differences, students may not understand the attitudes of the Kongolese regarding slavery. Domestic and other kinds of servitude and slavery existed in communities bound together by mutual obligation and internally differentiated along kinship lines.[82] As a political unit, the Kongolese kingdom was composed of diverse groups who shared varying degrees of kinship, and in other regions lineage ties created greater or lesser degrees of affinity. Villagers who raided other villages in the same region or political unit did not perceive themselves, necessarily, as *one* people (but then, neither did the Gauls, Vandals, or Visigoths of Europe).

The text also omits any explanation of the just wars, sanctioned by the Catholic Church, which gave the Portuguese (and other Europeans) the right, within the terms of their own cultural values and religious belief system, to foment and participate in wars and to buy and sell captive Kongolese prisoners as slaves.[83] Wynter notes that the historical significance of the just war as a legitimation for slavery among Christians can hardly be overstated.[84] Moreover, King Manual of Portugal's royal brother, as the Mani-Kongo called himself (he was baptized as Dom Affonso), appealed to a succession of Portuguese kings on the basis of their common Christian brotherhood for assistance to develop the resources to participate as an equal trading partner with the Portuguese. This is not made clear in the excerpt of one of his letters presented in *Across the Centuries*.[85]

The teachers' edition of *Across the Centuries* suggests the following lesson activity at the conclusion of this section on the Kongolese slave trade: "have students imagine they live in a Kongo village in the year 1577;...debate whether to sell slaves to the Portuguese...[and] discuss political, economic, and moral aspects of the issue."[86] In my public statement to the California Curriculum Commission,[87] I critiqued this particular role-playing exercise as Eurocentric, noting that the text failed "to raise the question of whether the Portuguese were right or wrong to *buy* Africans and promote warfare to get slaves."[88] In rebuttal, one of the coauthors of *Across the Centuries* explained that the intended purpose of this exercise was to get students "to understand the dilemma created for the Mani-Kongo by the actions of the Portuguese." This scholar further contended that "to have in that context stopped and asked the students to think instead from the point-of-view of the Portuguese would indeed have been Eurocentric!"[89] Yet the text is Eurocentric precisely because it focuses on a one-sided discussion that forecloses critical examination of relevant information students need to place the reasoning and actions of the Portuguese, and thus the dilemma they helped create, in historical context. Furthermore, to avoid blaming the victim, students need counterknowledge of the well-documented debates that took place in Spain and Portugal about the justness of the slave trade, events that significantly affected the decision to use enslaved Africans instead of Indians in New

World plantations. They must also be informed that the Portuguese ignored the Mani-Kongo's repeated requests, not only to halt the illegitimate enslavement of people from within the protection of the lineage and from noble families but for technical assistance as well. Moreover, to understand fully the dilemma faced by and the options available to the people of the Kongo, students need to understand why the Portuguese ignored the Mani-Kongo's appeals. To consider options from the perspective of the Kongolese, it must be possible for students to examine the motives and reasoning, not just the actions, of the kings of both Portugal and the Kongo.

The scenario depicted in *Across the Centuries* implies that the people of the Kongolese kingdom were free to choose a course of action. However, students role-playing this historical situation must be able to bring the cultural mode of rationality of the Portuguese into the discussion. Only then can they begin to reflect upon the parameters of action available to the Mani-Kongo, parameters that are inherently linked to why he (or the villagers) faced such a choice in the first place. Effective role playing requires exploration of relevant viewpoints involved in human dilemmas in their social contexts. The errors of omission and bias in this lesson are symptomatic of the entire history textbook series adopted by the state. Students are likely to grasp only partial and limited understandings from it.

As a systematic and deliberate process of forced cultural amnesia, the slave trade and the Middle Passage are apt metaphors for the travesty of alienating texts that suppress the cultural knowledge students need. The consequences when "black people forget everything they know" continue to be disastrous.[90] If the loss of cultural memory aided the process of chattel slavery, textbooks aid contemporary processes of mental enslavement by making the anarchy and terror slavery engendered seem to be a natural state of existence for African people. Poverty, hunger, homelessness, and other forms of societal violence among Black people today thus seem equally natural if not just to many within our present cultural mode of rationality.[91]

PARENTS AND EDUCATORS RESPOND

What I have been fighting for and am still fighting for is the possibility of black folk and their cultural patterns existing in America without discrimination; and on terms of equality. If we take this attitude we have to do so consciously and deliberately.

—W. E. B. DuBois, "Whither Now and Why?"[92]

To explore the usefulness of a Black studies scholarly critique of ideology in California's adopted textbooks, I convened two meetings, one with a group of Black parents and another with a group of Black multicultural education specialists. The responses of the participants after a presentation of my critique and after viewing the videotape of Wynter's lecture can be grouped this way: (1) self-reflection regarding their own educational and social experiences (e.g., with racism) and the needs of students and children, (2) reflections on experiences of struggle (collective and individual action) and strategies to use the information presented, (3) social analyses of schooling and power in society, and (4) disagreement with some aspect of the content of the videotape.

Prior to viewing the videotape I asked each group the following questions: "What comes to mind when you think of the Middle Passage; that is, do you think of Ellis Island?" No one did. One of the multicultural educators said: "I just see people huddled together on ships being whipped." I then asked if they had heard about Africans selling each other into slavery. Everyone had. No one in either group mentioned the diversity among the captives or the various ways Africans may have been enslaved in Africa. At the meeting with the educators, for example, one retired teacher said:

> All we knew about in school was slaves. We were taught nothing about
> Africa. All I knew was they [people] jumped from tree to tree with their wild
> and wooly hair and thick lips. That's what our white teachers taught us.
> But when we got to Fisk University, [Professor] Lorenzo Turner told us there
> are over 1,000 African words in the Indian languages. We didn't even
> understand what that meant then.

Viewing the video seemed to galvanize these educators, who talked excitedly about it for almost an hour and a half. They discussed how they could work more effectively with other teachers using this information, and they exchanged ideas about presenting it strategically in ways that would be of practical interest to those of their colleagues who are tired of hearing about multiculturalism. The tape also stimulated discussion of critical insights about society. For example, several of the educators described personal experiences with discrimination in school as well as in such places as department stores. They also suggested that ministers view the videotape as well because, as one teacher noted, "We need to get them educated."

Initially, the parents talked about how overwhelming it is to realize that "all this [bias in the curriculum] is still going on" and that "we are just chipping away at it." A mother who said she felt overwhelmed by how long the struggle has been going on shared her concerns about what her grand-children will experience in school. "Mary McLeod Bethune died," she said, "thinking this battle had been won." Soon the conversation turned to talk about the kinds of collective and community action group members were engaged in or that is needed to protect the children from biased texts and racism in education. Several parents talked about the need for strategies to help students resist subtle racism in school, for example, a curriculum for learning about stereotypes and providing students with counterknowledge such as that described in the textbook critique and the videotape. Parents and teachers alike suggested Saturday schools for parents and students. In a follow-up interview, one mother complained that the support group's focus was too oriented toward success rather than on preparing students to deal with racism strategically. As she explained, "We don't mention the 'R' word, but I'm happy to know someone cares and is working on this. I don't pay enough attention to what is being taught and I need to know more myself. What you presented is what our group should really be about."

In follow-up conversations, parents told me that the videotaped lecture was difficult to understand. "There's so much there!" one said. However, these discussions reveal that laypeople do immediately relate their own ex-periences to such presentations. Although none indicated feeling intimidated by the material, some suggested ways to make it more understandable. One mother, who said she has not "studied everything the professor is talking about on the tape," succinctly summed up Wynter's discussion of Wood-son's analysis of what the curriculum does to demotivate students: "This is about the way they are manipulating our kids' psyches. That's why the Black males end up hanging out together in school." She continued, "I don't know about all this, but I can feel it in terms of what is happening to my children." Another mother explained: "My daughter tells me, 'They [teachers] try to invalidate me as a person, when I try to share what I know about our history.'" This mother stated bluntly, "They know what they are doing. This is about the perpetuation of White supremacy." Similarly, the parents talked about the publishing industry and why state officials ignored my critique of the textbook controversy. "This shows," said one parent, "that they are not ready to deal with a total change in the culture. And here are all these kids riding around with guns—and it's the White kids, too."

Evidently, parents and teachers are interested in this Black studies ideology critique because it serves as an effective framework for discussing concrete experiences and issues they want to understand better and deal with more effectively. They see themselves within the perspective of society that the critique presents and they want to develop alternatives. Parents and teachers want opportunities to understand the theoretical concepts in a presentation format that is digestible but not watered down.

However, one parent participant, a retired college biology teacher, objected to Wynter's critique of her discipline and call for a rewriting of the knowledge in all the disciplines. "The information was totally fallacized," she told me. "Anyone with a science background would reject it out of hand." She further commented that the information Wynter presents is "too complicated for the average parent" and added that "they [parents] are not interested in this anyway." (She left before the discussion period.) I later discussed this participant's comments in a follow-up interview with a multicultural educator, who had also viewed and discussed the videotape, who said

> We have to remember that educated specialists have been taught to think the way they think. They have to come to terms with the falsehood in their own disciplines. And we need respect for the common person; respect for the human spirit made it possible for us to survive slavery. . . . This is truly revolutionary because our people have built their lives on these lies and they are threatened by the truth.

THE POSITIVE USES OF CONTROVERSY: A CHANGE IS GONNA COME

> As far as the great masses or classes of people learnt anything, they learnt it concretely in struggle against some concrete thing.
> —C. L. R. James, *Notes on Dialectics: Hegel-Marx-Lenin*[93]

This exploratory study, although it focused the attention of parents and educators on the textbook controversy, reveals a deeper crisis of legitimacy within the academic disciplines and in the nature of schooling itself. In the case of California's textbook adoption controversy in the 1990s, the issues were so distorted that the decision to adopt the textbooks may appear to have been a victory for bureaucracy and manipulation and a defeat for popular resistance to miseducation. The deeper issue underlying this controversy continues to be Black survival, that is, how Black people will live in this society. For one paradox in this post–civil rights era is that social cohesion, the cherished "unum," can only be realized if their education permits Black students to become literate in and construct social identities grounded in their actual history. (Witness the identification, cohesion, and belonging that gangs and the military provide.) This collective identity is integral to their human consciousness and is not be confused with essentializing or totalizing racial nationalism.

By contrast, the adopted textbooks are likely to promote individualistic assimilationist strategies that will undermine community solidarity and leave corporate interests and White supremacy racism unchallenged. For the Black struggle for justice to continue, it must be collective and community based. Moreover, all students need educational opportunities to identify with communities of interest that sustain life and humane values.[94] This requires re-thinking representations of our history, particularly within the African context, that effectively deprive Black students of a rational basis for identification with their African heritage and with their local and global "communities of destiny."[95] Appeals to "well-grounded canons of historical scholarship" in defense of half-true historical explanations are beside the point.

According to Alinsky, people are often not concerned enough to act unless there is a controversy.[96] He notes that "when people have a genuine opportunity to act," they begin "to think their problems through" and then "they have a reason for knowing."[97] Some of the parents and teachers I met with had been active in the struggle against the textbooks. Viewing and discussing the videotape critique gave the participants in this collaborative inquiry an opportunity to think through the critique of the textbooks, opportunities they sorely need to address such issues and discover possibilities for resistance and struggle. This study suggests some ways this might happen and how Black studies scholarship and intellectuals can help.

A frequently posed question regarding the textbooks was: "If these books aren't good enough, how do we create multicultural textbooks?" (Translation: "What do Blacks want now?" Answer: "Liberty and justice for all.") It was also often said that "these books are so much better than the ones we had before." Clearly, this judgment depends on the measurement standard used.[98] Parents who do not have precise knowledge of curriculum are acutely aware of how harmful schooling is for their children based on their concrete efforts to help them achieve and survive racism in education. Therefore, standards for measuring the progress of educational change need to reflect not what *was* but what education is for *now*. This exploratory study suggests that Black studies research and social action agendas should be informed by the concrete experiences of parents and students and should focus inter-disciplinary attention on all subjects. As Weinburg concludes, we know too little about "challenging students' beliefs about history."[99] This applies equally to the beliefs and miseducation of teachers and to scholars who write textbooks.[100] Black studies scholars need to be wary of invitations to join the consensus and concentrate on generating deciphering social analyses that help people differentiate between competing educational reform agendas using this standard-for-the-standards.

The Middle Passage is somewhat analogous to current social realities. In many ways, the violence in African American communities today recalls the violence of slavery.[101] If the overseas passage into enslavement of African people is analogous to abductive schooling, the problem now, as Woodson pointed out in 1933, is one of mental slavery to the dominant intellectual paradigm and school knowledge that promotes assimilation and self-abnegation.[102] This hegemonic intellectual paradigm slanders people of African descent, causes Black children to disidentify with their history, deprives them of their heritage, and distorts their humanity as well—all of which is a postmodern way of death of the psyche, if not a physical one.[103] What are children learning about the Middle Passage, the origins of the transatlantic slave trade, and the African diaspora here and there? Further analysis of the empirical relationship between ideology, domination, and alienation is needed to understand the educational experiences of Black students and the role of textbooks under conditions of White supremacy racism. Educators, parents, and students could benefit from studying these issues together. Indeed, one role of intellectuals is to uncover ways ideology conceals domination and supports alienation in the educational process. This will make a vital contribution to the realization of the historical potential of Black struggle that depends on "self-knowing subjects,"[104] whose authenticity is not obliterated by alienating school knowledge.

Both diaspora literacy and consciousness are needed to decipher the regime of truth represented in school texts. From the perspective of dialectical social theory, the validity of the Black studies perspective must be determined in the practical application of the ideology critique and social action this intellectual perspective generates. Hopefully, then, the sojourn of Africa's children in the New World will transcend the enduring vestiges of slavery and global racism, and out of the Middle Passage a radically more human mode of being and world-class standards for an equitable and just social life will emerge.

NOTES

1. J. C. Miller, "The Slave Trade in the Congo and Angola," in M. Kilson and R. Rotberg (eds.), *The African Diaspora* (Cambridge, MA: Harvard University Press, 1976), 75–113.

2. Carl Degler is noted for advancing the proposition that people with darker skins (i.e., Africans) have been universally looked down on. See St. Clair Drake, *Black*

Folk Here and There, vol. I (Los Angeles: UCLA Center for Afro-American Studies, 1990) for a refutation of the Degler-Gergen propositions. Comments made on the MacNeil-Lehrer News Hour, November 28, 1991.

3. E. C. L. Adams, "The King Buzzard," in E. C. L. Adams and R. G. O'Meally (eds.), *Congaree Sketches* (Chapel Hill: University of North Carolina Press, 1987), 120–121; Georgia Writers Project, *Drums and Shadows* (Athens: University of Georgia Press, 1940); A. Haley, *Roots* (New York: Doubleday, 1976); C. Johnson, *Middle Passage* (New York: Atheneum, 1990); J. Lester, *To Be a Slave* (New York: Scholastic Books, 1968); L. Levine, *Black Culture and Black Consciousness* (London: Oxford University Press, 1977); J. Mellon, *Bullwhip Days* (New York: Weidenfield and Nicholson, 1988); J. Winter, *Follow the Drinking Gourd* (New York: Knopf, 1988).

4. H. Courlander, *The African* (New York: Crown, 1967).

5. Ibid., 149.

6. C. G. Woodson, *The Mis-Education of the Negro* (Washington, DC: Associated Publishers, 1933).

7. See Web site http://www.APIECENJ.org. Accessed April 17, 2006.

8. Abena Busia (p. 197) borrows the concept of "diaspora literacy" from Clark, who recently defined it as "the ability to comprehend the literature of Africa, Afro-America, and the Caribbean from an informed, indigenous perspective" (p. 42). I also draw on Vévé Clark's use of the concepts *lieu de mémoire* and *milieu de mémoire*, which refer to settings for researching and remembering the history of the other that are adapted from an essay by the French historian Pierre Nora. See: A. Busia, "What is Your Nation?: Reconstructing Africa and Her Diaspora through Paule Marshall's *Praisesong for the Widow*," in C. Wall (ed.), *Changing Our Own Words* (New Brunswick, NJ: Rutgers University Press, 1989), 196–211; Also see: V. Clark, "Performing the Memory of Difference in Afro-Caribbean Dance: Katherine Dunham's Choreography, 1938–1987," paper presentation at the Dunham Symposium, Stanford University, Stanford, CA, May 12, 1989; V. Clark, "Developing Diaspora Literacy and *Marasa* Consciousness," in H. Spillers (ed.), *Comparative American Identities* (New York: Routledge, 1991), 41–61; P. Nora, "Entre Memoire et Histoire. La Problematique des Lieux," in P. Nora (ed.), *Les Lieux de Mémoire* (Paris: Gallimard, 1984), xvii–xiii.

9. S. Wynter, "Re-Thinking Aesthetics: Notes Toward a Deciphering Practice," in M. Cham (ed.), *Ex-iles: Essays on Caribbean Cinema* (Trenton: Africa World Press, 1992), 237–279; J. S. Wills, " 'Some People Even Died': Martin Luther King, Jr, the Civil Rights Movement and the Politics of Remembrance in Elementary Classrooms," *International Journal of Qualitative Studies in Education* 18, no. 1 (2005): 109–131.

10. Wynter, "Re-Thinking Aesthetics," 266.

11. A. Giddens, *Central Problems in Sociological Theory* (Berkeley: University of California Press, 1979), 173, 187.

12. Ibid., 170, 174.

13. Ibid., 194.

14. Ibid.

15. R. Eyerman, *False Consciousness and Ideology in Marxist Theory* (Atlantic Highlands, NJ: Humanities Press, 1981).

16. C. L. R. James, *Notes on Dialectics: Hegel-Marx-Lenin* (Westport, CT: Lawrence Hill, 1948/1980); J. King and C. A. Mitchell, *Black Mothers to Sons: Juxtaposing African American Literature with Social Practice* (New York: Peter Lang, 1990).

17. R. Yin, *Case Study Research: Design and Methods* (Beverly Hills, CA: Sage, 1984).

18. S. Wynter, "America as a World: A Black Studies Perspective and a Cultural Model Framework." Letter and essay to the California State Board of Education, 1990; S. Wynter, *"Do Not Call Us Negros": How Multicultural Textbooks Perpetuate Racism* (San Jose, CA: Aspire Books, 1992).

19. J. King and S. Wynter, *Diaspora Literacy and Curriculum Change: A Black Studies Perspective* [Videotape] (Santa Clara University, Santa Clara, CA. 1991).

20. Wynter, "America as a World"; Wynter, "Re-Thinking Aesthetics."

21. G. Breitman (ed.), *Malcolm X Speaks* (New York: Grove Press, 1965), 198.

22. Busia, "What Is Your Nation?" 197.

23. J. King and T. L. Wilson, "Being the Soul-Freeing Substance: The Legacy of Hope in Afro-Humanity," *Journal of Education* 172, no. 2 (1990): 9–27.

24. J. Anyon, "Ideology and United States History Textbooks," *Harvard Educational Review* 49, no. 3 (1979): 361–386; P. R. Mattai, "Rethinking the Nature of Multicultural Education: Has It Lost Its Focus or Is It Being Misused?" *Journal of Negro Education* 61, no. 1 (1992): 65–77; R. Sims, *Shadow and Substance: Afro-American Experience in Contemporary Children's Fiction* (Urbana, IL: National Council of Teachers of English, 1982); N. Wa Thiong'o, *Decolonizing the Mind: The Politics of Language in African Literature* (London: James Currey, 1986); Woodson, *The Mis-Education of the Negro.*

25. H. Kohl, "Rotten to the Core," *Nation* 254, no. 13 (April 6, 1992): 457–461.

26. K. B. Jones, "Authority and Representation: Sisterhood Is Complicated," paper presented at the Jing Lyman Lecture Series, Stanford University, Stanford, CA, January 1992.

27. C. McCarthy, *Race and Curriculum: Social Inequality and the Theories and Politics of Difference in Contemporary Research on Schooling* (New York: Falmer, 1990).

28. B. Ollman, *Alienation: Marx's Conception of Man in Capitalist Society* (London: Cambridge University Press, 1971).

29. Eyerman, *False Consciousness*, 283.

30. Ibid.

31. Wynter, "America as a World"; King and Wilson, "Being the Soul-Freeing Substance."

32. W. Strickland, "Identity and Black Struggle: Personal Reflections," in *Education and Black Struggle: Notes from the Colonized World, Harvard Education Review*, Monograph no. 2 (Cambridge, MA: Harvard University, 1974), 137–143.

33. J. King, "Dysconscious Racism: Ideology, Identity and the Mis-education of Teachers," *Journal of Negro Education* 60, no. 2 (1991): 133–146.

34. See Cynthia Hamilton's discussion of authenticity in C. Hamilton, "A Way of Seeing: Culture as Political Expression in the Works of C. L. R. James," *Journal of Black Studies* 22, no. 3 (1992): 429–443. Human consciousness is consistent with the possibilities for authentic self-knowledge within Afrocentricity (not to be confused

with ethnocentrism or ethnic chauvinism) as I have discussed it elsewhere (King and Mitchell, *Black Mothers to Sons*; King and Wilson, "Being the Soul-Freeing Substance). See also M. K. Asante, "The Afrocentric Idea in Education," *Journal of Negro Education* 60, no. 2 (1991): 170–180.

35. V. Harding, "The Vocation of the Black Scholar and the Struggles of the Black Community," in *Education and Black Struggle: Notes from the Colonized World*, Harvard Education Review, Monograph no. 2 (Cambridge, MA: Harvard University, 1974), 10.

36. California State Department of Education, *History/Social Science Framework* (Sacramento: California State Department of Education, 1988).

37. J. King, unpublished letter to the California Curriculum Development and Supplemental Materials Commission (Sacramento, CA: July 11, 1990).

38. I took a public stance against the adoption by mailing my letter and textbook critique to educators and citizens throughout California and in New York and Texas, two influential states also scheduled to make textbook decisions.

39. King, "Dysconscious Racism"; J. King, "Unfinished Business: Black Student Alienation and Black Teachers' Emancipatory Pedagogy," in M. Foster (ed.), *Readings on Equal Education* (New York: AMS Press, 1992), 245–271.

40. H. Heyser, "New Text Survives Bias Debate," *Peninsula Times Tribune* (July 19, 1991): A1, ff.

41. K. E. Epstein and W. F. Ellis, "Oakland Moves To Create its Own Multicultural Curriculum," *Phi Delta Kappan* 73, no. 3 (1992): 635–638; Heyser, "New Text Survives Bias Debate."

42. The Rochester, NY, Public Schools Multicultural Office, TACT (The Association of Chinese Teachers, in San Francisco), CURE (Communities United Against Racism in Education in Berkeley), TACTIC (Taxpayers Concerned About Truth in the Curriculum, in Sacramento), NABRLE (National Association of Black Reading and Language Educators, in Oakland), and the Rethinking Schools Collective (in Wisconsin) are some grassroots groups in which teachers, parents, and students worked collectively around these issues.

43. In 1992, Sylvia Wynter's essay was reprinted and published for a lay audience as *Do Not Call Us Negros: How Multicultural Textbooks Perpetuate Racism.* (Note: "Negros" is the Spanish-language spelling of the word.)

44. A. Sanford, "An Education Agenda," *Essence* (August 1990): 126; J. King, "Nationalizing the Curriculum or Downsizing Citizenship?" in E. Eisner (ed.), *The Hidden Consequences of a National Curriculum* (Washington, DC: American Educational Research Association, 1995), 119–144.

45. R. Hughes, "The Fraying of America," *Time* (February 3, 1992): 44–49.

46. A. K. Armah, *Two Thousand Seasons* (Portsmouth, NH: Heinemann, 1973), 1.

47. R. Reinhold, "Class Struggle," *New York Times Magazine* (September 29, 1991): 26–29, 46–47, 52; D. Waugh, "California's History Textbooks: Do They Offend?" *California Journal* 22, no. 3 (1991): 121–127.

48. V. Harding, *Hope and History* (Maryknoll, NY: Orbis Books, 1990).

49. Giddens, *Central Problems in Sociological Theory*, 193.

50. Comments made on *The Peter Jennings News Hour* (ABC), September 14, 1990; emphasis added.

51. *Textbook Adoption Recommendations* (Sacramento: California State Department of Education, 1990), 7.

52. One of these established scholars, historian Arthur Schlesinger Jr., defends the California textbook decision, warning that one of the "bad consequences" of the "eruption of ethnicity" is that "fragmentation and apartheid" will replace "America's historic purposes" of "assimilation and integration" [A. Schlesinger Jr., *Reflections on a Multicultural Society* (Washington, DC: President's Committee on the Arts and the Humanities, 1991), 7]. Confessing a nostalgia for a "unifying American identity," the idealized "melting pot," Schlesinger claims that the "rising rate of intermarriage across ethnic, religious, even (increasingly) racial lines" is a "telling indicator" that the majority of people prefer this unum of one people, to what he calls the "cult of ethnicity" or the "artificial ethnic chauvinism" that is disuniting America (p. 11). Hughes's article is another recent example of mainstream reaction to the epistemological challenge Black studies represents (Hughes, "The Fraying of America").

53. F. D. Peat, *Blackfoot Physics: A Journey into the Native American Universe* (Grand Rapids, MI: Phanes Press, 1994).

54. D. Reynolds, *John Brown, Abolitionist. The Man Who Killed Slavery, Sparked the Civil War and Seeded Civil Rights* (New York: Knopf, 2005).

55. Wynter, "America as a World."

56. C. Sleeter, "The White Ethnic Experience in America: To Whom Does it Generalize?" *Educational Researcher* 21, no. 1 (1992): 33–36.

57. Hamilton, *Apartheid in an American City.*

58. This was seen in the civil insurrection in Los Angeles following the trial of the White police officers accused of brutally beating Black suspect Rodney King. Andrew Hacker's observations support this analysis of relations between Blacks and Koreans [A. Hacker, *Two Nations: Black, White, Separate, Hostile, Unequal* (New York: Scribners', 1992), 176, 202]. As Hacker notes, "when its rolls need expanding, the White majority is ready to absorb upwardly mobile Hispanics and Asians, who are already being encouraged to separate and differentiate themselves from black Americans." Yet Hacker points to "political motives for stressing the immigrant origins of certain white citizens" which can be "useful for politicians who seek to divert attention from economic issues." He states that the manipulation of White ethnic identity has been a favored strategy of the right—deployed by presidents Reagan and Bush senior.

59. Courlander, *The African*, 173.

60. Consider one exercise many teachers in elementary and secondary schools use, which asks students to trace their family's immigrant roots. Black students cannot answer questions like: "What country did your ancestors come from?" or "When did they first arrive?" These questions also appear in the fourth-grade Houghton Mifflin text. *Oh, California* [B. Armento, G. Nash, K. Salter, and K. Wixson, *Oh, California* (Boston: Houghton Mifflin, 1991), 138–139]. It is noteworthy that teachers are advised to have children who are adopted or whose "biological families have gone through painful experiences" to participate in discussion of these questions "at any level that is comfortable for them" (Teacher's Edition, 139).

61. A. C. Bailey, *African Voices of the Atlantic Slave Trade: Beyond the Silence and the Shame* (Boston: Beacon, 2005).

62. King and Mitchell, *Black Mothers to Sons.*

63. J. A. Hawkins, "The Cries of My Ancestors: The 'Uncomfortable' Story of Slavery Must Be Told Honestly," *Teacher* (June/July, 1990): 8–9.

64. See report of the National Council on Education Standards and Testing to Congress, the Secretary of Education, the National Education Goals Panel, and the American people titled *Raising Standards for American Education* [National Council on Education Standards and Testing, *Raising Standards for American Education* (Washington, DC: U.S. Government Printing Office, 1992)]; see also J. Leo, "Teaching History the Way It Happened," *U.S. News and World Report* (November 27, 1989), 73.

65. Adams, "The King Buzzard," 121.

66. Bailey, *African Voices of the Atlantic Slave Trade;* Georgia Writers Project, *Drums and Shadows;* Lester, *To Be a Slave.*

67. W. Rodney, *West Africa and the Atlantic Slave Trade* (Dar es Salaam: East African Publishing House, 1967).

68. J. Rawley, *The Transatlantic Slave Trade* (New York: Norton, 1981), 432–433.

69. J. C. Miller, *Way of Death* (Madison: University of Wisconsin Press, 1988).

70. Wynter, "America as a World"; Wynter, "Re-Thinking Aesthetics."

71. J. C. Miller's analysis of the slave trade in Angola describes this diversity and attempts a portrayal of the trade "from the virtually unrecorded perspectives of the slaves themselves" (Miller, *Way of Death,* xv; see also 23–39).

72. B. Davidson, *Black Mother* (Boston: Little, Brown, 1961), 6.

73. B. Armento, G. Nash, K. Salter, and K. Wixson, *Across the Centuries* (Boston: Houghton Mifflin, 1991).

74. Ibid., 153.

75. As Anthony Giddens contends, "an ethnocentric conception ... takes the standpoint of one's own society or culture as a measure to judge all others" [A. Giddens, *Sociology: A Brief but Critical Introduction* (New York: Harcourt, Brace, Jovanovich, 1983), 42]. It also involves using one's own culture as the standpoint from which to interpret the experiences and actions of others (Asante, *The Afrocentric Idea*).

76. Armento et al., *Across the Centuries,* 151.

77. Miller, "The Slave Trade in the Congo and Angola."

78. Wynter, "America as a World."

79. Davidson, *Black Mother,* 18.

80. Ibid., 29.

81. Miller, "The Slave Trade in the Congo and Angola"; Miller, *Way of Death.*

82. J. A. Carney, *Black Rice: The African Origins of Rice Cultivation in the Americas* (Cambridge: Harvard University Press, 2001); Rawley, *The Transatlantic Slave Trade.*

83. Miller, *Way of Death,* xiii.

84. Wynter, "America as a World."

85. Armento et al., *Across the Centuries,* 144.

86. Ibid., 152.

87. King, unpublished letter.

88. Ibid., 7.

89. J. Ridley and G. Nash, unpublished letter and appendix to the State Superintendent of Public Instruction (Sacramento, CA: April 21, 1990).

90. Courlander, *The African.*

91. Wynter, "America as a World."

92. W. E. B. DuBois, "Whither Now and Why?" in H. Aptheker (ed.), *The Education of Black People: Ten Critiques, 1906–1960 by W. E. B. DuBois* (New York: Monthly Review Press, 1973), 150.

93. James, *Notes on Dialectics*, 93.

94. S. Alinsky, *Rules for Radicals* (New York: Random House, 1971); D. W. Orr, "What Is Education For?" *In Context* 27 (1991): 52–55; D. W. Orr, *Ecological Literacy* (Albany: State University of New York Press, 1992).

95. P. B. G. da Silva, "Black-Women-Teachers' Resistance to Racism in Sao Carlos (Sao Paulo, Brazil)," paper presented at the annual meeting of the American Educational Research Association, San Francisco, CA, April 1992.

96. Alinsky, *Rules for Radicals*, 117.

97. Ibid., 106.

98. King, "Nationalizing the Curriculum or Downsizing Citizenship?"

99. S. Weinburg, "On the Reading of Historical Texts: Notes on the Breach between School and Academy," *American Educational Research Journal* 28, no. 3 (1991): 518.

100. G. Ladson-Billings, "Beyond Multicultural Illiteracy," *Journal of Negro Education* 60, no. 2 (1991): 147–157; G. Ladson-Billings, "Distorting Democracy: Social Studies Curriculum Development and Textbook Adoption in California," paper presented at the National Council of Social Studies, Washington, DC, November 1991.

101. Miller, *Way of Death.*

102. King and Wilson, "Being the Soul-Freeing Substance."

103. Miller, *Way of Death.*

104. Wynter, "Re-Thinking Aesthetics."

10

Demystifying Our Reality: Deconstructing Our Politics of Nonengagement

Rudolfo Chávez Chávez and Jeanette Haynes Writer

Is real history the history of people's consciousness, the history of how people were aware of their contemporary scene and of events, or is it an history of how events really occurred and how they *had to be* reflected in people's consciousness? There is a double danger here: one can either recount history as it *should have* happened, i.e., infuse it with rationality and logic, or can describe events uncritically, without evaluation, which of course amounts to abandoning a fundamental feature of scientific work, namely the distinction between the essential and the peripheral, which is the *objective* sense of facts. The existence of science is based on the *possibility* of this distinction. There would be no science without it. . . . Mystification and people's false conscious-ness of events, of the present and the past, is a part of history.

—Karel Kosík, "*Dialectics of the Concrete: A Study on the Problems of Man and World*" (emphasis in original)

INTRODUCTION

The country recently commemorated the fiftieth anniversary of *Brown v. Board of Education* and yet we live in neo–Jim Crow times. Now at age ninety-one, the chairperson of the Leadership Conference on Civil Rights and President Emeritus to the National Council of Negro Women,

Dr. Dorothy I. Height, was one of the first women leaders of the movement. She says that because blatant segregation made racism and discrimination much more overt in years past, it was clear why people were so committed to the struggle. Today, however, she maintains the struggle is harder work. "The inequality is more subtle now," she says. "And we are fighting for different things. Today it is more of an accelerated kind of dedication."[1] The complexities of the confounding contextual issues of an accelerated kind of dedication add a dualistic irony. On the one hand, we have many post-Brown babies included within the highest halls of power, the White House staff: African American, Latino, Asian, Caribbean, European American, some women, but mostly rich White men. And on the other hand, we have policies and practices that create neo–Jim Crow philippics handed down as carefully crafted hegemony, pronouncements that by and large we accept but are nothing more than supremacists' deeds for control and power. Privilege and equality are not color-blind—racial profiling is still a destructive and controlling police practice on brown and Black folk. Tim Wise, a White antiracist whose consistent essays on ZNet are keepers, recently wrote, "We [white folk] take for granted that we won't be racially profiled even when members of our group engage in criminality at a disproportionate rate, whether the crime is corporate fraud, serial killing, child molestation, abortion clinic bombings or drunk driving."[2]

More people of color are imprisoned and their disproportionate over-representation is a disease that bedevils our sense of the common good. Three neo–Jim Crow examples are worth reporting.

- Montana ranks third in the country for overrepresentation of Native Americans in their prison population. Nationally, Native Americans make up only 1 percent of the population, yet comprise 1.6 percent of the federal prison population and 1.3 percent of prisoners in state prisons.[3]
- Blacks are incarcerated severely out of proportion to their numbers in every state in the Western region. Research has shown that African Americans are treated more harshly at every juncture in the criminal process. Nationally, Blacks make up 50 percent of our country's prison population.[4]
- Latinos are incarcerated at rates nearly double their representation in the population in Idaho, Utah, and Wyoming. Nationally, Latinos are the fastest growing ethnic group. Between 1990 and 2000, the Latino population in Idaho grew by over 92 percent — in Utah, the figure is 138.5 percent. These are the two states with the highest rates of Latinos in prison in the Western region.[5]

Neo–Jim Crow is best exemplified in the rise of segregation in our schools. An exceptional report researched and written by the Civil Rights Project states:

The data show the emergence of a substantial group of American schools that are virtually all non-white, which we call apartheid schools. These schools educate one-sixth of the nation's black students and one-fourth of black students in the Northeast and Midwest. These are often schools where enormous poverty, limited resources, and social and health problems of many types are concentrated. One ninth of Latino students attend schools where 99–100% of the student body is composed of minority students.[6]

Implicit within these issues and the ones to follow are the gradations of exclusion found within the hegemony of the everyday; these are issues of mystification needing demystification. For example, affirmative action and its lukewarm yet ironically enough significant recent wins; major demographic changes skewing the codifications minority and majority; the living of everyday civil rights under the police state of the Patriot Act; the gross racial and ethnic disparities in the criminal justice system, including the possibility of juvenile offenders on death row and the overwhelming criminalization of children coupled with the unconscionable overrepresentation of People of Color within the prison industrial complex; the legislative impact of FAIRNESS: The Civil Rights Act of 2004; the noble acts of teaching and learning and its implicit joy obscured by the heavy-handed one-size-fits-all policies of No Child Left Behind (NCLB); the distortion and sabotage of gay, lesbian, bisexual, and transgender antidiscrimination information on official publications to fit the Bush administration's ideological notions of relationships; the need to document hate crimes, which are down from an all-time post–September 11, 2001, high of 9,726 in 2001 to 7,462 in 2003 (a 23.3 percent decrease)[7]; housing and lending disparities that challenge equity in a pluralistic society; protecting and stabilizing the civil rights of both undocumented and documented immigrants; reclaiming and stopping the erosion of sovereignty by the remaining Native Nations that are federally recognized; and the inadequate rights and privileges of children of which eleven million children attend broken-down schools every day.[8] Simultaneously, according to a study funded by the Poverty and Race Research Council, Jianping Shen found that

in comparison to other schools, schools with the highest level of minority enrollment, i.e., those with 50% or greater minority enrollment, were and continued to be disadvantaged in terms of having a proportionate share of quality teachers. Cross-sectionally, when [Shen] analyzed the most recent data collected (1999–2000), [she] found that schools with 50% or greater minority enrollment had: (a) the highest rate of teachers who were not certified in their primary teaching fields; (b) the highest rate of teachers who had low level of certification (i.e., temporary and emergency); (c) the highest percentage of new teachers; and (d) the highest rate of teacher attrition....[9]

Additional issues are the rights and privileges of the elderly—in 1970, there were just over twenty million enrollees in Medicare, whereas by 2001 there were forty million; this healthcare reality is a backdrop to emphasize that we now have 43.6 million people who do not have health insurance,[10] a living wage, or protected employment benefits. "Every day in America, 85,444 workers lose their jobs. 14.7 million people are jobless, underemployed or have given up looking for work...[and] 12,878 workers are injured or made ill by their jobs. Six million eight hundred thousand people are in the workforce but are still poor."[11] And one final issue that places the proverbial inclusionary cherry on the exclusionary sundae, the UCLA Chicano Studies Research Center researching prime time TV characters per genre reported: "White characters account for over 75% of all roles on prime-time television and can be found on 95% of all prime-time series, while Latinos remain highly segregated on the programming schedule, appearing on only 15% of series and on just 5 out of 12 genres."[12]

These are a few of the many issues that in our minds create inclusion for some and exclusion for many and should serve as the ethical determinants that inform teaching and learning to passionately engage our cultural work as teacher-scholars and scholar-activists within the multicultural education terrain. "Such exclusions" in the words of Terry Eagleton, "can be profoundly hurtful for a great many people. Whole masses of men and women have suffered the misery and indignity of second-class citizenship."[13]

Two reports add to the contextual exclusionary gauntlet. The first report is by the Civil Rights Project called "*Brown* at 50: King's Dream or *Plessy's* Nightmare?" As suggested by "*Brown* at 50, there have been major strides toward integration of our public schools, yet at the same time, "there has been a major increase in segregation."[14] This report, focused in its approach and doing an adequate job of exploring some of the reasons for segregation, desegregation, and resegregation and the power plays against integration (mostly at the judicial level), as well as addressing the demographic data facts, leaves one with an uneasy feeling that somewhere deep in the discourse is the textual glue of greed, money, and White supremacy that holds all this together. In a significant section of this report are the U.S. Census Bureau data that show, from shore to shore and border to border, dramatic public school enrollment changes. For example, from 1968 to 2001, there has been a 308 percent increase of Latino children in the public schools at the same time a 18 percent decline of White children.[15] Last, the report reviews the broad sweep of segregation changes nationally, regionally, and by state since the 1954 Brown decision. It shows that the movement that began with the Supreme Court decision has had an enduring impact but that we are experiencing the largest backward movement in the South, where the court decisions and civil rights laws had produced the most integrated schools in the nation for three decades.[16]

The second report is a joint release by the Civil Rights Project at Harvard University, the Urban Institute, Advocates for Children of New York, and the Civil Society Institute titled *Losing Our Future: How Minority Youth Are Being Left Behind by the Graduation Rate Crisis.*[17] I quote from the report three general findings:

- "Nationally, highschool graduation rates are low for all students, with only an estimated 68% of all those who enter 9th grade graduating with a regular diploma in 12th grade." For Whites the rate is 74.9 percent but rates are significantly lower for most minority groups, and particularly for minority males. "According to the calculations used in this report, in 2001 only 50% of all Black students, 51% of Native American students, and 53% of all Hispanic students graduated from high school."[18]
- Graduation rates for Black and Hispanic males are averaging under 50 percent nationally. "Black, Native American, and Hispanic males fare even worse: 43%, 47%, and 48%, respectively." The gender differences within racial groups can be as large as ten points, with males of every racial group consistently faring worse than females. The data on minority males are rarely reported although they are clearly experiencing the deepest crisis.[19]
- At the national and state level, the racial gap in graduation rates between Whites and most minority groups is pronounced: The national gap for Blacks is 24.7 percentage points; for Hispanics 21.7 percentage points; for Native Americans 23.8 percentage points. Despite wide ranges within some states, nearly every state shows a large and negative gap between whites and at least one minority group.[20]

These are just some of the many interweaving issues that we in the two courses, both called Multicultural Education,[21] connect to the everyday practices of racism, classism, sexism, and heterosexism within the socially accepted rubrics of low expectations, silencing, and the pernicious and many times invisible practice so coined the "pobrecito syndrome" within our schools;[22] that is, the victimization of the many other. The data are illustrative of what happens when the pobrecito syndrome is in full swing. Now mind you, do not think for one minute that good schools do not exist—*they do*! During the sixteen weeks of the respective courses, we read about and show videos of some exemplary schools and outstanding teachers out there; however, if liberating and transformative praxis was consistently the case, we would have no need to provide the realities that face so many in the everyday within the "land of the free and home of the brave," nor would we really need courses named Multicultural Education.

McLaren and Farahmandpur have so aptly described this politics of exclusion as

> a politics of representation that has deftly outflanked the issue of socioeconomic redistribution (Fraser, 1997). The postmodernist and postsocialist assumption that culture [of exclusion] has suddenly found ways of winning independence from economic forces and that somehow the new globalized capitalism has decapitated culture from the body of class exploitation by constructing new desires and remaking old ones in ways that are currently unmappable and unfactorable within the theoretical optics of political economy.[23]

We are multicultural teacher educators; the scene is our classrooms, with their actors (teachers and learners both) in the struggle for agency to create a pedagogical imaginary for democracy, equity, and social justice practices. We envision, hope, and have faith that our practices contest and assist our students to interrogate the neoliberal times we live in that silently and ruthlessly spread their capitalistic tentacles like indeterminant rhizomes that codify and commodify the culture of exclusion. "For instance," writes Geneva Gay in her book *Culturally Responsive Teaching*, "if society really stopped being racist, it would insist (and enforce the expectation) that all its institutions, including schools [would stop with its racist practices]."[24]

This is our cultural work as teachers, to contest and interrogate our terrain of engagement, to demystify what is mystified. We connect such contestations and interrogations to what Kosík addresses as "hypostatizing." That is, where many but not all learners hypostatize and favor the whole reality over its parts—over the many facts that make reality what it is, which leads to a false totality instead of to a concrete one. Kosík argues:

> If the whole process represented a reality which would be indeed genuine and higher than facts, then reality could exist independently of facts, independently in particular of facts that would contradict it. . . . Emphasizing the whole process over facts, ascribing to tendencies a reality higher than to facts, and the *consequent* transformation of a tendency of facts into a tendency independent of facts, are all expressions of a hypostatized whole predominant over its part, and thus of a *false* totality predominant over the concrete totality.[25]

Demystification is then an active process where both teacher as student and student as teacher engage the many facts that make our reality and where, we so hope, ensuing transformations into the complexity of teaching and learning in a diverse society will arise.

ENGAGEMENT AND NONENGAGEMENT

In his well-known 1897 educational essay called "My Pedagogic Creed," John Dewey spoke to the importance and power of engagement with others to establish connection to and learn from a social community. Dewey believes

> that the only true education comes through the stimulation of a child's powers by the demands of the social situations in which he finds himself. Through these demands he is stimulated to act as a member of a unity, to emerge from his original narrowness of action and feeling, and to conceive of himself [sic] from the standpoint of the welfare of the group to which he belongs. From the responses which others make to his own activities he comes to know what these mean in social terms.[26]

Since the time of Dewey's essay, conceptualizations of the term *engagement* have metamorphosed as various educators critiqued and further problematized engagement in educational settings, such as in the field of critical multicultural education. In their edited book *Speaking the Unpleasant: The Politics of (Non) Engagement in the Multicultural Terrain*, Chávez and O'Donnell provide discussion of the complexities of the concepts of engagement and nonengagement.[27] "The process of engagement refers to those who do not accept the status quo and begin to unconsciously conscious and/or consciously unconscious transform themselves to understand the status quo and place themselves into a location for liberatory action based on a praxis of social justice."[28]

Whereas those who engage, disown, and critique the status quo, those who practice nonengagement, "accept the status quo and reject and resist challenges to the status quo."[29] Thus transformation does not occur for the individual, which inhibits transformation in a larger context, such as the classroom.

Pohan and Mathison add to the conversation on engagement through their work concerning student resistance and defensiveness. Resistance is defined as "an act of opposing, counteracting, withstanding, or attempting to defeat," whereas, defensiveness is "an act of defending or protecting."[30] Resistance and defensiveness often occur when students are confronted with unsettling challenges to their belief systems. Using pedagogical skills to create an environment where students may form a safe learning community and making oneself available to the students, a teacher educator can engage students as they traverse through the initial phase of resistance and defensiveness.[31] Setting ground rules (including respect and speaking from one's experience) for discussion and facilitating sharing and problem-solving activities in small groups enhances engagement between students.

McIntyre speaks to the careful balance, one that is often difficult to attain, between the method of critique with engagement. Using self-critique to assist preservice and in-service teachers to explore the complexities of self to examine how those manifestations of self-impact teaching, McIntyre asserts that "white educators who engage in self- and collective reflection and critique about their racial identities can rework their pedagogy and disrupt racist teaching practices, thereby reinventing teacher education programs."[32]

Farris addresses engagement in her university-level literature courses as events in which her diverse students enter into critical, and sometimes heated, discussions of constructs of race, the manifestations of race in language, and literary representation.[33] These discussions serve as points of identifying who has authority and who has authority to speak and providing opportunities to cast out silences while creating spaces to extend one's voice through verbal or written exchanges. Students engage with each other and their professor in the classroom as well as outside of class. Farris states,

> It's important for me to remember that the culturally diverse classroom often feels like unexplored territory to students as well as teachers. Contentious issues are present both in the physical (the bodies and voices of a diverse population) and the abstract (the ideas, stories, languages of a multicultural curriculum). ... Students don't come ... already knowing that territory, issues of cultural difference already resolved. But face to face, there is possibility.[34]

Cruz-Jenzen and Taylor, in their discussion of urban preservice teachers' experiences in an introductory educational foundations course heavily infused in multiculturalism, also found that engagement was enhanced through discussion opportunities.[35] The discussions were purposefully structured through "dyads between two candidates, small groups of 5–7 candidates, whole class, and individual written reflections" as well as through the formation of small support groups.[36]

A barrier to engagement is the willingness and readiness of the students themselves.[37] An individual cannot force another to learn what he or she does not want to learn. Temporal maturity to interact with and understand certain information is essential to multicultural engagement. Research shows that it is not feasible to expect students to totally transform themselves in one semester through one multicultural course.[38] They have a limited amount of time to devote to the course and its content;[39] as multicultural educators we must be "impatiently patient" and "patiently impatient."[40]

THE PRAXIS OF ENGAGEMENT

In what may be one of Paulo Freire's final works recently published in Buenos Aires (and simultaneously in Mexico) called *El Grito Manso* (*The Gentle Scream*), in a chapter titled "The Practice of Critical Pedagogy," Freire reinvents himself by reaffirming the importance that we are historical beings—"we are incomplete, unfinished, inconclusive."[41] This is very much a natural state of being. As teachers and as learners, we can attest to this as well. In all this uncertainty, in our infallible incompleteness we are reinventing our humanity and what humanity can be—"*nos pusimos de pie, liberamos las manos y la liberación de las manos es en gran parte responsible de lo que somos*" (we stand, we free our hands, ourselves, and by freeing ourselves, in large part, makes us responsible for what we can be).[42] To continue with the notion Friere states, "As human beings we know we are unfinished. It is precisely this point—in this 'radical' moment of the human experience—that resides the possibility of teaching and learning . . . education is thus something special to humans."[43]

It is our incompleteness—the humble realization that the world is not us; I am not you; you are not me; and the indeterminant presence that is around each of us, this world, our world—that creates me, you, us. It is precisely, Freire argues, the consciousness of the world that creates our conscience conscientiousness. And of course, this is all connected to the infinity of relationships that we create, nurture, and want to know more about. This interrogation leads us to our inquiry, to find out, discover, and make us more complete. "This creates our intention to comprehend the world and to comprehend our position in the world."[44] Thus Freire's clarity and our mantra, "reading the world" precedes "reading the word." Context visible or not, denied or not, named or not, is the world, our world as teachers, and the worlds of the learners we work with where the engagement of the many facts rather than the mystified whole becomes our terrain of engagement.

The praxis of engagement is a dialectical-materialist encounter with our realities. Our stance can be signified by three interconnected moments of engagement:

1. deconstruction of the pseudoconcrete (i.e., of fetishist and fictitious objectivity of the phenomenon) and cognition of its real objectivity;
2. the cognition of the dialectic of the unique and of the generally human; and
3. the cognition of the objective content and meaning of the phenomenon, of its objective function and its historical place within the social whole.[45]

It is a process where we do not consider fixed cultural and traditional artifacts, formations and objects prevalent in schooling—such as Black history month and the reciting of the "I Have a Dream" speech of Dr. Martin Luther King Jr.; or Cinco de Mayo, where all Mexicans in this case dance, drink, and are carefree; or the coming together of Pilgrims and Indians who sit down and break bread in harmony during Thanksgiving, to name only a few of the many obvious points of fetishist, fictitious, and reductionistic encounters that lead to contestation and interrogation. Engagement is problematized to include both the material world of things and that of ideas and routine thinking.[46]

Such thinking, which abolishes the pseudoconcrete to reach the concrete, is also a process that exposes a real world under the world of appearances, the law of the phenomenon behind the appearance of the phenomenon, real internal movement behind (external) appearance of the phenomenon, real internal movement behind the visible movement, and the essence behind the phenomenon.[47]

We find that the entrenched notion of teacher authority has been unconsciously established and maintained in many of our postsecondary students' early years of the traditional schooling paradigm through what Freire speaks to as the banking concept of education and thus significantly impacts their dialogic engagement.[48] Whereas many of our students find their voices, begin to name and practice their agency, and prosper within our education program (which is grounded in social justice and critical multicultural education philosophies), some do not. Some are still immersed, mind, body, and spirit, in the paradigm of the pseudoconcrete; they are content with and pacified by the mystified whole. Some are even angry that their false realities are exposed and that we do not provide a simple how-to multicultural education course. For example, one student admitted, "At first, I was annoyed that he [Rudolfo] asked so many questions and answered our questions with questions. I would leave here very agitated at the feeling that I was 'left hanging' and never got any concrete answers."[49]

It is easier to accept prepackaged knowledge and lessons rather than have to contest and interrogate everyday realities of oppression and how such realities impact the educational process. It would be indeed much easier to not challenge the realities of oppression, granting learners what Ladson-Billings names "permission to fail" by simply doing what is acceptable by the status quo.[50] Our desire is that students critically engage with the contextual world around them via the disciplined understanding of multicultural education subject matter, each other, and us to break out of this indoctrinated process, to critically think and critically act contrary to their own essentialist desires. One of our everyday goals is to have students begin to understand how each of them constructs their idiosyncratic notions of the pseudoconcrete. Our hope, via the dialectical dialogic processes we aspire to, is to provide each of them mechanisms for transformation while simultaneously embracing the integrity of diversity, equity, and social justice within the praxis of a multicultural education. After more time in the multicultural education course, the same student reflects,

> Now I understand that there are no concrete answers to my questions and that every day situations will arise that are different from yesterday. Creating our own "dialog" is important to help each of us construct our own meanings in the things we talked about. *This* model will be invaluable to me as a teacher. This is a teaching method that must be *lived* to be learned.

DECONSTRUCTING THE POLITICS OF NONENGAGEMENT

Engagement versus Nonengagement

As part of our labor as teachers and learners, we engage learners in the process of a multicultural education that envisions democratic agency coupled with integrating sociocultural and contextual experiences that concretize learners' identities (ontological), knowledge bases (epistemological), and ethical understandings (axiological).[51] This translates into the combination of one's sociocultural experiences with a theoretical knowledge base to develop individual multiculturally equitable and just teaching strategies, both abstract and applied. Such strategies have continued to be central to the foundations of our course for students' transformative democratic experience, which moves learners from nonengagement to engagement to deconstruct and engage their personal politics about race, class, gender, and sexual orientation. Our work is to facilitate learning in such a way that students construct their own knowledge bases based on their idiosyncratic understandings on race, class, gender, and sexual orientation.[52] Haynes Writer's notes speak to the process of doing a multicultural education, where transformative demystification is indeed possible.[53]

> Engagement was the cornerstone of multicultural understanding and development in this course; one had to engage with others, materials, and concepts in order to progress and grow. Through his development of the classroom environment, use of transformative democratic pedagogies and careful selection of reading materials and videos, Rudolfo thoughtfully attempted to engage his students. Nonetheless, students could always resist engagement in ways that were visible and invisible to Rudolfo and Jeanette.

The dialectical conception of reality further concretizes our work as multicultural teacher educators and as engaged learners. Students do and will resist engagement, this is their democratic right. Notwithstanding, our explicit role is to engage learners in the "process of *concretization* which proceeds from the whole to its parts and from the parts to the whole, from phenomena to the essence and from the essence to phenomena, from totality to contradictions and from contradictions to totality."[54] The phenomenon so named is multicultural education, its essences (i.e., facts, issues, concepts, etc.) are those addressed earlier in this chapter's introduction and the many more discussed during any given semester. Kosík explains:

> Such cognition is not a summative systematization of concepts erected upon an immutable basis constructed once and for all, but is rather a spiral process of interpenetrations and mutual illumination of concepts, a process of dialectical, quantitative—qualitative, regressive—progressive totalization that transcends abstractness (one-sidedness and isolation). A dialectical conception of totality means that the parts not only internally interact and interconnect both among themselves and with the whole, but also that the whole cannot be petrified in an abstraction superior to the facts, because precisely in the interaction of its parts does the whole *form* itself as a whole.[55]

Recently, Chávez created an exam that placed this into practice. Figure 10-1 is page two of the midterm exam for graduate Multicultural Education, EDUC 515.[56]

The Activity Question/Problem in Three Parts:

As you are now well aware, teaching and learning are complex interactions that happen within the "thoughtful, respectful, and democratic process of engagement" and always within a diverse & pluralistic community (think of the diverse complexity of the *"I Am From..."* pieces.).

➢ Part I (Meta-Cognitive): Deconstruct your selected Case Study Student from Nieto (this will begin within the class as an activity)...the case analysis will include...

- What is the Point of View of the *Case Participant* and, if need be, the *Case Writer*

  ✓ Inform yourself: Nieto 5; Adams et al., Section 1

- What are the Issues, Problems, & Possibilities within the case: narratives & counter narratives

  ✓ Inform yourself: Nieto 3, 4, & 5; Adams et al., Sections 2, 3, & 4. *The Voices!*

- What are the Solutions to resolve and/or to understand the case issues, Problems, & Possibilities (See Part II)

  ✓ Inform yourself: Geneva Gay; Nieto 4, 5, 6, & 7; Adams et al., Sections 2, 3, & 4, and *The Voices, Next Steps, & Action!*

- Once your resolution/reconstruction is reached that meets your expectations

Figure 10-1   Page Two of the Midterm Exam for Graduate Multicultural Education

via Nieto, Chapter 10, you are now ready to determine the implications for the vast community of teachers & learners whom you/we will engage. A multi-faceted analysis is now needed which applies the insights acquired to your "Self", that is, "Your 'Self' as a cultural/ethnic entity who is a Learner" and is in struggle to create relational connections to the "Other" (See Part III). Consider the following concepts many times are gate-keepers in one's ability to commit and be responsible to the teaching/learning process in a diverse and pluralistic society: essentialist, reductionist, and dogmatic thinking.

     ✓ Inform yourself: Rethinking Schools short pieces; Adams et al., *Next Steps & Action*

➢   Part II: Rationale of Understanding as Learner (maximum four pages): Using at least 4 readings from the four Adams et al. sections; and Nieto Chapters 3 & 4, create your "rationale of understanding" that describes, critiques, and provides analysis to the external appearance(s) of your reality (specific essences that inform your rationale). This "rationale of understanding" will include at least 4 to 5 concepts that have challenged you to create 'real internal movement' as opposed to 'visible movement' (politically correct) (See Section 1 of Adams et al.) you believe fundamental to your growth as a learner.

➢   Part III "To Be a Multicultural Educator" (maximum four pages): Provide an integrated rationale that will assist you "to be" an awe-inspiring teacher who has begun or desires to begin the struggle for true consciousness by your focused desire to analyze and critique the dynamics of race and/or ethnicity, class, gender, sexual

Figure 10-1 (continued)

orientation and much more in a pluralistic/diverse setting based on your readings, your reflexive & reflective journal entries, your in/out of class conversations, class activities, videos, and popular culture media. Consider pertinent videos; plus, additional readings

Make sure to include a reference page. This page will not count toward your total pages.

Figure 10-1   (continued)

Learners realize that demystifying our reality is a responsibility that only each of us as teacher-learners and learner-teachers can accomplish. The transformative experience is indeed idiosyncratic based on the individual contexts learners are willing to contest and interrogate. Both Chávez Chávez and Haynes Writer are familiar with learners being initially angry and resistant to the uncovering of their realities using an array of facts to discover the phenomenon so named multicultural education. Students come to realize that to demystify their socially constructed reality, ready-made answers will not suffice. Through the process of our course and its explicit praxis of demystification, students become conscious of the fact that they possess and can deconstruct knowledges for themselves. In responding to the exam, Student A, a White female student from a small town located close to a Native American reservation, says, "Using the example discussed in class, I stand on a moving conveyer belt that symbolizes acts of prejudice, discrimination and racism, and while I stand still the conveyer belt continues to move. My acts of silence and conformity give consent to these acts and make me an accountable agent in its progression."

Student B entered the same course with a quiet reluctance, which challenged her internal movement and how she began to rethink what responsibilities she had to contest within her chosen reality:

This concept [discrimination] is the first thing that challenged me to create a real internal movement in the beginning of this class. I felt that if everyone would just be more respectful and appreciate every one's differences then everything would be better and there would not be any more discrimination or oppression. I wish it was this easy. Unfortunately, it goes deeper than just our actions; the most difficult discrimination to stop and overcome is structural and institutional. . . .[Speaking directly about one of our EDUC 515 readings Student B continues] This has been another challenging concept for me in order to create a real internal movement of this complex phenomenon [structural and institutional discrimination]. How can you put an end to discrimination when you have no idea how it is happening and who is actually responsible for it? Before this class, I never realized how bad the discrimination is on the institutional and structural level. In order to make a real internal movement it is necessary that we all understand the roots of this discrimination in order to make changes.

Students A and B are both struggling to create their dialectical conception of a newly discovered totality. Note as well how the parts they are just beginning to interrogate internally are somewhat interconnecting both among themselves and with the whole. The whole—that is, their chosen realities—is no longer within a petrified status, nor is the abstraction of equality in "the land of the free and the home of brave" superior to the facts about racism or discrimination born out via our readings and dialogues. It is precisely the interaction of these disparate but now connected parts that form themselves into a whole, where both Students A and B are demystifying their respective realities and dialectically moving from the pseudoconcrete to the concrete via the gathering of facts. Kosík explains that the process of reality, which is dialectical conception, corresponds with an epistemological principle that in its simplest form assists us to "grasps reality as a structured, evolving and self-forming whole."[57] Our role as engaged learners or teachers, or both, is to ground ourselves with the realization that "social reality is known in its concreteness . . . when the character of social reality is exposed, when the pseudoconcrete is abolished and when social reality is known as the dialectical unity of the base and the superstructure, with man as it objective, socio-historical subject."[58]

Because reality and our wherewithal to expose such is always in movement, always evolving, each sociohistorical subject will be on a continuous journey. This is exemplified well by Student A:

In the video *The Shadow of Hate*,[59] we saw evidence of white Americans striving for white supremacy by massacring hundreds of unarmed Native Americans at Wounded Knee Creek, forcing Chinese immigrants to build our rail roads for meager wages and not allowing them to be considered citizens, lynching of African Americans, and many other horrendous acts. The traces of these deep roots of ethnocentrism are still visible in society today. . . . [She then quotes from a course article by Gay, then she continues] Being a multicultural educator also includes as Gay states, "providing students with information about the history and contributions of ethnic groups who traditionally have been excluded . . . replacing the distorted and biased images of those groups that were included in the curricula with more accurate and significant information."[60] This means correcting false images that students have developed based on their monocultural education, and informing them of the perspective[s] that have so long been pushed aside and ignored.

The qualities that Students A and B display, although limited in many ways, is illustrative of actors who are in struggle. Important here is that these learners are willing to question their reality; to question how social reality is formed. It is what Edward W. Said powerfully addresses as creating a "beginning."[61] Kosík argues "this type of questioning, which establishes what social reality is by way of establishing how it is formed, contains a revolutionary concept of society and man [sic]."[62]

Over time, we have learned that engagement and the act of demystifying our reality only happens when students fully participate in and own their discourse within our multicultural education courses. The many facts, such as those mentioned within this chapter's introduction, as well as the infinity of facts out there or yet to be discovered are comprehensible only in the contextual whole—"that the very concept of fact is determined by the overall conception of social reality."[63] As such, we struggle often with biting our respective tongues; we listen with the intent of simply listening. Praxis emerges when learners engage the opportunities constructed via dialogue and where they self-create opportunities to do the talking, or put another way, do the very work they may have avoided or ignored if not for critical subject matter mirrored in the social reality of race, class, gender, and sexuality situated within the multicultural education course. Haynes Writer asked Chávez Chávez a question concerning not only the pace, but the impatient patience of what may be characterized as learning, and he explained:

> I've learned to be really slow in [the multicultural education course] and give very little information . . . it [must] come from the students because if it's not theirs, if they're not authenticating themselves, if they're not authenticating their voice then it's very easy for a professor to say, "This is what you're supposed to be thinking."

There is a difference between the authority of the teacher and being an authoritarian.[64] As authorities, our teaching requires us to create, interrogate, and contest the myriad relational interconnections and interdependences between facts and their generalizations. According to Kosík, "just as generalizations would be impossible without facts, there are no scientific facts that would not contain an element of generalization."[65] Consequently, as we listen we must question implicit and explicit contradictions of the reality in question. Our teaching and our learning rests on how well we question the objective content and the significance of the facts before us. Hence, our role in decoding facts and placing them within the cognition of a historical reality is a process of theoretical appropriation; enter deconstructing the politics of nonengagement.

Deconstructing the politics of nonengagement is no more than each of us realizing that only each of us in engaged dialogue can and must seek to uncover contradictions—"without contradictions, totality is empty and static; outside totality, contradictions are formal and arbitrary."[66] As actors within and without the course so named Multicultural Education, we are always in the making of our dialectical character. As teachers wanting to understand the complexity of this political dance, we have encountered a certain multicultural correctness. For some students the appropriation of multicultural language and behaviors is genuinely practiced due to their desire to become multicultural; they are trying to understand the concepts and reflect that understanding even on the surface before the concepts and deep understanding has become incorporated. Others, however, began to act multiculturally correct because this allows them to mask not having to interrogate their perceived reality. In contrast to the engagement captured by those previous students, there is a small but significant number of students who practice what we coin performance engagement. Some students become sophisticated in this practice. One male student interviewed within a focus group spoke of his performance engagement almost in terms of naturalness.

> It's [this class] challenging, I kind of like that because most classes are pretty, I wouldn't say it's easy, but ... you know how to work it, you know what the teacher wants to hear, you know what the others want to hear, you know what to say, ... But in this class you have to let it out. It's not much of a, a lot of work but, I don't know. It's challenging to do something.

The politics of nonengagement is a dialectical result of nonmovement, of what we consider reproducing a deterministic role. Kosík on the other hand speaks to its insipid complexity:

> When cognition does not destroy the pseudoconcrete, when it does not expose the phenomenon's real historical objectivity under its fictitious objectivity, and when it consequently confuses the pseudoconcrete with the concrete, it becomes a captive of fetishist intuiting and results in a bad totality. ... In "bad totality," social reality is intuited only in the form of the object, of ready-made

results and facts, but not subjectively, as objective human praxis. The fruit of human activity is divorced from the activity itself.[67]

Performance engagement, although cloaked as engagement, is nonengagement, plain and simple. In a focus group when students were speaking of the concept of a teacher's responsibility within a classroom, Haynes Writer encountered a female student articulating the importance of being prepared; however, Haynes Writer also overheard her in class that same evening saying she had not done the reading. Here are her performed words on responsibility, revealing how the politics of nonengagement transpires; showing how a bad totality may be insidiously constructed:

> I know for me, I don't dare come in here and not read something and that right there is helping me with this whole class or with my whole program because I know some classes I just know I don't have to read or . . . I mean I have to because I not only inform him, I have to inform the group I'm in. I have to go to the new current table and act like I know what I'm talking about. I can't act if [I] don't read. So with him expecting that from us has helped me because I know that that's what I need to do and that's the way I'm going to learn, if I do that.

Another example of a bad totality or rather another of the many ways to construct the politics of nonengagement is appropriating power by speaking not only for self, but for all. For example, one student maintained a position of privilege throughout the duration of the same multicultural education in that when she spoke in classroom discussions and focus groups she did not position herself to speak for herself but for all members of the class.

Students become astute in multicultural correctness, Kosík would speak to this as a bad totality. This may be a conscious effort, that is, the creation of a bad totality, whether to please or self-deceive, to meet the expectations or requirements of the multicultural education course. This form of nonengagement is often undetectable unless situated in a discrepant context. "False consciousness, reification, subject-object relations, etc., lose their dialectical character when they are isolated, torn out of the materialist theory of history and severed from other concepts which together form a whole."[68]

CONCLUSION

In the creation of the Highlander School, Myles Horton in his autobiography spoke to his yearning to create a space where people could come together to address their respective realities, educate themselves, and challenge social systems that unjustly impacted their lives.[69] Reflecting on the challenge of providing such a space Horton addresses what may be our conundrum as multicultural educators when he writes, "I've never been able to define democracy. . . . it's a growing idea."[70] This growing idea requires not just a suspended judgment about what we may think is in the minds of those learners we work with and even within ourselves—infinitely illusive as it may be—but also requires us to imagine a democratic space where shared interests are respected and where there is a fullness to understand not only ourselves but the other with a freedom of interaction within and without all groups.[71] Implicit within this chapter, to expose the pseudoconcrete, demystify our reality, and deconstruct the politics of nonengagement, is to learn the praxis of listening. This is what Lisa Delpit speaks to as "taking a special kind of listening"; she continues, "listening that requires not only open eyes and ears, but open hearts and minds. . . . we must learn to be vulnerable enough to allow our world to turn upside down in order to allow the realities of others to edge themselves into our consciousness."[72]

Our dialectic-materialist stance as teachers and learners implicates an axiological and ethical imaginary; an authority of valuing the self and the other coupled with a moral authority of making ourselves vulnerable by turning ourselves upside down to see our destiny and our realities in the others' eyes. Angela Valenzuela in her study of U.S.-Mexican youth, *Subtractive Schooling*, eloquently argued the centrality of a moral authority where teachers and institutional structures "value and actively promote a search for connection, both between teacher and student, as well as among students themselves."[73] Our hope and, yes, our faith as teacher-scholars is to imagine insightful and intuitive practitioners willing to struggle and to be challenged to understand their unique realities and to decipher and connect for themselves and with the many other the undercurrents of the pseudoconcrete and the dynamics of the concrete. With the constant evolving and ever-changing nature of reality, we believe our dialectic-materialist stance presumes an imaginary of what, all too often, has not yet been imagined for a multicultural education to manifest, where our historical integrity creates a democratic space of trust and respect, and where, with caring and loving abandon, we will be courageous enough to fathom the possibility of such distinctions.

NOTES

1. R. Kelotra, "Inspired by Dr. King's Legacy, the Civil Rights Movement Continues." Available online at www.civilrights.org/issues/enforcement/details.cfm?id=17874; accessed on June 6, 2005.

2. *White Whine: Reflections on the Brain-Rotting Properties of Privilege.* ZNet Commentary (April 20, 2004).

3. The statistics reflect the prisoner population of the Western Region for 2000–2001. Western Prison Project, "Incarceration of People of Color in our Region." Available online at www.westernprisonproject.org/Publications/Factsheets/POC_In_ Pris_Region_2000-1.pdf; accessed on April 20, 2004.

4. Ibid.

5. Ibid.

6. E. Frankenberg, C. Lee, and G. Orfield, *A Multiracial Society with Segregated Schools: Are We Losing the Dream?* (Cambridge, MA: The Civil Rights Project, Harvard University, 2003). Available online at www.civilrightsproject.harvard.edu/ research/reseg03/AreWeLosingtheDream.pdf.

7. According to the Southern Poverty Law Center's Intelligence Project, they "counted 751 group chapters in 2003, up 6% from the 708 that were active the year before. Much of the gain was accounted for by improved counting of Black separatist groups—groups that probably already existed in prior years. But there were real rises in key sectors of the hate movement. Hate Web sites, meanwhile, rose from 443 in 2002 to 497 last year, a 12% increase." Available online at www.splcenter.org/intel/ intelreport/article.jsp?aid=374; accessed on April 21, 2004.

8. T. Matzzie, "Back on the Bus." Available online at hispanicvista.com/html4/ 041704ec.htm; accessed on April 19, 2004.

9. Jianping Shen, "Have Minority Students Had a Fair Share of Quality Teachers? Results from a National Longitudinal Study (1987–88 to 1999–2000)," special issue of *Poverty and Race* (July/August 2003).

10. Matzzie, "Back on the Bus."

11. Tom Matzzie is online mobilization manager at the AFL-CIO and rode the bus on the Show Us the Jobs tour. Go to www.showusthejobs.com or www.tompaine .com/feature2.cfm/ID/10260; accessed on April 19, 2004.

12. A. R. Hoffman and C. A. Noriega, "Looking for Latino Regulars on Prime Time Television: The Fall 2003 Season." UCLA Chicano Studies Research Center. An occasional series available in electronic format, Research Report no. 3, at www. chicano.ucla.edu/press/reports/documents/crr_03April2004.pdf.pdf

13. Terry Eagleton, *Figures of Dissent: Critical Essays on Fish, Spivak, Zizek, and Others* (New York: Verso, 2003), 18–19.

14. Gary Orfield and Chungmei Lee, "*Brown* at 50: King's Dream or *Plessy's* Nightmare?" Available online at www.civilrightsproject.harvard.edu/research/reseg04/ brown50.pdf, 3.

15. Ibid., 13.

16. Ibid., 2.

17. Gary Orfield, Daniel Losen, Johanna Wald, and Christopher Swanson, *Losing Our Future: How Minority Youth Are Being Left Behind by the Graduation Rate Crisis* (Cambridge, MA: The Civil Rights Project at Harvard University. Contributors: Advocates for Children of New York, The Civil Society Institute, 2004). Available online at www.civilrightsproject.harvard.edu/research/dropouts/LosingOurFuture.pdf.

18. Ibid., 2

19. Ibid.

20. Ibid., 4.

21. Students must take the Multicultural Education course with a passing grade before they are admitted into New Mexico State University's Teacher Education Program; EDUC 315 is the undergraduate-level course and EDUC 515 is the graduate-level course.

22. This word illustrates how many well-meaning teachers can victimize learners by having low expectation of them via implicit or explicit feelings of pity (i.e., "poor little things").

23. Peter McLaren and Ramin Farahmandpur, "Reconsidering Marx in Post-Marxist Times: A Requiem for Postmodernism?" *Educational Researcher* 29, no. 3 (2000): 25–33.

24. Geneva Gay, *Culturally Responsive Teaching* (New York: Teachers College Press, 2000), xix.

25. K. Kosík, "Dialectics of the Concrete: A Study on the Problems of Man and World," in B. S. Cohen and M. W. Wartofsky (eds.), *Boston Studies in the Philosophy of Science*, vol. 52, translated by Karel Kovan with James Schmidt (Dordrecht: D. Reidel Publishing, 1976), 27; emphasis in original.

26. M. S. Dworkin, *Dewey on Education: Selections* (New York: Teachers College Press, 1959), 20.

27. R. C. Chávez and J. O'Donnell (eds.), *Speaking the Unpleasant: The Politics of (Non) Engagement in the Multicultural Terrain* (New York: SUNY Press, 1998).

28. Ibid., 2.

29. Ibid.

30. C. A. Pohan and C. Mathison, "Dismantling Defensiveness and Resistance to Diversity and Social Justice Issues in Teacher Preparation," *Action in Teacher Education* 20, no. 1 (1999): 15–22.

31. We question the idea of creating a safe environment. As teacher educators, as with teachers, we cannot assume that our classrooms are always safe for all students at all times. Psychological safety is often elusive for students who have been marginalized or silenced.

32. A. McIntyre, "Constructing an Image of a White Teacher," *Teachers College Record* 98 (1997): 653–681.

33. S. Farris, "'Don't Go There': Exploring Unknown Territory in the Culturally Diverse Classroom," *Radical Teacher* 51 (1997): 31–35.

34. Ibid., para. 23.

35. M. I. Cruz-Jenzen and M. Taylor, "Hitting the Ground Running: Why Introductory Teacher Education Courses Should Deal with Multiculturalism," *Multicultural Education* 12, no. 1 (2004): 16–23.

36. Ibid., para. 11.

37. G. S. Cannella, "Fostering Engagement: Barriers in Teacher Education," in R. C. Chávez and J. O'Donnell (eds.), *Speaking the Unpleasant: The Politics of (Non) Engagement in the Multicultural Terrain* (New York: SUNY Press, 1998), pp. 87–107.

38. R. E. Bahruth and S. F. Steiner, "Upstream in the Mainstream: Pedagogy against the Current," in R. C. Chávez and J. O'Donnell (eds.), *Speaking the Unpleasant: The Politics of (Non) Engagement in the Multicultural Terrain* (New York: SUNY Press, 1998), 127–147; L. T. Díaz-Rico, "Toward a Just Society: Recalibrating Multicultural Teachers," in R. C. Chávez and J. O'Donnell (eds.), *Speaking the Unpleasant: The Politics of (Non) Engagement in the Multicultural Terrain* (New York:

SUNY Press, 1998), 69–86; M. Dressman, "Confessions of a Methods Fetishist: Or, the Cultural Politics of Reflective Nonengagement," in R. C. Chávez and J. O'Donnell (eds.), *Speaking the Unpleasant: The Politics of (Non) Engagement in the Multicultural Terrain* (New York: SUNY Press, 1998), 108–126; D. J. Goodman, "Lowering the Shields: Reducing Defensiveness in Multicultural Education," in R. C. Chávez and J. O'Donnell (eds.), *Speaking the Unpleasant: The Politics of (Non) Engagement in the Multicultural Terrain* x(New York: SUNY Press, 1998), 247–264; Sonia Nieto, "From Claiming Hegemony to Sharing Space: Creating Community in Multicultural Courses," in R. C. Chávez and J. O'Donnell (eds.), *Speaking the Unpleasant: The Politics of (Non) Engagement in the Multicultural Terrain* (New York: SUNY Press, 1998), 16–31; R. Smith, "Challenging Privilege: White Male Middle-Class Opposition in the Multicultural Education Terrain," in R. C. Chávez and J. O'Donnell (eds.), *Speaking the Unpleasant: The Politics of (Non) Engagement in the Multicultural Terrain* (New York: SUNY Press, 1998), 197–210.

39. Díaz-Rico, "Toward a Just Society."

40. Paulo Freire, *Teachers as Cultural Workers: Letters to Those Who Dare Teach*, translated by Donaldo Macedo, Dake Koike, and Alexandre Oliveira (Boulder, CO: Westview, 1998).

41. Paulo Freire, *El Ggrito Manso* (Argentina: Siglo Veintiuno Editores, 2003), 19.

42. Ibid., 20.

43. Ibid., 20–21.

44. Ibid., 20.

45. Kosík, *Dialetics of the Concrete*, 30.

46. Ibid.

47. Ibid., 6.

48. Paulo Freire, *Pedagogy of the Oppressed* (New York: Continuum, 1970).

49. Jeanette Haynes Writer interview with 315 students.

50. Gloria Ladson-Billings, " 'I Ain't Writin': Permissions To Fail and Demands to Succeed in Urban Classrooms," in L. Delpit and J. K. Dowdy (eds.), *The Skin that We Speak: Thoughts on Language and Culture in the Classroom* (Stamford, CT: Thomson Learning, 2002), 197–120.

51. See, for example R. C. Chávez, "A Curriculum Discourse for Achieving Equity: Implications for Teachers when Engaged with Latina and Latino Students," in W. Secada (ed.), *Hispanic Dropout Project Papers* (Washington, DC: National Clearinghouse for English Language Acquisition, 1997). Available online at www.ncela.gwu.edu/miscpubs/hdp/3; Chávez and O'Donnell, *Speaking the Unpleasant*.

52. Cameron McCarthy, *The Uses of Culture: Education and the Limits of Ethnic Affiliation* (New York: Routledge, 1998).

53. During the spring 1999 semester, Haynes Writer observed Chávez Chávez teaching one of his undergraduate courses as part of a research study to understand the disparate voices of students within a multicultural education class taught from a critical multicultural perspective. Haynes Writer observed several class sessions, surveyed the students about the course content and processes, held focus groups, and conducted self-expression exercises. She observed and interviewed Chávez Chávez to further clarify his pedagogical idiosyncrasies with the intent of determining his pedagogical groundings.

54. Kosík, *Dialetics of the Concrete*, 23.

55. Ibid.

56. Exam readings included the two core texts used across all EDUC 515 sections: Maruianne Adams, Warren J. Blumenfeld, Rosie Castañeda, Heather W. Hackman, Madeline L. Peters, and Ximena Zúñiga, *Readings for Diversity and Social Justice: An Anthology on Racism, Anti-Semitism, Sexism, Heterosexism, Ableism, and Classism* (New York: Routledge, 2000), and Sonia Nieto, *Affirming Diversity: The Sociopolitical Context of Multicultural Education* (Boston: Allyn & Bacon, 2004). Included as well were Geneva Gay, *A Synthesis of Scholarship in Multicultural Education* (Napierville, IL: North Central Regional Educational Laboratory, Urban Education Monograph Series, 1994) and various articles from Rethinking Schools Online, available online at www.rethinkingschools.org.

57. Kosík, *Dialetics of the Concrete*, 24.

58. Ibid., 25.

59. C. Guggenheim (Director), *The Shadow of Hate* (Teaching Tolerance, 1995).

60. Geneva Gay, *A Synthesis of Scholarship*, 11. Available online at www.ncrel.org/sdrs/areas/issues/educatrs/leadrshp/le0gay.htm.

61. Edward W. Said, *Orientalism* (New York: Vintage Books, 1979).

62. Kosík, *Dialetics of the Concrete*, 25.

63. Ibid.

64. bell hooks, *Teaching to Transgress: Education as the Practice of Freedom* (New York: Routledge, 1994).

65. Kosík, *Dialetics of the Concrete*, 25.

66. Ibid., p30.

67. Ibid., 30–31.

68. Ibid., p. 31.

69. Myles Horton (with Herbert Kohl and Judith Kohl), *The Long Haul: An Autobiography* (New York: Teachers College Press, 1990); B. J. Thayer-Bacon, "An Exploration of Myles Horton's Democratic Praxis: Highlander Folk School," *Educational Foundations* 18, no. 2 (2004): 5–23.

70. Horton, *The Long Haul*, 174.

71. Thayer-Bacon, "An Exploration of Myles Horton's Democratic Praxis."

72. Lisa Delpit, *Other People's Children: Cultural Conflict in the Classroom* (New York: New Press, 1995), 46–47.

73. Angela Valenzuela, *Subtractive Schooling: U.S.-Mexican Youth and the Politics of Caring* (Albany: SUNY Press, 1999), 255.

11

"If Only We Could Find Some!" The White Privilege of Teacher Education

Rasheeda Ayanru, Eugenio Basualdo, and Stephen C. Fleury

INTRODUCTION

It is not uncommon to hear fellow teacher educators lament the difficulty of identifying and retaining students and faculty of color. Not sensing themselves, their institutions, or the larger society in which we live as openly racist, few of us may recognize how our own participation in a system of power neutralizes the very social changes we advocate. Because most teacher educators are White and unaware of the social and professional privileges enjoyed because of this, the chances that the system will self-correct are few or perhaps even nil. Policies attempting to correct the ills of inequity within the system are often misguided because we design interventions and anticipate ramifications from our own privileged majority perspective.

For example, Whites have had (and will likely continue to have) greater access to undergraduate education, certification programs, and teaching positions; as untenured faculty, they are less susceptible to the vicissitudes of student and peer evaluations; and as instructional leaders and committee participants, they are less likely to be viewed as a historical anomaly, an anomaly even more pronounced in a profession grounded in cultural regulation. This chapter provides three stories about the way White privileges may create less than a welcoming environment for faculty of color, send contradictory messages about race and diversity in teacher education classrooms, and uphold institutional barriers against recruiting and retaining students of color for the teaching profession.[1]

THE TEACHER EDUCATION INITIATIVE

The teacher education initiative we describe typifies the effort of many colleges adjacent to sizable minority populations to recruit and retain more teachers of color for local urban schools. An objective look at the metropolitan area suggests it has many advantages that any typical midsize city might have in providing enlightened social and cultural leadership in successfully finding solutions for many of the problems besetting contemporary urban school systems: Its historical prominence in the nineteenth-century abolition movement has continually provided inspiration for the activities of many community organizations and individuals regarding local and global civil and human rights issues; the cultural milieu of the city and surrounding area is deeply influenced by the diversity missions and programs of multiple educational institutions, as well as its vibrant public and private school systems. Furthermore, compared to the large urban settings written about by Jonothan Kozol and others, midsize cities and their school systems are not so large as to be despairingly unmanageable. For this particular city, one often hears that it is large enough to provide urban amenities but still small enough to offer personal responses akin to small-town relationships. Yet a closer looks shows that it has many of the same problems as large urban areas.

Collaborations between the metropolitan school district and local colleges have existed in the past four decades to address problems in the education system, but the impetus for the latest education initiative began over ten years ago when a new dean of education of an area college extended an open invitation to meet with the metropolitan district's superintendent to explore ways the college could assist. The superintendent brought a large group of administrators and teachers to meet with their college counterparts to discuss solutions for what they perceived as their unique teacher preparation needs. The problems they brought forth, however, were not uncommon to urban education across the country and included declining state and local resources (in part, worsened by the privatization of education), increasing public pressure for higher student achievement, losing teacher candidates—as well as veteran teachers—to more attractive and highly paid positions in adjacent suburban districts, and, it seemed to this group, hiring new teachers who were not up to the challenges posed by teaching in an inner-city environment.

The demographic and pedagogical irony that the minority student population was now the majority was not lost on this group of mostly White administrators and teachers. There was general agreement of the need for "more professional role models in the schools," that is, hiring more teachers whose skin color and ethnicity more closely reflected that of the student, but there was a tacit understanding that the paucity of minority applicants was intractable. The percentage of African American, Native American, and Latino teachers had hovered in the range of 7 to 9 percent since the 1970s, despite the efforts of two previous urban education programs with area colleges. Over the years, there had been little change in this regard.

There was a strong sense among these educators that it took a "special kind of person" to successfully educate students from the inner city, and tacitly recognized among the participants as someone like themselves. Many in the group had gained their earliest teaching experiences in a preparation program designed specifically for this purpose in the 1960s and 1970s. Recognizing that federal and state funding for such a program was more difficult today, they proposed that the college and district pool resources to better prepare teachers for the school district. Their proposal resonated with the college educators at the meeting, who acknowledged that many of their own students, predominantly White and from suburban and rural areas, expressed resistance to applying for positions in an urban school. Yet the data emanating from state Education Department reports made it clear that the annual number of available nonurban teaching positions was low when compared to the high number of newly certified teachers. It was likely that many newly certified teachers would either begin, or eventually end up, teaching in an urban school, prepared or not.

Faced with this situation, a commitment was made on the part of the college administrators and faculty to collaborate with the district with the intention of better preparing their graduates for the needs of the metropolitan school district; a secondary commitment was made to recruit and prepare more teachers of color, perhaps as many as thirty each year. Elated at the apparent success in delivering their request for help, one school administrator punctuated their gratitude by promising that the district would "hire every minority candidate you send us." In reality, given the normal attrition rate of the large population of teachers in the school district, hiring thirty minority teachers annually would likely do little more than maintain the status quo, perhaps underscoring a latent function of the meeting. The subsequent influence of the dean of education helped define the college's response proactively.

Committing Higher Education

The dean's previous academic accomplishments of recruiting minorities into education resonated with the diversity themes in the school of education's mission statements and course syllabi, but the presence of a strong African American male advocating educational policies met with an admixture of fanfare and apprehension among the faculty and administration. The dean had taken the initiative to reach out to the school superintendent, but their discussions may not have yielded such a jubilant commitment by the group without the imprimatur of the president, also a dynamic leader supported by the college community for the educational vision he offered, recently including his strong voice on multicultural affairs. White privileges may be difficult to distinguish from the privileges associated with official positions of power.

The president personally emphasized the college's commitment to diversity by announcing the creation of a number of annual scholarships for minority students enrolling in teacher preparation who would commit to teach in the metropolitan school district. The president's action signaled to the education faculty, the school district, and the public a strong message of college support for improving the metropolitan district's education. His genuine goodwill promised to make a dramatic difference each year for the lives of the scholarship recipients who would otherwise be unable to attend college; the difference it would make for their future students and their own descendants was incalculable.

Public praises were rightfully given to the college, the president, and the school of education for actively recruiting and supporting minority teachers candidates. The college's mission to provide opportunity for people in the surrounding community was enhanced, as well as the president's and the dean's positions as bold and innovative leaders in this effort. So, it was a surprise for everyone involved in creating the scholarship program when acrimony and contentiousness arose among many of the recipients and some community leaders about the details of its implementation. In hindsight, this situation illuminates how the efforts conceived in goodwill and made possible within a system of privileges may be received and interpreted differently by those who live within the realities of less advantaged conditions.

College budgets are often very tight, and this case was no different. Creating the scholarships required rearranging college finances to avoid noticeable sacrifice from the current students, faculty, and administrators. The president offered to carry the scholarship program until the dean could generate subsidies from external sources. Conditionally, to receive the awards, students needed first to apply for any state and federal support for which they were eligible; the college's scholarship would then make up the difference between the aid the students' received and the tuition cost. Because the minority students for whom the scholarship was benefiting were mostly low-income, state and federal assistance was able to accommodate a large portion of the actual tuition cost.

The Partly Working Drawbridge

The time between the programs' announcement and the college's semester deadlines for enrollment and housing was relatively short. In fairness to everyone involved in the creation of this program, the rush to select candidates and implement the program provided ample opportunity for misinterpretations and misunderstandings. Confusion arose among the students over the phrase "full-tuition scholarship," with some moving onto campus in the belief that "full" included room and board, and others planning to use their state and federal aid for family expenses.

For older, nontraditional students, a tuition scholarship took care of part of difficulty in going back to school but left them with the problem of how to financially maintain their families while attending college. This was an especially poignant issue for those who were single parents, usually mothers in need of child care. Transportation was especially problematic, as the length of the commute made public transportation very costly in child-care time and very difficult in automobiles that were often unreliable (one African American student reported her frustration in attempting to attract road assistance for her disabled automobile for over two hours). Some had worked for years in low-paying positions such as teaching assistants and social workers. Few of the students or their families had sufficient financial reserves to support them through their time in college. In some cases, a previous academic or financial record made it difficult to find lending sources. There is an old saying that drawbridges that open only partway do not partly work; they are, in fact, useless. For students in great financial need, which is the case for many of the students from traditionally underrepresented groups in teaching, the effect of receiving a partial scholarship, even at very high amounts, can be tantamount to the partly working drawbridge.

Most ironically, the dean, as the most identifiable representative of the college to the students, found himself in a defensive position against charges of racism by some of the scholarship students. Perplexed by how the students had become rancorous and unappreciative over an education benefit program for which he had expended a great amount of energy and political capital to negotiate with the higher administration, the dean was further challenged when two self-appointed student leaders aggressively approached him about their rights as minority students. After describing his own experiences and personal sacrifices in the struggle for civil rights, the dean informed them that their scholarship rights were a product of his personal impact on the political decision making of those with power. He subsequently explained that the continuation of the scholarship program depended on his ability to maintain the college administration's support and respect. And in no uncertain terms, he made it clear that the students' personal continuation in the program depended on his continuing respect for them, which, at that particular moment, was rapidly diminishing.

Gender seemed to have a role in the direction of events. The female scholarship recipients were willing to accept and accommodate the conditions of the scholarship, but many of the male recipients viewed the situation more politically, perhaps reflecting their own previous experiences as community and campus leaders. Publicly expressing suspicion of the college and the dean's role in what they perceived as an unfairly limited scholarship, these students found sympathetic support from another African American faculty member. His influence as the aggrieved students' unofficial advisor and ombudsman accompanied their growing feelings that concerted political action at the college, in the school district, and in the community was needed to rectify what they perceived as racial injustice. The students demanded to meet with college, school board, and other community officials to air their concerns. Fearing that young African American male students would be given an inequitable hearing in a public forum, this faculty member played an admirable role as student advocate at each of the meetings. The students' accusations, however, increasingly came to be viewed as racial invective by school officials and even some African American school board members, eventually prompting the remark by one official that "none of you will be hired in this district if you continue to push this scholarship issue with the college."

Through the efforts of the dean, faculty, and school administrators, the atmosphere surrounding the scholarship confusion gradually stabilized as the recipients got on with their programs. The dean was highly respected and popular among the students, often the source of sustaining financial and academic support in personal financial emergencies. Especially notable were the spontaneous standing ovations he received at graduation ceremonies.

New challenges reappeared, and new solutions were created, but for a brief period of time, the different interpretations and actions of those with and those without privileges threatened to abort a well-intended, albeit limited equity program in teacher preparation.

Expanding the Collaboration

In addition to the scholarships, the college collaborated with the school district and a community college in securing a state grant to increase the number of minorities enrolling in the teacher education programs. Early in this effort it was recognized that the community college had a significant role to play in this collaboration because community colleges are recognized as a first-step institution for many minority students. This new initiative immediately attracted a higher enrollment of minority students into teacher preparation programs.

Three years later, the teacher education initiative was joined by two additional colleges with teacher preparation programs. The operation of this collaboration was moved to the metropolitan school district's teacher center, centrally located to the minority population. Expansion of this collaboration met with mixed success for these two colleges. Although there was little enrollment change for one college, significant gains have been made by the smaller college through a combination of tuition discounts, student book stipends, graduate assistantships, and the nurturing of a close working relationship with the director of the school district program that supports professional development. Among all three colleges, an annual rolling average of seventy-five students participates in any given semester, with ten to fifteen graduating as certified teachers annually. Although this number may not sound large, it represents at least a tenfold increase over the enrollment in the years previous to the creation of the teacher education initiative. As it turns out, more minority teachers than teaching positions are available in the metropolitan district each year.

ANOTHER STORY: "WE'LL HIRE ALL YOU SEND US?"

The metropolitan district hires well over a hundred new teachers each year, but in reality only a small number of them are graduates of the teacher education initiative. Where do the rest go? Many would prefer to teach in the metropolitan district but accept jobs elsewhere when local positions are not available for them. Where family circumstances allow it, some move to other regions of the country; some to a larger urban area in the state; and others, South. And some, still hoping for a tenure-line position in the metropolitan district, continue working as a daily substitute at lower pay, often for a long period of time. But by no stretch of the imagination can it be claimed that once certified, a minority candidate's access to a teaching position is ensured because of the district's involvement with the teacher education initiative. The metropolitan school district officials offer a number of plausible explanations, including that

- candidates are certified in the wrong areas;
- other district candidates who are teaching assistants have seniority as part of union-negotiated contracts;
- the district is unable to hire until the city's budget is finalized in late summer, often too late to secure the first-choice candidates; and
- the school principals who have the greatest influence on hiring decisions may not be familiar with the goals of the teacher education initiative.

Over the years, there have been continuing efforts to surmount many of the hiring barriers for minority candidates. A few of these include focusing the recruiting of teachers for high-need certification areas, involving the district's school principals in the goals of the teacher education initiative, and appealing to school board officials and local politicians for remedies to the budget restrictions. As one barrier is partly redressed, however, new ones seem to arise, making it appear that in spite of the any special collaborative effort, the district's earlier commitment to "hire every certified minority teacher you send" is better understood as abstracted goodwill, unrelated to the concrete and institutionalized barriers that exist for minority teachers candidates.

Institutional Resistance to Minority Retention

The first male graduate from among the scholarship recipients was hired by the metropolitan district with great fanfare, yet he could not meet the tenure hurdles. Although he has gone on to achieve great success in a tenured position in another prominent district, the process he went through before leaving the metropolitan district seems to have become the norm for a number of male graduates of the teacher education initiative. The participants of the teacher education initiative perform as well as or better than other students in the teacher education programs. Most have substantial experience as paraprofessionals, and many hold voluntary or salaried positions in agencies involving children, cultivating a high degree of ability to interact positively with students and parents, so it is difficult to discern why any have experienced difficulty in the tenure process.

A career interruption occurs unexpectedly and rapidly, usually within the first or second semester, with a flurry of supervisory evaluations that include a meeting where the evaluator outlines a professional development plan to remedy the deficits. If satisfactory progress is not made within a stipulated period, the teacher may be encouraged to resign, a seemingly generous offer allowing the teacher to preserve their professional reputation.

To an outsider, the district's professional development process appears to support new teachers in resolving difficulties, but for many new minority teachers, the district's help may seem tantamount to a teaching assassination squad. The assistance offered may be too little, too late, with the teacher left feeling that the process served less as professional development than as documentation for dismissal. Because a new teacher is in a subordinate position, most willingly agree to accept the recommended help; only later might they come to believe that their good-faith cooperation in a professional improvement plan also provided an admission of incompetence.

Equality over Equity

Representatives of the local teachers union have served on the advisory board of the teacher education initiative. In general, they agree that the education of the district's children should include more teachers of color for role modeling, yet when proposals are made for circumventing a particular hiring barrier for minority teachers, the representatives carefully avoid endorsing any strategy that would appear to provide preferential treatment of some teachers over others, even for redressing the racial imbalance of the students' educational experience.

A similar caution is taken by the school district administrators, some of whom themselves were recipients of affirmative action searches. There may be a palpable sensitivity among minority administrators to avoid the appearance of favoritism of minority teachers. For example, on first meeting the codirectors of the teacher education initiative, one new African American superintendent strongly expressed that that he was most interested in all teachers being superb teachers of urban children, not exclusively teachers of color. This even-handed approach may have also defined a passive endorsement of the teacher education initiative's activities in recruiting and retaining local minority teacher candidates.

THINKING, LEARNING, AND TEACHING ABOUT
WHITE PRIVILEGE: A BALANCING ACT

A final story concerns the college programs involved with the teacher education initiative. Each college has made greater efforts to recruit faculty from traditionally underrepresented populations. A tacit expectation by college students that they will be taught by White faculty is one critical element of White privilege in teacher education programs. It may be obvious that most participants in teacher preparation programs are overwhelmingly White; it is far less obvious that these students expect to see professionals who look like them and share their cultural experiences. What happens when faculty of color interrupt that expectation? And what does it mean to be an African American instructor within a program that does not reflect diversity with respect to its full-time faculty?

It is perhaps naive and idealistic to believe that promotion and tenure will naturally result from an objective and meritorious evaluation process of one's hard work and effort. Other factors external to the objective measures bear on the outcome, and one's gender and racial status can be part of this. How students and peers evaluate one's fit in a program weighs heavier on many (if not most) new faculty of color, especially African American faculty. Feeling confident about fitting in may not be easily conjured when there are few other professors of color in the whole institution. In addition, some new faculty express that the culture of individual survival mitigates seeking mutual support from other faculty on simply the basis of race. And for some, a further complication arises when faculty with lighter skin are promoted as academic role models or may seem preferentially selected for diversity representation on choice committees.

For an untenured professor, it would be a relief to believe that students will provide accurate and equitable representations of one's teaching abilities, regardless of skin color. Student evaluations are, after all, a key component of the tenure process. Yet African American professors in teacher preparation programs are constantly reminded that their evaluations are made by a predominately White group of students who are educated in all-White communities, from homogenous geographic regions, and worship in all-White faith communities with limited (or no) exposure to cultural diversity or any understanding of how White privileges shape their cultural landscape. "Sharon," a third-year faculty member of one of the teacher preparation programs involved with the teacher education initiative, explains that:

> The learning curve for an African American female professor as a junior faculty can be particularly daunting in a White institution. At the same time you are negotiating the typical new faculty status responsibilities and acculturation in the institution, race and gender becomes the added burdensome baggage that you must carry. At times it is [an] alienating and isolating experience.

Timeliness, force of voice, and other everyday behaviors can be easily misinterpreted or ascribed as cultural markers. Maintaining extraordinary sensitivity, awareness, and diligence exacts higher levels of energy that extend far beyond the work normally required of new professors. An early experience of this minority faculty member illuminates her work as a delicate balancing act, involving joyous, rewarding professional moments juxtaposed with contradictory messages and dilemmas.

Sharon had returned in late August from a month-long trip to an African country, accompanying her college-aged daughter, who had received a grant to study traditional healing practices. The trip had given her time to reflect on the mixed emotions she had experienced during her first year as a junior faculty. In her office mailbox was a package from a young female European American who teaches in an urban setting. The card read: "Thank you for reopening my eyes to my love for learning and my abilities as an educator. Very few people have had the amount of impact on my life like you have in such a short time. I admire your strength, empathy. I hope I can impact my students in the way you have done for me." With it was a plaque that read "Stand up for your principles even if you stand alone."

Feeling extremely pleased and validated in her teaching, Sharon checked messages and sorted mail with renewed resolve for her professional responsibilities when she noticed the light flashing for a phone message. Listening to a frantic message from a colleague who instructed her "not to be alarmed," she learned that "several students have made a complaint to the dean about you." Nothing more. She anxiously wondered what she had done. She couldn't recall any particular problem during the summer courses, and she had not even met her students for the fall semester yet. The students had become upset after waiting several minutes for an instructor to show up at their first class meeting a couple of days earlier. This was a surprise for this new faculty member, for, unable to return two days earlier, she had carefully prepared a folder and left it with the chair for the first class. But something had gone wrong, and she was now left owning a problem with potentially serious implications for her professional status.

The department chairperson subsequently visited the class to apologize for his omission, but the die was cast. Sharon explains:

Group talk among the graduate students occurs. I believe the students were well aware of who I was. I can't help but be skeptical about their motives. Why complain to the dean and overstep the department chairperson? It would have been great if upon contacting the dean, they were referred to the chair of the department and encouraged to follow some semblance of protocol. In my other course, an individual did contact the department chair and the class was covered. Students did not feel the need to "report to the dean." For me this represents an attitude of power and privilege that translates into the classroom.

This is an example of student behavior that seems to occur frequently when instructors who are racial or cultural minorities first become part of the faculty, manifesting the potentially unequal politics of the teacher and student relationship. The students' deep-seated feelings of racial and cultural superiority are thinly concealed by their emphasis on consumer rights. When a college instructor speaks with an accent from a foreign language, students may complain of their inability to receive the information they have purchased; when an instructor is an African American for whom some of the students feel should not have equal privileges of power, identifying incompetence by exaggerating a classroom incident serves as a form of White resistance.

For Sharon, the group's attitude reflected in class participation during the semester: "I found them sullen and disengaged despite my best efforts. This particular course I've taught several times and had developed excellent practical assignments related to coteaching and differentiated instruction. My most recent evaluations were strong. However, at the end of the semester, I received weak evaluations in the course."

Sharon's concerns represent far more than a missed class. The hectic pace of the start of the new semester for the chairperson most likely accounts for his original omission to protect her reputation with the students. Yet Sharon was left having to dispel the possible racist overtones. Her experience in this situation is a good example of the potentially unnerving and, in reality, diminishing aspect of being an African American junior professor working in a racially monolithic institution of higher education. The questions Ladson-Billings poses are questions that White college professors are privileged in not needing to ask about themselves, their students, or the ideas presented in class: "Am I accorded the same deference they do to White male professors? Must I be doubly gracious and accommodating so as to not appear embittered and militant? Do they want me to wear a mask so they will not have to?"[2] Sharon narrates another compelling incident that further illustrates the racial dynamics of classroom teaching:

Throughout the semester, I became increasingly aware of Tom's lack of cultural competency. He often referred to a negative experience he'd had with a female African American professor at a nearby regional institution. According to Tom, he had "issues with terms such as African American, Mexican American, and Native American." He continually used the language "people of a darker persuasion" to address all people of color, and felt this was perfectly acceptable because a European American public school teacher had instructed him to use this terminology to help him with his struggles. She assured him this would be acceptable and shared the fact that she was the proud mother of what she termed a "beautifully blended child." The father of the child is African American. Tom seemed to take issue with anything that he could throughout the course. However, when he wrote a scathing final reflection paper that lacked professional tone, I felt it was time to express my concerns to the chairperson. The meeting consisted of a colleague, the chairperson, Tom, and me. The chairperson started with sharing our accreditation claims that we would seek to produce caring, competent teachers. She then asked him if his writing reflected that mission. With tears, Tom narrated how his family and community were racist and how he was emotionally raw from a negative experience with a previous African American professor. Through our discussions, we tried to get him to see that these experiences may have shaped his perception of my teaching and his learning experiences. Reluctantly, he conceded. We eventually hugged and the meeting was concluded. Afterward, my chairperson remarked poignantly that even though Tom's feelings were out in the open, it raises the question of how many other students preparing to be teachers sit silently in the class but share Tom's attitudes about race? At the end of the semester, despite a couple of negative remarks, I received an overall strong evaluation which was also noted by the dean in my yearly evaluation. Tom is currently substitute teaching and has accepted a teaching position in the fall.

Ladson-Billings advises that despite the dilemmas faced, being an African American does not discharge one from the important responsibility to critically examine one's practice in determining effective strategies to engage students. Sharon adheres to this professional wisdom, and it enables her to exert more personal control over her professional situation.

For example, in her teaching, Sharon has instituted a process of having students complete weekly CIQs (Critical Incident Questionnaires) adopted from Brookfield's work on critical reflective teaching.[3] Because they are completed anonymously, students are free to express themselves. The feedback helps her understand how students experience the course and whether she needs to make adjustments to support their learning. She finds that, overall, students respect her professional experiences in the public schools and appreciate the ways she structures class to encourage their sharing ideas. One student expressed, "Hopefully you will not take this the wrong way but I was most surprised about you as the professor. I heard from other students that you were a tough teacher with your own strong opinions. I thought you were very understanding about all our different backgrounds in education as well as sympathetic to our questions." Sharon also finds that integrating technology has become an excellent organizing tool for strengthening her teaching. On their online blackboard site, she is able to post the week's lectures, class activities, handouts, and grades. Most important, in addition to creating both the sense and reality of strong and efficient organization to her instruction, the online work approach has become invaluable in penetrating the silences and student resistance that often occur when topics of race and class are discussed in class. She comments that:

> I am hopeful about my professional development as junior faculty of color, especially balancing issues of race with my professional responsibilities. It takes more than recruitment to create a diverse climate in an institution. Struggles for professional recognition and identity are real barriers that exist in White institutions. Surely greater institutional change is important, and one important step would be the recognition that students might be affected by their feelings of racial superiority.

SUMMARY

Each of the stories emanating from the activities of the teacher education initiative suggest how White privileges operate in a differential manner in upholding some of the institutionalized barriers of preparing and retaining African American, Native American, and Latino students and faculty in the field of teacher education. The first two stories describe how, through a combination of privileges and power, educational leaders were able to initiate an equity program in teacher preparation; yet an analysis of the delimited structure of the program suggests its creation and implementation was never a serious threat to the institutionalized patterns of preparing, hiring, and retaining a predominantly White teacher workforce. The college president adeptly understood how to make changes in what remained a primarily White institution; likewise, he also understood the limits within which he could act and remain a vibrant and magnanimous leader. This interpretation is neither blame nor criticism but merely an observation of how White privileges serve multiple and conflicting social ends. The reputation for the college and its leaders was greatly enhanced by the teacher education initiative for greater equity, yet the changes that were made at the college did not threaten the resources or expectations of the dominant group of White students.

Understanding how White privileges operate at an institutional level can be helpful in designing equity programs in teacher education. Tuition scholarships that do not threaten the existing privileges of other students may involve little actual cost for a college. Adding a dozen or so minority scholarship students to a population of thousands does not require the addition of new faculty; it does involve placing a few additional seats in a few scattered classrooms for students who would not have attended otherwise. And, as in the case we describe, the stipulation that scholarship winners contribute their eligible federal and state aid as a condition for the scholarship may enable the college to gain some additional resources for students who would not attend otherwise. Covering the living costs of students as well as the tuition would be a gift on the part of the college, but it might also create repercussions if it cut too directly into the resources of the majority of students.

Despite the early enthusiasm among some district and college educators to enlarge the availability and presence of minority teachers in the schools, the status quo remains. After the metropolitan district's superintendent, the college dean, and college president moved out of their positions, the political endorsement and visibility of the teacher education initiative diminished, and, consequently, less priority has been placed on the program's goals by midlevel administrators. Over the past decade, a greater number of African American, Native American, and Latino students have been recruited into teacher preparation programs that feed the metropolitan school district. Providing professional guidance, educational awareness, and personal encouragement to teacher candidates of color has served to help balance the opportunities afforded by the privileges the other students already have by virtue of being born White. Yet there is an irony in fact that the school district's institutionalized hiring and professional development practices may favor most the minority teachers who "learn how to be White."

In the final vignette, the faculty of most teacher education programs—mostly White—hold ideas and beliefs that reify the privileges they and most of their students enjoy. For the colleges involved with the teacher education initiative, their respective policies, affirmative action programs, and course syllabi amount to a resounding commitment to multiculturalism and diversity, providing the appearance that racism has little opportunity to appear or do harm. It may not be unreasonable to hold these beliefs, nor is it completely unreasonable to positively act on these beliefs, if you are a White, untenured professor. But the experiences of many untenured African American professors who have been involved with the teacher preparation programs affiliated with the teacher education initiative make these presuppositions tenuous. The story we provide exemplifies how one junior faculty member who is African American emancipates her own professional development by developing strategies to confront both the content and effect of White privilege in college classrooms.

NOTES

1. P. McIntosh, "White Privilege and Male Privilege: A Personal Account of Coming to See Correspondences through Work in Women's Studies," in M. L. Anderson and P. H. Collins (eds.), *Race, Class, and Gender: An Anthology* (Belmont, CA: Wadsworth, 1992), 70–81; Christine Sleeter, "How White Teachers Construct Race," in C. McCarthy and W. Crichlow (eds.), *Race Identity and Representation in Education* (New York: Routledge, 1993), 157–171; Alice McIntyre, *Making Meaning of Whiteness: Exploring Racial Identity with White Teachers* (Albany: State University of New York Press, 1997).

2. Gloria Ladson-Billings, "Silence as Weapons: Challenges of a Black Professor Teaching White Students," *Theory into Practice* 35, no. 2 (1996): 79–85. Quotation on p. 84.

3. S. Brookfield, *Becoming a Critically Reflective Teacher* (San Francisco: Jossey-Bass, 1995).

12

Avoidance, Anger, and Convenient Amnesia: White Supremacy and Self-Reflection in Social Studies Teacher Education

Luis Urrieta Jr. and Michelle Reidel

> Eliminating racism will require Whites to connect with their race, to make meaning of that connection by understanding the accompanying emotions, and to move on to take positive action.
>
> —J. Arminio, *"Exploring the Nature of Race-Related Guilt"* [1]

INTRODUCTION

This chapter highlights, like Loewen in *Lies My Teacher Told Me*, that the kindergarten through grade twelve social studies curriculum and pedagogy—and we would include social studies teacher education programs—generally have not changed in close to ninety years.[2] Although superficial inclusion of women and certain groups of color has occurred since the 1960s, meaningful contributions have been erased from the official history of the United States. We argue that this is consistent with the ideology of White supremacy that is at the foundation of U.S. society.[3] By White supremacy, we are referring

The authors thank Patrick S. DeWalt and Anissa Butler for careful feedback on this work. This research was funded by both the Implementation of Multicultural Perspectives and Approaches in Research and Teaching (IMPART) Awards Program and the School of Education at the University of Colorado at Boulder.

to the official and unofficial practices, principles, morals, norms, values, history, and overall culture that privileges Whites in U.S. society.

Using ethnographic data from a self-selected cohort ($n = 10$) of predominantly White preservice social studies teachers, this chapter reveals how critical multicultural and social justice issues in social education are often avoided, responded to with anger, or conveniently forgotten. Issues of inequality and diversity are especially made a problem of the other that is hurried through and not dealt with in-depth. Building on Boler's pedagogy of discomfort, we argue that "discomfort" is a necessary step toward self-reflection and trans/formative social studies education, but we question how race afects what we mean by discomfort.[4] How does the race of the instructor affect the effectiveness of a pedagogy of discomfort in helping White students deconstruct White supremacy through self-reflection in a secondary social studies teacher education course? We propose that social studies teacher education programs committed to social justice begin by making their students uncomfortable, by encouraging students to draw from this discomfort to self-reflect and commit to challenging the White supremacist system through their future teaching practices. From this study we offer some insights that question how we define discomfort and how the racial dynamics of a classroom affect.

White preservice teachers' disposition and willingness to learn from the discomfort.

BACKGROUND

Over the past twenty-five years, the U.S. teaching force has become increasingly monocultural and monolingual. Current estimates indicate that over 80 percent of all practicing and prospective teachers are upper- to middle-class White Americans.[5] At the same time, the student population of our nation's public schools has become more culturally, ethnically, and linguistically diverse.[6] These cultural differences can make the relationships that are at the heart of teaching and learning difficult to create and maintain.

A number of educators and scholars argue that until White teachers own their identity, connections between teachers and students, students and curriculum, and schools and communities will continue to falter.[7] This ownership must include both an understanding of how U.S. society is stratified by race, class, gender, and language and how our educational system often operates to support and sustain White supremacy. More important, owning one's identity requires prospective teachers to critically examine their own complex relationship to the White culture. To do so, Nieto argues that teachers need to "face and question their own racial, linguistic and social class privilege."[8] However, questioning cherished beliefs, unacknowledged assumptions, and one's identity is never easy, rarely voluntary, and almost always painful.

In *Racial and Ethnic Identity and Development*, Chávez and Guido-DiBrito argue that this type of critical self-reflection is especially difficult for White Americans.[9] These scholars suggest that White Americans practice and enact their racial identity in "mostly unconscious ways through behaviors, values, beliefs and assumptions."[10] As a result, race and ethnicity are both invisible and unconscious for most White Americans. Chávez and Guido-DiBrito argue that this invisibility is sustained and maintained by the ways in which societal norms have been constructed around White Americans "racial, ethnic and cultural frameworks," making them appear neutral, normal, and reflective of the "standard American culture."[11] This normalization of White supremacy makes it difficult—even painful—for White Americans to recognize the ways in which Whiteness is privileged or how they benefit from these privileges.

Making the invisible visible is hard work and rarely a task taken on voluntarily. Yet for many practicing and prospective teachers it is work that must be done if they hope to be effective educators with all students. To address this need, teacher education programs must provide opportunities for prospective teachers to investigate their own beliefs, assumptions, and cultural identity. Teacher educators in pursuit of this goal have used a variety of approaches and methods, all of which include an emphasis on self-reflection.[12] Strategies include the use of autobiography, narrative storytelling, and cultural portfolios or memoirs, and each is intended to foster critical self-reflection on both culture and identity and their relationship.

In *Walking the Road: Race, Diversity and Social Justice in Teacher Education*, Cochran-Smith argues that this type of inquiry must inform all aspects of teacher education if we hope to "bridge the chasm between school and life experiences of teachers and students."[13] Practicing and prospective teachers must interrogate the ways in which culture and identity inform not only their understanding of U.S. society and schooling but their conceptualizations of curriculum, pedagogy, and assessment. We argue that nowhere in our educational system is an exploration of the complex relationships between culture, identity, curriculum, pedagogy, and assessment more vital than in social studies education.

Social studies education has long been charged with the task of fomenting nationalism, even blind patriotism, without an analysis of race.[14] This has often been carried out primarily by teaching a victorious and teleological White supremacist version of history,[15] and by educating students to be good citizens.[16] Using assimilation and acculturation models, diverse populations were and are coerced to follow the White supremacist norms of U.S. society. Included is the adoption of a vision of democracy focused on passive spectatorship (voting) rather than active participation, resulting in what some scholars call a *spectator democracy.*[17]

To prepare social studies teachers to question the rationale for social studies education, work effectively, and form meaningful relationships with all students, we must help social studies teachers understand the racial narrative that generally underlies social studies curricula.[18] This type of understanding requires "intense self-critical reflection and analysis" that is best fostered when White preservice teachers collectively investigate their emotional investment in particular beliefs, assumptions, and worldviews.[19]

Megan Boler calls this form of critical inquiry a pedagogy of discomfort.[20] Boler argues that the discomfort, along with the anger and fear we feel when we question our beliefs and assumptions, is something to be investigated rather than ignored. We must investigate the cultural and historical reasons for our emotions and our emotional investment in particular worldviews because they are neither neutral nor natural. Boler argues that the discomfort, anger, and fear we feel when we critically examine our own identity and beliefs are in part shaped by the "effects of a specific cultural agenda" and are "embedded in cultural ways of seeing and not seeing."[21] Therefore if we are to see what our anger, fear, and discomfort prevent us from seeing, we must make these emotions the focus of our inquiry.

In this study, we focused our attention on making preservice social studies teachers uncomfortable with dominant conceptualizations of democracy, citizenship, and civic education and their own beliefs about social studies education. By teaching from a critical perspective the instructor designed the course around readings, activities, and projects that focused on diversity and questioned the legitimacy of White supremacy. Expecting that this would arouse the discomfort of the students, our goal was to ask them why they felt uncomfortable and investigate the cultural and historical sources of their discomfort. Our hope was that this would lead the students to become more self-reflective. The following sections provide an overview of the study.

THE STUDY

Secondary Social Studies Methods (SSSM) is typically the last teacher education course preservice social studies teachers take prior to student teaching in the College of Education at Mountain University (MU). MU is a prominent and predominantly White university in the Western United States. This study focused on SSSM as a bound system, grounded in detailed in-depth data collection that uses multiple sources of information.[22] As a bound system, the study is focused on those students who volunteered from the course and the events and activities connected to the course.

In preparation for this study the course emphasized a strong focus on multicultural issues and included a number of activities specifically designed to elicit thoughtful reflection about citizenship, democracy, and social studies educators' role in civic education. These activities include (1) structured observations of a (grade eight to twelve) social studies classroom and the compilation of fieldnotes based on these observations, (2) the design of and participation in a social action project, and (3) the development and implementation of a unit about citizenship.

A sample of self-selected students enrolled in this course for the fall 2004 semester constituted the population studied in this chapter. Although the study also included a second cohort of students enrolled in the spring 2005 course, those data will not be included in this analysis. The total number of participants for which data are here presented is ten ($n = 10$), five men and five women. All of the participants identified as White, except for a Native American female, Mary. All of the participants reported that their first language was English, four reported to be of upper-middle-class background, five of middle-class background, and one of upper-working-class background.

The course was taught by the first author, a male professor of Chicano heritage. However, all of the data were exclusively collected by the second author, a White female of working-class background who was especially meticulous about not revealing who the participants in the study were. Access to all of the data was restricted to the instructor by order of the human subjects committee until after the course grades were formally turned in to ensure that the students were graded fairly. Pseudonyms were used for all people and institutions in this study.

Methodology

Data Collection.   The data collected in this study over a period of sixteen weeks (one semester) included:

1. Interviews. Tape-recorded, semi-structured interviews were conducted at the beginning and also at the end of the course with each participant and the instructor. The format focused interview discussions on the topics of

democracy, citizenship, and civic education and preservice social studies teachers' cultural and civic identities. All tapes were destroyed after transcription and before the data analysis began to ensure anonymity.

2. Observations. Weekly two-and-a-half-hour observations and accompanying fieldnotes of the social studies methods courses were conducted by the second author. These observations served two purposes: to record how preservice social studies teachers enacted their understandings of democracy, citizenship, and civic education within the context of the course; and to record how activities, experiences, and guided reflection about democracy, citizenship, and civic education affected these understandings.

3. Documents/Artifacts. Copies of the following documents and artifacts produced by the participants were collected: (a) practicum observation fieldnotes, (b) written reflections about social action projects, and (c) unit and lesson plans on citizenship. These documents ideally would provide additional lenses to consider how preservice social studies teachers understood citizenship, democracy, and civic education and how cultural diversity was reflected in these understandings. The names of the participants were erased from all documents collected.

Data Analysis. Interviews were transcribed and all field notes were typed by the second author. A constant comparative method was used.[23] A constant comparative method "combines inductive category-coding with a simultaneous comparison of social incidents observed and coded."[24] This method provided a "thick description" of preservice teachers' beliefs about democracy, citizenship, and civic education.[25] Interview transcripts, fieldnotes, and classroom observation transcripts and documents were used to triangulate and develop categories for coding. Emerging themes were identified from interviews to inform the data analysis. Larger domains of data were later grouped according to the themes identified from all of the compiled data. Themes included conceptualizations of democracy, citizenship, social studies, and civic education.

FINDINGS

Overall, this study finds that a pedagogy of discomfort is only partially successful, when used by a professor of color, in helping White preservice teachers become more self-reflective about their privileges and teaching social studies in a White supremacist society. Despite all of the effort and compassion built into the course to induce self-reflection, the overwhelming majority of the students in this study found ways to resist the critical, multicultural, and social justice orientation of this course. This resistance prevented the instructor and students from interrogating the ways in which their responses to the course and the instructor were neither neutral or natural but a product of both historical and cultural dynamics. As a result, White students' emotional responses to the course became roadblocks to learning self-reflection rather than an entryway as Boler suggests.

In general, three patterns of resistant behavior emerged: (1) *avoidance* of engagement with the course material, the instructor, and the engaged students—especially Mary, an elder in her tribe; (2) expressions of *anger* by the most resistant students toward students who did engage; and (3) a *convenient amnesia* of the themes covered in the course. Each of these forms of resistance is discussed in this section.

Avoidance

In general, this study finds that some White preservice teachers primarily resisted the critical, multicultural, and social justice focus of the SSSM course by avoiding serious engagement or discussion about issues related to diversity and social studies education. Moreover, they refused to make the connections between theoretical constructs about democracy, citizenship, civic engagement, and how those relate to diversity, equity, and social studies curricula and pedagogy (methods). Throughout the semester, students insisted that what they called "theory" was not necessary and that what they needed were "practical ways of teaching." Thus they consciously or perhaps unconsciously engineered ways to avoid engagement in bridging theory and practice. Avoidance was carried out in three ways: (1) by engaging in a culture of silence, (2) by physical disengagement, and (3) by shifting the focus away from themselves and onto the other.

The culture of silence involved students being silent and not responding to the professor's questions, class discussions, or participating in small-group discussions. This was in part due to the fact that many of the students refused to do the assigned course readings and openly admitted this to the instructor. This was especially evident during small-group discussions when students were observed in silence because most of them had not read the assigned reading. On one particular occasion, fieldnotes recorded that none of the students in a given group had read the article assigned to their group for discussion and none of them, with the exception of one student had even brought a copy of the article to class that day. Subsequently, the student with the copy of the article quickly skimmed the article as the rest of the students sat silently. Silence also prevailed during whole-class discussions because a sizable number of students did not actively contribute to the discussion. For example, throughout the duration of the course, four students, all White males, engaged in a culture of silence by consistently sitting together alongside the windows and rarely engaging in class discussions. Most were observed to be consistently expressionless and occasionally chimed in to support more conservative perspectives.

Another way students avoided engagement was through physical disengagement when the instructor was speaking about social justice and equity issues or when other students who were engaged spoke. This pattern was especially evident when Mary, who happened to be the only student of color enrolled in the class and who was also very passionate about issues of equity and diversity, spoke. Observation notes reveal that students consistently physically tuned out when the professor was speaking about issues of diversity and equity. This disengagement was done by carrying on quiet conversations, drawing, reading, or looking out the windows while the professor was speaking. Subsequently, when the professor asked critical and self-reflective questions of the students, this was followed by long periods of silence without any response until the professor asked another question or changed the topic altogether.

Avoidance of Mary was especially pronounced as students physically turned away from her as she spoke in class. This student was physically isolated and sat by herself in the middle front of the room; rarely, even during group discussions, did other students include her in their groups until the instructor assigned her a group. One time when asked to engage in a paired discussion none of the students would pair up with her, so the professor sat with her instead. A number of inappropriate behaviors were also noted when Mary spoke, often including rolling of the eyes, teeth sucking, sighing, half smirks, and head shaking.

A third way that students avoided critical engagement was by shifting the focus away from themselves and onto the other. This means that instead of trying to seriously engage the material or be self-reflective about class issues, they often placed the burden on Mary or on the professor. This was noted on several occasions but was most pronounced in the following two examples. In the first example, the class discussion was focused on John Marciano's *Civic Illiteracy* which was assigned to the class to read.[26] *Civic Illiteracy* argues that U.S. society is kept civically illiterate and passive by means of social studies textbooks and the media that glorify wars and keep the general population ignorant and passive as the dominant elite continue to exploit the masses through corporate greed. The instructor chose to include this book with the hope that students would appreciate a counterargument and begin to question the use of textbooks and the focus on wars in their future social studies teaching.

The general response to the book, however, with the exception of Mary, was of very vocal disapproval. In fact, it stirred the most hostile response from the students of all the assigned reading. Because almost all of the students refused to even consider the idea of civic illiteracy seriously, and to try to engage the students in thinking critically about the book and model a practical teaching method, the instructor asked the students to simulate a trial and judge the *idea* of civic illiteracy. Students were equally assigned to either the prosecution or defense of the idea with two students playing the role of attorneys and a handful of students as judges.

The students assumed their roles, although a number of the students having to defend the idea openly expressed their distaste for the book. One student loudly exclaimed, "God, I have to defend this lunatic!" Mary happened to be on the defense and was pressured by the group to role play Marciano even though she expressed that she did not want to do that.

> Ann tells Mary that she should be Marciano since she *likes* him. Mary says she wants to be a different character. This causes a disagreement in the defense group. Several students are speaking at the same time because no one in the group wants to role play Marciano. No one will do it. They all look at each other and then look again at Mary with serious and expressionless faces. Finally Mary concedes.[27]

By way of diverting this role to Mary, the students shifted the focus away from themselves and onto the other—Mary. Had any of them had to play Marciano, would that mean that they would have to, at least for the role play, seriously consider his point of view?

A second example of shifting the focus away from themselves and onto the other that is important to highlight occurred when the professor expressed to the class his concern that many of them were not reading the assigned material. His main concern was that this was not enabling critical class discussions. Within a matter of minutes the focus of this conversation, which was aimed at the students for self-reflection, was refocused on the professor as the students, one after the other, with the exception of Mary and a handful of more engaged students, blamed him for their disengagement. A series of complaints followed, "There are too much readings assigned," "I am *alienated* from the topics!" "I feel like we keep reading the same thing over and over again," and "I *disconnected* when we kept doing the same thing." The overall message was that students did not want to engage in critical (or what they called theoretical) conversations about the whys of teaching but rather wanted hands-on activities about the how-tos of teaching.

Interestingly and conveniently, several students appropriated the language of the course—alienation, disconnection—to argue their positions, making it almost impossible for the instructor to counter their points. Not that the instructor could not, but to do so would go against the basic lesson on connected citizenship he was trying to teach through this course and he himself was trying to model as an inclusive teaching strategy. The students insisted, however, that this was a methods course and therefore there was not a high need for what they interpreted as theory. Although this did cause the professor to self-reflect and eventually incorporate more how-tos into the course, it amazed both researchers how quickly and swiftly the students diverted the attention to the instructor rather than engage in self-reflection.

Anger

Expressions of anger by the most resistant students toward students who did engage was also a form of resistance to the critical, multicultural, and social justice orientation of this SSSM course. Specific topics of conversation about issues of racism, sexism, sexual orientation, and classism and the relationship to social and citizenship education often manifested in anger for some students. At times students looked physically disturbed as they turned red and made disapproving gestures as certain students spoke, especially Mary, and at other times students verbally expressed their anger toward a specific reading or topic in class. In this study, resistant students expressed their anger in at least three ways: through (1) body language, (2) oppositional responses, and (3) the end-of-semester course evaluations.

Body language was the primary way that students expressed their anger. As mentioned already, this was done deliberately by making faces, rolling of the eyes, teeth sucking, smirking, laughing, or engaging in other tasks like reading, looking away, or literally turning away when comments were made they did not agree with. The image of the four silent men by the windows also comes to mind. In particular, one student in the class who was on active military duty, Bill, frequently engaged in physical responses that expressed anger.

Fieldnotes consistently reported Bill's occasional expressions of disapproval of certain points of view by sighing, laughing, or holding a pencil tightly by making a fist. Bill generally sat on the side where most of the class sat but kept to himself. Often he assumed a slouched position and looked down, rarely did he speak, except for one occasion when the professor was being observed (discussed later). Because of his open and proud affiliation with the military, his expressions could have been interpreted as intimidating, especially toward Mary. For example, during the attempted discussion about Marciano's book:

> Mary was quick to express her appreciation of the book and Marciano's ideas. Quickly, Bill sighed loudly and shook his head in disapproval. Mary continued by saying she particularly liked the human liberation concept and asked if Marciano was a communist? Bill stares at Mary from under his eyebrows without raising his head and listens intently as he begins to turn red. Shortly after he picks up his pencil and clenches it tightly in his right fist. A number of students look at Bill and then at Mary and then back at Bill. Silence prevails.[28]

On a number of occasions Bill physically expressed his disapproval of Mary's comments and often these expressions were followed with silence by the rest of the class.

On other occasions students were quick to respond with oppositional remarks about certain topics and readings. The overall accusation of most of these students who subscribed to the myth of neutrality in education and research was that the work was biased and therefore afforded their dismissal.[29] Oppositional responses included comments such as that the author or researcher was "unbelievably biased," that there was "little balance," that they "didn't like it," or that they thought the author was "mean." In response to these instances of anger, the professor wrote the following in his weekly journal:

> I am frustrated with the role I sometimes have to assume here at MU as a professor. Of course I think Marciano's work is great, but I have to downplay my enthusiasm because I know this type of perspective often puts some White students off. I chose to get them to tell me about their overall impressions to get a general feel for what they thought. Unfortunately, only Mary thought it was good, the rest thought it was bad. "Unbelievably biased" was a comment made that keeps ringing in my head. How could they so angrily say that Marciano is biased and *not* see that US society and history is also *unbelievably* biased as well? So, I have to hide my emotions and lead the discussion to a more appreciative ground. That is frustrating to me because I feel like sometimes I compromise who I am and what I believe in. But, it's either that and have them listen to me for a *little* while, or not listen to me at all. So, I wonder what I'm doing here teaching White students? I don't know, but there has to be some hope.[30]

The issue of compromise was one that often troubled the professor, especially when, after students expressed their anger with oppositional responses, he had to modify his tone in an effort to engage at least a few students.

As part of an effort to improve the racial climate at MU, a White female consultant was hired to observe classes and offer professors feedback about how to improve multicultural communication. To improve the climate in this class, the professor invited the consultant to observe. Purposefully, he introduced the consultant to the class as someone who was there to observe him teach without mentioning the reason why she was there. Interestingly, this happened to be the last class before the 2004 national elections. The professor was not secretive about his party affiliation and noted that a student was wearing a bright beanie with "W '04" stitched on it. The focus of the class was on using Socratic seminars as a method to engage students in discussions in a social studies classroom. Contrary to his usually quiet, yet physically expressive manner, Bill was very talkative that day but focused mostly on challenging the professor.

Professor: You can also follow up a seminar with a position essay as a form of assessment. This is also a good way to allow students who don't participate in the discussion to take a stand.

Adam: What do you do with kids that don't have a ticket and can't participate?

Mary: Because of the way these seminars run and because they are supposed to be interesting to the students, they will begin to prepare their tickets to participate.

Bill: [in a loud and confrontational tone] You can't tell me this is a magical solution to kids not doing their work! [to the professor] Answer the question! He asked what do you do with kids that don't have a ticket!

Professor: You as a teacher should choose topics that kids will care about and of course there is no guarantee that it will work all the time or for everybody. Evidence does show however, that it gets students involved.

Bill: [angry] I still don't understand how kids who are not involved will get involved! You make it seem like this is the best thing since sliced bread! Besides, it seems like a lot of work!

[The professor tries to respond to Bill, but Bill continues to talk over the professor. In the end Bill slouches again and looks angry. The professor asks the class if anyone has anymore questions. Silence takes over.][31]

Despite his usual quiet manner, Bill used this occasion as the professor was being observed to challenge him. Through oppositional questioning, Bill was able to express his anger and disbelief about the general pedagogical approach the professor espoused.

A final, anonymous, and perhaps most damaging way that resistant students chose to express their anger was through end-of-semester course evaluations. Course evaluations are used at MU to measure yearly progress in the area of teaching for professors and also for career advancement such as yearly reviews and tenure and promotion decisions. For this course, the overall grade for the class was a C, which indicates that a high distribution of the evaluations were in the middle and low range. The compiled grade for the instructor was a C+, and the workload distribution on a scale from 1 to 10 was a 6.7. The numbers themselves, without the context of the course social and cultural dynamics, would indicate that the instructor was not effective in teaching the course content. The overall grade for the professor's attention to issues of diversity and women, an A, would indicate that the instructor focused disproportionately on such issues without an under-standing of why such an interpretation is inaccurate when issues of diversity and equity are infused as fundamental throughout the course. In a college of education where the majority of courses were graded highly, several ad-ministrators expressed concern for this professor's teaching abilities, sug-gesting pedagogical strategies and offering consolation, and thus shifting the focus of attention away from the White students and onto the other—the professor of color.

Written feedback on these evaluations also revealed that students were not happy about the course content and generally did not see the importance or relationship between larger concepts such a democracy, citizenship, di-versity, and equity and the social studies content and pedagogy (methods). Table 12-1 illustrates some of their written responses to the question of what was least effective about the course in the end of semester course evaluations.

Again, they focused on the "how-to" and divorced it from the "why" of teaching social studies. Although they did receive strategies of how to teach by using discussion-based activities, students indicated that they would have liked to receive such things as Venn diagrams, topics for journal entries, maps, and worksheets that the instructor indicated they could get from multiple sources including the Internet. Course evaluations have been repeatedly docu-mented as the place where professors of color are graded unfairly by angry and uncomfortable White students.

Convenient Amnesia

The final way students resisted the critical, multicultural, and social justice orientation of the SSSM course was through a convenient amnesia of the themes covered in class. By convenient amnesia we are not arguing that

Table 12-1   What Was Least Effective about the Course?

S 1	Social action project. More focus on teaching social studies and less emphasis on democracy/equality/action theme.
S 2	This entire class was about equality, something important, but we all took this class to learn about *methods*. I think Louis did a great job addressing issues of social inequalities and being conscious about how to portray equality and address issues from multiple angles, but this class was supposed to be about *methods*. This class was a total waste as far as that goes.
S 3	Although I enjoyed many of the ideas we discussed in class, I felt that this class somehow took on a negative atmosphere among students and the instructor.
S 4	This is not a theory course—teach methods.
S 5	Citizenship and democracy is good, preparing us for teaching is better.
S 6	Give us things that we can use in the classroom. This class was extremely heavy in theory and not so much the practical nature of teaching the social studies.
S 7	The topic of citizenship. The instructor didn't relate nor cover the topic of this course.
S 8	I think this would have been a great course if it was titled, "Citizenship and Democracy," but for a methods course it totally lacked in that instruction.
S 9	Too much reading every week. Too much emphasis on theories, not enough on the actual methods.

students forgetting that certain themes covered in class were important was deliberate, it was simply observed. In general, convenient amnesia manifested in three ways that we labeled as: (1) I wash my hands speech, (2) reinforcement of the culture of teacher neutrality, and (3) superficial appeasement engagement.

I wash my hands speech refers to student acknowledgment that U.S. society is not perfect but they had nothing to do with issues of past wrongdoings and it was therefore not their responsibility to remedy them. This was observed mostly when discussing James Loewen's *Lies My Teacher Told Me*. This book was chosen by the instructor because of the powerful way that traditional high school history texts are deconstructed by Loewen. Strategically, by offering counternarratives to the official versions of history, Loewen exposes the inaccuracies of curricular portrayals and this is often an effective strategy to get students to question the versions of history they themselves were taught. Although a lot of the material presented in this book made several students uncomfortable, their response to that discomfort was disengagement.

Although the responses varied, generally students seemed unwilling to accept the responsibility to engage in the struggle to undo the wrongs of the past as teachers. Similar reactions occurred when studying disconnections in U.S. citizenship and other topics throughout the course.[32] However, it was noted that perhaps the students engaged in *I wash my hands speech* because the issues covered did not personally affect them, or people like them. This is illustrated in the following quotation offered by Doug, one of the generally quiet men sitting by the window in response to the professor's question, "How do we make people more aware about issues of diversity and connected citizenship?"

> Sometimes the "times" [hand gesture for quotation marks] make people more aware and more active in their citizenship. Like, I remember after 9/11 [September 11, 2001], the banning of French fries and then Freedom fries. . . . that was like part of our citizenship and made people feel like they actually belonged! Columbine too—when things like that happen it raises your awareness that things need to change. I guess when it happens to you, you see it, or when it happens to people like you, you see it. It's . . . It makes you more aware.[33]

Through this response Doug was indirectly dismissing the professor's challenge to make people aware of issues of diversity and engaged citizenship that did not pertain to him or people like him. Doug implicitly conveyed through this message of *I wash my hands speech* that until certain issues do not affect him and people like him, his attention and awareness of them will not be affected.

Another way that students engaged in convenient amnesia was by reinforcing the culture of teacher neutrality. Although the instructor repeatedly deconstructed this myth, students seemed to forget often. When teaching about controversial public issues and especially historical controversial public issues, for example, the professor insisted that it was important for them to model taking a stand for their students. For which Kelly had the following response: "But, at the same time parents and the school board have a lot of control over what gets taught. If parents think only the positive version of U.S. history should be taught, I think we should respect that!"[34] Not only was Kelly suggesting that she was not going to take a stand, but that she felt committed to teaching the White supremacist version of U.S. history out of respect to parents.

Repeatedly, throughout the semester, students did not agree that teachers should model taking stands as a method of instruction and reinforced the culture of teacher neutrality. For example, later on during the semester, Bill strongly disagreed with the professor on the taking a stand issue by stating, "I disagree. Any time you put personal opinion into your classroom as a teacher, that creates a hostile environment and students won't feel safe. The purpose is to create a safe environment."[35] To that comment, the professor replied, "Most of what happens in the classroom is an imposition of beliefs. There is no neutral stance and that is why self-examination and reflection is very important." Although the students had heard this exchange before, they looked perplexed and several shook their heads in disapproval of the professor's comment, again reinscribing the culture of teacher neutrality.

A final way that students resisted the critical, multicultural, and social justice orientation of the SSSM course was through a culture of superficial appeasement engagement. Superficial appeasement engagement refers to the students engaging in limited conversations about diversity and equity issues in social studies education at a very basic and superficial level. This type of engagement illustrates convenient amnesia because the same basic conversations were still being had even toward the end of the course. The depth of the conversation never advanced, and it seemed as if every time was the first time these ideas were being discussed. This was especially true when the instructor asked the students to discuss diversity and equity issues as they relate to democracy and citizenship and social studies standards, curricula, assessment, and other topics.

Superficial appeasement engagement was also a way of simultaneously appeasing the instructor and not really delving deeply into the issues they were being encouraged to explore. This form of convenient amnesia was most obvious when students were asked to prepare a mini-unit with a focus on citizenship in groups of four or five people. In general, the topics covered in these units did not delve into critical issues about citizenship and democracy and stayed at a superficial level. The topic of citizenship itself was not treated as a fundamental part of social studies education but as an add-on subject, similar to what some people perceive multicultural education to be. In general, the topics ranged from lessons to have students organize a mock protest for getting more varieties of snacks at their school (shifting the focus away from social justice to a more consumerist focus on individuals' wants and needs) to teaching about how events in U.S. history helped Americans "unite under a common cause," with the examples used being Pearl Harbor and the terrorist attacks of September 11.

Although all of the units were problematic and superficial, the unit on "national unity" was the most worrisome. This group consisted of five men, four of whom belonged to the group of silent men that sat by the windows, and focused on how attacks by foreign entities fomented citizenship by bringing in a sense of national unity. In each lesson, the unit explored with the students how these events caused by "them" helped "us" become united—rhetorically, these lessons praised the importance of this unity but did not address that what often unites people in this position is an us-versus-them mentality or hysteria. Importantly, the issue at hand—citizenship—was not addressed in any degree of complexity but was couched under the rubric of blind patriotism. Finally, this group created as an exemplar of a final project for this unit, a poster that they created with crossed bars in the form of an elongated X with stars inside the bars, that to both researchers resembled the Confederate flag. On this poster, they depicted the images of bombs falling over Pearl Harbor and of the Twin Towers being hit by planes all neatly decorated in red, white, and blue.

All of the units, but especially this one, superficially engaged the topic but mostly to appease the professor and fulfill the class requirement. Despite having been assigned several readings on connected, disconnected, and multicultural citizenship, civic engagement, democracy, and books like *Rethinking our Classrooms*,[36] and *US and THEM*, what the students produced exemplified convenient amnesia because there was little evidence that students had familiarity or critical engagement with these topics. Although, when it was to their advantage, the students did conveniently appropriate the language of the course—alienation, disconnection—to divert the focus of self-reflection away from themselves as they did when the professor expressed to them his concern for them not doing the course reading.

DISCUSSION

Overall, the White preservice social studies teachers in this study found ways to not fully engage in a critical, multicultural, and social justice analysis of social studies education in the SSSM course. Specifically, White preservice social studies teachers disconnected issues of why teach from issues of how to teach to divert attention away from the challenge of critically thinking about teaching and about their positions as White people of middle- and upper-middle-class backgrounds. This is important because educators frequently complain that there is a disconnect between theory and practice, and yet when given the opportunity to try to make those connections, these preservice social studies teachers consistently refused to engage.

The students in this study focused on asking for practical teaching tools rather than engaging in conversations about the rationale for teaching social studies and how that relates to standards, assessment, curricula, and pedagogy (methods). Although a practical method was taught at each class session, most of the strategies taught in SSSM focused on discussion-based approaches to engage students in dialogue and deliberation in social studies classrooms, the students hoped to receive artifacts like worksheets, timelines, Venn diagrams, and other materials they referred to as methods. Clearly, there was a misunderstanding of what methods meant for the instructor and for the students in this course, perhaps the angst of student teaching prevented the students from seeing the relationship between the whys and how-tos. Although the instructor on several occasions spoke extensively about how the rationale for teaching social studies directly influenced how (pedagogy) and what (content/curriculum) teachers teach.

Another important observation with larger implications for social studies education is the fact that the students in this SSSM course did not see how social studies education is embedded in issues of citizenship and democracy. As the course evaluation comments reveal, the students perceived citizenship and democracy to be separate content areas and altogether a separate course, not a fundamental part of social education. Furthermore, when instructed to create a mini-unit focused on aspects of citizenship, all of the groups focused superficially on the specific topic of citizenship, completely devoid of an analysis of how through the content and pedagogy teachers use in the classroom they are in essence modeling and teaching about citizenship and democracy to their students.

Finally, although some of the students that did engage in self-reflection reported benefits from the SSSM course, it seemed like a Pyrrhic victory to the instructor, raising important questions about Boler's pedagogy of discomfort and other pedagogies created to teach White students about issues of privilege, equity, and social justice. The primary concern is that such pedagogy is often diffuse of a strong racial analysis, or the race of the instructor is not factored into how effective the pedagogy will be for instructors of color. The findings suggest that a pedagogy of discomfort may not be as effective for professors of color working with predominantly White students. Important questions arise about whether this pedagogy is most appropriate for White instructors working with White students, and why, in this case, it did not work as well, bringing about "a negative atmosphere between the students and the instructor." Critical analysis and evaluation is necessary to judge the value of specific pedagogical approaches and how those relate to teaching White students about critical, multicultural, and social justice issues and if those strategies are equally effective for instructors of color as they are for White instructors.

Implications for the Study of Race and Ethnicity in Education

For the study of race and ethnicity in education, this work raises important questions about pedagogies that aim to use discomfort to trigger self-reflection from White students about critical, multicultural, and social justice issues in education. The specific question that arises is about how we define discomfort, and how the racial dynamics of a classroom affect White preservice teachers' disposition and willingness to engage and learn from the discomfort. Specifically, do White teacher educators and theorists like Boler define discomfort like a professor of color would define discomfort? Is the fact that the professor is a person of color uncomfortable to begin with for White students? To use an analogy, would a male professor make male students as uncomfortable about gender issues in the same way that a woman professor would, and would both of these (man and woman) professors define discomfort about gender issues in the same way?

The data from this study reveal that perhaps reflecting on the definition of discomfort is a good starting point in the quest to expose White supremacy in teacher education and education courses and programs. There is no question that both White professors and professors of color should be dedicated to this task, especially because this study also reveals that students view issues of equality, diversity, citizenship, and democracy as detached from issues of teaching, and especially of teaching the social studies. To advance not only in the study of race and ethnicity in education, but most important, to expose and work toward dismantling White supremacy, all teacher education courses should make the critical examination of multicultural and social justice issues the foundation of the course and not relegate these issues to one day on the syllabus.

Like Boler we also argue that students' emotional responses to curricula are an important and vital space to investigate if we hope to promote self-reflection, but getting beyond the resistance stage may be difficult for professors of color in predominantly White contexts. Likewise not making White students uncomfortable enough may also be an issue for White professors working with these pedagogies in predominantly White contexts as well. In either case, for both White professors and professors of color, the proper mechanisms of support should be put in place to help them challenge White students to be self-reflective. There should, however, be a full acknowledgment that the needs of these professors are fundamentally different. Equal opportunity color-blind support mechanisms (such as abundant material resources) and methods for evaluating teaching (such as end of course evaluations) are not appropriate for either White professors or professors of color in a White supremacist society.

CONCLUSION

As we reflect on our work and what we learned over the course of this project, we are somewhat humbled. Questioning cherished beliefs and unacknowledged assumptions and challenging White supremacy—in all its forms—is hard emotional work. It is also work that belongs at the heart of social studies education. We hoped that by making students uncomfortable with their unexamined assumptions about citizenship and democracy we could begin this work, but instead we met with resistance, avoidance, and hostility. As a result, we began to consider the ways in which race affects what we mean by discomfort and how we react to this discomfort. It also caused us to consider how the racial dynamics of the classroom can support or inhibit an investigation of these feelings. More investigations into the emotional terrain of teaching and learning are vital if we hope to both broaden our understanding of the complex relationship between race, ethnicity, and education.

NOTES

1. J. Arminio, "Exploring the Nature of Race-Related Guilt," *Journal of Multicultural Counseling and Development* 29 (2001): 240.

2. J. W. Loewen, *Lies My Teacher Told Me: Everything Your American History Textbook Got Wrong* (New York: Simon and Schuster, 1995).

3. Eduardo Bonilla-Silva, *White Supremacy and Racism in the Post–Civil Rights Era* (Boulder, CO: Lynne Rienner, 2001).

4. Megan Boler, *Feeling Power: Emotions and Education* (New York: Routledge, 1999); Megan Boler, "Teaching for Hope: The Ethics of Shattering World Views," in D. Liston and J. Garrison (eds.), *Teaching, Learning and Loving: Reclaiming Passion in Educational Practice* (New York: Routledge, 2004), 117–135.

5. H. Hodgkinson, "Educational Demographics: What Teachers Should Know," *Educational Leadership* 58, no. 4 (2001): 6–11.

6. J. A. Banks, *Educating Citizens in a Multicultural Society* (New York: Teachers College Press, 1997); M. Cochran-Smith, *Walking the Road: Race, Diversity and Social Justice in Teacher Education* (New York: Teachers College Press, 2004).

7. J. A. Banks, "Teaching Multicultural Literacy to Teachers," *Teaching Education* 4, no. 1 (1991): 135–144; Cochran-Smith, *Walking the Road*; G. Ladson-Billings, "Preparing Teachers for Diverse Student Populations: A Critical Race Theory Perspective," *Review of Research in Education* 24, no. 2 (1999): 11–27; S. Nieto, *The Light in Their Eyes* (New York: Teachers College Press, 1999).

8. Nieto, *The Light in Their Eyes*, 138–139.

9. A. Chávez and F. Guido-DiBrito, "Racial and Ethnic Identity and Development," in M. Clark and R. Caffarella (eds.), *An Update on Adult Development Theory: New Ways of Thinking about Life Course: New Directions for Adult and Continuing Education*, no. 84 (San Francisco: Jossey-Bass, 1999), 39–47.

10. Ibid., 39.

11. Ibid.

12. See, for example, Cochran-Smith, *Walking the Road;* S. Florio-Ruane, "The Future Teachers' Autobiography Club: Preparing Education to Support Literacy in Culturally Diverse Classrooms," *English Education* 26 (1994): 52–66; G. Gay, "Developing Cultural Critical Consciousness and Self-Reflection in Preservice Teacher Education," *Theory into Practice,* (2003): Nieto, *The Light in Their Eyes*; C. E. Sleeter, "Preparing Teachers for Culturally Diverse Schools: Research and the Overwhelming Presence of Whiteness," *Journal of Teacher Education* 52, no. 2 (2001): 94–106.

13. Cochran-Smith, *Walking the Road,* 5.

14. G. Ladson-Billings, *Critical Race Theory Perspectives on Social Studies* (Greenwich, CT: Information Age, 2003).

15. Loewen, *Lies My Teacher Told Me.*

16. L. Cary, "The Refusals of Citizenship: Normalizing Practices in Social Educational Discourses," *Theory and Research in Social Education* 29, no. 3 (2001): 405–430.

17. E. W. Ross, "Social Studies," in D. Gabbard (ed.), *Knowledge and Power in the Global Economy* (Mahwah, NJ: Lawrence Erlbaum, 2000).

18. Cochran-Smith, *Walking the Road.*

19. Ibid., 98.

20. Boler, *Feeling Power*; Boler, "Teaching for Hope."

21. Boler, *Feeling Power,* 180; Boler, "Teaching for Hope," 7.

22. J. Creswell, *Qualitative Inquiry and Research Design: Choosing among Five Traditions* (Thousand Oaks, CA: Sage, 1998), 66.

23. Ibid.

24. M. LeCompte and J. Preissle, *Ethnography and Qualitative Design in Educational Research,* 2nd ed. (San Diego: Academic Press, 1993), 256.

25. C. Geertz, "Thick Description: Toward an Interpretive Theory of Culture," in C. Geertz (ed.), *The Interpretation of Cultures* (New York: Basic Books, 1973), 3–30.

26. J. Marciano, *Civic Illiteracy and Education: The Battle for the Minds of American Youth* (New York: Peter Lang, 1997).

27. Fieldnotes, September 22, 2004.

28. Ibid.

29. Ross, "Social Studies."

30. Professor's journal, September 29, 2004.

31. Fieldnotes, October 27, 2004.

32. T. Howard, "Connection and Democracy," *Theory and Research in Social Education* 29, no. 3 (2001): L. Urrieta Jr., "Dis-Connections in 'American' Citizenship and the Post/Neo-Colonial; People of Mexican Descent and Whitestream Pedagogy and Curriculum," *Theory and Research in Social Education* 32, no. 4 (2004): 433–458.

33. Fieldnotes, October 6, 2004.

34. Fieldnotes, September 15, 2004.

35. Fieldnotes, October 27,2004.

36. B. Bigelow, L. Christensen, S. Karp, B. Miner, and B. Peterson (eds.), *Rethinking Our Classrooms: Teaching for Equity and Social Justice,* 4th ed. (Milwaukee, WI: Rethinking Schools, 1994); Jim Carnes, *US and THEM: A History of Intolerance in America* (Oxford: Oxford University Press, 1996).

Overcoming Disparity: Repositioning Leadership to Challenge the Conceptual Underpinnings of Antiracist Education

Carolyn M. Shields and Russell Bishop

INTRODUCTION

Disparity constitutes one of the greatest challenges for educators in this century—a challenge that confronts educators in both developed and developing countries. Moreover, although many types of difference may be found in the rapidly changing contexts and communities of many schools, it is not diversity but rather the disparity that comes from the power imbalances so often present in diversity that constitutes the challenge. In North America, educational policy and reform efforts often advocate forms of multicultural or antiracist education as ways of addressing the needs of students who, due to recent demographic trends, come from increasingly diverse sociocultural and linguistic backgrounds. In the United States, the greatest manifestation of these efforts is the 2002 Elementary and Secondary Education Act, more commonly known as No Child Left Behind. But the United States is not alone. In Canada, educators decry the gaps in achievement between indigenous students and their Caucasian counterparts. In New Zealand, Maori students who constitute approximately 21 percent of the school population (but 47 percent of students suspended) too often fail to graduate from secondary school with credentials that permit them to access higher education. In China, with massive educational reform well under way, educators express concern about the growing disparities between urban and rural education and the inadequate opportunities provided for millions of students. In less developed areas, such as Bali (Indonesia), formal schooling, even at the primary level, is beyond the financial ability of many families.

Of equal concern is the fact that most current approaches to redressing disparities have failed. In this chapter we argue that this is because we have too long relied on strategies that tend to be individualistic, superficial, and limited in focus. We have focused too much on students and their families and ignored the roles of teachers firmly situated within specific institutional and social contexts. As we demonstrate later, current approaches ignore the deeply seated cultural and structural inequities that have developed in societies and institutions over decades, indeed centuries, of unchallenged inequality, and they fail to disrupt the patterns of thought and action that constitute our unquestioned realities—our *habitus*, as Bourdieu would call it.[1] Bourdieu explains that our dispositions and understandings are so deeply ingrained that they constitute structures that organize and perpetuate societal norms often at a subconscious level.[2] Because we rarely question these understandings, the culture of schooling that clearly reflects and represents those values, practices, and knowledge perspectives is often erroneously deemed to be neutral.

In this chapter, we reflect on ways in which dominant conceptions of educational leadership and antiracism may be challenged and changed for educators at all levels—teachers, school administrators, and policy makers—to overcome disparities in the educational attainment of diverse learners in this century. We first examine some of the literature, which provides scaffolding for this chapter; we then present an explanatory approach that has the potential to advance both the theory and practice required to overcome the disparities currently associated with diversity. We illustrate this approach with examples from schooling in several countries but primarily with the story of Mrs. Lake, an experienced secondary school science teacher from New Zealand. We conclude by identifying some implications for how educational leaders may use the repositioning we advocate to create school communities that are more socially just and academically excellent for all students.

First, we comment on the concepts of diversity and disparity. Diversity is a reality. It is not something we see as a problem. It is not a challenge. It just is. Without diversity, our world would be colorless and boring. There would be none of the exquisite variety of species we find in the plant and animal kingdoms, no stunning mountain ranges, canopied forests, sparkling waters, or towering cliffs to enhance our enjoyment of nature; and there would a remarkable uniformity of ability, interests, positions, and talents among our human colleagues. In other words, all of creation constitutes a glorious, richly designed tapestry within which each educator and student is a stitch. Yet each stitch is critically important; unless it is strong, well anchored, and adequately and appropriately connected to the whole, the complex weave of the tapestry begins to unravel.

Unlike diversity, disparity in itself is a problem. It is not only a challenge; overcoming disparity based on race, ethnicity, religion, language, and socio-economic status (to identify only a few areas) constitutes perhaps the greatest moral and ethical imperative facing educators in this century. We can no longer be complacent about the overrepresentation in many countries of indigenous, minoritized, and impoverished children in special education programs. We can no longer be complicit in their overrepresentation in lower-level, less challenging, and dead-end courses in many schools. We can no longer tolerate inequitable programs, policies, and resource allocations that create learning environments in which some children feel respected and valued and others continue to be marginalized, unable to develop a sense of belonging or find a place to stand. In fact, we can no longer countenance the often unequal power relations within heterogeneous populations that result in educational and social disparities.

UNDERSTANDING CURRENT APPROACHES

In this brief section, we do not provide a comprehensive overview of the vast bodies of literature related to leadership, multiculturalism, and antiracism, for to do so would be a virtual impossibility. Instead, ignoring some of the important nuances of the debates between antiracism and multiculturalism, we focus on the work of several authors that has led us to our present position. This literature persuades us that we do not need new strategies, new programs, or even new resources. Instead, we argue that what will be most advantageous in the drive to address disparity is an informed and morally purposeful form of leadership that understands the need to build community within schools. It is leadership that works with the broader communities in which schools are located to reposition thinking about antiracism in deeper understandings of how racism persists and how it may be disrupted in educational institutions, communities, and the wider society.

Repositioning Leadership

To successfully address the disparities currently present in educational systems requires educational leaders imbued with a sense of moral purpose and driven by a moral imperative for transformation.[3] Such transformative leadership is described by Astin and Astin as an essentially value-based approach designed to

> enhance equity, social justice, and the quality of life; to expand access and opportunity; to encourage respect for difference and diversity; to strengthen democracy, civic life, and civic responsibility; and to promote cultural enrichment, creative expression, intellectual honesty, the advancement of knowledge, and personal freedom coupled with responsibility.[4]

There is a convincing body of literature that demonstrates the importance of educational leadership in effecting change. Silins and Mulford write: "The contribution of school leadership to past and current high school reform efforts have been found to be undeniably significant, even if these contributions are indirect."[5] Moreover, the increasing emphasis on shared or distributed leadership in no way diminishes the role or importance of the educational leader. We argue, therefore, that the role of educational leaders—both formal and informal—is critical in changing both cultures and structures to ensure more equitable educational outcomes.

Understanding Racist Discourses

In a seminal book, Valencia and others traced the origins of deficit thinking,[6] including various manifestations such as intelligence testing, constructs of "at-riskness,"[7] and "blaming the victim."[8] More recently, Shields, Bishop, and Mazawi detailed, through their examination of the experiences of American Navajo, Israeli Bedouin, and New Zealand Maori children's schooling, how educators and policy makers continue to pathologize the lived experiences of children.[9] In general, these authors critiqued the common practice of attributing school failure to individuals because of their affiliation with a minoritized group within society. They defined pathologizing as a process "where perceived structural-functional, cultural, or epistemological deviation from an assumed normal state is ascribed to another group as a product of power relationships, whereby the less powerful group is deemed to be abnormal in some way."[10] They then go on to state that "pathologizing is a mode of colonization used to govern, regulate, manage, marginalize, or minoritize primarily through hegemonic discourses."[11]

Deficit thinking and pathologizing the lived experiences of children is therefore a form of power that, as Foucault explains, works on and through individuals as they take up positions offered to them in discourse and as they become objects of discourse.[12] To put this argument another way, discourses provide each of us with a self-narrative that we use to describe and think about our positioning within society. We construct meaning out of our lives and experiences in an interactive social process that locates us within sense-making frameworks, discourses, and languages in action. Hence our words, actions, and attitudes are "manifestations of discourses, outcrops of representations of events upon the terrain of social life. They have their origin not in the person's private experience, but in the discursive culture that these people inhabit."[13]

Struggles over representation of what constitutes appropriate knowledges are struggles over whose meaning or sense will prevail. Meaning does not lie in images as such, nor does it rest entirely with those who interpret what they see; "rather it emerges in the dialogue between those who do the interpreting and the images they perceive."[14] Thus those who are positioned within the dominant discourse have recourse to generally accepted means of framing how "subordinate groups live and respond to their own cultural system and lived experiences."[15] Furthermore, they rarely recognize how this practice marginalizes others and fails to take account of their own sense-making images and narratives. This represents a challenge for educational reformers in that, as Bruner acknowledged, it is not just a matter of intervening in part of the system; what is necessary is that we challenge whole discourses and move ourselves beyond our current positionings to alternative discourses.[16]

Schuerich and Young reinforce these points when they suggest that overt and covert individual, institutional, and societal racism all have their roots in what they term "civilizational racism"—the totality of our deepest assumptions about what constitutes "the real, the true, and the good," assumptions that consciously or unconsciously privilege dominant groups and cultures and disadvantage others.[17]

RECONSIDERING ANTIRACISM AND MULTICULTURALISM

In the second part of this chapter, we argue for repositioning educational leadership with respect to diversity and inequity. In this brief overview of some related literature, our rationale becomes clear. For when one considers the adoption of either antiracist or multicultural approaches, one is immediately confronted by myriad competing and often conflicting definitions, strategies, and theoretical underpinnings. Moreover, although advocates of one or other approach make clear theoretical distinctions between them, in practice, these distinctions often blur, with both antiracism and multiculturalism being introduced in relatively superficial ways that fail to address the underlying systemic issues related to power inequities that lead to disparity of educational opportunity or outcome.

Gale and Densmore, for example, argue that "multiculturalism often defined in terms of racial minorities," ignores power relations.[18] Moreover, they explain that in early conceptions of multiculturalism, the emphasis was on individual prejudice rather than on systemic problems.[19] Multiculturalism was critiqued for essentializing and homogenizing culture and failing to recognize its dynamic nature. Alternative forms of multiculturalism soon arose in attempts to address these early problems, with Kincheloe and Steinberg, for example, describing five distinct approaches.[20] The most promising, perhaps, is critical multiculturalism—a form that "concerns itself with issues of social justice and change and their relation to the pedagogical."[21]

At the same time as multiculturalism was evolving, antiracist approaches emerged to address some perceived shortcomings. Antiracism took up some of the wider questions related to class and gender and the ways in which "economic structures and relations influence people's perspectives at least as much as cultural traditions."[22] Proponents claimed to reject notions of culture that were "reduced to distinct, exotic groups of people with a shared descent and fixed customs."[23] Yet others critiqued them for this same failing, claiming that they, too, "share beliefs about the essentialist nature of racial categories and imply rigid divisions among groups of people."[24] May stated that in the United States, "the privileging of racism over other forms of inequality in early articulations of anti-racist education has resulted in a preoccupation with 'colour racism' and the black-white dichotomy."[25] He explained that "the unwillingness of antiracists to incorporate a culturalist approach . . . has also meant that they have been . . . inadequate in addressing new, multiple racisms and the particular historical and contextual dimensions which underpin them."[26] Moodley extended the critique in the following way:

> All too often antiracist advocates display a self-righteous superior morality that by definition exempts the speaker from the sins of racism. Antiracist pedagogues patronizingly lecture others in proper behaviour, spread enlightenment about neglected voices and hope that their own indignation or alleged victimhood will either persuade or cow racists into submission.[27]

It is the tendency to exempt oneself from participation in racism that we believe must be addressed if the conceptual underpinnings of antiracism are to be successfully challenged.

Overall, we are concerned that no matter how carefully the terms are defined or how earnestly they are translated into educational programs and pedagogical strategies, the risks of ignoring the fundamentally inequitable beliefs about what is real (ontology), what is worthwhile (axiology), and what is true (epistemology) that underlie disparity and inequity are simply too great. Moreover, educators need to acknowledge that disparities include but are not limited to those related to race and culture. For that reason, we argue that antiracism and antiracist education need to begin with discursive repositioning that takes into account the pervasive power differentials that result in disparities in individual behavior, institutional structures and practices, as well as in society as a whole. Unless educators start with a recognition of our own roles and responsibilities and take steps to reposition ourselves, disparities in educational attainment will not be overcome.

A More Promising Approach

To achieve education that is socially just, offers to all children learning opportunities that permit them to bring the totality of their lived experience to make sense of both formal and informal curricula, enables them to achieve their potential, and opens doors of opportunity and windows of understanding, educators and educational leaders must pay "explicit attention to beliefs, norms, and pedagogical principles."[28] We must understand that difference and discrimination exist in various forms and on multiple levels, including the individual, institutional, societal, and cultural. Moreover, we argue here that to make strides in addressing these fundamental educational problems, educators (including ourselves) must work simultaneously on several fronts. We must challenge and better understand individual positioning (beliefs, discourses, and practices) as well as collective norms and assumptions; we must examine our own positioning and, at the same time, work to disrupt inequities in both the cultures and the structures of our educational institutions.

We introduce for the consideration of our fellow educators a framework that consists of four elements: context, structures, attitudes and positionings, and relationships.[29] Here, we use the word *attitudes* as Burr does to refer to "manifestations of discourses, outcrops of representations of events upon the terrain of social life. They have their origin not in the person's private experience, but in the discursive culture that these people inhabit."[30] We use the concept of *positioning* to mean a discursive process "whereby selves are located in conversations as observably and subjectively coherent participants in jointly produced story lines. There can be interactive positioning in which what one person says positions another. And there can be reflexive positioning in which one positions oneself."[31]

We use the concept of *discourse* to refer to not only words but the meanings we have adopted and manifest in our positioning—our thoughts, words, and actions that are shaped by power relations and provide a complex network of images and metaphors that determines in large part how we think and act. Education is offered by individuals with unique positionings within institutional structures that are further embedded in social contexts that are enmeshed in dominant cultures. Each of these influences how we think about and relate to the students who have been entrusted to our care.

Dominant Cultures and Contexts

We start with the most ignored element of the framework: the dominant social and cultural modes of thought and behavior that shape all other aspects of educational life. Deeply held beliefs and values that have developed over time create assumptions about the correct ways to live and be in the world— assumptions that tend to privilege dominant groups and disadvantage others who have not historically held equal power or status within a given society. This dominance can and does occur whether the group in question is in the numerical majority (as, for example, the Caucasian population—Pakeha—in New Zealand) or the numerical minority (as is evident in the dominance of White, middle-class topics in schools whose population is 80 or 90 percent aboriginal). This phenomenon has given rise in the United States to the curious phrase "majority-minority" and the theoretically more accurate concept of minoritized populations—groups that although in the numerical majority have been so historically marginalized that they are not treated as equal partners, capable of agency or self-determination. The mores of the dominant groups come to be seen as normal and those groups within society who deviate in any way to be seen as abnormal, deprived, or deficient. Over time, the deeply embedded social and cultural practices are also shaped and constrained by political processes that often result in unequal allocation of resources and social benefits.

In society, the dominance of one set of norms and beliefs over all others often leads to inequities that are rarely identified as racism or prejudice, but most commonly seen as simply the way the society has developed historically. In the United States, a Human Rights Watch report released on February 27, 2002, found, for example, that incarceration rates revealed striking racial disparities; "blacks and Hispanics make up 62 percent of the incarcerated population, though comprising only 25 percent of the national population." It further found that "Hispanic youth are incarcerated at rates seven to seventeen times greater than those of Whites in Connecticut, Hawaii, Massachusetts, and New Hampshire, while the incarceration rate for Black youth is between twelve and twenty-five times greater than those of Whites in Connecticut, Delaware, Iowa, Massachusetts, Montana, and New Jersey."[32]

Often policies to redress social inequities, although well intentioned, serve to perpetuate rather than overcome societal racism and disparities. Don Brash, well-known and controversial leader of the New Zealand National Party, critiqued the race-based policy instituted by one local health organization of "making free taxi rides available to all Maori and Pacific Island patients regardless of their income, but only to some low-income Pakeha [European, caucasian New Zealanders]." He wrote, "The system cannot be justified unless the Primary Health Organisation staff hold the view that there is no such thing as a successful Maori."[33] Although the policy was an attempt to recognize and provide redress for long-standing inequities in the health and welfare of the Maori population, it functioned more to perpetuate deficit stereotypes than to address the current needs of the society. The point here is that new policies, strategies, and approaches in and of themselves do not, and likely cannot, bring about the necessary equitable opportunities for all members of society. In fact, practices that suggest all Maori (or all members of any other minoritized group) are in need of special financial assistance tend to perpetuate deficit thinking and create conflict rather than to change the status quo.

Too often, we accept statistics such as these as a simple refection of the ways things are without examining the underlying conditions that result in such disparities. Perhaps more disconcerting for our present reflections on educational disparity, are the ways in which societal beliefs and assumptions influence educators' beliefs about the ability of children from various sociocultural groups to succeed or fail in schools and the ways in which these beliefs determine how we allocate and distribute educational resources to groups of children.

Institutional Structures

In education, the dominance of certain beliefs and assumptions plays out in pervasive but sometimes subtle ways to advantage some students and disadvantage others; moreover, deficit mindsets are often reflected in policies and practices as well as their underlying assumptions. Historically in many countries, early programs for aboriginal students (for example Navajo,

Maori, Canadian First Nations) were conceived as vocational preparation for work rather than academic in nature. They reflected the underlying societal assumptions that although students from these groups needed to be educated, they could not handle the challenging academic curricula offered to students from the dominant culture. Similarly, it has become normal to assume that children from advantaged families will perform well at school, constitute the majority in classes for the gifted and talented, and garner the large majority of academic awards as well as places in the most prestigious universities. Little attention is paid to how giftedness is defined or assessed or the ways in which the programs are marketed to children whose families are not from the middle-class, dominant culture. The rare presence of a child from one of the less represented classes is cause for celebration and perhaps more unsettling is touted as proof that when others apply themselves equally hard, they too may be successful. This emphasizes once again the importance of individual effort but downplays the need for a critical reexamination of the ways in which societies and institutions as well as individuals constrain and circumscribe the opportunities of minoritized groups.

Institutional constraints may be as obvious as a teacher failing to recognize the value of a student's home language and consequent belief that a less-than-perfect ability with English (or other primary language of instruction) reflects less academic ability on the part of the student. It may be reflected in dominant attitudes toward students whose lived experiences differ from the norm. They may live with grandparents or in extended family situations, dress differently (i.e., wear turbans or headcovers), or come from cultures in which asking questions of adults is seen as a sign not of curiosity but disrespect. In each case, the student rarely finds himself or herself reflected in the formal curriculum of the school and hence receives the implicit message that he or she does not belong or is valued less than the "mainstream" counterpart.

These prejudices and mindsets are also reflected in national or regional the educational statistics such as the following. In the United States in 2001, students living in low-income families were six times more likely than their peers in high-income families to drop out of high school. In fact, an October 2001 National Council for Educational Statistics survey found that 27 percent of Hispanic youth ages sixteen to twenty-four had dropped out of high school compared to 7.3 percent of White non-Hispanic and 10.9 percent of Black non-Hispanic students.[34] In 2003, in the Canadian province of British Columbia, for example, only 46 percent of aboriginal students completed high school compared to approximately 80 percent of their non-native peers.[35]

Although these statistics are race-based, we do not find in them an argument for race-based educational initiatives such as multicultural or antiracist strategies. In fact, because programs coming from these approaches focus on ethnicity and culture, they tend to overlook other forms of related disparity including fiscal equity and socioeconomic status. Most important, they permit educators to focus on individuals and groups of minority students without ever considering either their own role or the underlying institutional norms that help determine academic success or failure. Educators must become aware of the underlying societal norms, beliefs, and values that support and legitimate such statistics. They must understand, for example, how socioeconomic status is perpetuated by dominant discourses of power and how it commingles with other societal advantages such as good health, stable living conditions, and educational opportunities.

Current approaches to parent involvement in education are also good examples. Much research demonstrates that when parents are involved in their children's education, the children tend to perform better at school.[36] There are several problems with this approach. The first is that it suggests a causal relationship—one that has not been proven. In other words, it may be equally accurate to say that when children do well at school, their parents are more involved in its processes—a concept to which we shall return shortly. Current thinking also makes assumptions about what parental involvement means and how it should look. Lopez and colleagues, in their study of Hispanic migrant parents of children who were successful at school, found that although the parents had never interacted with their children's teachers nor entered the school at any time, they felt they were very interested and involved in their children's education.[37] They talked to them about the importance of education in helping them have multiple occupational opportunities and career choices; they took their children to the fields and orchards to ensure they experienced what awaited them if they did not succeed at school, and generally ensured that they attended school fed, rested, and ready to learn.

As educators, we constantly make assumptions about what children can learn based on what they have already learned, failing to distinguish between ability to learn and opportunity to learn. In developed countries, this is particularly true when we are dealing with children whose home situations differ from the White middle-class norm. We assume that a child who has learned to print her name, recognize letters of the alphabet, count to twenty, or color within the lines has more intrinsic ability than the child who comes to school without those skills. We do not value the skills the latter child may have learned—to operate kitchen appliances and prepare a simple meal, speak more than one language, go to the corner store on his own—and we too often suggest a lower-level placement or remedial help. And of course, this occurs most often when we are considering the needs of children from ethnic, linguistic, or socioeconomic minorities within the school community.

Attitudes and Positionings

When educators begin to deconstruct the dominant societal discourses about what is normal and understand how some groups of children have been marginalized and pathologized by common understandings and interpretations, they have the basis for challenging their extant attitudes and positionings and for developing new approaches to the education of all children. Although the outcomes may be consistent with the aims of many multicultural or antiracist programs, we argue that this is a very different approach. The starting point is the educator who must first grapple with the ways in which he or she perpetuates inequity and disadvantage, often unknowingly.

This belief in the critical importance of repositioning and of identifying new and empowering discourses is fundamental to a widespread national reform effort going on in New Zealand: Te Kotahitanga.[38] The approach is less than three years old, but already almost every educator in the nation recognizes the term and many identify their school as a "Te Kotahitanga school." In his intensive training and coaching program, Bishop begins by asking educators to identify the reasons why Maori (and other minority children) perform less well than their Pakeha peers. Educators most frequently identify factors related to students' home and family lives and the intrinsic motivation or ability of the Maori students themselves. The next most numerous factors relate to institutional constraints—ways in which teachers believe their work with minoritized students is made more difficult (lack of resources, constraining rules, etc.). Very few recognize personal responsibility as a contributing factor. Bishop then presents educators with accounts written by students themselves in which they identify a sense of not being valued or included and most especially a sense that the teachers do not feel they can be successful and thus pay less attention and give less assistance and support to them than to their non-Maori classmates. There is not space here to fully describe the ways in which Bishop and colleagues help teachers understand and change their discursive practices and positioning, but every evaluation to date of the program has found it to be successful in changing educators' awareness and rapidly creating a climate in which Maori student performance improves.

The account of one experienced secondary school teacher, Mrs. Lake, is sobering. She reported that she had been an educator for over thirty-two years and thought she had been doing a good job. "Then," she said, "Along came Te Kotahitanga . . . and I became part of an exciting program in New Zealand. I had never thought of myself as being racist," she continued, "but I guess I was a deficit thinker of the soft type. I used to say 'if only' a lot. . . . If only the students had more caring and involved parents. If only the children had a quiet place and someone to help them with their homework. If only they cared more about education."

Lake went on to say that with help from the program's pedagogical coaching and evidence gleaned from its observational strategies, she changed her pedagogy. When she began to question her assumptions and view her minority students as learners, she changed her discursive practices and thus changed the interactions and relationships in the classroom. She asserted that within one year, all the children in her classroom had become "excited about education and about learning." They had begun to ask questions and take the classroom conversations home to share them with their families. In turn, the conversations from home came back into the classroom with comments and queries from family members.

One child reported a conversation with a parent who said "I don't think I agree with your teacher about why the sky is blue." The child went on to describe proudly how she informed her parent that it was not the teacher's claim but that it was something the students had worked out themselves. As the teacher changed her discursive practices, the students began to take ownership of their own learning. And, perhaps not surprisingly, parents became more involved—on their terms, sending questions back to school with their children, "Your teacher might be able to help with this."

Lake reflected, "I was overwhelmed with a sense of my power and my responsibility. Nothing else changed. The child was the same. The family life was the same. The ethnic and cultural background and socioeconomic situation were all unchanged." What changed was the teacher's positioning and, as a consequence, her pedagogical approaches. She had not adopted a new program. She had not turned to either research or practices related to multiculturalism or to antiracism. She had, instead, examined her own beliefs and values—beliefs and values that were part of the dominant culture. She had begun to challenge the dominant discourses of the society in which her school was located. In this way, she had started to peel back the layers of racism that had prevented the Maori students in her classroom from performing as well as their non-Maori peers.

Relationships

Fraser argues that a politics of recognition helps address sociocultural inequities by instituting both affirmative remedies that correct "inequitable outcomes of social arrangements without disturbing the underlying framework that generates them" and transformative remedies that are "aimed at correcting inequitable outcomes precisely by restructuring the underlying generative framework."[39] We would argue that these approaches must be inextricably interconnected and infused into our understanding of pedagogical relationships. When educators begin to see their students as colearners on a journey of discovery, everything changes, but perhaps most important the power relationships both within the individual classroom and among all members of the school community are transformed. When the implicit "if only's" are removed, then relationships among equals take their place. The affirmative strategies described by Fraser become the norm within the school and classroom, respecting and valuing who the students are, recognizing and affirming the worth of what they bring to the learning situation, and acknowledging and supporting what they are learning. Furthermore, when repositioning and new discursive practices are at the root of the affirmation, transformation soon follows.

Relationships between student and teacher are changed as they begin to learn from and with each other. Relationships between the minoritized and dominant students in the school change as the gaps in student outcomes are overcome and all students are seen to be capable and agentic learners. Teachers from the minoritized groups no longer sit silent and separate in the staffroom but make suggestions and offer explanations that help their colleagues reposition their pedagogical practices. And parents become involved in their children's learning, not because of new parental involvement programs, but because the children are engaged in and excited about learning. As students are encouraged to bring the totality of their lived experiences into their educational conversations and inquiries and to build on them in new and often unexpected ways, the school community becomes more united. Those members of the community who had previously been marginalized by educational discourses that considered them less able, less engaged, and less willing to participate become fully participating members of the school community.

Overcoming Disparity

The new attitudes and positionings expressed by Lake and experienced by other educators in the Te Kotahitanga project reflect Coburn's beliefs about change. Coburn states that to be at scale, "reforms must effect deep and consequential change in classroom practice." She elaborates:

> By "deep change," I mean change that goes beyond surface structures or procedures (such as changes in materials, classroom organization, or the addition of specific activities) to alter teachers' beliefs, norms of societal interaction, and pedagogical principles as enacted in the curriculum. By *teachers' beliefs*, I am referring to teachers' underlying assumptions about how students learn, the nature of the subject matter, expectations for students, or what constitutes effective instruction. [40]

We have argued that it is a change of belief and discursive practice that brings about many of the goals of multicultural and antiracist pedagogical approaches. Yet antiracist pedagogy fails because it does not explicitly require educators to confront their own complicity in the continuing educational disparities of minoritized youth. We posit that unless educators are willing to confront their own discursive positioning shaped by decades, often centuries, of societal and cultural assumptions, norms, and practices, the deeper structures of disparity and inequality in our educational systems will not change. As educators, it is critical to understand how pervasive images of unequal ability, dysfunctional behavior, or inappropriate outcomes have shaped the ways in which we interact with and teach students from minoritized groups. Educators who recognize the inequitable power arrangements of the status quo begin to acknowledge that instead of finding ways to change the learners, the pedagogical context, or even the institution itself, they must start with themselves. They no longer adopt programs that attempt to address the learning needs of individuals or groups of students in ways that do little more than make them feel better about themselves, or that promote tolerance and understanding between groups (although these are not inconsequential outcomes).

Coburn asks, "Do teachers' encounters with reform cause them to rethink and reconstruct their beliefs?"[41] We argue here that this is the fundamental first step toward offering to all students education that is just, inclusive, and equitable—one in which all students attain high performance standards. Moreover, it lays the foundation for disrupting the pervasive and destructive norms and practices, beliefs and values that undergird our individual attitudes, institutional policies and practices, and society as a whole. Both cultural practices and institutional structures that perpetuate inequity and disparity must be challenged and troubled if we are to move beyond the current emphasis on programs to the deeper cultures and structures from which new programs arise.

The challenges for educational leaders are multiple and complex. New conceptions of antiracist education require educators to start with themselves, recognizing how they have been shaped by the dominant discourses of their sociopolitical contexts and the structures and norms of their institutions. We will no longer focus on programs or strategies but on the discursive practices and positionings that adversely affect the academic performance of minoritized children. We must also help others embark on a similar journey of self-discovery and exploration—modeling, encouraging, facilitating dialogue, asking questions, never being content with discourses that disempower or marginalize. We must examine the policies, practices, and pedagogies that guide us and help others within the school to do the same. And we must be agents of change—not in terms of leading the charge for new practices, strategies, or programs but for the creation of new, inclusive, respectful, agentic school communities in which people story and restory their lives and educational experiences; construct and reconstruct knowledge and understanding; and develop new, respectful, learning relations with others.

As we reposition ourselves discursively, we can transform the educational experiences of students who have traditionally been marginalized and unsuccessful. As we empower all learners, we develop new knowledge, understanding, norms, beliefs, and assumptions. As we reposition ourselves, we disrupt the inequities in power, participation, resource allocation, and achievement that have challenged educators for so long. We invite educators everywhere to take up the challenge of restorying and repositioning antiracist education in ways that address deep-seated beliefs and values and, perhaps most important, that help us overcome the disparities so often inherent in the diversity of our school communities.

NOTES

1. D. Swartz, *Culture and Power: The Sociology of Pierre Bourdieu* (Chicago: University of Chicago Press, 1997).

2. Michel Foucault, *Power/Knowledge: Selected Interviews and Other Writings*, edited by C. Gordon (New York: Pantheon, 1980).

3. Michael Fullan, *Change Forces with a Vengeance* (New York: Routledge/Falmer, 2003); G. C. Furman and Carolyn M. Shields, "Leadership for Social Justice and Democratic Community," in W. A. Firestone and C. Riehl (eds.), *A New Agenda: Directions for Research on Educational Leadership* (New York: Teachers College Press, 2005).

4. A. W. Astin and H. S. Astin, *Leadership Reconsidered: Engaging Higher Education in Social Change*. Available online at www.wkkf.org/documents/youthed/leadershipreconsidered, p. 6. Accessed December 2004.

5. H. Silins and B. Mulford, "Leadership and School Results," in K. Leithwood and P. Hallinger (eds.), *Second International Handbook of Educational Leadership and Administration* (Boston: Kluwer, 2002), 564–565.

6. R. R. Valencia (ed.), *The Evolution of Deficit Thinking* (London: Falmer, 1997).

7. Beth Blue Swadener and Sally Lubeck (eds.), *Children and Families "At Promise": Deconstructing the Discourse of At-Risk* (Albany: State University of New York Press, 2003).

8. Peter McLaren, *Life in Schools: An Introduction to Critical Pedagogy in the Foundations of Education*, 4th ed. (Boston: Pearson Education, 2003).

9. Carolyn M. Shields, Russell Bishop, and Andre E. Mazawi, *Pathologizing Practices: The Impact of Deficit Thinking on Education* (New York: Peter Lang, 2005).

10. Ibid., x.

11. Ibid.

12. Foucault, *Power/Knowledge.*

13. V. Burr, *An Introduction to Social Constructionism* (London: Routledge, 1995), 50.

14. J. Ryan, *Race and Ethnicity in Multi-Ethnic Schools: A Critical Case Study* (Clevedon, UK: Multilingual Matters, 1999), 5.

15. McLaren, *Life in Schools*, 77.

16. Jerome Bruner, *The Culture of Education* (Cambridge, MA: Harvard University Press, 1996).

17. J. J. Schuerich and M. D. Young, "Coloring Epistemologies: Are Our Research Epistemologies Racially Biased?" *Educational Researcher* 4, no. 26 (1997): 4–16.

18. T. Gale and K. Densmore, *Just Schooling: Explorations in the Cultural Politics of Teaching* (Buckingham: Open University, 2000), 135.

19. Ibid.

20. J. L. Kincheloe and S. R. Steinberg, *Changing Multiculturalism* (Philadelphia: Open University Press, 1997).

21. Ibid., 27.

22. Gale and Densmore, *Just Schooling*, 136.

23. Ibid.

24. Ibid.

25. S. May, "Introduction: Towards Critical Multiculturalism" in S. May (ed.), *Critical Multiculturalism: Rethinking Multicultural and Antiracist Education* (Philadelphia: Falmer, 1997), 2.

26. Ibid., 3.

27. K. Moodley, "Antiracist Education through Political Literacy: The Case of Canada," in S. May (ed.), *Critical Multiculturalism: Rethinking Multicultural and Antiracist Education* (Philadelphia: Falmer, 1997), 141.

28. C. E. Coburn, "Rethinking Scale: Moving beyond Numbers to Deep and Lasting Change," *Educational Researcher* 6, no. 32 (2003): 5.

29. This is the framework we used, in collaboration with our colleague Andre Mazawi, when we wrote about the need to depathologize educational practices (see Shields, Bishop, and Mazawi, *Pathologizing Practices*).

30. Burr, *An Introduction*, 50.

31. B. Davies and R. Harre, "Positioning the Discursive Production of Selves," *Journal of the Theory of Social Behaviour*, 20(1997): 43–65. Reprinted in M. Wetherell, S. Taylor, and S. Yates (eds.), *Discourse Theory and Practice: A Reader* (London: Sage, 2001), 261–271. Quotation from p. 264.

32. Human Rights Watch, "U.S.: Incarceration Rates Reveal Striking Racial Disparities." Available online at www.hrw.org/press/2002/02/race0227.htm. Accessed January 2005.

33. D. Brash, *Don Brash Writes—No. 47*. Available online at www.national.org.nz/don_brash_article.aspx?ArticleID=3355. Accessed January 2005.

34. National Center for Educational Statistics, *Drop-Out Rates in the US: 2001* (Washington, DC: U.S. Department of Education, 2001). Available online at nces.ed.gov/pubs2005/dropout2001/sec_2.asp. Accessed April 20, 2006.

35. BC Education. Available online at www.bced.gov.bc.ca/abed/; accessed January 2005.

36. P. Coleman et al., "Learning Together: The Student/Parent/Teacher Triad," *School Effectiveness and School Improvement* 7, no. 4 (1996): 361–382; J. P. Comer, "Is 'Parenting' Essential to Good Teaching?" *NEA Today* 6, no. 6 (1988): 34–40; and J. L. Epstein, L. Coates, K. C. Salinas, M. G. Sanders, and B. S. Simon, *School, Family, and Community Partnerships* (Thousand Oaks, CA: Corwin, 1997).

37. G. R. Lopez, J. D. Scribner, and K. Mahitivanichcha, "Redefining Parental Involvement: Lessons from High-Performing Migrant-Impacted Schools," *American Educational Research Journal* 38, no. 2 (2001): 253–288.

38. Russell Bishop, M. Berryman, S. Tiakiwai, and C. Richardson, *Te Kotahitanga: The Experiences of Year 9 and 10 Maori Students in Mainstream Classrooms* (Wellington, New Zealand: Ministry of Education, 2003). Available online at www.minedu.govt.nz/goto/tekotahitanga. Accessed April 20, 2006.

39. N. Fraser, "From Redistribution to Recognition? Dilemmas of Justice in a 'Post-Socialist' Age," *New Left Review* 212 (1995): 568–593. Quotation on p. 582.

40. Coburn, "Rethinking Scale," 4.

41. Ibid., 5.

Index

Abstract liberalism, 5–6

Accountability, 120. *See also* High-stakes testing

Achievement gap, xviii–xxi

Across the Centuries (Armento et al.), 223–26

Adams, E. C. L., 222

Affiliation, 192

Affirmative action, 5–6, 9, 12

Africa, teaching children about, 201

African, The (Courlander), 210

African American teachers, 191–93, 203; committed to social justice, 195–203; ideals in the pedagogy of, 192; resistance from colleagues and authorities, 195–96, 202. *See also* Social studies teacher education; Teacher education initiative

Afrocentric feminist thought, 192, 193

Afrocentric womanist pedagogy, 192, 193

Alexander v. Sandoval, 130–31

Alienation, 60, 62–63

Anarchism, 100; individual, 104–7

Anarcho-capitalism, 102–4

Anderson, James, 192

Anger of resistant students toward students not engaging, 285, 288–91

Antiracism, 26, 29, 39, 68, 166; race and, 30–32; reconsidering multiculturalism and, 305–16

Antiracist education, 165, 185–86; building it in majority White schools, 172–85; importance in majority White schools, 167–70; nature of, 166–67

Antiracists, 26

Antiracist White role models, 179–80

Anyon, Jean, 46

Apartheid schools, xx

Arminio, J., 279

Astin, A. W., 304

Astin, H. S., 304

Attitudes, 307, 312–13

Autobiography, 175–76

Baldwin, James, 71, 78

Banks, James, 183

Bell, Derrick, 198, 202

Bell Curve, The (Murray and Herrnstein), 74–76

Bigotry *vs.* racism, 48

About the Editor and the Contributors

EDITOR

E. **Wayne Ross** is a Professor in the Department of Curriculum Studies at the University of British Columbia. He is interested in the influence of social and institutional contexts on teachers' practices as well as the role of curriculum and teaching in building a democratic society in the face of antidemocratic impulses of greed, individualism, and intolerance. A former daycare worker and secondary social studies teacher in North Carolina and Georgia, he has also taught on the faculties of the State University of New York (at the Albany and Binghamton campuses) and the University of Louisville, where he was Distinguished University Scholar. Ross is also cofounder of the Rouge Forum (www.rougeforum.org), a group of educators, students, and parents seeking a democratic society. He is coeditor of the journals *Workplace: A Journal for Academic Labor* (www.workplace-gsc.com) and *Cultural Logic* (www.eserver.org/clogic) and the former editor of *Theory and Research in Social Education*. He is the author or editor of numerous books including: *Defending Public Schools (Vols. 1–4)*; *Neoliberalism and Educational Reform* (with Rich Gibson); *The Social Studies Curriculum: Purposes, Problems, and Possibilities*; *Image and Education* (with Kevin D. Vinson); and *Democratic Social Education: Social Studies for Social Change* (with David Hursh). You can find him on the web at: www.weblogs.elearning.ubc.ca/ross.

CONTRIBUTORS

Rasheeda Ayanru is an Assistant Professor in the Education Department at Le Moyne College. Ayanru recently earned her doctorate in education with an emphasis in curriculum and instruction and special education from West Virginia University. She was the recipient of the highly competitive W. E. B. DuBois fellowship for academic excellence at WVU. Her research interests include equity issues related to race, class, and disability, and the influence of biography on the practice of teachers. She has presented at various workshops and conferences on multicultural education and preparing teachers to meet the needs of learners with diverse abilities.

Eugenio Basualdo is Professor of vocational and technical education at the State University of New York College at Oswego and director of a faculty and student exchange program with the University of Havana, Cuba. For the past thirty years Basualdo has sought to bring a liberating and mindful experience to the preparation of vocational and career-oriented teachers, so that they in turn may bring about a greater social consciousness in their own students.

Russell Bishop is a Foundation Professor and Assistant Dean for Maori Education in the School of Education at the University of Waikato, Hamilton, New Zealand. He is also a qualified and experienced secondary school teacher. Prior to his present appointment he was a senior lecturer in Maori education in the Education Department at the University of Otago and Interim Director for Otago University's teacher education program. His research experience is in the area of collaborative storying as Kaupapa Maori research, having written a book called *Collaborative Research Stories: Whakawhanaungatanga* and published nationally and internationally on this topic. His other research interests include institutional change, critical multicultural education, and collaborative storying as pedagogy. This last area is the subject of the book, coauthored with Ted Glynn and published in 1999, *Culture Counts: Changing Power Relationships in Classrooms*, which demonstrates how the experiences developed from within Kaupapa Maori settings—schooling, research, and policy development—can be applied to mainstream educational settings. His most recent book, *Pathologising Practices: The Impact of Deficit Thinking on Education*, coauthored with Carolyn Shields and Andre Mazawi and published by Peter Lang, investigates how deficit thinking pathologizes the lived experiences of children and prevents minoritized children from achieving their full potential in schools. He is currently the project director for a large New Zealand Ministry of Education–funded research and professional development project that seeks to improve the educational achievement of Maori students in mainstream classrooms.

Eduardo Bonilla-Silva is a Professor of Sociology at Duke University. Bonilla-Silva's 1997 article in the *American Sociological Review*, titled "Rethinking Racism: Toward a Structural Interpretation," challenged sociologists to analyze racial matters from a structural perspective rather than from the typical prejudice problematic. His research has appeared in journals such as the *American Sociological Review, Sociological Inquiry, Racial and Ethnic Studies, Race and Society, Discourse and Society, Journal of Latin American Studies*, and *Research in Politics and Society* among others. To date he has published three books: *White Supremacy and Racism in the Post-Civil Rights Era* (co-winner of the 2002 Oliver Cox Award given by the American Sociological Association); *Racism Without Racists: Color-Blind Racism and the Persistence of Racial Inequality in the United States*; and *White Out: The Continuing Significance of Racism* (with Ashley Doane). He is currently working on two books: *Anything but Racism: How Social Scientists Minimize the Significance of Racism* (Routledge) and *White Logic, White Methods: Racism and Methodology*. He is also working on a project examining the characteristics of the emerging racial order titled "We Are All Americans: The Latin Americanization of Race Relations in the USA."

Linda Turner Bynoe is a Professor in the College of Professional Studies at California State University, Monterey Bay. Her research focuses on empowering education and multicultural community partners. Her recent chapter, "Strategies for Teaching Caring and Empowerment" in the book, *Educating for a Culture of Peace*, edited by Riane Eisler and Ron Miller (Heinemann Press), was published in 2004.

Rudolfo Chávez Chávez is Regents Professor in the Department of Curriculum and Instruction at New Mexico State University. He teaches undergraduate, graduate, and doctoral courses in critical multicultural education, curriculum theory and foundations, and critical pedagogy and learning foundations. Chávez Chávez is the author of *Multicultural Education in the Everyday: A Renaissance for the Recommitted* plus chapters and articles that address multicultural teacher education issues from a critical perspective. He co-edited *The Leaning Ivory Tower: Latino Professors in American Universities* (with Ray Padilla); *Ethnolinguistic Issues in Education* (with Hermán García); *Speaking the Unpleasant: The Politics of (non)Engagement in the Multicultural Terrain* (with Jim O'Donnell), which was awarded 1999 Honorable Mention by Gustavus Myers Outstanding Book Awards; and more recently *Social Justice in These Times* (with Jim O'Donnell and Marc Pruyn).

Also, with Jeanette Haynes Writer, he co-edited the Summer 2002, ATE *Journal of Teacher Education* Special Theme Issue "Indigenousness Perspectives of Teacher Education: Beyond Perceived Borders."

George J. Sefa Dei is a Professor and Chair of the Department of Sociology and Equity Studies in Education at Ontario Institute for Studies in Education/University of Toronto. His teaching and research interests are in the areas of antiracism education, development education, international development, indigenous knowledges, and anticolonial thought. He has written extensively on antiracism education and minority youth schooling. His most recent books are: *Playing the Race Card: Exposing White Power and Privilege* (with Leeno Luke Karumanchery and Nisha Karumanchery-Luik) (Peter Lang Publishing, 2004); *Critical Issues in Anti-Racist Research Methodology* (co-edited with Gupreet Johal) (Peter Lang Publishing, 2005); and *Anti-Colonialism and Education: Politics of Resistance* (co-edited with Arlo Kempf) (Sense Publishers, 2006).

David G. Embrick is a doctoral candidate in the Sociology Department at Texas A&M University and a current American Sociological Association Minority Fellowship Program (MFP) Fellow. His current research is on the discrepancies between corporations' public views and statements on diversity and their implementation of diversity as a policy. His argument is that corporate managers are using diversity as a mantra while they maintain highly racially inequitable environments. He has published in a number of journals, including the *Journal of Intergroup Relations, Race and Society, Research in Political Sociology*, and *Sociological Forum*, and is an active member of several organizations, including the Association of Black Sociologists, Sociologists Without Borders (where he was awarded the Beatrice and Sidney Webb Award), Society for Women in Society, as well as the American Sociological Association.

Stephen C. Fleury is Professor of Education at Le Moyne College in Syracuse, New York. He currently attempts the Sisyphian task of subverting institutional racism in education through advising, teaching, lobbying, and publishing. Formerly a social studies teacher, Fleury wishes to apologize to his former students for any cultural and conceptual damage because of forcing their complicity with the subject matter.

Rich Gibson is a Cofounder of the Rouge Forum, a former organizer for the National Education Association, the American Federation of State, County, and Municipal Employees (AFSCME), the Service Employees International Union (SEIU), and an educator and social worker. He is now an Associate Professor of Education at San Diego State University and the author of *How Do I Keep My Ideals and Still Teach?* published free online, at Heinemann.

Jeanette Haynes Writer is an Associate Professor in the Department of Curriculum and Instruction at New Mexico State University. Her areas of specialization include critical multicultural teacher education, Native American identity, and social justice education.

Jay P. Heubert is a Professor of Law and Education at Teachers College, Columbia University. His scholarly interests include legal issues in education, equal educational opportunity, high-stakes testing, law and school reform, and interprofessional cooperation. He is the author or editor of numerous books including *Understanding Dropouts: Statistics, Strategies, and High-Stakes Testing*; *High Stakes: Testing for Tracking, Promotion and Graduation*; and *Law and School Reform.*

Joyce E. King holds the Benjamin E. Mays Chair for Urban Teaching, Learning and Leadership at Georgia State University. Recognized here and abroad for her contributions to the field of education, her publications include *Black Education: A Transformative Research and Action Agenda for the New Century*; *Preparing Teachers for Diversity*; *Teaching Diverse Populations*; and *Black Mothers to Sons: Juxtaposing African American Literature with Social Practice.* Numerous articles and book chapters address the role of cultural knowledge in effective teaching and teacher preparation, black teachers' emancipatory pedagogy, research methods and black studies theorizing in curriculum change. King is the former Provost and Professor of Education at Spelman College; she was Associate Provost and Professor of Education at Medgar Evers College (CUNY) and Associate Vice Chancellor for Academic Affairs and Diversity Programs at the University of New Orleans. She also served as Director of Teacher Education at Santa Clara University.

Marvin Lynn is an Assistant Professor and coordinator of the Minority and Urban Education Program in the Department of Curriculum and Instruction at the University of Maryland, College Park. He has published numerous articles and book chapters on issues of urban education and critical race theory in education and is a key figure in the development of critical race theory in education.

Michael Peterson is a Professor in the College of Education at Wayne State University in Detroit, where he teaches in the special education program. Peterson is the coauthor *Inclusive Education: Creating Effective Schools for All Learners* and the founder and coordinator of the Whole Schooling Consortium, an international network of schools, teachers, parents, administrators, university faculty, and community members who promote excellence and equity in schools throughout the world to build inclusive and democratic societies (www.wholeschooling.net).

Michelle Reidel is Assistant Professor of Social Studies Education at Georgia Southern University. Her current research interests include social studies education and high-stakes testing, and the relationships among power, knowledge, and emotion.

Carolyn M. Shields is a Professor and Head of the Department of Educational Organization and Leadership at the University of Illinois, Urbana–Champaign. Her research focuses on issues of leadership and social justice in diverse contexts. She has conducted various studies including research into transformative leadership in cross-cultural communities and the role of dialogue and spirituality in creating more holistic and inclusive school communities. She has also studied in the potential of year-round schooling (modified or balanced calendars) to facilitate more equitable achievement (broadly conceptualized) for all students. Her research in this area has focused on the role of leaders in implementing change and the potential of these calendars to provide more equal and more inclusive learning environments for students who, by virtue of membership in specific social classes, ethnic groups, home language other than English, and so forth, tend to be the least successful in more traditional school settings. Her current research relates to summer learning loss in balanced calendar schools, the motivations of educators for doing social justice work, and leadership issues in diverse and bilingual schools.

Christine Sleeter is Professor Emeritus in the College of Professional Studies at California State University, Monterey Bay. Her research focuses on antiracist multicultural education and multicultural teacher education. Sleeter has received several awards for her work including the California State University at Monterey Bay President's Medal, the National Association for Multicultural Education Research Award, and the AERA Committee on the Role and Status of Minorities in Education Distinguished Scholar Award. She currently serves as a Vice President of Division K of AERA. Her journal articles appear in publications such as *Review of Research in Education, Journal of Teacher Education, Teacher Education Quarterly,* and *Social Justice.* Her most recent books include *Un-Standardizing Curriculum* (Teachers College Press); *Culture, Difference and Power* (Teachers College Press); *Multicultural Education as Social Activism* (SUNY Press); and *Turning on Learning* with Carl Grant (Wiley). She has just completed a book on multicultural curriculum in the context of the standards movement, to be published by Teachers College Press.

Luis Urrieta Jr. is an Assistant Professor of Cultural Studies in Education at the University of Texas at Austin. Urrieta's general research interests center on issues of identity and agency, activism, altruism, new social movements, and social practice theory. He is specifically interested in Chicano and *Indígena* identity, and in activism as a social practice in educational spaces both in the United States and internationally. Methodologically, his work is grounded in anthropology and qualitative research methods. Urrieta's work specifically makes claims for native anthropology and native educational research as a political practice and method. Some of his articles have appeared in *Educational Studies, Educational Foundations, High School Journal, Journal of Latinos and Education, Urban Review, The Social Studies,* and *Theory and Research in Social Education.*

John F. Welsh is a Professor of Higher Education at the University of Louisville, where he mentors dissertation students and teaches courses in higher education finance and administration. He has won several teaching awards during his career, including the Red Apple Award from the University of Louisville for outstanding teaching. He has published widely in the major international higher education research journals. He has also been a contributor to important volumes on the future of public education and the neoliberal transformation of higher education. He is an advanced student of Krav Maga, and has written on self-defense and martial arts.